GLOBALIZING THROUGH
THE VERNACULAR

GLOBALIZING THROUGH THE VERNACULAR

Kothis, *Hijras*, and the Making of Queer and Trans Identities in India

Aniruddha Dutta

BLOOMSBURY ACADEMIC
LONDON • NEW YORK • OXFORD • NEW DELHI • SYDNEY

BLOOMSBURY ACADEMIC
Bloomsbury Publishing Plc
50 Bedford Square, London, WC1B 3DP, UK
1385 Broadway, New York, NY 10018, USA
29 Earlsfort Terrace, Dublin 2, Ireland

BLOOMSBURY, BLOOMSBURY ACADEMIC and the Diana logo are trademarks of
Bloomsbury Publishing Plc

First published in Great Britain 2024

This book was made possible with generous support from the University of Iowa's Office
of the Vice President for Research and College of Liberal Arts and Sciences.

For legal purposes the Acknowledgements on p. xi constitute an extension of this
copyright page.

Cover design: Adriana Brioso
Cover image: Kolkata Pride Walk, India, 17th Dec, 2023. (© Dipayan Bose/SOPA Images/
Sipa USA/Alamy Stock Photo)

A catalogue record for this book is available from the British Library.

Library of Congress Cataloging-in-Publication Data
Names: Dutta, Aniruddha, author.
Title: Globalizing through the vernacular: kothis, hijras and the making of queer and trans
identities in India / Aniruddha Dutta.
Description: New York, NY: Bloomsbury Academic, 2024. | Includes bibliographical
references and index.
Identifiers: LCCN 2024015816 (print) | LCCN 2024015817 (ebook) | ISBN 9781350382770
(hardback) | ISBN 9781350382817 (paperback) | ISBN 9781350382787 (epub) |
ISBN 9781350382794 (ebook)
Subjects: LCSH: Sexual minorities–India. | Transgender people–India. |
Gender identity–India.
Classification: LCC HQ73.3.I4 D87 2024 (print) | LCC HQ73.3.I4 (ebook) |
DDC 306.760954–dc23/eng/20240615
LC record available at https://lccn.loc.gov/2024015816
LC ebook record available at https://lccn.loc.gov/2024015817

ISBN: HB: 978-1-3503-8277-0
ePDF: 978-1-3503-8279-4
eBook: 978-1-3503-8278-7

Typeset by Deanta Global Publishing Services, Chennai, India

To find out more about our authors and books visit www.bloomsbury.com and sign up for
our newsletters.

To my kothi–hijra–trans sisters and elders

CONTENTS

FIGURES

MAP

TABLE

ACKNOWLEDGMENTS

It takes several communities to create a book. I owe my greatest thanks to the trans-*kothi*–*hijra*–queer communities and organizations who made this work possible—particularly, the communities and activists associated with Nadia Ranaghat Sampriti Society, Moitrisanjog Coochbehar, Madhya Banglar Sangram, Dum Dum Swikriti Society, Kolkata Rista, Koshish, SAATHII, Samabhabona, Pratyay Gender Trust, Bandhan, ATHB, and the Kolkata Rainbow Pride Walk. Among my community friends, interlocutors, sisters, and elders, especial gratitude and love to Bikash-da, Sumi, Arghya, Sushanta-da, Kanchana, Priyanka, Raina, Aruna, Rajorshi-da, Heena, Disha, Honey, Babu, Khushi, Santosh, Sanjana, Iswar, Bappa-da, Maitreyee, Saptarshi, Ram-da, Anindya, Ranjita-di, Madhu-di, Aparna-di, Pawan-da, Rudra, Souvik, and so many others for their incredible generosity, insights, and support.

Among several academic communities, my teachers and colleagues at Jadavpur University, the University of Minnesota, and University of Iowa deserve special mention—my heartfelt thanks go to Richa Nagar, Jigna Desai, Ajay Skaria, Simona Sawhney, David Valentine, Rushaan Kumar, Naomi Greyser, Leslie Schwalm, Rachel Williams, Philip Lutgendorf, Nilanjana Deb, Supriya Chaudhuri, Kaustav Bakshi, and Paul Greenough, among many others. I am sincerely grateful to the colleagues, mentors, and friends who supported this project in the wider academic world, including Anjali Arondekar, Geeta Patel, Rohit Dasgupta, Debanuj DasGupta, Paul Boyce, Dia Da Costa, Enakshi Nandi, Kareem Khubchandani, Meghna Chaudhuri, Claire Pamment, Adnan Hossain, Gayatri Reddy, Ila Nagar, Sayan Bhattacharya, Srila Roy, Dipika Jain, David Gramling, Chloë Taylor, Vaibhav Saria, and others too numerous to thank individually but each uniquely important to the book. Meena Khandelwal, Sahana Ghosh, Sohini Chatterjee, Brady G'Sell, and Prerna Subramanian offered incisive and helpful comments on the manuscript. The editors and anonymous reviewers offered invaluable feedback for improving the book; all remaining faults are mine.

My natal and chosen families tolerated so much and helped out in immeasurable ways. Ma, Baba, Prosenjit, Henglu, Botam, Sanjay, Manju-di, Shukla, Diya, Bubu, Didibhai, Neha, Parjanya, Jaime, Sumi, Tara, Arghya, Kishan, my aunts, my late grandmothers—to you, I owe my and this book's existence.

ABBREVIATIONS

ATHB	Association of Transgender/Hijra in Bengal
CBO	Community-based organization
DDSS	Dum Dum Swikriti Society
DFID	Department for International Development, UK
HST	Humsafar Trust
KRPW	Kolkata Rainbow Pride Walk
KSMF	Karnataka Sexual Minorities Forum
MBS	Madhya Banglar Sangram
MSJE	Ministry of Social Justice and Empowerment
MSM	Men who have sex with men or males who have sex with males
NACO	National AIDS Control Organization
NACP	National AIDS Control Programme
NFI	Naz Foundation International
PUCL-K	People's Union for Civil Liberties, Karnataka
SAATHII	Solidarity and Action Against the HIV Infection in India
UNDP	United Nations Development Programme
WBSAPCS	West Bengal State AIDS Prevention and Control Society

INTRODUCTION

TOWARD A THEORY OF VERNACULARIZATION

2nd of July is indeed a historic day . . . when the first ever pride walk was held in India . . . Pawan Dhall, a leading gay rights activist (was) one of the participants . . . 15 bravehearts walked down the roads of Kolkata.

—"A Walk to Remember," *Gaylaxy* Magazine, 2010

In memory of the Stonewall riots . . . on July 2, 1999, fifteen front-rank activists from different Indian cities came together to hold this historic event (the first pride walk in India).

—Bengali Pamphlet for the Kolkata Rainbow Pride Walk
(KRPW), 2010 (my translation)[1]

Susanta was born in a small town near Kolkata, the capital city of the eastern Indian state of West Bengal.[2] Today, he is an activist associated with a community-based organization (CBO) that works for the rights and sexual health of LGBTQ+ (lesbian, gay, bisexual, transgender, queer, etc.) people. Usually described as a gay man in middle-class activist circles, his first exposure to LGBTQ terminology came from reading Bengali and English newspapers in the 1980s. As he told me in an interview, "gay is one of the first terms I heard about." As a young man in the 1990s, Susanta migrated to the city and became part of an early generation of urban Indian LGBT activists who started coming out, representing their identities in the media, and networking with their counterparts abroad at a time of economic liberalization and globalization.[3] As the preceding quotes indicate, the first Indian pride walk in Kolkata in 1999 marks a defining moment in this journey, signaling a larger process of organizing among activists from different cities who draw inspiration from Western precedents like the Stonewall riots and become part of a globalizing LGBTQ (especially gay) movement. Such metropolitan and mostly middle- or upper-class activists become positioned as pioneering leaders—"bravehearts," "front-rank activists"—of the Indian LGBTQ movement.

However, having grown up in a lower middle-class family in a small town, Susanta also participates in less elite communities of people who refer to themselves as *kothi*, *dhurani*, or *hijra*, although younger generations may also identify as gay or transgender. The contextually varied relations, overlaps, and distinctions between *kothi* (also spelled *koti*), *dhurani*, and *hijra* are explored later in the book. For now,

I will provisionally gloss them as multivalent, loosely overlapping terms used across various South Asian regions that indicate a diverse spectrum of people, usually assigned male at birth, who variously describe themselves as women or like women, as feminine males, as a separate gender, or as a fluid combination of such subject positions. While *kothi, dhurani,* and *hijra* are not necessarily rigid or singular identities and may be flexibly adopted alongside other LGBTQ terminology, people who enter these communities generally share some sort of identification with variably interpreted ideas of femininity and also, often, desire men. *Hijra*, the best-known of these terms, denotes a subset of these communities characterized by distinctive religious practices, forms of elective kinship, and professions that involve blessing people for money. Notwithstanding much diversity in *hijra* identities, *hijras* are popularly regarded as physically masculine-appearing people who wear culturally feminine attire and are distinguished by certain characteristic gestures like a loud clap, which may be used to greet other community members, emphatically punctuate sentences, or retaliate against abuse. People who call themselves *kothi* or *dhurani*—who may wear male or female attire—may or may not also identify as *hijra*, and vice versa.[4]

In the late 1980s, before entering Kolkata's gay circles, Susanta discovered a community that he described as a *shomaj* or society of *dhuranis* while visiting a public park beside a lake in south Kolkata—a cross-class haunt for cruising or sexual networking where people had sex behind bushes, sex workers solicited clients, and gender nonconforming persons hung out in groups despite threats of police violence. Susanta took pains to learn the *bhasha* (language) used within these communities, called Ulti (literally, inverted) or Dhurani Bhasha (*dhurani* language)—basically, an intra-community lexicon of words that are inserted within the grammatical framework of mainstream languages like Bengali or Hindi to create a somewhat clandestine mode of communication that may, however, be used in public and taught to trusted outsiders.[5] As Susanta told me: "I didn't want to be excluded from this *shomaj*—I took notes and practiced the language at home!" Later, while employed in transnationally funded HIV-prevention projects for MSM (men who have sex with men) run by LGBTQ nongovernmental organizations (NGOs), he worked extensively with *dhurani–kothi–hijra* communities, who provided both lower-level staff and target groups for the projects. While most such people were from working class and/or Dalit (oppressed caste) backgrounds, marginalized both due to their gender/sexual nonconformity and socioeconomic status, Susanta's participation in these communities indicates that group affiliation was not strictly restricted by class.[6]

Indeed, as a nonbinary trans feminine ethnographer, I, too, have been gradually included within these communities despite my middle-class, dominant-caste background and US-based employment. In conversations over the years, several *kothi* friends and sisters have casually asked me questions like, "How do *kothis* in America live?" As elaborated later, some *kothis* even map queer or trans feminine characters they encounter in English films or shows as "*bideshi kothi*" (foreign *kothis*). *Kothis* might thus imagine the category as not only extensible across class, but even as transnationally generalizable. However, in the discourse of NGOs and institutionalized activism, such terms are often mapped as local relative to globalizing categories like transgender. As one report on transgender communities in eastern India states: "Transgender . . . is an umbrella term which includes transsexuals, cross dressers, intersexed persons . . . In eastern India there are various local names and identities, such as Kothi, Dhurani" (SAATHII 2009: 17). Yet, as we shall see, these communities do not neatly conform to such categories of scale as "local," and varied discourses of gender/sexual difference intersect in ways that belie stratifications between "global" and "local" languages of gender and sexuality.

Globalizing through the Vernacular studies the relation between nonelite forms of gender/sexual variance and LGBTQ+ politics in India, particularly focusing on eastern India. Drawing on over a decade of ethnographic research, interviews, and textual analysis, the book goes beyond well-studied spaces such as urban Indian LGBTQ movements and *hijra* communities, and explores how the networks, discourses, and practices of relatively underrepresented groups like *kothis* and *dhuranis* in nonmetropolitan India intersect with LGBT representational politics—the political processes through which categories such as transgender, gay, or MSM are constituted for public representation and institutional recognition.[7] This intersection is shot through with hierarchies of class, caste, location, scale, and language. Processes of institutional representation are typically led by middle-class and dominant-caste sections of gender/sexually variant communities, who play a salient role in articulating dominant versions of LGBTQ identities based on both transnational and South Asian discourses of gender/sexuality.[8] Such activist formations tend to be centered around urban hubs of capital and resources, while *kothi–dhurani–hijra* community networks are less organized around metropolitan centers, stretching between rural areas, small towns, and cities.

Analyzing these intersecting formations, the book makes several interwoven arguments. First, even as nonelite communities like the *kothi–dhurani–hijra* spectrum interact with the expansion of organized LGBTQ politics and become more consolidated as identities, the book contends that various aspects of their discourses and practices—including both non-English linguistic practices and rearticulations of terms like gay or transgender—remain irreducible to dominant identitarian categories or frameworks as represented by elite LGBTQ constituencies or recognized by institutions like the state and mainstream media. Second, I argue that articulations of gender/sexual difference that come into tension with dominant representational frameworks often become subordinated through hierarchies of scale and language that position these discourses and related communities as local and vernacular—for instance, as local versions or vernacular articulations of the transnational MSM or transgender categories. I offer the analytical framework of vernacularization, elaborated later in the introduction, to theorize the subordination of communities and discourses as local and/or vernacular through intersecting hierarchies of scale and language. Third, the book studies some of the effects of this process—vernacularization may deny "local" communities an equal role in national and transnational processes of LGBT organizing, subsume their discourses under dominant identitarian frameworks aligned with capitalist and/

or nationalist formations, and delegitimize or efface aspects that are not entirely legible within such frameworks. Further, this process might reinforce existing hierarchies within *kothi–dhurani–hijra* communities and restrict legible subjects of rights and welfare. For example, as shown in Chapter 6, people who are seen as breaching categorical divisions between cisgender homosexual maleness and transgender womanhood may be seen as ineligible for state benefits for trans people. Finally, the book studies how some discourses and practices within *kothi–dhurani–hijra* communities contest dominant understandings of identity and rights and offer alternative framings of difference and resistance—including rearticulations of Anglophone and dominant Indian-language discourses—even as such contestations are often precarious and effaced. The book does not move through these foci in a linear sequence but interweaves them through studies of multiple identitarian frameworks such as institutionally recognized versions of *hijra* identity, the MSM category, varied elite articulations of transgender politics, and urban gay identities—always locating these formations in terms of their relation to the aforementioned communities.[9]

Figure 0.1   Trans-*kothi–hijra* people from Murshidabad, West Bengal, at the Kolkata Pride Walk, 2008. Courtesy author.

These relations involve both overlaps and hierarchies. Susanta's contextually shifting position as a gay activist and participant in *dhurani* communities indicates that interactions between institutionalized LGBT politics and nonelite communities are not between neatly separated sides: people cross over; identities and discourses overlap. Thus, part of my project involves tracing how the aforementioned communities enter into a productive relation with LGBT representational politics, contributing to and being transformed by the (trans) national emergence of LGBTQ identities—a mutually constitutive interaction or mediation that contributes to the expansion of contemporary forms of gender/ sexual identity. *Kothi–dhurani–hijra* community networks connect eastern India with adjoining regions of India, Bangladesh, and Nepal, and help expand identity- and rights-based politics outside urban centers and across class/caste divides. They bring nonmetropolitan participants to urban events like pride walks, and translate between older discourses of gender/sexual variance and emergent identities. Seemingly "local" communities, therefore, help the transregional and transnational expansion of globalizing categories like MSM and transgender across South Asia, partly enabling their globality—and in turn, are themselves partially transformed.

Yet, such interactions are deeply asymmetric and hierarchical, resulting in the exploitation of *kothi–dhurani–hijra* labor in the development sector (NGOs and funders), and the subordination of their discourses of gender/sexual variance within hierarchies of legibility and legitimacy. Scholars such as James Scott and Judith Butler have critiqued how modern states and societies produce grids of legibility through which social realities or subject positions are rendered intelligible, precluding other epistemologies (Scott 1999; Butler 2004, 2009). I trace how, even as communities and languages mediate each other, certain epistemologies or ways of understanding gender and sexuality become more legible to institutions like NGOs, the state, and the media, while others are delegitimized. While dominant epistemologies may crystallize around Anglophone terms or concepts, they are not a simple diffusion or transplantation from Western sources, but rather are translated, transformed, or coproduced by domestic elites.[10] Indeed, these epistemologies may selectively incorporate certain aspects of *kothi–dhurani–hijra* communities and languages while effacing others.

Irrespective of their provenance, dominant frameworks of representation bear a hierarchical relation with the aforementioned communities. Nonelite discourses and practices may be rendered illegible if they contradict or do not neatly translate to such frameworks, which tend to be aligned with the late capitalist conceptualization of LGBTQ categories as clearly bounded minorities and stable interiorized identities and/or with Indian middle-class, dominant-caste, and culturally nationalist understandings of gender/sexual variance.[11] Such subordinating or delegitimizing processes intersect with the languages and practices of *kothi– dhurani–hijra* communities, especially intra-community tensions or divides— extant hierarchies are often reinforced through vernacularization while egalitarian or fluid relations between subject positions may become suppressed. Some gender/sexually marginalized people fit better within dominant representational categories than others, and certain versions of *hijra* (and sometimes *kothi*) identity gain institutional recognition while other *kothi–dhurani–hijra* narratives are marginalized or elided—even as communities contest or rearticulate dominant discourses. Such multilayered hierarchies signal not only the subordination of specific forms of gender/sexual variance, but also broader epistemic shifts such as the increasing conceptual separation between gender and sexual identities evident transnationally (Valentine 2007; Jackson 2009).

Examining the relation between emergent epistemic frameworks and intersecting hierarchies of scale, language, class, and caste, I analyze the subordination of *kothi–dhurani–hijra* discourses as symptomatic of a broader process that I call *vernacularization*, which reveals tensions within dominant modes of LGBTQ activism and larger formations of capitalism, nationalism, liberal democracy, class, and caste that inform such activism. Vernacularization is often glossed as the adaptation of global or cosmopolitan discourses *into* local or vernacular idioms, or the rise of vernacular literatures that challenge the cosmopolitan (Merry and Levitt 2017; Michelutti 2007; Pollock 2006). Instead, I expand on a less common sense of the term as the reduction of a language to vernacular status in contexts where the vernacular occupies lower prestige or power within tiered linguistic hierarchies (Chimhundu 1993; Annamalai 2014). I use vernacularization to describe the intersecting construction of hierarchized dichotomies such as cosmopolitan versus vernacular and global versus local, and the relegation of communities and discourses as spatially local and/or linguistically vernacular relative to discourses of gender and sexuality that emerge as dominant at transnational, national, and/or regional levels of scale. Both LGBTQ discourses in English that claim transnational or national status and middle-class, dominant-caste articulations of gender/sexuality in "regional" languages like Bengali may position nonelite discourses as local or vernacular, resulting in a compounded, multilayered, and unstable stratification between various scalar levels. Despite contradictions and ambiguities within multiple superseding representational frameworks, overall, the vernacularization process serves to contain tensions within Indian and globalizing formations of LGBT activism by subsuming, devaluing, or delegitimizing apparently local forms of gender/sexual variance that contravene dominant discourses even as they intersect with and contribute to "global queering"—the transnational but regionally differentiated expansion of LGBTQ identities (Jackson 2009; Chiang and Wong 2016). The following sections contextualize the aforementioned arguments, situating the book's conceptual framework of vernacularization with respect to my position as an ethnographer; scholarship on Indian LGBTQ communities; and relevant queer, trans, feminist, postcolonial and sociolinguistic literatures on scale, language, and the vernacular.

Beyond Metrocentric Representations

My initiation into this project was deeply personal. Like Susanta, I grew up in a small-town middle-class family north of Kolkata but lacked exposure to queer communities. Gaining some freedom as a college student, I was initially drawn to the seemingly utopian promise of LGBTQ liberation in metropolitan cities (Weston 1995; Boyce and Dasgupta 2017). However, while volunteering with funded NGOs in Kolkata, I discovered their linkages with CBOs scattered across suburbs, small towns, and rural areas. Metropolitan NGOs acted as intermediaries channeling funds from transnational and national funders to smaller CBOs. These CBOs and related communities provided me with a support network that enabled my return to nonmetropolitan milieus. Later, I drew upon this network to begin ethnographic fieldwork spanning Kolkata and ten districts north of the city—particularly Nadia, Murshidabad, and Cooch Behar—places that evidenced extensive interactions between nonelite and nonmetropolitan communities and metropolitan activism, and thus provided appropriate sites to explore the issues central to this book. My choice of fieldwork location was further informed by my cultural and linguistic familiarity with the region and its prominence as an early site of Indian LGBTQ activism.

My research was spurred by my privileged and yet ambiguous position between metropolitan activism and these communities, which made me increasingly aware of their subordination and exploitation. My privilege as an English speaker means that I am often asked to fill out forms, send emails, or prepare reports for small-town CBOs, since funders or the state often require such documents to be in English although most nonmetropolitan community members are more fluent in Bengali or Hindi. Simultaneously, I often need to deliberate with community members on how to represent them as MSM, *kothi*, transgender, and so on, to such institutions. Such experiences have constantly reminded me of the linguistic, spatial, and epistemic hierarchies through which nonelite, nonmetropolitan communities must negotiate institutional representational politics and transnational languages of gender and sexuality. Media and activist narratives often privilege metropolitan middle-class activists as sources of gender/sexual transformation and reinforce modernist and developmentalist teleologies where gender/sexual progress is seen as expanding from globalizing metropolitan centers to supposedly backward or less developed peripheries, ostensibly less connected to globalization and Western influence.[12] There are many recursive variations of this narrative: in 2005, the Kolkata pride march is cited as an example of westward-looking liberalization and globalization awakening a conservative city (Sengupta 2005). In 2009, the BBC describes Mumbai as the "San Francisco" of India, leading its gay rights struggle (Ahmed 2009). Contrastingly, rural areas may be mapped as monolithic sites of gender/sexual repression, patriarchy, and caste hierarchy (Patel 2016). Even attempts to reclaim Indian precedents of same-sex desire or gender variance have typically focused on relatively elite (often Hindu dominant caste) literary, artistic, and religious archives (Vanita and Kidwai 2000; Pattanaik 2012). The role of nonmetro and nonelite communities in social and historical transformation is thus commonly elided, whether explicitly or implicitly.

Responding to calls within queer and trans studies to interrogate the privileging of metropolitan centers and to consider the rich possibilities enabled by queer/trans vernacular cultures (Halberstam 2005; Brown 2012; Omni and Harris 2023),

I go beyond metrocentric discourses of social change by studying communities and networks in nonmetropolitan India as constituencies that help produce "global queering." Much ethnographic literature has analyzed both the possibilities and limits of Indian LGBTQ movements in urban spaces, including the (eventually successful) campaign for the decriminalization of nonheterosexual intercourse, interventions for the prevention of HIV transmission, and lesbian feminist mobilizations (Dave 2012; Puri 2016; Lakkimsetti 2020; Vijayakumar 2021; Roy 2022). Some texts offer rich analyses of both online and offline metropolitan queer spaces and related class, caste, linguistic, and gender hierarchies, including discrimination against *kothis* (Dasgupta 2017; Khubchandani 2020). Drawing on such analyses as needed, I focus on areas and communities studied less often in relation to urban mobilizations. I draw inspiration from some scholarship that has countered metrocentric representations, such as a recent anthology on "regional expressions" of queerness in texts in the "vernacular languages" of India (Chakraborty and Chakraborty 2023: i). Others have studied how the everyday lives of same-sex desiring people in small towns "trouble urban-oriented queer utopian narratives" (Boyce and Dasgupta 2017: 211), or how rural *hijras* do not conform to liberal secular ideas of futurity or activist discourses of safer sex (Saria 2021). Some critiques of identity-based conceptions of sexuality evoke working-class and/or nonmetropolitan spaces for examples of fluid, ambiguous, and non-identitarian idioms of sexual desire and gender, which may be effaced or reductively represented as fixed minority identities by legal, epidemiological, and activist discourses (Boyce and Khanna 2011; Khanna 2016). Similarly, Navaneetha Mokkil (2019) shows how vernacular sexual subjectivities in Kerala (South India) exceed dominant frameworks of legibility, identity, and rights. While building on these critiques, this book brings greater focus on processes of identity and community formation in nonelite and nonmetropolitan contexts—especially within the *kothi–dhurani* spectrum—and how such processes contribute to or mediate metrocentric, elite-led forms of LGBT representational politics and vice versa. Some studies do analyze the relation of *kothi* communities to the HIV-prevention NGO sector, but largely focus on how the transnational political economy of HIV activism facilitates the adoption and dissemination of the *kothi* identity among working-class males (Khanna 2016; Katyal 2016; Cohen 2005; Boyce 2007). In contrast, as I show in Chapter 2, older *dhurani–kothi* networks and related languages partly enabled the expansion of categories like *kothi* and MSM, and of the HIV-prevention sector itself. This suggests the necessity and scope of studying such communities as agents of gender/sexual transnationalism who partially shape formations of organized activism, while being partly reshaped themselves.

Hence, I am not just invested in a critique of metrocentrism that turns to nonmetropolitan areas as sites of difference from or resistance to urban or elite identity politics. Rather, the book analyzes the imbrications of metrocentric and top-down forms of LGBT politics, and associated structures like the development sector, with non-metrocentric transregional community formations that both extend and disrupt their hegemony. This approach resonates with a critical queer regionalism that pays attention to both vertical logics of globalization and more horizontal intra- or transregional "traffics of queerness" (Chiang and Wong 2016: 1645). The book thus traces the mutually constitutive interlinkages between metrocentric activist formations and more loosely scattered transregional networks, connecting trajectories of urban activism with gender/sexual transformations outside big cities to show how global queering and related identities are both enabled and interrupted in nonmetropolitan India.

Here, I do not use "metropolitan" and "nonmetropolitan" to imply rigidly distinct or oppositional spaces, but as flexible referents for relatively privileged and subordinated locations within spatialized relations of power—urban centers where infrastructure, resources, and capital are concentrated, as contrasted with less well-resourced rural areas, small towns, and city slums.[13] Further, the relation between spatial and socioeconomic location is nonlinear—relatively elite sections in nonmetropolitan areas such as dominant-caste CBO activists or *hijra gurus* (leaders) may wield more institutional power than underprivileged *kothi–dhurani–hijra* people in bigger cities, though such elites may still be considered "metropolitan" in the sense of greater access to metrocentric circuits of discourse and capital. "Metropolitan" and "nonmetropolitan" are thus provisional designations for contextually shifting poles of intersecting spatial and socioeconomic hierarchies, rather than "binary geographies" of static cores and peripheries (Ramamurthy 2004: 764–5). Analogously, terms like "nonelite" also designate shifting relationalities, not static groups: internal differentiation and upward mobility within *hijra–kothi–dhurani* communities mean that some benefit from metrocentric institutional politics more than others.

Moreover, urban Indian LGBTQ spaces are diverse, and hence there is no singular interface between a monolithic form of metropolitan LGBT politics and nonelite communities, but varied forms of interlinkage studied specifically over the chapters. I focus more on forms of LGBTQ politics that have intersected *both* with institutions like the state or media *and* nonmetropolitan *kothi–dhurani–hijra* communities. For instance, *hijra* leaders have undertaken forms of representational politics that influence media discourse and trans activism while also impacting *kothi–dhurani–hijra* communities. The HIV industry constitutes another specific conjuncture: since the 1990s, HIV-prevention funding for MSM and trans feminine people from the Indian state and development agencies like the World Bank has aided the growth of NGO networks working on sexual health and rights (Khanna 2016; Vijayakumar 2021). These networks have extensively drawn on *kothi–dhurani–hijra* communities as both cheap labor and target populations. Urban activist spaces like pride walks and related middle-class gay and trans communities also intersect with *hijra–kothi–dhurani* community networks, and increasingly, online gay spaces also factor in. Contrastingly, urban lesbian and trans masculine activism have impacted nonmetropolitan *kothi–dhurani–hijra* communities less despite growing interactions, given that such activism has been marginalized within the LGBTQ development sector due to factors like the direction of HIV-related funding to male-assigned "high-risk groups" (HRGs) and the relative newness of trans masculine community networks (Nagpaul 2017). Hence, one limitation of the book is its lack of focus on people assigned female at birth. Another tendency I regrettably explore less is the increasing emergence of urban Dalit–Bahujan (oppressed caste) queer activism, even as my arguments draw upon Dalit feminist, queer, and trans critique. Many *kothis*, *hijras*, and *dhuranis* are from oppressed caste backgrounds, and as later chapters show, aspects of their discourses and practices that contravene caste and gender norms are particularly susceptible to subordination through vernacularization. Yet, intersections between these communities and explicitly Dalit-identified activism are still nascent at the time of writing, especially in eastern India—although the afterword notes some emerging interlinkages.

While attending to variegated interactions, my focus remains on the asymmetries that broadly characterize mediations between nonelite communities and institutionally impactful LGBTQ politics—asymmetries that take forms specific to eastern India, yet suggest transregional patterns. Multiple forms of urban Indian activism and LGBTQ expansion outside urban hubs draw on nonelite labors of spatial networking and discursive translation while systemically exploiting and devaluing them. As some progressive activists have critiqued, working-class feminine-identified people typically occupy the lowest rungs within NGOs and HIV projects, often earning below legal minimum wage (Aneka and KSMF 2011). This falls within a larger tendency of the silencing, subordination, or tokenistic inclusion of Dalit–Bahujan voices and communities within Indian LGBTQ spaces (Kang 2016; Thakur and Zaffar 2023). The book explores various ways in which such exploitation and erasure affect nonmetropolitan *kothi-dhurani-hijra* communities—for instance, through activist condemnations of their articulations of gender, sexual desire, or resistance as disreputable, uncivil, backward, or incorrect.

In studying the contradictory location of these communities, I seek to bridge the ethnographic study of these communities as sociocultural *groups* with a study of their position as mediators of broader *processes*. Ethnographies of gender-variant communities in India, which have particularly focused on *hijras* and to a lesser extent on related identities, provide nuanced representations of these communities as internally diverse groups with intersectional identities and complex negotiations with social norms (Cohen 1995; Nanda 1999; Reddy 2005; Hall 2005; Nagar 2019; Saria 2021). Some ethnographies locate *hijras* as dynamically evolving communities who are not backward relative to "modern" gay/lesbian identities (Reddy 2005). Extending this, Hossain explores how *hijra* subjectivities in Bangladesh are being transformed through "agentic adaptations and appropriations" of state and NGO discourses by *hijras* (2021: 182). However, there is much scope for corresponding work on the *kothi–dhurani–hijra* spectrum in nonmetropolitan India as an interactive constituency mediating (trans) national LGBTQ activism. The few ethnographies that specifically focus on *kothis* or similar groups like *jananas* provide insightful analyses of their identities and languages but do not focus on the mediation between intra-community dynamics and activist discourses, while noting their coexistence with NGOs (Nagar 2019; Nandi 2024). In that context, the book explores how intra-community tendencies intersect with dominant discourses and representational frameworks.

For example, *kothi–dhurani–hijra* communities evince linear gradations and hierarchies between "less" and "more" overtly feminine people. Similar linear spectra of identity in the West have been critiqued by scholars of queer, trans, and disability studies, who seek alternative nonlinear frameworks (Halberstam 1998; Thomas and Boellstorff 2017; Castleberry 2019). However, *kothi–hijra* communities also show how linear tropes can be deployed nonlinearly—for instance, people in male attire (clothes socially assigned for men) may be described as "more feminine" than female-attired persons. But institutional activism and processes of vernacularization may reinforce linear hierarchies while effacing nonlinear deployments, undermining the non/linearity—fluid interactions between linear and nonlinear tendencies—within these communities. In that context, an interrogation of hierarchies of scale and language is necessary for both countering the devaluation of these communities as agents of LGBTQ activism and "global queering" and for appreciating their diversity and complexity, which exceed not only dominant representational frames but sometimes even critical queer/trans theoretical lenses.

Vernacularization, Language, and Scale

As the book demonstrates, dominant modes of LGBTQ politics tend to reinforce multilayered hierarchical constructions of scale, which, more broadly, also characterize Indian nationhood and globalizing formations of capitalism and liberalism. Certain discourses and categories of gender/sexuality are sought to be established as global, transnational, or national, while others—such as *kothi–dhurani* articulations of gender/sexual variance—are positioned as localized vernaculars relative to globalizing categories or as local/regional versions thereof. Scholarship in transgender studies has critiqued how activist or media discourse may subsume *hijra* or *kothi* as local variants of a putatively global or universal transgender identity (Dutta and Roy 2014; Chatterjee 2018; Billard and Nesfield 2020). But this is only a recent iteration of a longer, broader process. In HIV prevention discourse of the 2000s, terms like *kothi* were positioned as local subgroups of the transnational MSM category (Boellstorff 2011). While they never occupy the global mantle of Anglophone terminology, *hijra*—and less commonly, *kothi*—may be positioned as national terms within South Asia. The *hijra* is often seen as the quintessential Indian "third gender" identity (Cohen 1995: 276–9). Indeed, it may be projected as an overarching national identity with local variants across India (Tom and Menon 2021). Meanwhile, even as *kothi* was subsumed as a subtype of MSM, some HIV activists positioned terms like *dhurani* as "local variations" of the *kothi* (Praajak 2005). The specific position of *hijra* and *kothi* within multilayered scalar hierarchies is thus unstable and variable—though, at best, they gain limited access to the higher scalar levels associated with transregional, cross-cultural mobility or even universality.

The recurrent positioning of certain articulations of identity as local or regional elides how subordinated communities and discourses are part of alternative transregional or transnational scales—*kothi–dhurani* networks may stretch across eastern India, Bangladesh, and Nepal—which are not legible as per the aforementioned scalar hierarchies. It also effaces how the expansion of LGBTQ discourse across South Asia has partly depended on nonelite forms of transregionalism, and that *kothi* may see the term as applicable across cross-cultural and trans-spatial scales, as evidenced when they read trans feminine people abroad as *kothis*. While Sheldon Pollock notes that some South Asians have historically conceptualized their languages as local relative to the "larger world" (2006: 20), Sudipta Kaviraj shows regarding medieval Bengali devotionalism that cultures situated within specific regions may also conceptualize themselves as cosmopolitan (2015: 68). Elsewhere, Evelyn Blackwood notes how *lesbi* (lesbian, trans masculine) communities in Indonesia see themselves as part of a global *lesbi "dunia"* or world (2010: 190). Given that terms like transgender and gay are often universalized and projected onto non-Western communities irrespective of whether they adopt such terms themselves, such counter-projections by *lesbis* or *kothis* cannot be dismissed as incorrect or aspirational. Indeed, as we shall see, the willingness of *kothi–dhurani* communities to see their identities as continuous with people elsewhere has facilitated their adoption of transgender as a term that some of them use interchangeably with *kothi* or *hijra*—an imagined *kothi–hijra–dhurani* universalism may thus facilitate the material globalization of Anglophone terms. More broadly, all languages arguably have an irreducible "semantic capacity" to generate generalized meanings, even as concepts always carry traces of their context (Sartori 2008: 46). Hence, no language, whether mainstream or queer/trans, is entirely reducible to scalar categories like local.

Thus, *kothis* and similar communities may be seen as evincing a form of situated non-locality: situated in specific sociocultural sites but not simply containable as local. The elision of these alternative scales parallels the conceptual erasure or devaluation of articulations that do not neatly translate to identitarian rubrics sought to be established at higher scalar levels, as when *kothi* subject positions overlapping between feminine maleness and trans womanhood are effaced by the homosexual–transgender divide.[14] The critique of hierarchical formations of gender/sexuality thus necessitates an interrogation of normalized categories of scale.

The scalar hierarchization of gender/sexual discourses parallels the positioning of world languages along levels of scale: specifically, the tiered hierarchy between the "global" lingua franca (usually English), national languages, and subnational regional or local vernaculars—a tiering that characterizes both the operations of transnational capital and the Indian national public sphere. I adapt the analytical rubric of *vernacularization* to theorize the intersections between scalar hierarchies, linguistic ranking, and epistemological particularization. My deployment of the term departs from its typical interpretations in the social sciences and humanities, where vernacularization often denotes the localized adaptation or translation of transnational discourses or phenomena like democracy or human rights (Michelutti 2007; Okafor and Krooneman 2011). For instance, the "vernacularization of women's human rights" is described as how "global human rights ideas" are translated into "local understandings" (Merry and Levitt 2017: 214). Another influential sense is Sheldon Pollock's theorization of vernacularization as the rise of "local . . . literary languages" that "challenge" cosmopolitan languages like Sanskrit (2006: 1). Across these usages, the distinction between the global/cosmopolitan and the local/vernacular is taken as a neutral empirical description of an externally existing difference in scale. While Pollock and some other scholars who reference his theorization note that the vernacular–cosmopolitan relation emerges dynamically from shifting historical processes of linguistic expansion, domination, and subordination, such that some languages may move from vernacular to cosmopolitan status or even occupy overlapping positions, their focus remains more on linguistic assertion or resistance from the position of the vernacular rather than a deconstruction of the categorization of particular languages as such (Pollock 2006: 20; Kullberg and Watson 2023: xv–8). Contrastingly, the Zimbabwean linguist Herbert Chimhundu and Tamil linguist E. Annamalai separately deploy vernacularization to denote the social positioning of nonelite languages as vernaculars and critique it as an ongoing process of subordination (Chimhundu 1993; Annamalai 2014). As Chimhundu writes: "To vernacularize a language is to reduce it to a vernacular" (1993: 35). While they do not connect their critiques of vernacularization with scale, I draw on several literatures that interrogate the apparent empirical reality of scale to expand on this sense of vernacularization as a process through which scalar and linguistic distinctions are actively constructed: how categories like "vernacular" and "local" are produced in the first place, and how particular communities and discourses are subordinated through relegation to such scalar and linguistic positions.

In questioning the construction of the local/vernacular, I am inspired by feminist, queer, and trans interrogations of gendered binaries between the "global" and the "local" and related hierarchies of scale (Mountz and Hyndman 2006; Boellstorff et al. 2014; Brady 2022). Feminists have critiqued how common conceptualizations of capitalism and globalization cast the scale of the "global" as an overwhelming force that dominates and penetrates the "local," which is essentialized, feminized, and rendered passive (Gibson-Graham 1996; Mountz and Hyndman 2006). Feminist, queer, and postcolonial approaches to scale have undone such dichotomies, demonstrating how scalar levels are relational and mutually constitutive—the local inflects or infiltrates the global and vice versa (Mountz and Hyndman 2006; Blackwood 2010). Further, multiple scales inform particular sites and subjects; nothing is purely local or global. People situated within specific locales in the Global South may well be "transnational" by participating in "processes that extend globally" (Blackwood 2010: 19); the apparently local subjectivities of *kothis* are informed by intersecting local, national, and global processes (Boyce 2007: 175). While the "global" in such discussions often references West-centric forms of transnationalism, some scholars of queer and transgender studies deploy concepts such as "queer regionalism," "critical regionality," or "minor transnationalism" to analyze interregional circuits of queer and trans discourse within the Global South and move past the binary of Eurocentric globalization versus local cultures (Chiang and Wong 2016: 1645; Chiang, Henry, and Leung 2018: 307). By attending to lateral traffics, (dis)continuities, and inequities across regions in the South, queer regionalism seeks to shift focus from both West-centric transnationalism and spatial imaginaries centered on the nation, providing an alternative frame of reference for understanding gender/sexual variance (Chiang, Henry, and Leung 2018: 308; Chiang 2021: 83).

My arguments are enabled by these approaches. But beyond describing nuanced intersections between global, regional, and local scales, or alternative scalar frameworks that better encompass *kothi–dhurani–hijra* transregionalism, my aim is more to interrogate the a priori construction of phenomena as local, regional, (trans)national, or global. Recourse to alternative scalar frameworks focused on the regional might not be adequate to deconstruct scalar hierarchies in the Indian context. As discussed in Chapter 4, activist discourse in "regional" languages like Bengali constructs normative representational categories such as *rupantarkami* (literally, transformation-desiring) by adaptively translating globalizing terms like transsexual, and positions *rupantarkami* as a universal identity and other terms as relatively local or vernacular—thus reconstructing scalar and epistemic hierarchies, even if from a non-Western standpoint. Further, the very legibility of categories like "regional" implicitly assumes a distinction from the "local" and thus implies a stratification of scale that cannot recognize how apparently local discourses and formations may be interregional or transnational in potentially effaced ways.

In that context, I take my cue from geographical, feminist, and sociolinguistic scholarship that suggests that, beyond better scalar descriptions, we must approach scale itself "not as an ontological structure which 'exists,' but as an epistemological one—a way of knowing or apprehending" (Marston, Jones, and Woodward 2005: 416). While not simply reflecting reality, the "performative epistemology of scale" has hierarchical effects (Springer 2014: 414). Scale, especially in its dominant Western form as a nested hierarchy that orders space "from the local to the regional to the hemispheric to the global," is an integral part of colonial imagination, enabling the rise of empires that sought to conquer and unite the world (Brady 2022: 18). This suggests that scaling, or categorizing phenomena in scalar terms, is a dynamic, power-laden, and contestable process with material consequences: scalar analysis must address the "social and material effects" of scaling practices without treating scale as "an objective reality" (Canagarajah and De Costa 2016: 2–7). In that regard, I deploy vernacularization as a particular form of scalar analysis that reveals how discourses or practices are not simply local or vernacular in reality but rather are actively *localized* and *vernacularized* through scaling processes that merit analysis and critique.

Unpacking the Vernacular

The "vernacular" is a useful heuristic for such analysis as a multivalent term that can variously denote scalar, linguistic, and conceptual hierarchies and suggest their interlinkages. In one sense, "vernacular" connotes the linguistic distinction between standardized registers of languages and more informal or everyday usages (Coupland 2009). Further, a "pejorative connotation" marks some senses of the vernacular as per its etymological association with enslaved people, while it also simply means local or native (Pollock 2006: 22). These senses are useful to describe both distinctions and hierarchies between different languages or linguistic registers. Emergent Dalit queer voices in urban India have critiqued how Dalits face exclusion in queer spaces due to lack of English fluency (Thakur and Zaffar 2023)—although English may also be reclaimed for Dalit emancipation (Saxena 2022). Samya, a middle-class gay/queer person I met in online groups, told me in an interview in 2021 that in some metropolitan queer spaces, "speaking in a vernacular language is a very shameful thing." In that context, vernacularization is useful to denote the creation or maintenance of hierarchies between LGBTQ discourse in English (and prestige varieties of Indian languages) and the subcultural languages of *kothi–dhurani–hijra* communities, which may be effaced or delegitimized by formal, public activist discourse and/or sought to be contained within informal, private spaces, as shown in subsequent chapters.

Moreover, the "vernacular" carries senses of the "local," "culturally specific," and "parochial" as contrasted with the "universal" and "cosmopolitan" (Werbner 2006: 496). Thus, it suggests how scalar distinctions between the global and local intersect with other conceptual dichotomies such as cosmopolitan/provincial and universal/particular. Here, my focus is not on concepts such as vernacular cosmopolitanism that seek to bridge apparently opposed ideas (Werbner 2006)— but rather, on the a priori construction of global/local and universal/particular distinctions and their interlinkages. For instance, expansionist discourses of capital and liberalism may justify scalar supersession through normative universalism by conflating West-centric forms of globalization with the expansion of universal human rights. Hegemonic LGBTQ discourse tends to assert identities like "gay" as both spatially global and as universal human ontology, implicitly positioning other conceptualizations of sexuality as cultural and particular—as Hillary Clinton declared while announcing US diplomatic support for LGBT rights abroad, "being gay is not a Western invention, it is a human reality" (Gray 2011). In that regard, vernacularization can connote distinct linguistic, scalar, and conceptual processes of hierarchization but also suggest their interlinkages.

Further, in designating a process rather than a set structure, vernacularization helps to conceptualize a contextually variable multilayered hierarchy rather than a static binary. Languages in India are variably ranked as local or regional relative to the national language (Hindi, a contested claim) and the transnational lingua franca (English).[15] Scholarship in South Asian studies has critiqued linguistic hierarchies and sometimes noted the inadequacies of "vernacular" or "regional" as descriptors that undermine the scope and reach of these languages (Iyer and Zare 2009; Sadana 2012; Shankar 2012). Some show how English, rather than always being elite or colonizing, may be localized or function as a vernacular in India (Sadana 2012; Saxena 2022). However, a systematic critique of the reduction of less powerful South Asian languages to the position of the vernacular, as offered by Annamalai (2014), is perhaps less common. Yet, like *kothi–hijra–dhurani* discourse, these languages are not reducible to static scalar categories—as evidenced by the transnational span of languages like Tamil across multiple Asian countries and diasporas (Shankar 2012: 146). Even going by official scalar ranking, some languages occupy contextually variable positions—Bengali is "regional" in India, officially recognized in certain states, but "national" in Bangladesh. Further, the tiered hierarchies of vernacularization may extend within languages themselves. Sanskritized registers of languages like Bengali or Hindi—standard varieties infused with words deriving from Sanskrit, a prestige language in precolonial India—have state recognition at national or regional levels, but "local" or colloquial varieties of these languages, commonly used by nonmetropolitan and nonelite people including many among *kothi–dhurani–hijra* communities, do not. Thus, not all subordinate linguistic positions are equally vernacularized, and may be contextually less or more vernacularized (see Table 0.1.).

This contextual variability in degrees of vernacularization is also apparent in gender/sexual terminology. Certain versions of *hijra* identity acquire a publicly recognized national position, and may be used to challenge or modify the globalizing transgender rubric, even as *hijra* is also subsumed under transgender. Sometimes, as shown in Chapter 2, *kothi* also emerges as a "national" term, but its status is more unstable, and it may be recast as local. Further, subordinated discourses may include non-hegemonic senses of "global" English terms like gay and transgender, which acquire a variety of meanings in nonmetropolitan and nonelite spaces, suggesting that putatively Western categories spread in horizontal and not just top-down ways (Boellstorff 2005; Jackson 2009). However, such variant senses, especially usages where "gay" and "trans" are not clearly distinguished, may not acquire acceptance or legibility in activist or state discourses, and remain vernacularized relative to globalizing epistemes of LGBTQ identity. Vernacularization therefore does not designate a neatly linear hierarchy or a singular subordinating relationship, but variable processes of scalar and epistemic supersession and subordination that sometimes contest or contradict each other.

Table 0.1 Scalar Positions of Indian Languages and LGBTQ Terminology: The Same Language or Word May Occupy Multiple Scalar Levels and Positions May Be Contested

Scalar Level	Language	LGBTQ Terminology
Transnational/global	Standardized US/UK English	Gay, transgender, queer, LGBTQIA, etc.
National	National languages: Indian English; Sanskritized Hindi (contested); Bengali in Bangladesh, Nepali in Nepal, etc.	LGBTQIA, hijra/kinnar, third gender, kothi (contested), samlaingik ("homosexual" in Hindi), etc.
Regional	State-recognized "regional" languages: Sanskritized Bengali in West Bengal, Nepali in India, etc.	Samakami, rupantarkami ("homosexual" and "transgender" in Bengali), etc.
Local/vernacular	"Dialects" like Bangal, Sylheti, Khortha, etc.	Codes like Ulti, terms like kothi and dhurani

These hierarchies of scale may thus be described as "queer," not only in the sense of referring to gender/sexual identities—"queer" is often used as an umbrella term for LGBTQ communities in metropolitan Indian activism—but also, insofar as "queer" indexes an irreducibility to binaries and stable categories, it references the instabilities within these hierarchies.[16]

Vernacularization, Culture, and Class

The multivalence of Anglophone terms suggests that vernacularization is not a matter of *cultural* opposition between Western and South Asian languages of gender/sexuality. Naisargi Dave has critiqued the anthropological essentialization of non-Western gender/sexual identities as culturally different from Western ones in some previous scholarship: "Following from the presumption of cultural alterity is the idea that most non-Western queer people are preoccupied not with the politics of identity, but with commensurating their sexuality with culture, religion, or nation" (Dave 2012: 16). My critique of vernacularization does not follow from the assumption of an essential incommensurability between cultures; the process of epistemological hierarchization is not reducible to binaries between "foreign" versus "indigenous" or "culturally authentic" terms since translinguistic flows and mediations defy such dichotomies. "Transgender" or "gay" may be used in rural India as perfectly "authentic" identities; however, not all articulations of such identities gain equal transnational recognition or legibility. As we see in later chapters, such terms, during their very spatial expansion, intersect with vernacularized discourses of gender/sexual variance and acquire senses that contravene established (trans)national epistemologies of gender/sexuality and thus may become elided or delegitimized relative to their dominant articulations. Meanwhile, some non-English identity terms, like some versions of the *hijra*, gain recognition at the national level. Thus, vernacularization signals a dynamic process through which, during the messy multidirectional translations between various terms and discourses, epistemologies of gender/sexuality are variably universalized or particularized in scalar and conceptual terms, irrespective of their "origins."

While Anglophone terms are not oppositional to nonelite or nonmetro contexts, entirely sidestepping the question of identitarian difference or commensurability may elide hierarchies of intelligibility. Dave's approach, which treats terms like queer as translatable, "widely accommodating" rubrics creating solidarity across linguistic and spatial locations, may efface discursive and spatial differences of power: "'Queer' . . . has come to India largely through the migratory movements of young, cosmopolitan scholar-activists . . . then gained currency as a widely accommodating, radical political frame" (2012: 20). But not all locations and languages have equal capacity of asserting such potential translatability and currency. Indeed, vernacularization is precisely the denial of such potentiality: while terms spread by "cosmopolitan scholar-activists" can be advanced as potential sites for translinguistic and transregional commonality, *kothi–dhurani–*

hijra terminologies are typically denied that scope by being positioned as spatially and culturally particular, despite their transregional scales and contributions to transnational processes.

Just as the vernacularized is not simply the "indigenous" or non-Anglophone, it is also not simply the nonelite. Rather, vernacularization is a subordinating mechanism that is contingently aligned with class or caste hierarchies without being deterministically linked to them. Working class and Dalit gay men or trans women who do not experience incommensurability vis-à-vis accepted models of homosexual and transgender identity may still face various forms of oppression, in which case the vernacularization of languages or identities may be a less salient factor (as exemplified by Dalit transgender activists who fluently articulate themselves as trans women).[17] However, scalar and epistemological hierarchies, where applicable, may intensify socioeconomic subordination by preventing access to identitarian legibility and related rights, as for Dalit *kothis* who may be seen as breaching MSM/transgender or cis/trans divides and thus ineligible for transgender benefits. While upward social mobility might happen despite or even through vernacularization, a systemic critique of class and caste hierarchies necessitates an interrogation of vernacularizing processes, which is not a rejection of LGBTQ identity politics in nonelite contexts, but rather problematizes how such political possibilities are restricted by scalar and linguistic hierarchies.

Capital, Noncapital, and Vernacularization

The book further analyzes vernacularization as symptomatic of tensions or contradictions between ascendant forms of LGBT representational politics informed by dominant social formations, processes, or discourses—including capitalism, nationalism, and caste—and more effaced logics of identity and community formation that contribute to but are not entirely legible within such representational frameworks and related normative logics.

Early theorizations of the cross-cultural emergence of LGBTQ identities ("global queering") often saw capitalist globalization as a dominating, universalizing force that to varying extents brought about a homogenization of sexual identities based on the Western model of homosexuality and the hetero–homo binary—whether this was seen affirmatively or critically (Altman 2001; Massad 2007). Subsequent scholarship nuanced such views—showing that emerging LGBT identities in the non-West are not simply derivative of the "West," that globalization and global queering evidence both cross-cultural convergences and variegation, and that non-Western forms of nationalism and capitalism, not only imperialist forms of Western capital, also inform the emergence of modern non-Western LGBT identities (Boellstorff 2005; Jackson 2009; Farmer 2011). Some of this scholarship has, however, emphasized the interlinked logics of capitalism and national modernity as dominant factors that inform the emergence of non-Western LGBT identities (Boellstorff 2005; Jackson 2009; Farmer 2011). As Blackwood argues, such emphasis on "transnational" or "national" processes might result in the relative neglect of local and regional scales (2010: 18)—or, in my framing, factors that are not recognized as national/transnational and relegated to local/vernacular scales. Contrastingly, the growing literature on queer regionalism emphasizes the "regional" but not so much the "local" (Chiang, Henry, and Leung 2018).

The representational frameworks that are sought to be established over vernacularized discourses are not simply determined by a homogenizing global capitalism, nor by any one form of nationalism. Rather, a variety of ideologies, processes, and logics—including biopolitical power targeted at the welfare and management of populations, neoliberal forms of capitalism, Hindu right-wing and liberal secular nationalism, and varying (trans)regional ideologies of caste and patriarchy—contingently inform multiple ascendant gender/sexual discourses that gain varying levels of dominance or hegemony. Countering tendencies within leftist theorizing that tend to see sociocultural multiplicity as part of the overarching totality of capital, Vinay Gidwani (2008) argues that "capital" is not a sovereign totality, but parasitically interacts with other socioeconomic logics not entirely reducible to its terms, such as gender, race, or caste.[18] Revising Kalyan Sanyal's (2013) theorization of the "capital not-capital complex," which describes the coexistence of capitalist and noncapitalist production in contemporary societies, Gidwani and Wainwright state: "the law of value, which structures capitalist social relations, is a normative logic that is parasitic on other (often effaced) normative logics (including non-capitalist ones) . . . other normative logics (of gender, caste, race, region, and religion, to name some) . . . traverse, enable, and interrupt . . . capitalist and non-capitalist forms of production" (2014: 44).

I find this formulation of the parasitic relation between capital and relatively effaced logics that both enable and interrupt it useful to understand the relation between dominant (trans)national formations of gender/sexual identity and ones positioned as relatively local/vernacular. As marginalized subjects demand rights and recognition, certain forms of gender/sexual identity and politics become legible at higher scalar levels through contextually varied articulations with various dominant capitalist and noncapitalist structures, processes, or discourses, even as LGBTQ movements contest and transform these formations in some respects. However, nonelite and/or nonmetropolitan communities and discourses tend to occupy more precarious positions relative to these various normative logics—neither entirely outside them, nor entirely recuperable or intelligible in their terms.

In that context, vernacularization or scalar-epistemic subordination serves to manage tensions that arise during mediations between multiple normative (non)capitalist logics and sociocultural formations like the *kothi-dhurani-hijra* spectrum that might both enable and contradict them. Most broadly, vernacularization serves to efface the contradictory dependence of "global queering" on irreducible forms of gender/sexual variance by casting them as local or regional. Further, vernacularization signals more specific tensions between discourses of gender/sexuality that fit biopolitical, nationalist, and/or liberal framings of identity and rights and articulations of gender/sexual difference that potentially contravene them. For instance, *kothi-hijra* networks help translate and expand MSM and transgender, yet interrupt dominant models of MSM and transgender as well as a neat separation between these categories, challenging their biopolitical reification as bounded populations. Their forms of self-expression may also contravene nationalist, dominant-caste, and liberal framings of rights through which LGBTQ political claims are asserted. Thus, their vernacularization as regional or local variants of MSM/transgender may serve to elide aspects that contradict these rubrics, which activists may dismiss as regressive, disreputable, or incorrect. Thus, these communities and discourses are circumscribed as localized versions of global, national, or regional LGBTQ formations inasmuch as they facilitate articulations between dominant (non)capitalist logics and gender/sexual difference, but may be effaced when they destabilize articulations between (non) capitalist logics and LGBTQ politics. Some tensions become more salient than others in particular contexts, and thus vernacularizing processes take multiple forms that are specifically explored over the chapters.

Entering the "Field"

The book draws on about forty-eight months of ethnographic fieldwork conducted over fourteen years (2007–21) across urban and rural West Bengal, supplemented by interviews and textual analysis. Since 2007, I have been closely involved as a volunteer, advisor, and participant observer with several CBOs in ten districts of West Bengal—mostly in Kolkata, Nadia, Murshidabad, and Cooch Behar (or Coochbehar), with supplementary fieldwork in North 24 Parganas, Hooghly, Malda, North and South Dinajpur, and Jalpaiguri (see Map 0.1). Since the community networks in these locations have connections with their counterparts in North India, Bangladesh, and Nepal, I also occasionally visited such adjoining regions.

In my interactions with *kothi–dhurani–hijra* communities, I represent class and caste privilege, metropolitan location, and transnational mobility, yet I am also a "native" co-inhabitant of the region. Despite my complicity in class, caste, and locational hierarchies, the boundaries between "researcher" and "subject" have often been destabilized as I have been interpellated into these communities as a friend, sister, or daughter—requiring complex navigations between my roles as a "participant" and an "observer." The political critique of vernacularization in this book emerges from the constant realization of the inequities and yet kinship that mark our collaborations.

The chapters draw upon detailed field notes of quotidian interactions and conversations among my interlocutors and myself, as well as recorded interviews, and often make use of quoted excerpts from notes—not to claim verbatim accuracy, but to indicate a sense of the linguistic dynamics of the exchanges. All translations are mine; throughout, italicized words within translated dialogue indicate words (including English terms) reproduced from the original quote. I realize that there remains a certain strategic empiricism in the attempt to render the "original" dynamics of such speech. Even as I critique the various representational frames used to describe these communities, a claim to verisimilitude (and its attendant responsibility) remains unavoidable if one is to critique dominant epistemologies from the vantage point of narratives that may not be "heard" within hegemonic scripts of legibility (Spivak 1988)—not as a heroic quest to "recover" such narratives from loss, but as an aspirational attempt to learn from below (Arondekar 2023).

Representing My Interlocutors: Gender, Sexuality, Caste, Class, Religion

While it interrogates institutional discourses of gender/sexuality, this book is itself an institutionally constrained act of representation that, in a sense, brings the difference it describes into being. This becomes especially fraught when describing my interlocutors in terms intelligible to Anglophone audiences, an act that inevitably risks vernacularization in potentially rendering "local/vernacular" communities as "evidence" for transnational theory-making in English (Arondekar and Patel 2016: 155)—even as I offer the critique of vernacularization as a way to interrogate the attempted containment of such life worlds through elite representations.

When referring to particular individuals, I try to follow their self-designation as *kothi*, *hijra*, transgender, and so on. However, I use broad, overlapping phrases like "gender/sexually variant" to describe the *kothi–dhurani–hijra* community spectrum overall. While LGBTQ movements have distinguished between gender identity and sexual orientation to guard against a conflation of gender variance and same-sex desire, "gender" and "sexuality" are not universally separable as categories of experience (Valentine 2007). While acknowledging varied configurations of gender and sexual desire, the book problematizes rigid distinctions between gender and sexual identities, which might serve to elide and vernacularize *kothi–dhurani–hijra* discourses where gender and sexual desire often overlap.

Given the spectral, overlapping nature of identities and subject positions, pronoun use is another complex issue. In the aforementioned intra-community "languages," community members may be referred to using feminine markers irrespective of sartorial presentation or nuances of identification (e.g., Susanta may be called a "sister" despite identifying as a gay man). Further, while called *bhasha* or "language," they are not fully distinct languages, but specialized vocabularies inserted into the grammatical framework of languages like Bengali or Hindi (Nandi 2024). Standard Bengali does not have gendered pronouns, while Hindi does. Thus, preferred pronouns may be difficult to determine and situationally variable. I try to consider both individual preference and situational context when using English pronouns for my interlocutors, using the gender neutral "they" for indeterminate cases.

A related issue is the use of *kothi*, *dhurani*, or *hijra* as stand-alone monikers, for example, "the *kothi*" or "a *hijra*," which accords with community practice and previous literature (e.g., Saria 2021: 46). While "a gay" or "one transgender" might be considered disrespectful in English, in *kothi–hijra* languages, *kothi* or *hijra* are typically stand-alone words distinguished from genders like "man" or "woman" (*tonna* and *laharan* in Ulti). Hence, saying *kothi* woman or *hijra* person would not convey their actual usage and the sense of legitimacy they hold as stand-alone descriptors.

In socioeconomic terms, my interlocutors are diversely located. *Hijra* lineages (which have hybrid religious practices), *dhurani–kothi* communities, and related CBOs may include members across class, caste, and religion, but most community members tend to be working class (Gupta 2005; Hossain 2021). While some middle-class gay men I encountered in cities sometimes jocularly referred to each other as *kothi*, people in my field areas who evinced more consistent or public identification as *kothi*, *dhurani*, and/or *hijra* were usually working class or lower middle class (*nimnobitto* or *nimno-moddhobitto* in Bengali). Many were also Dalit; however, asking about caste was not always possible given the personal and potentially stigmatizing implications of such questions. In Murshidabad, a Muslim majority district, many interlocutors were Muslim, while largely from Hindu backgrounds elsewhere. I specify these variable intersections between class, caste, and religion individually where relevant.

Mapping the Book

The chapters proceed roughly from earlier to later forms of vernacularization, but not in a neatly linear sequence since vernacularizing processes may return or overlap over time. The first chapter studies the emergence of the *hijra* as a national "third gender" identity in India, situating this as an early case of vernacularization through which the *hijra* emerges as more transregional or transnational relative to apparently more localized communities. Surveying the diversity within transregional *kothi–dhurani–hijra* networks, the chapter delineates how contested attempts to standardize representations of *hijras* at higher scalar levels efface contrary articulations of *hijra* identity, elide *hijra–kothi* overlaps, and reinforce intra-community hierarchies. Such processes influence later forms of vernacularization, even as the *hijra* itself is vernacularized: first as a regional variant of the colonial "eunuch" category and later of transgender. The chapter thus demonstrates vernacularization as an unstable, multilayered process.

The second chapter surveys the expansion of *kothi* identity parallel to the spread of LGBT activism and HIV-related NGOs since the 1990s. It traces how HIV activism drew from and transformed gender-variant networks spanning eastern India and adjoining regions, subsuming them and the *kothi* as a national subcategory of the globalizing MSM rubric. The transregional expansion of the *kothi* represents a consolidation of extant community networks and languages, which MSM seeks to fix into a stable identitarian cartography but fails to. The role of transregional *kothi–dhurani–hijra* networks in the expansion of NGO activism and related identities is effaced by the positioning of their discourses as undervalued "local" knowledges, while intra-community discourses that contradict biopolitical categories mediated by development capital are often elided in official representations, reinforcing their status as informal vernaculars. Such vernacularization attempts to contain contradictions between dominant categories and *kothi–dhurani–hijra* discourses.

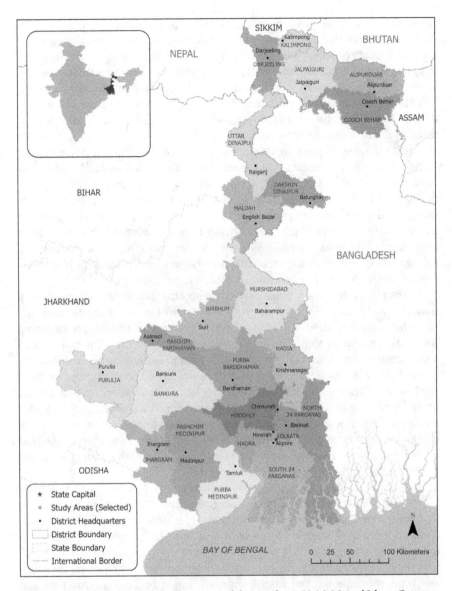

Map 0.1 Map of West Bengal showing internal districts by A. H. M. Mainul Islam. Courtesy of the artist.

The third chapter investigates how discourses on femininity within *kothi* communities intersect with vernacularization. *Kothi* communities evidence distinctions and hierarchies between "more" and "less" feminine members based on caste and gender norms but also contravene linear gradations of femininity. While LGBT and HIV activism utilize *kothi* participants and labor, dominant models of MSM and homosexual identity and liberal nationalist discourses of

LGBT rights come into tension with aggressive or sexualized forms of *kothi–hijra* public expression that contravene caste/gender norms. The vernacularization of *kothi* as a localized subtype of MSM or homosexual and the relegation of *kothi–hijra* linguistic practices to informal, private registers relative to activist discourse attempt to contain such contradictions and reinforce hierarchies between acceptable and excessive femininities. However, *kothis* also flout intra-community divides and contest hierarchies, sometimes utilizing ambiguities within activist discourses and vernacularizing processes.

The subsequent chapters turn to the much-debated globalization of transgender identities. Chapter 4 studies biomedical discourses of transsexuality and their rearticulation through Bengali terms like *rupantarkami* (transformation-desiring), which herald new models of interiority and linear male-to-female transition that both overlap and contrast with *kothi–hijra* discourses of interiority and embodiment. Both English and Bengali trans narratives often vernacularize *kothi–hijra* discourses as localized subtypes of transgender or transsexual, delegitimizing aspects that contradict normative models of identity, while *kothi–hijra* communities variably inculcate or contest trans discourses.

Chapter 5 shows how trans narratives become pluralized beyond binary transitional models. While linear models of transition are countered through *kothi–hijra* rearticulations of transgender as a separate gender, an emerging "national" version of third gender identity, modeled on the *hijra* and aligned with Hindu nationalism, may serve to elide or vernacularize other articulations of thirdness. Simultaneously, transgender politics heralds new avenues to claim rights and citizenship, but *kothi–hijra* strategies of public assertion that disrupt liberal models of formal equality may be condemned as violating transgender ontology. However, activist discourses also increasingly encompass more substantive understandings of equality, permitting bolder resistance. *Kothis* and *hijras* also contest vernacularization, utilizing tensions between multiple dominant discourses and resignifying dominant identities.

The sixth chapter studies how, even as transgender emerges as an "umbrella term" including binary and nonbinary identities, activist and legal discourses seek to cleanly distinguish it from sexual categories like MSM or gay. The MSM–trans divide is translated vis-à-vis *hijra–kothi* and intra-*kothi* splits, facilitating the expansion of transgender as a transnational term over its vernacularized "local" variations. *Kothi* subject positions that overlap between homosexual maleness and trans womanhood, and even *kothi* itself, might become controversial and erased from official discourse. While transgender people become conceptualized as subjects of substantive equality, MSM–trans and cis–trans binaries delimit the legible subjects of such equality. Variant *kothi–hijra* articulations of transgender contradict its distinction from cisgender and MSM categories but may be elided through vernacularizing processes. Simultaneously, middle-class gay communities articulate masculinized versions of gay identity as global and progressive, positioning *kothi* and related terms as localized, backward, and/or incorrect vernaculars. Contrastingly, relatively inclusive and "fluid" versions of gay or queer identity may position the *kothi* as too rigid, even as *kothis* rearticulate and resignify gay identity.

Together, these chapters critique the construction of rigidly bounded identities that tend to reify the dynamic distinctions within *kothi–hijra* communities into fixed categories, but do not valorize fluidity unconditionally. Some elite articulations of androgyny and queerness, for instance, demonstrate that metropolitan understandings of gender/sexual fluidity might not really be inclusive of the dynamicity of *kothi–hijra* communities that encompass both fluid and stable senses of selfhood.

The Afterword explores some ways in which nonelite, nonmetropolitan communities and discourses subordinated or effaced through scalar and linguistic hierarchies persist and even thrive, continuing to rearticulate and disrupt dominant models of identity. Specifically, *kothi* communities might intersect with emergent nonbinary discourse and Dalit queer/trans activism in ways that contest vernacularizing processes. These intersections signal an uncertain future, rife with contrary political possibilities.

Chapter 1

THE SCALAR EMERGENCE OF THE *HIJRA*

Just as we are hijras with penises, she is a hijra with a vagina!

—Heena, Nadia district, West Bengal

Heena was raised as a boy in a working class and Dalit family in an urbanizing village in Nadia. Over several conversations in 2012, she described herself as having been very *meyeli* (feminine) in her childhood, when she would surreptitiously dress in feminine clothes "like a typical girl," despite rebukes from her family. Isolated and teased at school, she gradually discovered a community of other feminine "boys" like her through contacts with older community members from her area, who call each other *kothi* and *dhurani*. Heena lives with her family, who have grown to accept her. At the time of our conversations, she stayed part-time in culturally "male" attire like men's T-shirts and jeans—partly due to habit, partly to avoid negative attention from neighbors. As she told me: "I don't like wearing feminine clothes always—I feel everyone is looking!" But occasionally, farther from home, she donned *sarees*—a common South Asian feminine garment—and blessed passengers in commuter trains for money, known as doing *chhalla* in community parlance. In such contexts, she identified and was perceived as a *hijra*, a member of the so-called third gender community of South Asia—feminine-attired people who may be distinguished from cisgender women by "masculine" features like facial structure or voice (Reddy 2005: 14). *Hijras* are commonly thought to be castrated or intersex, and associated with professions that involve blessing people in return for money or gifts (Reddy 2005; Hossain 2021). The epigraph above refers to the *guru* (guide/leader) of the *hijra* group with whom Heena did *chhalla*. This *guru*, whom we will meet later, was assigned female at birth and lives partly as a married woman with children, while presenting elsewhere as a *hijra*.

Heena's statement—which renders genitalia and assigned sex almost irrelevant for being *hijra*—contradicts long-standing academic and media representations of *hijras* as feminine-identified people assigned male or intersex at birth. *Hijras* often serve as "essentialized icons" of transgender or "third gender" identity in India (Cohen 1995: 276–9). International media have depicted *hijras* as "India's third gender" or the preeminent Indian example of transgender, specifically trans feminine, identity (Khaleeli 2014; Mok and Linning 2015). Much academic literature has discussed *hijra* identities and embodiments, debating whether *hijra* groups comprise castrated males, intersex people, impotent non-castrated men, feminine men, or some combination of such subtypes (Gannon 2009). Later ethnographies describe how *hijra* communities include diverse gender/sexual identifications and embodiments, but emphasize certain typical characteristics: *hijras* are mostly male-assigned (rarely intersex) people who dress in culturally feminine attire, follow distinct customs that blend Islamic and Hindu practices, and identify as like women or as neither men nor women (Reddy 2005). Ideally, they renounce sexual desire and, if not intersex, undergo physical emasculation (castration and penectomy) dedicated to a mother goddess—a sacrifice of reproductive potential for which they are divinely granted the power to bless or curse others with fertility or infertility, and which confers higher intra-community status relative to non-emasculated *hijras* and *kothis* (Nanda 1999; Reddy 2005).

Such *hijras* may garner more social respect too. Both male effeminacy and *hijra* identity are often stigmatized across South Asia—*hijra* may be used as a "derogatory epithet" for effeminacy, impotence, or effeteness (Hall 1997: 444). Yet, embodiments distinct from procreative sexuality may also have socioreligious connotations of an auspicious or powerful position—especially when such difference is perceived as congenital, since belief in the powers of sacrificial emasculation is less widespread outside these communities (Zimman and Hall 2010; Hall 2005). In a conversation in 2022, Silk, one of Heena's *kothi* friends who frequents *hijra* households in Nadia, shared that although people increasingly knew that most *hijras* were not "*jonmogoto*" (inborn) or even emasculated, "yet, even today, people believe there are some *ashol* (real) *hijras!*" Some still approached local *hijra gurus* believing they were congenitally "real" and had the power to bless people with fertility or even heal sick people. As Zimman and Hall state, *hijras* "claim that they are a people 'born without genitals' . . . because the *hijras* exist outside normative structures of sexual kinship they have earned the mystique of having power over procreation" (2010: 175).[1] However, given that congenital status is not always easy to ascertain, a much larger variety of people identify and are perceived as *hijra*. In that context, the position of Heena's *guru* as a community leader suggests relatively obscured narratives of *hijra* identity and practice—the literature mentions female *hijras* only marginally.[2] Further, countering the association between emasculation and intra-community status, Heena's group—mostly non-emasculated *kothis/hijras* with a female *guru*—illustrates the widely variable power dynamics within *hijra* communities.

This chapter explores how the public figure of the *hijra* as an iconic "third gender" corresponds to different, and sometimes clashing, logics of identification and community formation. I examine processes that tend to standardize certain narratives of *hijra* identity at national or transnational scales, and relatively invisibilize or elide others.[3] I argue that the attempted establishment of a consolidated, definable *hijra* identity over variable narratives of *hijra* identification constitutes a form of vernacularization—the construction of discursive and scalar hierarchies between (trans)nationally and institutionally recognized discourses of gender–sexuality, and practices, identities, or communities that become positioned as relatively local or vernacular. The process of establishing standardized *hijra* definitions begins at least from colonial times when British authorities enlisted *hijra* as a "vernacular rendering" of the pejorative "eunuch" category, and tried to determine whether *hijras* were "natural" (congenital) or "artificial" (castrated) eunuchs (Hinchy 2013, 2017). *Hijra* definitions were mediated through governmental and biopolitical technologies of power that emerged alongside colonial modernity and capitalism, and attempted to classify, enumerate, and manage population groups and regulate their conduct (Foucault [1976] 1990; Chatterjee 2004). In the postcolonial period, hegemonic versions of *hijra* identity are established through mediations between transregional *hijra* communities; institutions like the state, police, and media; and more diffuse social logics of gendered legibility (how people are read as particular genders). Hegemonic versions tend to reinforce status hierarchies within *hijra–kothi* communities and ideas of authenticity in public discourse that delimit social legibility as a "real" or respectable *hijra* as per normative ideologies of gender, class, and caste. However, attempts to produce hegemonic narratives are plural and sometimes contradictory, resulting in both narrowly bounded and broader definitions of *hijras* in the public sphere.[4]

Before elaborating my ethnography, I start from the extensive literature on *hijra* communities, which has increasingly de-essentialized *hijra* identities and documented their intersectionality and diversity, enabling more open descriptions beyond idealized criteria like emasculation or asexuality (Reddy 2005; Hossain 2021; Saria 2021). However, I am less invested in producing more complex or diversified representations of *hijras* as an empirically describable group or even multiple groups, and more in examining the production of representations as a dynamic negotiation between the spatial and discursive consolidation of *hijra* identity and variation in identitarian logics. If, as Adnan Hossain (2021) argues, *hijra*-hood is processual rather than a fixed set of attributes, I examine the negotiations and contradictions between multiple processes of *hijra* identity formation. Vernacularization here serves as an attempted strategy for managing tensions between contrasting logics of identification by establishing some *hijra* representations at higher scalar and discursive levels than others—particularly those that better fit social and governmental rubrics of identity and capitalist logics of gendered labor. The attempted scalar establishment of a (trans)national *hijra* identity across South Asia signals a representational politics that predates but continues through institutional LGBTQ activism and later informs other expanding identities like transgender and attendant forms of vernacularization, examined in later chapters.

Hijra *Representations and Scale*

Academic representations of the *hijra* raise intriguing questions regarding the scale of the category and its relationship with related groups. While the *hijra* often appears as a national, even supra-national community, there are regionally varied accounts of its overlap or distinction with terms like *kothi*, suggesting shifting cartographies of identity. Several scholars note how *hijra* communities are organized into "houses" or "lineages"—structured formations of non-blood kinship based on relationships between *gurus* and *chelas* (disciples)—that are connected across South Asia despite regional variations (Cohen 1995; Hall 1997; Reddy 2005; Hossain 2021). Contrastingly, feminine males or male-assigned persons outside or on the fringes of *hijra* lineages—and corresponding terms like *kothi, zenana,* and *jankha*—occupy a more variable and often localized scale, appearing in different regions under various names, but usually not depicted as part of comparable transregional networks (Cohen 1995; Reddy 2005; Hossain 2021). Indeed, when the *kothi* appears in activist discourse as a (trans)national category in the 1990s, its emergence is interrogated, and it may be seen as being spread via HIV-prevention projects or *hijra* lineages (Cohen 2005; Khanna 2016). Contrastingly, the historical continuity of the *hijra*—seemingly dating to precolonial times—and its supra-local expansiveness are not comparably interrogated.

Yet, the overarching transnational figure of the *hijra* is complicated by regionally variable mappings of the *hijra* vis-à-vis other categories. Sometimes, *kothi* is an umbrella term that includes male-attired *kada-catla kothis* and feminine-attired *hijras* as subgroups (Reddy 2005). Elsewhere, *kothis* are a "fourth" gender separate from *hijras* (Hall 2005: 128). *Hijras* may be seen as largely distinct from *zenanas* or *jananas* (Nanda 1999; Nagar 2019). Elsewhere, *janana* designates a subtype of *hijra* (Hossain 2021). Several scholars note that the boundaries between these identities are flexible (Reddy 2005; Nagar 2019; Hossain 2021). Gayatri Reddy notes fluid or overlapping identities across the *kothi* spectrum, but this apparently does not destabilize the identitarian schema itself, which provides a common frame of reference across which individual fluidity happens: "Most of these people recognize differences among these identities, but that does not . . . preclude the enactment of two or more of them" (2005: 76). However, the above contrasts suggest that the referential grid itself shifts spatially and contextually.

The same goes for logics of community formation. As Shane Gannon demonstrates, early studies of the *hijra* attempted to ontologically define them in terms of fixed gender/sexual or socioreligious attributes, producing conflicting representations (2009: 106). Subsequent literature critiques essentializing epistemologies of the *hijra* as a singular third gender, showing their diverse and intersectional identities. For Reddy, *hijra* is not merely a gender/sexual identity; several axes—gendered embodiment, ritualized kinship, profession, religious practices—multiply determine *hijra* subjectivities (2005: 34). However, scholars describe certain idealized markers of authenticity within *hijra* communities, particularly embodied distinctions from reproductive masculinity such as impotence, intersexuality, emasculation, or asceticism. These may be contravened by *hijras* in practice, but are nonetheless valued as ideals and invoked to distinguish "real" *hijras* from allegedly fake male pretenders to *hijra* identity and to claim higher status within the community (Reddy 2005: 15). Serena Nanda describes how, despite gender/sexual diversity among *hijras*, the lack of "reproductive capacities as either men or women" remains central to *hijra* identity: *hijras* are either born intersex, or must be impotent and undergo emasculation (1999: 141). Non-emasculated *kothis* among Reddy's interlocutors in Hyderabad may claim *hijra* identity, yet "sexual 'dysfunction'" and asexuality serve as imagined axes of distinction between *hijras* and non-*hijras*: "All *hijras* claim to be impotent, or physically impaired" (2005: 57). Supposedly ascetic and *nirvan* (emasculated) *hijras* claim more *izzat* (respect) within the community relative to non-emasculated and sex worker *hijras* (Reddy 2005: 40). Ideals and hierarchies of authenticity and respect prompt contestations: *kothis* mock *hijra* claims of sexual asceticism or congenital difference (Hall 2005: 130); *jankhas* contest bodily emasculation as a criterion for third gender status (Cohen 1995: 276); male-attired *kothis* claim more *izzat* (respect) for their ability to integrate within society (Reddy 2005: 228).

However, recent ethnographies contest the centrality of such embodied ideals for *hijra* identity. Hossain demonstrates how Bangladeshi *hijras* prioritize skill in *hijragiri*—the conduct of *hijra* professions and customs—over anatomical emasculation, such that non-emasculated *hijras*, even heterosexually married ones, may acquire higher intra-community rank than *nirvan hijras* (2021: 49). Thus, beyond non-*hijras* contesting hierarchies between *hijras* and themselves, the *hijra* itself shifts. Vaibhav Saria shows how *hijras* in Odisha cite shifting criteria to claim greater authenticity than other *hijras*—some cite their intersex or emasculated status, others cite their affiliation with *gharana*s (lineages), while those deemed inauthentic by such criteria cite their consistent feminine presentation and disparage those in male attire (Saria 2021: 100). As this chapter shows, the axes used to legitimize oneself as a *hijra* vary between embodiment, attire, lineage affiliation, psychic identification, and professional performance, some of which permit overlap with categories like *kothi*—further, the concern with *hijra* authenticity or status may itself be contested.

However, despite diverse logics of *hijra* identification, not all identities have equal social legibility. Sociocultural logics for distinguishing "real" *hijras* often hinge on some version of embodied difference, especially genital status and/or distinction from reproductive sexuality, although such understandings evidence ambiguities too. Thus, despite referencing non-anatomical criteria internally, Bangladeshi *hijras* "publicly claim to be born . . . with defective or missing genitals" (Hossain 2021: 49). I contend that the contradiction between variable *hijra* identities and relatively restrictive scripts of social legibility may foster vernacularization as senior *hijras* try to establish legitimized narratives of *hijra* identity at higher scalar and discursive levels, seeking to contain *hijra–kothi–dhurani* overlaps within informal and localized intra-community discourses.

Such vernacularizing attempts often reinforce a hierarchical linear continuum of subject positions over nonlinear, anti-hierarchical tendencies within *hijra–kothi–dhurani* communities. My analysis of linearity draws from Jack Halberstam's critique of the "masculine continuum" (1998: 151), which describes a linear arrangement of lesbian/butch identities from less to more masculine positions, with contested borders between transgender and cisgender categories (here, *hijra* vs. men or feminine males like *kothis*). Normative versions of *hijra* identity often construct linear hierarchies based on criteria like emasculation, asceticism, and lineage affiliation, which intersect with governmental and sociocultural distinctions between "real" and "fake" *hijras*. However, nonlinear tendencies, like male-attired *kothis* becoming *gurus* to emasculated disciples, disrupt such hierarchies. Such tendencies may indicate temporal shifts—*hijras* in Hyderabad complain about the increasing relaxation of membership norms, corresponding to declining public belief in their spiritual role and the rise of prostitution (Reddy 2005: 83–92). But I contend that such tendencies have older precedents, given the historical unevenness of *hijra* lineages and norms across regions.

The following sections interweave ethnography, interviews, and previous scholarship to sketch how such hierarchies and anti-hierarchical tendencies are negotiated among *dhurani-kothi-hijra* people. Providing an introductory overview of transregional community networks, I then analyze tensions within processes of community and identity formation—relatively powerful sections within these communities, in mediation with social and governmental rubrics of legibility, seek to establish clear divides and linear hierarchies between *hijras* and feminine men in public discourse, while nonlinear tendencies may be contained through scalar-discursive subordination or vernacularization. This process attempts to manage tensions between both varying logics of identity and different forms of transregionalism, such as uneven, locally diverse *kothi–dhurani–hijra* networks versus more systematized transregional lineages that may try to scale up a more homogenized identitarian schema. The aforementioned contrast between the transnational figure of the *hijra* and regionally divergent cartographies of identity signals such tensions between spatial consolidation and variation.

However, vernacularizing attempts cannot always contain alternative logics of *hijra* identification that destabilize *hijra–kothi–dhurani* distinctions. Further, increasing transgender visibility has fostered the governmental recognition of psychological gender identity, challenging biological understandings of *hijra* authenticity. The conclusion notes how *hijra* self-representations negotiate such shifts through changing strategies of vernacularization.

Dhurani–dhunuri–kothi: Introducing Transregional Community Networks

Terms like *kothi*, *dhurani*, and *hijra* as used in West Bengal are embedded within the larger linguistic context of the region. Bengali features a rich variety of regionally diverse expressions describing femininity in persons assigned male at birth. *Meyeli* (feminine) and *meyeli chhele* (feminine boy, male) are commonly used in the colloquial language of southern West Bengal, which has a relatively high prestige status and forms the basis of standard written Bengali (Kaviraj 2015). Analogous words like *maigga* (feminine, womanlike) and *maigga pola* (feminine boy/male) are used in the Bangal or Eastern Bengali language varieties of Bangladesh, which I often heard in districts like Nadia that border Bangladesh. Madhuri, a *hijra* and transgender-identified activist, recounted in an interview that her Bangal-speaking aunt had berated her for being *maigga* as a child. Another such term is *meye-noshka*—literally, patterned like a girl/woman—which I heard south of Kolkata. Beyond Bengali, *mowga* may be used to connote male effeminacy in the

Bhojpuri language spoken among migrants from the neighboring states of Bihar and Uttar Pradesh in West Bengal.

While these terms are used to describe others pejoratively or neutrally, they are also used for self-description—sometimes seen as a behavioral trait, sometimes as a form of personhood. Lal, a young man whom I met at a community organization in Nadia, described himself as having "*alpo meyeli bhab*" (a little feminine affectation or demeanor) in his childhood. But it was "only a little, not much," becoming less discernible as he grew up; for him, *meyeli* was a *bhab* that may wear off. However, others describe being *meyeli* as a more integral part of selfhood and use *meyeli chhele* to mark a type of person or community. Bikash, a senior participant in the aforesaid organization who grew up in a poor Dalit family in the small town of Ranaghat in Nadia during the late 1980s and 1990s, described herself over several conversations as being "*ekdom*" (totally) like girls in her childhood—she loved staying at home and wearing her sisters' dresses, "just like how *meyeli chhele* typically are!" She also gradually became aware of her desire for men and would surreptitiously check them out. She was abused at school as *homo*, *boudi* (sister-in-law) and *ladies*—all common derogatory terms for effeminacy. *Homo*, a colloquial derivative of "homosexual" dating back to at least the 1980s, suggests the social conflation between effeminacy and same-sex desire. However, *meyeli* could also be dissociated from same-sex desire: Bikash spoke of a Brahmin (highest-caste) priest in Ranaghat who was commonly perceived as *meyeli* but was happily married to a woman.

Like Heena, Bikash gradually discovered other *meyeli chhele* in her area in the early 1990s, a decade before community-based NGOs arrived there, which helped her to overcome her isolation: "initially, I did not know there was such a large *dal* (group) of us!" Bikash discovered a neighbor at whose house *meyeli chhele* would congregate, from whom she came to know that people like her called themselves *dhurani*, a term unknown in standard Bengali, and had an intra-community *bhasha* (language) called Dhurani Bhasha. *Dhurani* could also specifically mean someone who has a lot of sex or a sex worker—being related to the verb *dhurano* (to have sex) in the language—but Bikash's friends typically used it more generically for their community. They called the men they desired or partnered with *parikh*—*parikhs* were typically not *meyeli* and did not use any such terms; words like *dhurani* remained relatively private, intra-community usages despite the visible femininity of people like Bikash. Through her seniors, Bikash was gradually exposed to a transregional *dhurani–hijra* network and later learned terms like *kothi* from younger community members, which, as the next chapter elaborates, she treats as synonymous with *dhurani*.

Oral histories from the Murshidabad district north of Nadia and Kolkata in the south reveal similar, but locally varied, processes of community formation. In Murshidabad, gender-variant persons who grew up in the 1980s formed communities that called themselves *dhunuri*, which seems to be related to *dhurani*. They similarly called their male partners *parikh*; here, the language was called Dhunuri Bhasha. In Kolkata, Raina, who works today as a transgender activist, faced childhood isolation for being *meyeli*. But during her adolescence in the 1990s, she discovered the same cruising area in south Kolkata that Susanta, the activist we met earlier, had visited. There, she was introduced to a larger community who used both *dhurani* and *kothi* to designate themselves. Relative to mainstream terms like *meyeli* or *maigga*—which may or may not correspond to personal identity and same-sex desire—these terms thus signal a more consolidated sense of community, organized around an intergenerationally inherited vocabulary, an interlinked sense of gender and sexual variance, and distinction from mainstream men.

However, *dhurani–kothi* communities are also diverse and locally varied in terms of gender and sexual desire. For example, while Raina's friends primarily desired *parikhs* outside the community, there were also people like Bindiya, who described how she would visit public parks and cruise for *kothis* as a "handsome young man," but gradually entered these circles, felt drawn to feminine attire, and eventually joined a *hijra* lineage. Moreover, some *kothis/dhuranis* may be married to women, whether willingly or due to familial pressure. Some, like Heena and Raina, avow a consistent femininity since their childhood. Others, like Silk's friend Trishna, take pride in their ability to switch between masculine and feminine presentations, which may be useful to blend within working-class professions—Trishna supported her family as a male construction worker before taking to *chhalla*. In a 2012 conversation, Trishna, who had recently undergone emasculation without joining a *hijra* lineage and still sometimes wore male attire, told Silk and me: "I can still work as a man—I don't have any problem! They don't need to know I'm emasculated!" Indeed, the "languages" include multiple adjectives to indicate varying forms of gender variance, like *kodi* (less overtly feminine, male-attired) and *bheli* or *bhelki* (flamboyant, feminine-attired). Ajit, a "daughter" of Bikash in the Ranaghat circle, once explained to me: "*Kothis* are of many types: some are *kodi*, some *bheli*, some even half-*kodi*, half-*bheli* (*adha-kodi, adha-bheli*)!"

These networks overlap with *hijra* communities, and the language, called Ulti or Farsi by *hijras*, is shared too.[5] Madhuri claimed to me that *hijra* communities were historically older and *kothi–dhuranis* have taken their language from *hijras*. However, according to *dhunuris* in Murshidabad, they learned the language primarily from *dhunuri* seniors. Countering the claim of *hijra* precedence, a *kothi–dhurani* idiom found across several districts states: "*Hijras* are made from *kothis*, just as rice is made from paddy." While individuals may join *hijra gharanas* without passing through *dhurani–kothi* communities, many come from these communities. Bikash described how some *dhuranis* joined *hijra* groups permanently, while others temporarily undertook *hijra* professions like *chhalla* without joining *gharanas*, even remaining *kodi* at other times. *Guru–chela* (teacher–disciple) relations are also paralleled outside *hijra* lineages. Bikash accepted her neighbor Shombhu as her *guru-ma* (mother *guru*) and Shombhu's *guru-ma*, Shyamoli, became Bikash's *naan-guru* (grandmother *guru*), but without a formalized initiation process, unlike the *gharanas*. Shyamoli had moved to Ranaghat from her natal village and made her living through *lagan* or *launda nach*—a cultural practice found in Bihar and Uttar Pradesh where *laundas* (boys) dance at weddings in feminine attire (Morcom 2013). While Shombhu and Bikash wear male attire and live with their families, Shyamoli lived independently and dressed in feminine attire (she passed away in 2007). Described variably as a *dhurani* or *hijra* by community members, Shyamoli had contact with *hijra gurus* but remained outside the *gharana* system. Meanwhile, in Raina's circle, some *bhelki kothis* joined *hijra* lineages and underwent emasculation; others like Raina did not, although they wear feminine attire and may be socially perceived as *hijra*.

These practices do not indicate an unproblematic diversity or fluidity, as there are intra-community tensions around gender and respectability. Raina narrated that after she began wearing feminine clothes, she was distanced by some *kodi* acquaintances, especially those from dominant-caste, middle-class households, who regarded public feminine attire as *hijra*-like and disreputable. As elaborated in Chapter 3, *hijra*-like presentation carries not just gendered stigma but also contravenes caste respectability, since the social status or honor of a family within a caste-based and patriarchal social order is linked to the transmission of the male line through endogamous marriages, and a *hijra* son brings shame to the family through his supposed impotence (Hall 1997: 444). Meanwhile, some *hijras* and *bhelki kothis* regard *kodi kothis* with suspicion for their access to social masculinity and related privileges, which might be seen as *shubidhebadi* (opportunistic). Further, as detailed later, feminine-attired *kothis/dhuranis* may be regarded as fake *hijras* both by *hijra* lineages and mainstream society. Such tensions are uneven across locations. Bikash remarked that some of her male-attired *dhurani* friends maintained a masculine facade and did not want to be seen publicly with *hijras* or *dhuranis*. However, the towering presence of Shyamoli-*ma* (mother Shyamoli) at Ranaghat also inspired *kodi* (male-attired) *dhuranis* to become her *chelas*, such as Bikash and Shombhu themselves, who are publicly *bheli* (flamboyantly feminine) in their mannerisms. Therefore, subjectivity and kinship within the community also cross *kodi–bheli* divides.[6]

These communities thus evidence both transregionally shared characteristics and variations in language and community dynamics. The "languages" have spatially variable names—Dhurani Bhasha, Dhunuri Bhasha, Ulti—yet, terms may be analogous or cognates, like *dhurani* and *dhunuri*. Further, several words are transregional—*kodi* (describing masculine-presenting *kothis*) seems to correspond to *kada* in Hyderabad and *kare* in Delhi; *parikh* likewise corresponds to *panthi*.[7] When Raina traveled to Delhi for work, she found that *zenana* was a common name for the community, used simultaneously with *kothi*. In North Bengal and the neighboring country of Nepal, the term *meti* may be used synonymously with *kothi*. However, these languages are not uniformly present across Bengal or India. Debgopal, a filmmaker who has worked in the western districts of Birbhum and Bankura, recounted to me that such communities and languages were not widespread there up to the 2010s.[8] Yet, since the expansion of NGO-based activism from the 1990s, there has also been an increasing consolidation of community networks and languages, such that Ulti has become the most common name for the language in Bengal while *kothi* has often replaced *dhurani/dhunuri* among younger generations—as the next chapter elaborates. For now, I will treat *dhurani*, *kothi*, and so on, as loosely overlapping terms, given that they connote a flexible and transregionally overlapping spectrum rather than rigidly bounded categories.

Hijra *Transregionalism: Colonialism and the* Gharanas

The contrast between translocal connection and local variation is manifested through the variable relation between *kothi–dhurani* networks and *hijra* lineages: sometimes overlapping, sometimes rigidly distinct. Many, but not all, *hijras* in West Bengal belong to lineages known as *gharanas*, each organized into tiered ranks of *gurus* (teachers/leaders) and *chelas* (disciples). In conversations with my *hijra* interlocutors, I was told of three *gharanas* in Bengal—Shyambajari, Mechhua or Machhua, and Gunghor or Gumghor. Each *gharana* comprises several senior *gurus* (*nayaks* or chiefs) who lead independent households shared with their *chelas*, called *hijra khol* or *dayyar*. *Chelas* become second-tier *gurus* to *nati-chelas* (*chelas* of *chelas*) who in turn take their own *chelas*, gradually ascending in the hierarchy, while people of equal rank are *gotiya* (friends, sisters).[9] Each household nonlegally claims a territory (*bireet* or *elaka*) that demarcates the area where its members may undertake *hijra* occupations; *chelas* give the household's leading *guru* a share, usually *adhiya* (half), from their earnings. Among senior *gurus*, some control larger areas, multiple households, and more disciples, and accordingly hold more intra-community power and prestige—thus, *gurus* often compete over and try to expand their territories. Despite overall stigmatization, senior *hijras* may acquire wealth and attempt to fit within "respectable" society, as detailed later. Low-ranking *chelas* are typically expected to live with their *gurus*, but some also live independently, especially after they acquire more *chelas* and income. While *gharana* members use *hijra* or *brihannala* (in literary Bengali) to publicly represent themselves, *chhibri* (literally, emasculated) is used as a synonym for *hijra* in intra-community languages. However, many *hijra* household members, particularly junior *chelas*, are *akua* (non-emasculated), and some are intersex or female, with variable status.

Occupationally, the ritualized performance of *badhai* is the primary *gharana*-sanctioned *hijra* profession in West Bengal—it is typically undertaken by junior *chelas* who visit households with newborn children within their territory, sing celebratory songs and proffer blessings, and demand money or gifts in return.[10] A secondary, less respectable occupation is *chhalla*—proffering blessings and asking for money in shops, trains, or streets. As detailed later, *chhalla* is a site of tension, as *kothis* or *hijras* outside lineages also do it. Some *hijras* also perform *khajra* (sex work) with men at cruising spaces, which (like *chhalla*) is seen as disreputable relative to the asexual religiosity of *badhai* in Bengal.[11] However, in some cities like Mumbai, sex work is a legitimate occupation for some *gharana*-based *hijras*, suggesting regional variations in *gharana* norms. My *hijra* interlocutors mentioned at least fifteen *gharanas* in India. Bindiya, who is affiliated with the Gunghor *gharana*, explained to me that the *gharanas* are assembled into supra-regional clusters, sometimes classified as the *poorvi* (eastern) and *paschimi* (western) branches, which congregate in meetings where territorial disputes and other conflicts are arbitrated.[12] Some lineages have transnational connections— for instance, Madhuri's *gharana*, Shyambajari, extends into Bangladesh, and Bangladeshi members sometimes attend meetings in India. *Gharanas* thus exemplify more systematized transregional linkages relative to the more loosely organized *dhurani-kothi* circles.

Even so, *gharanas* have a spatially uneven presence in eastern India. Some *hijra* narratives claim Gunghor as the first "*srishtikorta*" (creator) *gharana* of Bengal, established by Gangaram, a *hijra* who arrived from North India some centuries ago, from which the other *gharanas* broke off later. While *hijra* narratives are often vague about dates, senior *gurus* of Gunghor claim that they were recognized by Mughal rulers in the eighteenth century. Madhuri explained to me that the reach of *gharanas* was historically more limited in the eastern and southern regions relative to North India—*hijra gharanas* arrived later in Bengal and are still absent in parts of Northeast India.[13]

This suggests that the *hijra* does not correspond to a historically or spatially uniform community across South Asia. Indeed, the spatial expansiveness of the contemporary *hijra* category emerges in mediation with colonial governmentality and classificatory practices. Modern forms of power are distinctively marked by the proliferation of biopolitical and governmental techniques that have sought to achieve the "subjugation of bodies and the control of populations" through ways of knowing, enumerating, and classifying people (Foucault [1976] 1990: 140). Jessica Hinchy (2013, 2019) and Shane Gannon (2009) examine how colonial administrative and ethnological discourse attempted to describe, classify, and regulate people they called "eunuchs" and *hijra*. Although these scholars do not specifically interrogate constructions of scale, their accounts suggest that colonial narratives helped establish eunuch and *hijra* as transregional terms, positioning others as relatively vernacular or local. In colonial archives, "eunuch" served as a pejorative category that indexed various forms of "failed masculinity" including impotence, emasculation, and cross-gender attire (Hinchy 2013: 197). "Eunuch" was used as an official category in administrative discourse, in relation to which other terms were positioned as "vernacular" equivalents. Hinchy notes: "In 1883, a police official outlined 'the meaning of several vernacular renderings of the English term eunuch'" (2013: 199). Further, various historical categories of gender/sexual variance were translated as eunuch: "translating various Sanskrit and Pali terms—*kliba, shandha, pandaka, napumsaka, tritiya prakriti*... to mean eunuch, the colonial translators created a class ... largely defined by exclusion" (Gannon 2009: 21). "Eunuch" thus became positioned as a transhistorical, supra-local category, subsuming diverse terms.

Among these categories, *hijra* was further established as a transregional term, suggesting tiered layers of vernacularization: "The category of the *hijra* became a primary one, under which a plethora of other social groups were included" (Gannon 2009: 22). Laurence Preston (1987) chronicles British interactions with a community known as *hijra* (or *hijda*) in western India as an early colonial encounter with "eunuchs." The British curtailed their hereditary rights such as revenue shares under the precolonial Maratha regime, impoverishing them (Preston 1987: 371–87). Colonial accounts thus enlisted *hijra* as one of the first "vernacular renderings" of the eunuch. As Hinchy notes, the colonial policing of eunuchs particularly focused on North India where the term *hijra* was common, such that colonial accounts used *hijra* and eunuch interchangeably, although this "obscured the internal diversities . . . of the eunuch category" (2017: 4). While colonial ethnological compendia indexed various other regional names for "eunuchs" including *khoja*, *pavaya*, *khasua*, and *mukhanas*, they sometimes cross-referenced these terms with *hijra*—for example, by redirecting an entry on the *hijra* to one on the *khoja*—thus treating regionally diverse terms as analogous or equivalent to *hijra* (Dutta 2012a: 829).

Yet, *hijra* is not a stable referent in colonial texts, gathering contrasting meanings. Reddy notes that colonial accounts evidence an overarching epistemological concern with physiologically classifying eunuch bodies (2005: 28). Several ethnological compendia distinguish between "natural" eunuchs, congenitally deformed or impotent, and "artificial" castrated eunuchs, but ethnologies from different regions contradict each other regarding which vernacular term corresponds to which category—sometimes *hijras* are "natural" while other groups like *khojas* are "artificial," but elsewhere, *hijras* are artificial while *khasuas* are natural (Dutta 2012a: 829). Rather than a transregionally uniform category corresponding to a fixed eunuch subtype, *hijra* seems to index regionally divergent groups.

Despite contradictory definitions, the colonial literature did set a precedent for the use of *hijra* (rather than *khoja*, *khasua*, etc.) as a transregional moniker. *Hijra* was a term historically prevalent in the North Indian languages of Urdu and Hindi (Reddy 2005: 243). Postcolonial Indian nationalism projected Hindi as national over supposedly more regional languages (Sadana 2012). Reddy notes that the Telugu term *kojja* is used synonymously with *hijra* in Hyderabad, but uses *hijra* as the overarching name given its greater recognizability (2005: 243). A media article notes, "there are a number of terms used throughout India, Pakistan, and Bangladesh . . . but for consistency purposes, these communities will be referred to here as *hijras*" (Gupta 2015). Positioned within a "national" language, *hijra* thus gains an expansive transnational referentiality through the loose synecdochical collapse of various apparently equivalent terms.[14]

Beyond the role of (post)colonial regimes, the terminological expansiveness of the *hijra* seems to be also undergirded by the transregional *gharana* or lineage system. Reddy, for instance, notes seven *hijra* lineages spread nationwide, to which Hyderabadi *hijras* also belong (2005: 9). Yet, this span is not spatiotemporally uniform. Madhuri offered me a historical narrative of lineage expansion, gleaned from her *gharana* seniors. Apparently, ancient Bengal suffered from "*matsyanyaya yuga*," a period of chaos or anarchy lacking strong rulers, which was later stemmed by the medieval Sena kings, following which *hijra gharanas* entered Bengal. Madhuri's narrative, whether historically accurate or not, suggests that some *hijras* associate the expansion of organized *hijra* lineages with the consolidation of medieval monarchical regimes and centers of power, from which lineages may have sought patronage. Significantly, medieval Bengal saw the rise of monarchies that reinforced caste hierarchy, the decline of Buddhist-influenced socioreligious movements that challenged caste, and the increasing migration of dominant castes from North India (Bandyopadhyay 2004: 18). *Hijra–kothi* interlocutors have pointed out to me that border areas of West Bengal like the western district of Purulia, which has a prominent presence of Adivasis or "tribes" outside the caste order, are still not entirely covered by *hijra* households and territories. *Kothis* from the north-eastern district of Coochbehar—an area with prominent Dalit and tribal groups such as the Koch–Rajbongshi—report that *gharanas* established households there only in the 2010s. In that context, Madhuri's narrative suggests a correlation (whether imagined or real) between *gharana* expansion and spaces where mainstream Indian sociopolitical orders have historically been centered, and contrasts hierarchy with anarchy. As Reddy demonstrates, although *hijras* are stigmatized as outside social norms, *hijra* lineages claim legitimacy through codes of *izzat* (respect) and related intra-community hierarchies (2005: 43). But given the spatial unevenness of *gharanas*, we will see that such hierarchies, and how they affect *hijra–kothi* relations, vary contextually.

Hijras *versus* "Men": The Real–Fake Distinction

While the presence of *akua* (non-emasculated) *hijras* within *gharanas* suggests their overlap with *kothi–dhurani* communities, whether such overlaps are seen as legitimate or not is related to both *gharana* norms and wider public understandings of *hijra* authenticity, which are contextually variable and contradictory. As Kira Hall notes, "real" *hijras* may be publicly perceived as born with ambiguous, defective, or missing genitalia and lacking sexual desire (2005: 125). However, contrasting social ideas contradict this narrative, such as stories about children being forcibly castrated to be made *hijra*, or *hijras* as impotent men (Cohen 1995: 283). The involvement of some *hijras* in sex work also undermines the narrative of biologically determined asexuality (Zimman and Hall 2010: 175). Some contradictions are more reconcilable than others—as several *kothi/hijra* sex workers told me, some men who saw their "male" genitalia during sex still believed them to be anatomically *hijra* since they had convinced their clients that their genitals were nonfunctional. Such credulity might be linked to a cultural belief that being penetrated anally causes impotence (Nanda 1999: 14). Once, a sex worker friend from Nadia laughingly described how one man even asked her to bless him after the sex was done, which both shocked and amused her. However, masculine reproductive potency, exemplified by *hijras* who marry and have children, may be harder to reconcile with anatomical or congenital ideas of *hijra* difference.

Such ideas may have been historically reinforced through the intersection of colonial governmentality with community and social narratives. Hinchy (2017) notes that colonial authorities in North India suspected "emasculated" *hijras* of kidnapping and castrating children. The government "intensified efforts to prosecute emasculation from 1865" and criminalized "eunuchs" through the

Criminal Tribes Act in 1871 (Hinchy 2017: 8).[15] Thus, Hinchy surmises that "eunuchs may have described themselves as a eunuch by birth to . . . avoid prosecution," but also notes that this might have been "a wider . . . form of public self-representation" predating colonial policing: "the 1865 Muzaffarnagar register reported that certain 'eunuchs' were '*said to be* a eunuch by birth', suggesting that this was how they had described themselves to local people" (ibid.). Hinchy concludes, "the eunuch-by-birth category emerged out of a convergence of the self-representations of so-called eunuchs, the knowledge of local people and the bureaucratic need to produce regular classifications" (ibid.).

However, in recent decades, media reports, documentaries, and autobiographies featuring NGO-affiliated *hijra* activists such as A. Revathi and Laxmi Narayan Tripathi have undercut the congenital narrative in favor of psychologized narratives of gender, associating *hijra* identification not with anatomy but with an inherent sense of gender identity that may be expressed through transition (Revathi 2010; Tripathi 2015). As later chapters examine, this brings the *hijra* closer to transnational discourses of transgender identity that have gained increasing state recognition since the 2000s.

Despite these shifts, the idea of *hijras* being anatomically and even congenitally distinct may continue to be evoked for the social and governmental policing of the *hijra*–male distinction. Hall documents several media reports of people who publicly present as *hijra* being shamed as "fake" and exposed as "men" based on their genitalia—sometimes even punished through public or police intervention abetted by *hijras* who claim to be "real" (2005: 125–6). I heard of several more recent incidents during my fieldwork. In July 2016, railway police arrested three *kothis* who were doing *chhalla* at a railway station in Kolkata as unauthorized encroachers. A transgender activist who tried to intervene told me: "The policeman said, 'these are not real *hijras*, they are *artificial* . . . they dress up for money; I will strip them and show you that they are not real!'"

While such policing may recall colonial practices, such actions go beyond the state. In 2015, Bikash told me about an incident where some women thrashed a *kothi/hijra* person doing *chhalla* in a commuter train after it was accidentally revealed that she had "male" genitals: "they said, don't you feel ashamed to do this as a *marad* (man)?" As per this biologically deterministic logic, assuming *hijra* identity is shameful for any anatomical "man," and male effeminacy does not legitimize *hijra* identification. Such trends are exacerbated by media narratives. A 2014 article in a prominent Bengali newspaper cautioned people against "*bhejal brihannala*" (fake *hijras*), men who dress as *hijras* and harass people for money, including some who are heterosexually married (Pramanik 2014). Marriage often serves to prove fakeness, as it contravenes the assumed lack of male reproductive capacity (Hall 2005: 126). However, *kothi–hijra* community members report that mainstream men posing as *hijras* for money are rare in West Bengal. Heena asserted that men without any internal (*bhetorer*) femininity would not be able to work as *hijras*, whereas Ajit stated that she had indeed seen *berupia* (impostor) troupes comprising mainstream men in cities like Mumbai. But both agreed that "fake *hijra*" claims mostly target *akua hijras* and *kothis*—married or not.

Sometimes, *hijras* reinforce such media narratives, as exemplified in a 2015 viral video that showed one *hijra* publicly thrashing and stripping another to prove the latter was male and thus "fake" (Daily Bhaskar 2015). *Hijra* deployments of the real–fake distinction are partly economically motivated—used to undercut competitors and fit within social imaginaries that connect congenital reproductive lack to the power to bless or curse (Cohen 1995: 286). Indeed, *hijras* may even strip and expose their genitalia (or the "lack" thereof) to prove their authenticity (Cohen 1995: 296).

Beyond *hijra* castigations of fakeness, the figure of the fake *hijra* gains legibility within the broader social shaming of feminization and emasculation. One article accompanying the aforementioned video stated: "It's disgusting for a perfectly healthy and young man to beg as a transgender and not work hard" (Daily Bhaskar 2015). The distinction from "healthy" maleness casts *hijra*-ness (here conflated with transgender) as a bodily deformity—an idea that *hijras* have occasionally played up to demand concessions from the government (Cohen 1995: 297). Even emasculation may not suffice to be deemed authentically *hijra*. In 2017, a Bengali notice signed by "concerned passengers" posted inside commuter trains near Kolkata alerted people to not give money to *hijras* in trains because they had become *hijras* by cutting off their penises (*"lingo kete"*) for easy money. Recently, even some *hijras*, who express discontent with intra-community conflicts and say they wish to quit the community, have stated to the media that inborn *hijras* are nonexistent or rare and most *hijras*, including themselves, are actually *"byatachhele"* (men) who were compelled to get emasculated by unscrupulous *gurus* looking to expand their business (News18 Bangla 2023).

The recurrent trope of faking *hijra* presentation for economic gain suggests that biological determinism and anxieties around emasculation converge with gendered and capitalist logics of productive work. "Fake" *hijras* may be condemned as part of illegitimate begging rings that seek to escape "hard work" (Daily Bhaskar 2015), which is masculinized in capitalist and patriarchal labor economies. Real–fake distinctions thus mark the convergences of varied social, subcultural, governmental, and economic logics, which we might understand as particular iterations of capital–noncapital complexes (Gidwani and Wainwright 2014). These convergences serve to erase or delegitimize the figure of the *meyeli chhele*—male yet not conventionally man—and the possibility of noneconomically motivated transition to *hijra* identity.

Yet, *hijra* and *meyeli* subjectivities may also be perceived as more continuous in Bengal. Since the 1990s, Bengali media and books have increasingly spread knowledge of feminine males transitioning to *hijra* through emasculation, undercutting the myth of *hijra* congenital difference among middle-class audiences (Ahmed 1995; Majumdar and Basu 1997). Further, there are older discourses of *meyeli–hijra* overlap found in more colloquial, quotidian registers. Annie, a *kothi* from the South 24 Parganas district, described that in her youth, she had heard people remarking on the association between *meye-noshkas* and *hijras*: they might say, "see, how that *meye-noshka* is walking with a *hijra*!" This suggests a public recognition of a certain affiliation or kinship between the two. In parts of Coochbehar, where *gharana* households have entered recently, the idea of *hijra* congenital intersexuality is not widespread among working-class and Dalit villagers. Sumi, a Coochbehar-based *kothi* and trans-identified activist, told me that in Ghughumari, her village, "people don't necessarily think that *hijras* don't have anything down there—rather, they think that their penises are small or inactive!" The lack of a rigid congenital *hijra*–male distinction means that people may use *hijra* as a loose term for a spectrum of feminine male-assigned persons, whether tolerantly or disapprovingly. As Sumi said: "Here, people call those of us who wear feminine clothes as *meye hijre* (girl *hijra*) and those in male clothes as *byatachhele hijre* (boy *hijra*)!" Some *kodi* (male-attired) *kothis* in Coochbehar have even appropriated these terms, and sometimes jocularly refer to themselves as *byatachhele hijre*. I also heard this phrase sporadically in southern Bengal, suggesting its uneven transregionality.

Further complicating such variable perceptions of the relation between male effeminacy and the *hijra*, *kothis/dhuranis* are often socially read as *hijra* if they dress in feminine attire, irrespective of transition or self-identification. As Sujoy, a *kothi* from Murshidabad, once told me: "If we dress up, people will call us *hijras* only, not girls!" Thus, despite discourses of *hijra* authenticity, who the *hijra* "really" is remains ambiguous in practice. The amorphous social legibility of the *hijra* permits shifting cartographies and logics of identification, including variable overlaps or distinctions between the public *hijra* category and more intra-community terms like *dhurani/kothi*. This may prompt attempts to standardize the distinction.

Homogenizing Cartographies: Policing Distinctions between *Hijra* and Non-*hijra*

For some community members, there is a clear, unambiguous distinction between *hijras* and *dhurani/dhunuri/kothi* people. In Murshidabad, Shyam and Annapurna both grew up in villages near Berhampore, the district headquarters, and discovered the *dhunuri* community in the 1980s. From a relatively middle-class background, Shyam remained in male attire and pursued mainstream professions, though avowing a strong internalized femininity. Contrastingly, as Shyam described in a 2011 conversation, "Annapurna and her friends danced and performed female roles in *alkap* (a regional 'folk' operatic form). Then, some of them started living together, away from their families, and wore *satra* (feminine attire) more freely. . . . Then, they joined a *hijra* house and got emasculated (*chhibralo*)." Annapurna told me that she had been *meyeli* (feminine) since childhood, enjoyed dancing, and was learning tailoring work, but was attracted by the wealth she saw in *hijra* households: "It went to my head—suddenly, one day, I got myself emasculated, and became a *hijra*." By Annapurna's time, most *hijras* underwent *nirvan* or *chhibrano* (emasculation) secretly through illicit doctors rather than the *dai*, *hijras* who specialize in the operation.[16] Later, Annapurna became the *guru-ma* (mother *guru*) of one of the two *hijra* households in Berhampore, which belong to the Mechhua *gharana* and perform *badhai* within their respective territories.

In Shyam and Annapurna's accounts, there is a linear, unidirectional transition from *dhunuri* to *hijra*, but no simultaneity between the categories. Further, while *dhunuri* networks are relatively open, permitting the entry of diverse people, access to *hijra* identification is more restricted, entailing both initiation into *hijra* households and emasculation.

Hijra gharanas in Bengal and beyond have sought to preserve such clear distinctions between *hijras* and feminine males and, despite the aforementioned exposés by renegade *hijras*, have tried to prevent the public exposure of transitions between these positions. While Nanda (1999) notes that *hijras* may cite certain Hindu myths to claim sacrificial emasculation as the source of their powers over fertility, public belief in or even knowledge of this process has not been historically widespread in north and eastern India (Majumdar and Basu 1997; Hall 2005). Bahuchara Mata, the form of the Hindu mother goddess worshipped by *hijras* to whom the emasculation is dedicated, has a public temple in Gujarat (western India), but the relationship between the goddess and *hijras* is known only to some locals and not widely (Kunihiro 2022). Belief in *hijra* powers seems to derive not from mainstream Hindu legitimation of *hijra* emasculation—but rather, from the mystique around their being allegedly *born* with ambiguous, defective, or missing genitals (Zimman and Hall 2010). Even such beliefs have been declining in Bengal since the 1990s (Majumdar and Basu 1997). As noted earlier, increasing public knowledge of emasculation need not translate to legitimacy—emasculated *hijras* may be seen as economically motivated rather than legitimate *hijras*. In 2012, when Shyam and I visited Hasina, the other *hijra guru* of Murshidabad, she complained that some *kothis* were telling people about emasculation: "They lessen our earnings; people say, these people become *hijra* by cutting their penis off, there's no need to give them anything!" Thus, publicly, *hijras* may stress their congenital distinction from *kothis/dhuranis* and disseminate real–fake binaries, while reinforcing hierarchies based on emasculation, *gharana* affiliation, and asexual religiosity inside the community.

Significantly, this is a project of spatial homogenization and scalar supersession—lineages seek to expand their territorial control so as to spread *hijra* versus non-*hijra* distinctions and establish uniform cartographic divides over local variations. Attempts to establish the more rigid version of the distinction, which suppresses transition from *kothi–dhurani* to *hijra*, involve at least two spatialized strategies. Several *hijras* have told me that *hijra* households avoid recruiting *murad* (members) from nearby areas to prevent the knowledge that feminine males may become *hijras*. Madhuri noted that this practice was stricter earlier, when *hijra* households maintained a greater distance from *kothis*. Second, *gharana*-based *hijras* may try to prevent *kothi–dhurani* people from donning feminine attire within their territories. In a 2012 conversation, Shyam described how some *hijra gurus* in a neighboring district objected to *kothis* outside *gharanas* wearing *satra* (feminine attire)—"one *guru* told me she'd beat up any *kothi* who dared to wear *satra* in her area!"

The erosion of public belief in *hijra* congenital difference may intensify anxieties about *kothi–dhurani* visibility. In 2008, Srijan, a *kothi* in Murshidabad, told me: "*Hijras* fear that *kothis* will spoil their market, because how many are born *chhibri* (*hijra*) anyway? People are realizing that *chhibris* are made from *kothis*." In other conversations, *kothis* from Nadia remarked that given the increasing public knowledge of transition, people give money to *hijras* less out of *bishwash* (belief) in spiritual powers and more out of *bhoy* (fear) of losing *shomman* (respect) due to their insulting behavior or of being shamed through contact with them.[17] Given the aforementioned link between caste–patriarchal order and the maintenance of heterosexual reproductivity, ethnographers note that *hijras* may be imagined as below or even outside conventional social rankings due to their supposed non-procreativity (Hall 1997; Nanda 1999). Not having much status to lose, *hijras* have developed survival tactics wherein they utilize their marginalized position to breach social norms of decency or modesty without shame or fear of losing respectability, deploying "indecent" behavior like hurling sexualized insults at abusers or people unwilling to pay, which may embarrass their interlocutors who are more constrained by the bounds of respectability (Hall 1997; Nanda 1999). In one conversation, Silk recounted stock statements that she had heard *hijras* use while visiting houses with newborn children to perform *badhai*—if the parents refused to pay, *hijras* might say loudly before their neighbors: "why, didn't you remember while fucking and producing this child that we'd come?"[18] South Asian norms of modesty, while spatiotemporally shifting, generally constrain the public expression of sexuality, especially for women (Gilbertson 2014). Feminine yet immodest, *hijras* threaten to undo the proper containment of sexuality and to implicate respectable householders in their shamelessness by exposing private sexual acts, embarrassing people into paying up.

Beyond shaming, *hijras* and *kothis* also use affective reactions like shock, fear, or disgust that people manifest toward disruptions of binary gender (Reddy 2005: 137)—asserting gender/sexual difference in ways that weaponize people's phobic reactions against themselves. During a community gathering in 2012, the *hijra* activist Madhuri explained: "see, people are afraid of *hijras* because they think that we are like women, so we'll be soft and meek . . . but when we are not, when we react like this (she loudly performed the *thikri* or *hijra* clap)—they get scared!" Clad in the typically feminine *saree*, Madhuri thickened her voice while speaking to suggest a masculine tone—signaling how *hijras* both evoke and transgress conventional femininity through embodied behaviors, purposely eliciting shock and fear. The most extreme transgression of both femininity and modesty that *hijras* are known for is the "thoroughly unfeminine" gesture of exposing their genitals, or the threat thereof (Nanda 1999: 18). This carries the threat of transmitting infertility—people may fear that looking at ambiguous or missing genitalia could render them impotent or infertile (Reddy 2005: 140). While such exposure was rare in my experience, I noticed when out in public with *hijra* and *kothi* friends that some responded to disrespectful behavior by issuing threats like "someone like us will be born in your family too"—thus threatening a less direct transfer of stigma. Overall, these strategies, sometimes called *bila kora* (insulting or making trouble) in Ulti, utilize various forms of social anxiety around non-reproductivity and gender non-conformity, not all of which involve congenital difference. However, the decline of the congenital narrative pushes *hijras* further toward such tactics by undercutting belief in their auspiciousness, while potentially also undermining the fear they elicit as purveyors of infertility.

This may prompt attempts by *hijra* households to reestablish the congenital myth. Hasina, for instance, sponsored a play on *hijras* by a Murshidabad-based theater group that toured West Bengal in 2014, which depicted its *hijra* protagonists as intersex. Meanwhile, during a conversation with local *kothis* in 2011, Annapurna advised them: "it is better if *kothis* wear *pant-shirt* . . . let them stay in *kodi-besh* (male attire)!" While rebuking *kothis* for wearing feminine attire, both *gurus* were affectionate to some *kodi* (male-attired) *kothis*, inviting them to their houses.

Such tendencies are unevenly transregional. I heard from several *kothis* who lived in feminine attire in Delhi in the 2000s that *gharana*-based *hijras* tried to convince them to either revert to male attire or join *gharanas* and completely present as *hijra*. In her autobiography, transgender activist A. Revathi (2010: 43) notes that Delhi *hijras* were anxious not to be perceived as forcibly feminizing boys, which recalls the colonial kidnapping and castration narrative—such pejorative perceptions might prompt *hijras* to conceal transition and overlap between *kothis* and themselves.

However, in areas with many visible *kothis* where their suppression is difficult, *hijras* may instead publicly disseminate categorical distinctions. In a 2016 conversation on an incident in which the police harassed some *kothis* for being "artificial" *hijras*, Heena pointed out: "*hijras* spread these divisions—when they visit any neighborhood that has *kothis*, *hijras* tell people, these are men, not *jonmoshutre* (inborn) *hijras* like us!"

In contexts where it is difficult to disseminate the congenital narrative due to growing public awareness, *gharana*-based *hijras* may emphasize emasculation as the axis of distinction instead. In 2012 at Kolkata, I visited an area frequented by *kothi* sex workers with Bindiya. Talking to some local women, Bindiya explained how *hijras* were different from the *kothis*: "We are *katano* (cut, emasculated)—those ones are not!" Conversely, *hijras* may try to hold on to the congenital narrative by conceding that while some *hijras* are emasculated, they are inborn and more legitimate. In 2022, a *hijra* household in Nadia, who had a longstanding territorial conflict with a rival household, sent representatives to meet municipal officials and request them to arbitrate. A *hijra* representative told them: "You know, there are two kinds of *hijras*: some are *jonmogoto* (inborn), some become *hijra* through *surgery*—those *hijras* used to be men, our household is of inborn *hijras*!"

Within the community, *gharana*-based *hijras* may try to perpetuate hierarchies based on formal *gharana* affiliation, emasculation, and/or gendered consistency. In 2012, Heena and I met Mishti, a *hijra* from Nadia, at another *kothi*'s house. At one point, Mishti told us derisively: "You guys are *bohurupis* (chameleons, pretenders); even if you dress up, you take the *anchal* (the loose end of the saree) on your shoulders one day, and then shrug it off! But we have taken the *anchal* for life." Besides feminine attire, "taking the *anchal*" (*anchal newa*) also connotes undertaking a *rit* or initiation under a *gharana*-based *hijra guru*. While Mishti conceded that both *kothis* and *hijras* "take" feminine attire—undoing the anatomical *hijra*–male binary—the contrast between *bohurupi* and *hijra* suggests a linear gradation of femininity from lesser to greater consistency and correlates the latter with *gharana* affiliation, accusing *kothis* of opportunistic gender fluidity. However, the *bohurupi*–*hijra* distinction conceals contradictions within lineages. While presenting in feminine attire publicly, senior *gurus* may assume patriarchal forms of authority vis-à-vis their *chelas*—assuming traditionally masculine titles like *nayak* (chief, leader)—and some even wear masculine or androgynous dress inside the community (Nandi 2024). I also observed that when facing member shortages, *gharana* households may temporarily recruit *kothi–dhuranis* from other areas. The recruit pays *chitpon* (a token fine) to be allowed to work as a low-ranking *chela*; she may remain *kodi* (male-attired) in her home area as long as she is consistently feminine-attired in the work area and does not publicly disrupt the *hijra*–male distinction.

Despite such private overlaps, the *hijra*–male divide is compounded by other hierarchized distinctions which *gharana*-based *hijras* disseminate inside and outside the community, particularly between *hijra* asceticism and *kothi* promiscuity (Reddy 2005: 64). In 2008, I visited Annapurna's house on the outskirts of Berhampore with some *kothis*. The conversation turned to *parikhs* (male partners). Annapurna said: "I have stopped doing *parikhs*, it's a matter of respectability (*man-shombhrom*). I would do *parikhs* earlier, some other *hijras* here have *parikhs*." She continued, "if *parikhs* visit too much, neighbors may create trouble; I live in a *bhadro* (genteel, respectable) neighborhood! One must maintain *shomman* (respect)." She then berated the *kothis* for chasing *parikhs*. Her mention of respect (*shomman*) evokes *izzat* as a hierarchizing logic among *hijras* in Hyderabad (Reddy 2005: 43). Beyond *hijra* norms, Annapurna suggests that such hierarchies draw from social imperatives of respectability. While *hijras* breach sexual modesty in some contexts, senior *hijras* may precariously try to maintain social respectability by concealing their sexuality. In 2013, I witnessed a conversation between Dipika, a high-ranking *guru* in the Hooghly district, and some *kothis*, whom she chided for openly soliciting men: "See, both us *hijras* and you *kothi–zenanas* like imagining ourselves as women and flirting with men, and people increasingly know this, yet, we still have some *ijjot* (*izzat*, respect) in society, so I ask you—have sex, but maintain the *porda* (purdah, veil) over our activities, don't reveal everything publicly!"

Significantly, the ascetic-sexual hierarchy is also internal to lineages. Annapurna mapped both *kothis* and juniors (the "other *hijras*") as more sexual: indeed, it is junior disciples who typically go out to perform *badhai* and deploy strategies like sexualized insults. Respect-based hierarchies within *gharanas* may also legitimize the exploitation of *akua* (non-emasculated) *hijras*, who occupy ambiguously variable positions. At Ranaghat, Bikash mentioned in several conversations that *akuas* fulfill specific functions within *hijra* rituals like worshipping the *dhol* (the drum used to accompany *badhai* songs), for which *gharanas* need them. At Kolkata, Bindiya once described how some *akua hijras*, including heterosexually married ones, ascend to high ranks within *gharanas*: "One need not become *hijra* by emasculation—one can also become *hijra* by being skilled in *hijra* politics!"[19] However, several of Bikash's *kothi* daughters who joined *hijra* households as *akua* complained that they were given more work but received less *hissa* (share) of the daily earnings; sexual relations were also restricted. These factors built the pressure to become *nirvan* (emasculated) irrespective of their desires.

While *hijra* sexuality is conceded privately, in public, *gharana*-based *hijras* may project sexual desire wholly onto non-*hijras*. Annapurna often complained about a particularly promiscuous feminine-attired *kothi* at Berhampore whom people perceived as *hijra*: "People ask me about her—I say, no, those people are *homosex* [*sic*] and we are *hijra*." This categorical distinction reiterates the common association between feminine maleness and homosexual desire, while dissociating *hijras* from such imputations.

Such a desexualized *hijra* identity is particularly challenged by *kothis/hijras* who undertake *khajra* (sex work) in feminine attire. Although (as noted earlier) clients may perceive them as impotent, they potentially threaten both the congenital myth and the ascetic-sexual distinction. In a 2014 conversation, Sajani, a junior *hijra* at Murshidabad, complained about *khajrawalis* (sex workers): "So many do *khajra* at the railway station, now the railway police know that they are all *likamwali* (penis-bearing); policemen call us and want to fuck!"

Anxieties about sex work may prompt attempts to suppress *khajra* within territories claimed by *gharanas*. In 2012, Hasina beat up a poor, Dalit *khajrawali* who had done *khajra* within her territory. As Sajani explained: "people think *hijras* are doing all this, though these *khajrawalis* don't belong to any *hijra* house—so *hijras* make trouble for them!"

Apart from *gurus*, some *kothis* also support the maintenance of *hijra–kothi* distinctions. During a gathering at Berhampore in 2015, Shundori, a *kothi*, cautioned her friends: "Several of us go around as men (*byatachhele*) in the day and then wear feminine dress at night; this is not right . . . *hijras* are being exposed (*kachchi-pakki hochhe*)." The phrase *kachchi-pakki* literally means spoiling or undoing (*kachchi*) something ripened, matured, or cultivated (*pakki*). Here, it refers to "spoiling" the *hijra*–male distinction that *hijras* take pains to "ripen" or "cultivate."

The process of "cultivating" authenticity binaries in contrast to overlaps that are sought to be kept private—such as *gharanas* incorporating *akua hijras* or *kothis* who switch attire—suggests that like some administrative and media narratives, *hijra gharanas* may simplify the complex, variable axes of *hijra* identification to construct public distinctions and fit social or governmental logics of legibility. This signals a form of representational politics preceding the institutional LGBTQ movement, though *hijras* may increasingly seek NGO and media collaborations for such purposes. In 2014, Sumi, the Coochbehar-based activist, recounted how some *hijras* requested her CBO to organize a press conference to denounce a rival *hijra* household as fake (she refused).

Such politics contributes to processes of vernacularization both spatially and discursively. Spatially, *gharana* leaders attempt to expand their territorial control, spread distinctions, and produce a uniform cartography of *hijra* versus (feminine) men, seeking to scale up hegemonic identitarian rubrics and contain variations. Simultaneously, Ulti words that describe diversity and overlap within the *hijra–dhurani–kothi* spectrum—like *akua*, *kodi*, or *bheli*—remain private, intra-community usages relative to public terms like *hijra* or analogous words in Sanskritized literary Bengali, such as *tritiyo lingo* (third gender) or *brihannala*, a mythical character used as a generic name for *hijras* in Bengali media. Both *tritiyo lingo* and *brihannala* are often understood as per anatomical difference from maleness. A 2014 op-ed in a leading Bengali newspaper glossed *tritiyo lingo* as people who are either intersex or impotent (Bhaduri 2014). Other media articles interview *hijra gurus* and depict them as "*prakrita brihannala*" (true/real *brihannalas*) who castigate *hijras* who do *chhalla* as "*purush*" (men) who are faking *hijra* identity to extort money (Pramanik 2014; "Nokol Brihannala" 2019). Thus, *hijra gurus* may reinforce concepts of anatomical thirdness and *hijra*–male distinction in formal, higher registers of Bengali, while maintaining Ulti, which contradicts such ideas, as a relatively vernacularized language—not in the sense of a devalued language but of a domestic, spatially contained, and noninstitutional one (Pollock 2006: 454). Indeed, I witnessed in Nadia and Kolkata that while younger *kothis* were often willing to teach Ulti to trusted outsiders like *parikhs* or non-*kothi* friends, senior *hijras* chided them and cautioned them to maintain Ulti as a secret, intra-community language.[20]

Beyond West Bengal, *hijras* have sought to establish their non-procreative status in national political discourse. Reddy describes how some *hijras* who entered electoral politics in the 2000s emphasized "their lack of genitalia and subsequent reproductive capacity" to claim exemplary status as politicians, uncorrupted by familial ties and nepotism (2003: 170). Since the 1980s, *hijra gurus* have also sought state recognition as a "third sex" (Cohen 1995: 297). When such recognition arrives in the 2010s, the "third gender" may be conflated with *hijra* authenticity—as when in 2018, the chief minister of West Bengal promised jobs for the "third gender" but specified that only "*prakrita* (real) *brihannalas*" would get them ("Morey Morey" 2018).[21] In Bangladesh, the governmental recognition of *hijras* as a third gender has hinged on a narrative of congenital disability, such that even emasculated *hijras* have been denied administrative recognition (Hossain 2017).

Despite such transnational tendencies, significant contradictions undercut the attempted homogenization of identitarian distinctions. Socioeconomic factors prompt variations between *hijra* households and lineages, pluralizing *gharana* norms. As Annapurna once remarked cynically, "*hijras* are giving up their *iman, man, shomman* (creed, respect) for money." For instance, in Mumbai, sex work is a lucrative occupation and *gharanas* there treat it as a legitimate *pon* or profession. Many non-emasculated *kothis* from West Bengal thus migrate there as *hijra* sex workers. Such variations disrupt uniform logics of authenticity or respect and signal a dynamic negotiation between the attempted establishment of hegemonic *hijra* narratives and alternative cartographies of identity, to which we now turn.

Territorial Ruptures and Alternative Cartographies

On the train from Kolkata to Berhampore, I often encountered two young people seeking *chhalla*—dressed in *sarees*, performing the characteristic *hijra* clap (*thikri*) loudly for attention, asking passengers for money, and sometimes blessing them in return. Like other passengers, I took them to be *hijras* like any other. *Kothis* at Berhampore called them the "Beldanga *chhibris*"—*chhibris* or *hijras* from Beldanga, a nearby small town. In 2010, Shyam accompanied me to their *chhibri khol* (*hijra* house). One of them, Suleiman, welcomed us into their small hut near the railway station, which, unlike typical *hijra* households, had no sign of a *guru* or other *chelas*. Shyam noticed some household male clothing lying around and expressed surprise, as both Suleiman and her friend were dressed in typically feminine attire:

> Shyam (pointing):   Who has left all this men's *satra* (clothes)?
> Suleiman: Why, I wear those clothes.
> Shyam (feigning scandal):   Oh, what are you saying!
> Suleiman (casually):   Yes, I wear these at home . . . (Starts changing into them)
> Shyam: Oh dear, what am I seeing! The sister has now become . . .
> Suleiman (smiling mischievously):   Why, make me your *parikh*!

Over the afternoon, I figured out that while Suleiman partly presented as *hijra* and *kothis* called her a *chhibri*, she was neither literally *chhibri* (emasculated) nor initiated under a *hijra guru*, living with her friend outside the *guru–chela* system. She used her natal male name and evidenced a playful overlap with masculinity (being *parikh*), breaking the *gharana* injunction of consistent feminine attire. Shyam explained how Suleiman's family, working-class Muslims, had become gradually used to her femininity since her childhood, and now accepted her feminine attire. She interacted with them daily; as Suleiman said, "they live over there—they send us two meals a day." Though lineage-based *hijras* in Dhaka may maintain family contacts and even live partly as married men, this is typically done in separate neighborhoods near the areas where they practice *hijra* professions (Hossain 2021: 151). Suleiman perhaps went further in violating the distance lineage-based *hijras* maintain from social maleness. During our conversation, neighbors casually dropped in; they clearly knew of her daily switch between *hijra* and male presentations, although the train passengers did not. To some extent, she publicly disrupted the association of *hijra*-ness with intersexuality or emasculation, and created an alternate form of legibility by habituating the area to her alternating presentations.

When I brought up the Beldanga *chhibris* with Annapurna, she predictably dismissed them as opportunistic, not really *hijra*: "Those ones sometimes call themselves *hijra*, sometimes *dhurani*, as convenient!" Despite her disdain, she did not intervene, though some of their working areas fell within the territory she claimed. Annapurna had a relatively relaxed attitude to territoriality—she even allowed some *hijras* to impinge on her own profession, *badhai*, in some poorer, less lucrative areas within her territory despite their lack of *gharana* affiliation.

Such departures from normative *hijra*-hood are also apparent elsewhere. Once, in 2011, I was on a train with some *kothis* in Nadia when we met one of their friends, Malati, who was then working as a *chhallawali* (*chhalla* seeker). The *kothis* teased her about her constantly changing *guru*. Laughing, Malati said: "There is no certainty to who my *guru* is!" She had taken initiation under a senior *gharana*-based *hijra* and done *badhai* for a few months. But this household was strictly hierarchical; she was given food last, after senior *hijras*. She rebelled: "When they asked me to get emasculated, I quarreled and came home; then I started doing *chhalla* and took Pinky (a *chhallawali* of Nadia) as my *guru*." Her refusal of emasculation corresponded to her fluid gender presentation. Malati boasted that many *kothis* had desired her earlier when she was male-presenting and sold snacks on trains (usually a male occupation). She added that she "might become a *tonna* (man) again" if *chhalla* did not work out. This fluidity paralleled her mobility between places and professions, dodging *gharana* norms.

Malati and Suleiman both challenged *gharana* definitions of the *hijra*—initiation into lineages, consistent feminine attire, and ideally, emasculation—which paralleled their dodging of *gharana* territoriality. Annapurna's relaxed territoriality permitted people like Suleiman, while Malati escaped from her *gharana guru*'s territory. If *hijra* norms are spread through the territorial expansion and consolidation of lineages, dodging norms and hierarchies may correspond to variations and ruptures in *gharana* territoriality.

In a 2011 interview, Annapurna reiterated this link between non-normative *hijra* figures, *kothi*–*hijra* overlaps, and territorial gaps:

> Suppose in a village where *hijras* don't go, a *dhurani* starts wearing *satra* (feminine attire) publicly. Maybe over the years, she starts posing as *hijra*. . . . Some locals regard her as a *hijra* . . . some still call her *mowga* (effeminate male, sissy). Maybe she buys a *dhol* (drum), and starts doing *badhai* . . . Once the actual *hijra* household of the area finds out . . . they go and ask her to stop. But maybe she's already too powerful, has local *chelas*, and resists them. So, they visit her again, but this time, offer her a position in the *gharana* system. After all, . . . she took a wild, uncultivated area, where *hijras* did not go, and cultivated it (*chash korlo*), made it suitable for us!

Thus, the unevenness of *gharana* territoriality allows for variant *hijra* figures outside lineages, which seek to reconsolidate their spatial control and reincorporate recalcitrant outsiders within their structure. Annapurna suggests that the social legibility of *hijra* subject positions is cultivated (*chash kora*) within particular spatiotemporal contexts, and thus contingently changeable—despite social scripts of *hijra* anatomical difference, a *dhurani* may gradually "cultivate" an area and make it amenable for *hijras* like herself. As the *gharanas* try to reconsolidate their territorial control and accommodate outsiders, *gharana* norms and *hijra* narratives may change, too.

Chhalla: *Inside/Outside the System*

It is not coincidental that Suleiman and Malati worked as *chhallawalis*. Professions like *chhalla*, *khajra*, and *lagan* symptomatize the tension between the territorial claims of *gharanas* over *hijra* identity and practice and variant claims to *hijra*-ness without emasculation or lineage affiliation. As Annapurna and Bindiya told me, conventionally, *gharana*-based *hijras* in West Bengal did *chhalla* only in market areas, collecting money from shops during festivals. In neighboring Bihar, *gharana hijras* also undertake *chhalla* in trains, but in Bengal till the 2010s, *gharanas* frowned upon train-based *chhalla*, though people outside *gharanas* did carry out *chhalla* in long-distance trains. Jyotsna, a *chhallawali* from Murshidabad, propagated train-based *chhalla* in North Bengal in the 1990s, without emasculation or *rit* (initiation) in a *gharana*. In other areas *chhalla* is even newer, especially on streets (soliciting money at traffic signals) and in short-distance commuter trains. In 2011, Annapurna told me that train-based *chhalla* in Murshidabad had been started recently by outsiders like Suleiman.

Gharana-based *hijras* often berated these developments. While Annapurna dismissed *chhallawalis* as opportunistic, in a conversation at Nadia, the *hijra guru* Mishti positioned them as outside legitimate *hijra* communities and professions: "We *hijras* are in the *pon* (*hijra* profession, *badhai*), and they are in *bepon* (invalid profession)." Contrastingly, Ronita, a Kolkata-based *hijra*, did not entirely invalidate *chhallawalis* as *hijras*, but claimed: "The *izzat* (respect) of a *ponwali hijra* (*hijra* following the *pon*) is much higher than that of a *chhallawali hijra*!"[22]

Despite the disdain, *gharana*-based *hijras* in West Bengal have not conventionally exerted territorial rights over *chhalla* as they do over *badhai*. In 2011, I spent a summer evening with Honey and Silk, two *kothi* friends of Heena from Kalyani, Nadia. They explained that they occasionally visited nearby *hijra* residences to maintain cordial relations, but were not formally initiated. During the conversation, we arrived near some derelict houses near a rail station, abandoned quarters for railway staff. Honey said, "a group of *kothis* used to live here—now they dance at *lagan* and have scattered to various places." They had taken over one of the abandoned houses, technically state-owned railway property, and did *chhalla* in trains, breaching the injunction against *kothis* donning feminine attire. While they visited local *hijra* residences, they had not undertaken the *rit* to become *chelas*. According to Honey, one needed the *rit* to do *badhai*, but not for *chhalla*—"nowadays, it's mostly *kothis* who wear *sarees* and do *chhalla*!" Silk added: "Even we do it sometimes! God has made us *kothi*—doing *chhalla* is my just right!" Honey continued, laughing, "how many *chhibrano* (emasculated) *hijras* are there anyway? If someone asks if I'm *hijra*, I'll simply lift my *saree*, make a *chipti* (vagina), and show them!" Later, she actually demonstrated this by tucking her genitalia between her thighs.[23]

Here, non-*gharana kothis* both parody and appropriate *hijra* claims of authenticity and the attendant gesture of genital exposure, performatively challenging real–fake binaries. This is not just a case of *kothis* doing parodic "*hijra*-acting" to position "themselves as normative . . . against the projected oddities of the other," as Hall observes in Delhi (2005: 126). Beyond *hijra* parody, *kothi* is posited as an innate, God-given subject position that grants rights to the social legibility of the *hijra* as a separate gendered position without emasculation or lineage affiliation. Cohen notes how *hijras* claim that the "hole," the physical and symbolic loss of castration, grants them special rights, particularly ticketless train travel (1995: 297). However, the same may be claimed by non-emasculated *kothis* or *hijras* in non-anatomical terms. As another *kothi* in Silk's circle once remarked about traveling ticketless: "We don't get the *shubidhe* (privilege/ benefit) of being men or women; won't we even take the *shubidhe* of being *hijra*?" In such claims, being *kothi* as an ontological and/or social condition takes precedence over the *hijra* subject position, encompassing and justifying presentation as *hijra*. The logic of *kothi* precedence is illustrated in another quote I heard in Murshidabad, where a *kothi* advised some *chhallawalis*, "if *hijras* challenge you, just say—it is from *kothis* that *hijras* are made!" This inverts the linear hierarchization of *hijra* over *kothi* based on *chhibrano* and consistent femininity—*kothi* becomes the more fundamental state from which *hijras* are derived (Hall 2005: 129).

For the aforementioned *chhallawalis*, such subversion was enabled by multiple forms of weakened territoriality—the weak *gharana* control over *chhalla* and gaps in the state's territoriality that permitted the communal takeover of abandoned government property. However, utilizing such gaps entails vulnerability to police violence—while *gharana hijras* often bribe the police to maintain good relations, less organized *chhallawalis* may lack such rapport and be harassed by railway police. Further, while some *hijras* disdainfully tolerate *chhallawalis*, sometimes *gharana*-based *hijras* evidence more hostile reactions when *chhallawalis* are seen as harming them economically or exposing *hijra*–male transition. At Berhampore, in a 2012 conversation, Hasina angrily accused *kothis* who did *chhalla* of "spoiling our market"—"People say, you people take money both in houses and trains . . . doesn't this spoil our image?" Meanwhile, Bindiya complained that *chhallawalis* were telling people about emasculation. Stock tactics for *chhalla*, like flirtation with young male passengers, also disrupt *hijra* claims of asceticism. The Kalyani *kothis* commonly approached men with phrases like "o *hero*, how are you doing"— implicating them in an eroticized interaction with themselves, which could entice or embarrass them into paying up. Sometimes *chhallawalis* also have sex with police to escape bribes. Such factors prompt attempts to reassert the real–fake dichotomy. In 2015, Sumi narrated how some *hijras* in North Bengal publicly reported *chhallawalis* in their territory as fake *hijras*: "The *hijras* called the media, beat up these people and stripped them to prove they were men!"

To protect themselves from such violence, some *chhallawalis* have formed hierarchical structures paralleling the *gharanas*. In North Bengal in the late 1990s, police harassment prompted Jyotsna and Kajori, her close associate, to organize local *kothis* who sporadically did *chhalla* and sex work, whom they recruited as disciples. As experienced *chhallawalis* with more income and police contacts, they negotiated bribes and protected newer entrants from police and *hijra* harassment. Kajori gradually acquired the status of a *hijra guru* among her *chelas*, though not initially recognized as such by *gharana* households.

However, from around 2010, *chhalla* in West Bengal has been increasingly brought into the *gharana* system, given changing economic motivations. I observed that despite their objections to *chhalla*, several *gharana*-based *gurus* started secretively recruiting *chhallawalis* from their areas as low-ranking *chelas* and pressurized them to give a *gawlla* (share) from their earnings, expanding their territorial control and making independent *chhallawalis* rarer. Bindiya explained that declining incomes from *badhai*, partly due to decreasing numbers of children per household, lured *gharanas* toward *chhalla*.[24] In North Bengal, Kajori told me that *badhai gurus* who previously harassed *chhallawalis* have begun inducting *chhalla gurus* into their *gharanas* to gain a share of their income. This process expands hierarchies: junior *chhallawalis* pay *gawlla* to their *chhalla guru*, who pays the *badhai guru*.

Despite such recognition of senior *chhalla gurus*, overall, *chhallawalis* retain a lower, ambiguous status within the *gharanas*. Shalini, a *chhallawali* who lived independently with her *parikh* in Murshidabad, told me that she had a *hijra guru* but did not attend *gharana* meetings as her presence would lessen her *guru's maan* (respect). Given the burden of paying *gawlla*, *chhalla* outside *gharanas* also persists—as Ronita told me, "many hide (from *hijra* households) and do it, but also get beaten up for it!" Indeed, *hijra gurus* have continued to denounce *chhallawalis* as fake to the media ("Nokol Brihannala" 2019). Kajori told me about one incident in North Bengal when *badhai* and *chhalla gurus* teamed up against independent *chhallawalis* who did not pay them *gawlla*, and exposed them to the media as men with penises. Ironically, one of the *chhalla gurus* herself lived as a married man in a different town.

Although *gharana* norms shift, such actions reconfigure and continue the vernacularization process. Relatively powerful *hijras* attempt to reestablish the *hijra*–male distinction in the Bengali media, containing unofficial, quotidian discourses of *hijra*–male overlap at the level of the intra-community vernacular. Such vernacularization serves to manage the contradiction between the socio-governmentally reinforced divide between *hijras* and men on one hand and professional affiliations between *gharanas* and non-emasculated *kothis/hijras* on the other. Vernacularization also addresses contradictions between permissible and impermissible forms of labor as per gendered and capitalist logics of productivity—while "begging" may be allowable for "real" *hijras*, "men" are not exempted from "hard work" (Daily Bhaskar 2015). Hence, *hijra–kothi* overlaps may be elided through the imposition of a more uniform territoriality over *chhalla*, spatially reconsolidating and homogenizing norms.

Challenging the Social Legibility of the Hijra

However, such reconsolidation of *hijra*–male divides is ruptured by the shifting sociocultural logics of legibility through which the relation between femininity and maleness is understood in different regional contexts. As Sumi told me in 2014, the aforementioned lack of a strongly biologized *hijra*–male distinction in rural Coochbehar meant that some people still perceived her as a *hijra* despite seeing her switching between attires. While she had long hair and wore feminine attire outside, she often wore T-shirts and shorts in her courtyard, visible to neighbors. Yet, locals occasionally approached her for blessings: "Neighbors see me in shorts, yet someone came for blessings because his son cannot walk properly; they think I have God-given powers." Laughing, she added, "so many people understand us in so many different ways!" Such contextual shifts in the social legibility of the *hijra* undo uniform authenticity criteria.

Even where the biologized *hijra*–male distinction is stronger, *kothis* outside *gharana* control may disrupt ideas of *hijra* authenticity and potentially create alternative scripts of *hijra* legibility based more on performance than embodiment or attire: for instance, by publicly performing typical *hijra* behaviors in male attire in commuter trains. Between 2012 and 2015, I frequently traveled with Heena, Honey, and Silk on local trains between Nadia and Kolkata. While Heena and Honey were more consistent in their feminine presentation, Silk often wore male attire. However, they commonly claimed a *hijra* positionality. For example, when reserving their place beside the gate in crowded "ladies" (female-only) compartments, Heena or Silk would proclaim: "No one should get into this spot, there are *hijras* here!" Silk also often cracked sexualized jokes with women commuters—"you will now go home, your husband will keep you warm . . . who will keep me warm, you tell me!"—thus making them laugh and befriending them, while disrupting the idea of *hijra* asceticism. On one occasion, Silk even approached a woman for *chhalla*, clapping and asking for money as *chhallawali hijras* do, despite her male presentation. The woman was somewhat surprised, but Silk, unfazed, complimented her about a beautiful blanket she was carrying, using exaggeratedly feminine hand and body movements while talking to her. The woman replied that she had bought the blanket as a gift for her daughter's wedding. She later even asked for Silk's *ashirvad* (blessings): "Give your *ashirvad* so that the marriage turns out well!" Later, Heena said admiringly: "There is a lot to learn from Silk . . . what confidence, doesn't get into trouble . . . even I wouldn't be able to carry this off!"

Thus, Heena conceded a certain nonlinearity to *kothi–hijra* gendered performance that disrupted the *gharana* hierarchy wherein consistent femininity is more respectable than *kothis* who switch between attires: Silk performed *chhalla* more adeptly in male dress than the more consistently feminine-presenting Heena. On another occasion, Heena remarked that while such incidents might be seen as *kachchi-pakki*—spoiling the cultivated *hijra*–male distinction—actually, they helped make people *pakki* (ripened, aware) about the reality of *hijras*. Heena thus hints at "ripening" or "cultivating" alternative modes of intelligibility not hinged on anatomical authenticity or sexual–ascetic binaries. Indeed, the establishment of bonds with women commuters may thwart attempts to reestablish hierarchical distinctions. On one occasion, a *gharana hijra* traveling on the aforementioned train route threatened to shame and expose a *kothi* as *nakal* (fake). She was stopped by a woman commuter who asserted, "we are all the same . . . we are all sisters!"

Displacing Authenticity Logics

Beyond broadening public perceptions of *hijras*, such refigured scripts of *hijra* legibility may also correspond to interiorized logics of *hijra* identification not based on external authenticity criteria. While Sumi entered the *hijra* subject position more as a situational performance, Heena claimed that she did not merely perform as a *hijra*—rather, she *was* a *hijra* in such situations. She made this point while describing the ritual role played by *hijras* in Chhath Puja, an annual festival worshipping the Sun God, popular in Bihar and among Bihari immigrants in West Bengal. *Hijras* play an important role by imparting blessings to women during the festival. Many *gharana*-based *hijras* temporarily hire *akua kothis* for the job, mediating contracts with households where Chhath is performed, in return for a share of their earnings. Heena described, "the women of the house lay down their *anchal* (part of the *saree*) on the ground, on which we *chhibris* dance; then we ask for money . . . although we are doing this while being *akua*, at that moment I am a *hijra* only!" Heena described such moments in terms of a situational affect, which she articulated as a legitimate claim to being a *hijra* or *chhibri*: "At that moment, I feel myself to be *chhibri* . . . in that situation, I *am* a *chhibri*!" She further asserted, "one is a *hijra* from one's *man* (mind, psyche), not from one's *tan* (body)!" This suggests that *hijra* may be reconceptualized as an internally or psychologically determined identity, not hinged on external criteria like anatomy or initiation. Notably, *gharana hijras*—ostensibly against *kothis* impersonating *hijras*—might facilitate such psychologized or performative claims on *hijra*-ness by hiring *kothis* contractually without initiation, partly because they perform in feminine attire for just a day in areas where their "male" identities are not known.

Heena also occasionally did *chhalla* under Najma, the aforementioned female *hijra guru*. In Bengal, female-assigned persons may enter *hijra gharanas* or professions in certain circumstances. As Bindiya explained, her *hijra guru* had adopted two young girls who grew up to do *badhai* alongside other *hijras* of the household. While they may be perceived as *hijras* during work, otherwise, the *guru* presented them as her adoptive daughters—not *hijras*. Najma, a Bihari Muslim woman, represented a different scenario. In a 2019 interview, she narrated that years ago, she was a destitute woman with young children, living in a makeshift tent on railway land, when a *chhallawali* working outside the *gharanas* took pity on her and offered to make her a *chela*. Under this *guru's* tutelage, Najma started doing *chhalla* in trains and later, started taking her own *chelas*. After her *guru* passed, Najma took discipleship under a senior *gharana*-based *hijra*, to whom she pays an annual share while living independently. As she stated proudly: "I've made my own space!" Although her femaleness was common knowledge among *hijras*, she described how she asserted her *hijra*-ness to *hijras* who challenged her: "I say—I am a *hijra* just as you are!" Later, Heena defended her claim to being *hijra*: "She takes her own *chelas*, imposes fines, does everything! You should see how she gives claps!" Heena continued, "If we can be physically male and still do *hijregiri* (*hijra* practices), why can't she do *hijregiri* being a woman?" Similar to the Bangladeshi *hijras* described by Hossain (2021), *hijregiri*—the performative conduct of *hijra* professions and rituals—here emerges as the central criterion for *hijra* identity, displacing anatomy, asceticism, and related hierarchies, even permitting women to claim *hijra* status.

While the recent expansion of *chhalla* may facilitate such deconstruction and pluralization of the *hijra*, there is no linear temporal trend, given how *gharana* territoriality and norms were perhaps even more uneven in the past. Professions like *lagan* seem to have permitted non-*gharana* claimants to *hijra* identity in the 1990s. Dilip, a former *laganwali* (*lagan* dancer) who is now a married householder at Kalyani and no longer wears female attire, narrated how he would present as *hijra* while traveling ticketless in trains decades ago, braving close brushes with the police. More recently, he claims a *guru* status to junior *laganwalis*, brokering dance contracts for them, and has even facilitated emasculation procedures for *kothis* who wish to transition without joining *gharanas*—displacing the classic ritual of *hijra* authenticity from the lineages. On one occasion, he boasted to local *hijras*: "I got a *kothi* emasculated and tended to her; you people have become *chhibris* through emasculation, but I'm sitting here as a bigger *hijra* with my penis intact!" Dilip's claim inverted the linear hierarchy articulated by *hijras* like Mishti between more feminine, ritually initiated *hijras* and inconsistently feminine *kothis*. However, Dilip's claim to *guru* status was also criticized by *kothis* like Heena, since he was not only married but even abusive to his wife—not all kinds of gendered fluidity are acceptable even to people who question *hijra* authenticity. Even so, Dilip's trajectory signals the immanent ruptures and contradictions within the *hijra–dhurani–kothi* spectrum that trouble any homogenized cartography of the *hijra*.

Conclusion: Changing Strategies of Vernacularization

In the 2010s, challenges to biologized notions of *hijra* identity within the *hijra–kothi–dhurani* spectrum are compounded by the increasing public visibility of transgender identity. Middle-class transgender activists in West Bengal have visibilized trans womanhood as an innate psychological rather than physiological identity (Das 2009); some reformulate *hijra* as merely a "profession" of some transgender people, not a distinct gender identity at all (Bandyopadhyay 2022). With the growing media and state recognition of trans identities, some *hijras* have managed careers as NGO-based trans activists and detailed their boyhood and transition (Tripathi 2015). While later chapters elaborate on these tendencies, here, I note how they may prompt shifts in *hijra* self-representations, while older tendencies also continue.

With growing trans visibility, the anatomical determination of *hijra* authenticity becomes increasingly unsustainable in liberal or progressive discourse. Critiquing the aforementioned video of a "real" *hijra* exposing a fake one in 2015, an article states: "Does having male genitals prove that the person is not transgender? . . . such videos . . . exacerbate misconceptions" (Mathew 2015). Other media articles describe *hijra* communities as including both transitioned and non-transitional embodiments. As per a 2014 piece in *The Guardian*, *hijras* are "eunuchs, intersex or transgender . . . part of South Asia's culture for thousands of years" (Khaleeli 2014). Here, a certain kind of scalar supersession—*hijra* as a transhistorical South Asian category containing various kinds of sex/gender variance—undermines another kind of supersession, the (increasingly untenable) standardization of a distinction between *hijras* and anatomical maleness.

In this scenario, some *gharana*-based *hijras* define *hijra* identity less in terms of gendered authenticity and more as per allegiance to a lineage-based culture or tradition. Madhuri, who straddles *gharana* and NGO worlds, told me in an interview: "The real criterion for becoming a *hijra* is not cutting off one's genitals. . . . If you have gone through the *rit* (initiation) . . . under a senior *hijra* in a *gharana*, only then are you a *hijra* . . . it doesn't matter what else you do!" This legitimated nontraditional occupations like her activism as having *gharana* sanction, marking emergent *hijra*–activist alliances. In a Bengali television interview in 2011, she positioned *gharana* affiliation as the primary criterion of *hijra* authenticity.[25] She stated: "My *gharana* is an *authentic* [*sic*] *hijra gharana* . . . Many people think that any man dressed in a *saree* or clapping in trains is a *hijra* . . . but they are not! . . . *Hijra* is a tradition . . . transmitted through a *guru–chela* system . . . They, too, are a kind of *hijra* but not part of *hijra* society!" Even as Madhuri broadens *hijra* definitions beyond anatomy, the distinction from non-*gharana chhallawalis* reappears—they are either entirely dismissed as cross-dressed men or conceded as "a kind of *hijra*" outside legitimate "*hijra* society."

Similarly, in 2015, a *gharana*-affiliated household near Kolkata gave interviews for an English article in the *Daily Mail*, which mentioned that many *hijras* are not emasculated (Mok and Linning 2015). The article then located lineages as a transregional, transhistorical site of *hijra* spirituality: "Their communities across south-east Asia date back more than 4,000 years . . . There is a firm social structure . . . (The) *hijra* comprise both communities in which spiritual meanings are preserved, and individuals who assume the identity of *hijra* to scratch out a living through begging" (ibid.). Paralleling Madhuri's distinction, lineages are positioned as the preeminent *hijra* community with "spiritual meanings," while outsiders "assume" *hijra* identity occupationally. Both representations implicitly perpetuate the aforementioned vernacularization of quotidian discourses around *chhalla* and non-*gharana hijras* relative to *gharana*-sanctioned narratives articulated in more formal registers of "regional" or "global" languages.

Thus, attempts to reestablish bounded narratives of the *hijra* at higher scalar and discursive levels may continue, even if reconfigured. While such attempts are sometimes contradictory—*hijra* as a supra-local category subsuming many kinds of gender variance undermines the homogenized distinction of *hijra* from feminine maleness—both broad and narrow representations of the *hijra* may involve forms of scalar supersession and attendant forms of vernacularization, eliding its spatially uneven, ruptured character. The transregional name of the *hijra* as the South Asian gender-variant category par excellence provides an appearance of continuity despite internal diversity, but this consolidated figure depends on concealing the *hijra* as a protean construction that variously (dis)connected people claim and articulate diversely—often through shifting relationalities with more localized or vernacularized categories like *kothi* or *dhurani*. People like Madhuri, Heena, and Najma conceptualize the *hijra* in disjunctive ways that trouble its scalar establishment as a governmental category or spatiotemporally continuous ethnographic object. The *hijra*'s position as a spatiotemporally more expansive category than *kothi*, *zenana*, or *dhurani* thus indicates contested processes of scalar consolidation and vernacularization, rather than pre-constituted scalar distinctions.

The shifting constructions of the *hijra* also mark how community-based processes intersect with (post)colonial institutions and social discourses to produce attempted identitarian consolidations. *Hijra* self-representations mediate and are mediated via institutional processes ranging from colonial governmentality to NGO activism, presaging other forms of institutional–subcultural mediation that subsequently characterize the LGBT development industry. As we shall see, the attempted (trans)national consolidation of *hijra* identity in distinction from non-*hijra* groups feeds into the expansion of the LGB–transgender divide in tandem with activism, law, and media. Simultaneously, the *hijra* is itself also vernacularized—first relative to the colonial eunuch category, and increasingly vis-à-vis the globalizing transgender rubric.

Chapter 2

KOTHI AND THE CARTOGRAPHY OF MSM

One day at the lake, I heard a young boy call out to me, "Hey, you are a dhurani!"... I went back and asked, "What did you call me? What is dhurani?" He said, "Oh, those who take it in the mouth or the butt." "But I don't do that!" I replied. "Well, you know, those who walk with a dancing gait, are a bit meyeli (girlish), like us." "But I am not like that, I don't do that either!" So finally, he said, "Well, anyone who loves to keep our company (amader shathe khub khatir), is dhurani!"

—Susanta, Kolkata

This excerpt from the interview of Susanta, the gay activist we met in the introduction, takes us to a scene of interpellation: a term that the French philosopher Louis Althusser famously used to describe quotidian rituals of recognition, such as calling out to people on the street, through which individuals are continually hailed into specific forms of subjectivity shaped by social ideologies.[1] During a visit to the lake area of south Kolkata in 1988, the seemingly masculine Susanta, usually socially recognized as a man, was quite literally hailed as a *dhurani* and sought to be inducted into the category through an increasingly broadening definition of the term—from those who perform specific sexual acts, to those who are a "bit" girlish, to anyone who keeps the company of the so-described. While initially indexing erotic practice, *dhurani* is thus used contingently and flexibly to reference multiple modalities of behavior and community affiliation, expanding to accommodate Susanta as a potential group member (the "us"). Earlier, in high school, Susanta had hesitantly confessed his desire for men to a visibly feminine classmate, but neither of them knew about *dhurani–kothi* communities yet. Subsequently, Susanta chanced across an article on gender-variant people in a Bengali magazine that mentioned the lake area. Visiting the lake, he learned various words that were not part of standard Bengali but used in the intra-community *bhasha* (language) spoken there, including *dhurani* and *kothi*—an increasingly common designation for the community. One day, he heard some *hijras* speaking in the language, known as both Ulti and Dhurani Bhasha in Kolkata, and indicated that he understood them. Surprised, they asked, "are you *kothi*?" He replied, "no, but I am of the *line*!"

The *line*, the English word adapted into Bengali, is another word of uncertain provenance that dates back to at least the 1980s as per oral histories. It may be used—as Susanta does—as a loose designation for people who participate in cruising spaces, described as *liner* (of the line). Shyamol, a middle-aged participant of *dhurani* circles in Nadia, told me in a conversation in 2010 about local cruising spots where people came to look for sexual partners or friends: "There are some places, like public bathrooms, where *liner* people come." Here, the "line" seems to mark a potential commonality or shared sexual interest, but not necessarily knowledge of Ulti or a preexisting sense of community or group identity.[2] But people who called themselves *dhurani* in Nadia, such as Bikash and her friends at Ranaghat, also used the "line" to designate their affiliation with specific communities and related practices: for example, by describing how they had entered the "the *dhurani line*." Speaking of cruising or sexual networking at the Ranaghat railway station in the 1980s, Sujit, a friend of Bikash, narrated how she could tell apart *dhuranis* from men: "Watching the passengers, I could tell by a glance who belonged to which *line!*" The *line* is thus not homogeneously gendered—encompassing both masculine-presenting and visibly feminine people—but may also signify a more consolidated sense of gender/sexual variance (Reddy 2005: 206).

I juxtapose the looser and more specific senses of words like *dhurani* and *line* to demonstrate the coexistence of both diffuse non-identitarian networks and communitarian or identitarian tendencies in the period preceding the organized LGBTQ movement in eastern India. Among these words, *kothi* emerged as the best-known category apart from *hijra* in the 1990s, supplanting terms like *dhurani* among younger generations in West Bengal. This chapter traces the attempted consolidation of the *kothi* as a nationally recognized identity within emerging networks of LGBT activism and NGOs, which drew from the increasing availability of transnational funding for HIV and AIDS prevention. This process entails a multilayered vernacularization—*kothi* becomes more institutionally and nationally recognized relative to terms like *dhurani*, but is simultaneously positioned as a regional subtype of the globalizing category of MSM (men who have sex with men), a term originating in Western HIV-related discourse that is translated and recast in South Asian terms by Indian activists writing in the (trans)national language of English. Sometimes, *kothi* also becomes subsumed under the homosexual/gay category. The scalar expansion of *kothi* and MSM starts later than that of the *hijra* but further reinforces divides between *hijra* and non-*hijra* identities, and between *kothis* and other MSM. The emergent institutional sense of the *kothi* is more circumscribed than the flexible usages sketched above: despite variations in activist interpretations of the term, its definitions become centered around sexual role, especially anal receptivity, which is associated with a high risk of HIV infection. Charting this development, this chapter asks: How does the transition to a more restrictively defined *kothi* identity take place? To what extent does such an identity become hegemonic, and how does it transform existing communities or foster new ones?

Beyond the Academic Vernacularization of the Kothi

My approach to these questions both builds on and departs from scholarship that emphasizes the role of the HIV and AIDS industry—transnational networks of NGOs, funders, and state departments working on HIV prevention—in the construction and dissemination of *kothi* identity. I show that older *dhurani* and *hijra* networks were also a crucial precondition for the rise of the *kothi* in West Bengal and beyond. While some scholars locate the *kothi* as historically continuous with precolonial times like the *hijra* (Hall 2005), others see the growth of *kothi*-identified communities as a recent phenomenon precipitated by transnational circuits of NGO activism and development capital (Cohen 2005; Boyce 2007; Khanna 2016; Katyal 2016). Some HIV-related NGOs posited the *kothi* as a more authentically South Asian identity than terms like gay, locating it within a putatively traditional gender/sexual binarism wherein *kothis* identify as feminine and desire sexual penetration by mainstream men, whom they call by various names like *panthi* or *giriya* but who do not use such terms themselves (Khan 2004). Several scholars critique such classifications as imposing reified categories on diverse and fluid forms of sexual life (Vijayakumar 2021: 2). Scholars interrogate the supposed cultural authenticity and homogeneity of the *kothi–panthi* schema, arguing that the *kothi*—at least in its form as a widespread, institutionally recognized identity— is produced by the HIV industry to fulfill its need for locally appropriate targets of HIV prevention (Khanna 2016: 105). Lawrence Cohen argues that the *kothi* usage, initially discovered among "young hustlers" in Chennai (South India), is picked up by the HIV industry and disseminated by NGO workers among communities that develop around these organizations; the emergence of such *kothi* communities as a "new social fact" serves to "fulfill funders' mandates for more and better sexual truth" (2005: 284–94). While *kothi* is presented in HIV activist discourse as a culturally intrinsic local term, its popular uptake apparently follows its dissemination via such activism (Boyce 2007: 184–97). Akshay Khanna avers that most *kothis* come to know themselves as *kothi* "after an interaction with the HIV/ AIDS industry"; it is thus "as much an artefact of 'modernity', 'globalisation' and neo-liberal expansion, as is the 'Gay' identity" (2016: 103–4).

While questioning reified notions of local authenticity, such interrogations perpetuate a certain hierarchy of scale, where the "transnational" HIV industry— and more broadly, the forces of global neoliberal capitalism—serve to mediate or even produce allegedly local categories. Some scholars concede preexisting histories of the *kothi*, but its previous articulations seem to be sporadic and localized (Cohen 2005: 284). Or, its circulation through older networks is briefly mentioned and does not seem to have much bearing on its institutional dissemination as an identity (Khanna 2016: 106). The scalar expansion of the *kothi* seems to largely follow from the socioeconomic conditions fostered by (trans)national formations of HIV activism, termed "AIDS cosmopolitanism" (Cohen 2005: 271–83). Thus, even as the expansion of the *kothi* is interrogated, the "cosmopolitanism" of the HIV industry is taken for granted. In effect, this vernacularizes the *kothi* and related formations by eliding their role in processes of scalar expansion. Curiously, the *kothi* seems to expand as an isolated term—this literature does not really explore the larger subcultural vocabularies within which words like *kothi* or *dhurani* are embedded, and how these languages spread. Further, while *kothi* expansion seemingly constitutes a sharp historical shift from previous discourses, the *hijra* seems more historically continuous and less determined by capitalist logics (but as we saw, is not so). This contrast between historical rupture and continuity evokes debates within South Asian historiography regarding how far colonial governmentality constructed new rigid forms of caste and religious identity in the region, and to what extent preexisting publics contributed to emerging identities.[3]

The subsequent sections complicate the scalar expansion of the *kothi* beyond such narratives, showing how the *kothi* spreads and consolidates as an identity through older, unevenly transregional community networks as much as through the development sector, and a complex mediation between these two phenomena facilitates the HIV industry's expansion and thus its "cosmopolitanism." Recent scholarship explores the contradictory relationship between the HIV industry and related communities (Vijayakumar 2021; Lakkimsetti 2020). The HIV industry opened up spaces where communities could contest the state regulation of sexuality, formulate new identities, and build solidarity between minoritized groups, but also reinforced intra-community hierarchies and exclusions (Vijayakumar 2021). However, this scholarship does not expand on the intersection between the HIV industry and the intra-community languages and practices of *dhurani–kothi* networks, which, as this chapter shows, predated and enabled its expansion in often effaced and devalued ways. In turn, these community formations were transformed in contradictory ways through mediation with HIV-related institutions, which extended networks, fostered new spaces for community formation, and enabled the emergence of *kothi* as a public identity that built on and transfigured older terms and subject positions. However, the *kothi* became subsumed within multilayered scalar and linguistic hierarchies of vernacularization, which fostered its circumscription within epidemiological models of sexual risk and the exploitative devaluation of *dhurani–kothi–hijra* languages and knowledges.[4]

The emergence of the *kothi* through this contradictory mediation is thus a dis/continuous process—neither simply descended from older discourses, nor an entirely novel emergence. Such (dis)continuity corresponds to the interaction of capitalist logics with formations not entirely reducible to capital. Gidwani and Wainwright see capitalism as "parasitic on other (often effaced) normative logics (including non-capitalist ones)" such as gender or caste that both enable and interrupt it (2014: 44). I adapt their framing to suggest how flows of capital and institutional networks that converged around HIV prevention parasitically utilized other gendered logics of community formation while effacing this reliance. While Boyce (2007) and Khanna (2016) critique how the HIV industry helps create conditions for the abstraction or reification of gender/sexual embodiments or idioms into categories that subsequently become adopted as identities, the following sections trace how the intersection of institutional and community networks both enables and interrupts the emergence of *kothi* as a sexual category mediated by but irreducible to official classifications. Subsequently, I trace contradictions between the institutional senses of the *kothi* and its protean quotidian usages within and beyond HIV projects, which often retain the contextual flexibility and variation of words like *dhurani*.[5] While the vernacularization of *kothi* as a subtype of the (trans) national MSM category attempts to contain such contradictions and circumscribe it as a bounded identity, the *kothi* often slips past categorical divides, undermining its scalar consolidation as a well-defined national category.

The Intergenerational Transition to the Kothi

In the 80s, I visited Delhi and heard people say *kothi* and *giriya* . . . I returned and spread these words in Kolkata!

—Chand, Kolkata

In some areas of West Bengal, *kothi* was known since the 1980s; elsewhere, it arrived later through both community networks and NGOs. Intergenerational and transregional processes of networking, evident in circles that developed outside *hijra gharanas* (lineages) since at least the 1970s, later facilitated *kothi* expansion. Previously, we saw that people like Bikash learned intra-community terms like *dhurani* from older people in their locality. Looking closer at this process, we find such intergenerational tendencies across metropolitan and nonmetropolitan areas—older people spot younger ones based on various gendered characteristics and hail them into their circle (as Susanta was hailed), who then interpellate their younger counterparts. Preceding NGOs and online networks, such intergenerational interpellation helps create community lineages beyond *hijra gharanas*, and disseminates categories and models of desire that anticipate the later *kothi–panthi* schema, despite much spatiotemporal variation in terminology. While *kothi* is not widely prevalent in older communities, they often treat it as interchangeable with terms like *dhurani* or *dhunuri*, thus helping its dissemination.

Witness the narratives of Govinda and Shyam, both from lower-middle-class families in small towns of Murshidabad. When I met Govinda in 2009, he was middle aged and unmarried, lived separately from his family, and managed a small business in spices. Govinda recollected the abuse he had faced in his youth: "People would say: see, a *magi* (roughly, woman or sissy) is going!" However, there was also a converse process of recognition; older community members "would notice our gait, our walk (*haanta-chola*), and recognize us." Govinda fondly narrated his initiation into this network in the 1980s. One day, he was taking a dip at a *ghat* (public bathing area) on the river Ganges at Berhampore when someone called out to him: "Hey *chhuri* (girl), do you have *nang* (husbands)? How many husbands?" Initially startled, he soon identified the person as "someone like me." Jaydip, the person who called out to Govinda, interpellated him both as feminine ("girl") and as desirous of masculine men ("husbands"). Govinda learned that people like them called each other *dhunuri* as well as *lavani* and *moga*—all indicative of femininity combined with the desire for men. His induction into this feminized circle countered his isolation and cemented his distinction from mainstream men: "First, I thought I was the only one . . . then I started going around with Jaydip and our friends. We would visit fairs, where we would find *parikhs* (male partners)!" Their shared femininity was evident in their humorous epithets for each other: Govinda was called *adawali* (ginger-woman) for his spice business.

Govinda, in turn, spotted Shyam, who was a few years younger. As Shyam put it, though she'd been "doing *meyelipona* (feminine behavior) since nine or ten years old," Govinda brought her into the *line*. "Govinda would say—first, you put one finger in, then two, then three, and then when you can take four fingers in there, you have entered the *line*!" The initiation into the *line*, here used in its narrower sense, thus links femininity with anal receptivity—though the evocation of self-penetration troubles the penetrative–receptive boundary, and suggests the agential rather than passive nature of this role. Though Govinda emphasized his relations with men, he also hesitantly admitted to taking the penetrative role with another *dhurani*. Shyam stuck to the receptive position more strictly. Unlike Govinda, she spoke of discomfort with her "male" genitalia: "Sometimes, I shudder—what has God given me there!" But like Govinda, she remained in male attire and feared being too visible. Instead of sartorial femininity, she boasted how she could entice men based on *kothar rosh*—the art of verbal seduction. Despite fears of harassment, their circle went far beyond a victimized position relative to men. Shyam fondly reminisced: "In the evenings, Govinda and all would congregate in a dark field near the municipality . . . they brought drinks, had sex with *parikhs* . . . . I had fun with so many men there!"

Shyam noted that their "language," Dhunuri Bhasha, had a limited vocabulary in the 1980s, not including *kothi*. Govinda claimed the language was their own "*abishkar*" (invention), and was not cognizant of similar terms like *dhurani* elsewhere. However, as Shyam's friend circle grew in the 1990s, her vocabulary expanded and she became more aware of transregional linkages: "We started hearing words like *kothi* after some *dhunuri* friends joined *hijra* houses . . . some of the language has come from (the state of) Bihar, some from Andhra Pradesh!" Though *kothi* arrived later as a relatively foreign term, Shyam sometimes humorously referred to her old *dhunuri* friends as "*British amoler kothi*"—*kothis* of the British (colonial) era—thus retrospectively mapping them as *kothi* and establishing a sense of historical continuity between *dhunuri* and *kothi*.

Shyam continued inducting younger people in the 2000s: "We are old-timers. . . . If we cannot recognize others like us, then who can?" Among the people she spotted was Anik, a middle-class college student who later became an NGO worker. However, the expansion of institutionalized activism in the 2000s also transformed the process of intergenerational interpellation. Before meeting Shyam, Anik had already met metropolitan activists who were expanding into Murshidabad, and learned words like *kothi* before *dhunuri*, resulting in a convergence between older and newer networks and languages, as detailed later.

At Nadia and neighboring districts, knowledge of the term *kothi* was uneven. At Ranaghat, Bikash averred that she learned the word *kothi* from younger community members in the 2000s, after NGOs entered the area. However, Babul, who lives in a neighboring district, told me in an interview that around 1985, when she was in high school, she was hanging out at a local railway station with friends when two strangers standing nearby noticed her and loudly remarked to each other—"*Oi dyakh, kothi lo* (hey, look, a *kothi*)!" Startled, Babul gradually made their acquaintance and learned that they called themselves *kothi*, and over subsequent visits, met "*duniar kothi*" (a "world" or large variety of *kothis*) from nearby towns who congregated at the station. Ranaghat was another pre-institutional hub of community networks—in Bikash's words, "*dhurani-der mohateertho*" (great pilgrimage spot for *dhuranis*). Babul gradually got acquainted with the Ranaghat *dhuranis* and learned to apply makeup from Bikash's *naan-guru* (grandmother *guru*), Shyamoli-*ma*. Together, they traveled to Bombay around 1987, where they did sex work along with other *kothis*.

Bikash described in a 2011 interview how her induction into the local *dhurani* circle by her neighbor Shivam involved adopting certain idealized gender/sexual roles. Shivam observed and recognized her as *meyeli* (feminine)—much as Jaydip had recognized Govinda—and later became her *guru*. Gradually, Bikash realized that Shivam and her friends "had physical relations with men just like *swami* and *stree* (husband and wife)." But Bikash wasn't sexually adept yet: "They would loudly tell each other: 'you know, today I had sex with a guy for money, took it in the ass!' They said such things to make me *pakki* (ripe, mature) . . . Meanwhile, a guy I liked wanted to fuck me, but he left because I couldn't do it . . . They told me, if you can't do this, you will never get a husband! You are a *kachchi dhurani* (immature, unripe *dhurani*)!" Bikash laughed, suggesting that their comments were lighthearted, and continued: "then, they explained how to do it!"

Thus, Bikash's maturation from an "unripe" to a "ripe" *dhurani* involved the adoption of a feminized sexually receptive role vis-à-vis masculine men, referencing sociocultural scripts of femininity and conjugality. *Dhuranis* who fulfilled such roles were sometimes called *akkhar* (extreme, ultimate) *dhuranis*. As in Murshidabad, though, such roles did not correspond to a subordinate position for Bikash: "We *dhuranis* would go around town with our heads high!" She then continued inducting younger members: "I noticed a junior boy in my school who was feminine. . . . One day I called out to the *dhurani*—'hey, listen!' He was initially scared . . . but gradually came into the group, and became my first daughter."

While such generationally reproduced communities were visibly gender variant, people like Bikash and Shyam kept their "language" private, not teaching it outside their circles and even to most male partners, which helped minimize outside interference and stigma. *Dhurani* or *dhunuri* functioned more as subcultural terms used in intra-community contexts than as public identity categories; outside their circles, they were perceived through the previously mentioned colloquial terms for feminine males such as *meyeli chhele* (feminine boy) or *maigga*.

Significantly, the gendered dynamics of *dhurani/dhunuri* circles were not confined only to non-Anglophone subcultural terms. In a 2015 interview, Swapan, a relatively affluent community member from Kolkata, narrated that in the 1970s, her friends did not know *kothi* and rather used *homo*, the colloquial derivative of homosexual, as well as *dhurani*. *Meyeli* from childhood, Swapan gradually

Figure 2.1 Bikash outside her home at Ranaghat, 2023. Courtesy author.

discovered others like her in north Kolkata with whom she discussed their common desire for men. Swapan would ponder to herself: "What does that mean, am I a man or a woman?" At a nearby cruising site, a community senior told her she was *dhurani*, and taught her about the anally receptive role. Meanwhile, her middle-class friends used *homo*: "They didn't know *dhurani*, they knew *homo* . . . We also didn't know words like *parikh*, we called our partners *swamis* (husbands). Sometime before the first NGOs, we heard terms like *kothi* at the Dharmatala *cruising spot;* then, NGOs spread these words more."

Swapan's *homo* is not equivalent to the homosexual or gay man who desires other men. Swapan insisted they did not have sexual relations among themselves: "Since we were *homo*, we were friends among ourselves, we liked only *purush* (men)!" Like *dhunuri* and *dhurani*, *homo* is cast as distinct from "men." Though *kothi* was a later arrival, during our conversations, Swapan sometimes referred to her older friend circle as "my *kothi* friends," and their "husbands" as *parikhs*, thus retrospectively establishing an intergenerational continuum between the *homo-swami* and *kothi–parikh* schemas. Later, she took a lead in teaching Ulti to younger community members—"they would take notes and write down words!"—thus further cementing these links.

Processes of transregional translation and inter-mapping between terms bolstered analogical correspondences between *homo*, *dhurani*, and *kothi* templates of desire. In a 2012 conversation, Chand, a participant of the Kolkata *dhurani* circles, told me how she visited Delhi in the 1980s and discovered similar communities there. Upon her return, she told her friends: "You know, in Delhi, *dhuranis* are called *kothi* and *parikhs*, *giriya!*"

While such spatial networking helped create a transregional linguistic continuum, it was highly uneven. Pintu from Coochbehar in North Bengal, where both *hijra gharanas* and NGOs entered later, narrated in a 2015 interview that her friend circle had no intra-community language up to the 2000s. They used Bengali phrases like "*meyeli bhaber chhele*" (boys of feminine attitude) or "*amader moton*" (people like us) for themselves. But there was already a sense of feminine sisterhood among them, and she claimed they only had sex with "men," not among themselves. This distinction was later mapped onto both the *kothi–parikh* schema and the analogous *meti–ta* dyad from neighboring Nepal. Pintu located Siliguri, the largest city in North Bengal, as the hub through which *kothi* and *meti* terminology traveled to Coochbehar. Even in areas with old *dhurani–kothi* communities, same-sex desiring males may interact outside such communities and models of desire. In 2009, *kothis* in a village in south Murshidabad introduced me to a group of men who had sporadic contact with them but did not use any particular name for themselves. They were mostly married and spoke of taking both penetrative and receptive roles; they spoke of feeling guilt at the "*paap*" (sin) of male–male sex but also of the lure of doing it again. Thus, terms like *dhurani* or *kothi* are neither homogeneously spread nor exhaustive of nonelite discourses in West Bengal, despite evidencing a remarkable pre-institutional range.

Further, even more consolidated *dhurani–kothi* circles evidence much sexual fluidity and variation. For instance, Dilip, the retired *lagan* dancer from Nadia whom we met earlier, claims seniority among *hijras* and *kothis* but also takes pride in his ability to take masculinized sexual roles. In an interview, Dilip narrated how, in the early 1990s, a feminine-attired *dhurani* met him in a train and initially took him to be a man: "because I was so handsome!" He subsequently had a sexual relationship with her, but also "learnt to apply makeup from her." For Dilip, pleasure in feminine self-expression did not preclude masculine roles, and penetrability was accorded less importance. Bindiya, from the Kolkata *dhurani* networks, stretched such role-switching further. From a poor Dalit background, she grew up in city slums and gradually began dressing in feminine attire in the late 1990s, eventually joining a *hijra gharana* and undergoing emasculation. But, as she once told me proudly, "I was an *arial tonna* (very masculine man) to begin with! All the *dhuranis* were crazy for me!" Nandini, a *hijra* acquaintance of Bindiya, told me disapprovingly: "She was not like us, you know . . . she'd dress up to entice the *parikhs*, and then instead of getting fucked, she would fuck them!" Bindiya, however, is unrepentant of her erstwhile fluidity: "When I would see a *kothi*, I would become more *parikh*—deepen my voice and change my walk; when I saw a *parikh*, I acted more like a *kothi*!"

Bikash, despite her lighthearted indoctrination into feminine receptivity, took delight in charting such diversity, and often remarked to me with relish: "There are so many kinds of *dhuranis*!" She called more masculine-presenting *dhuranis* "*byatachhele dhurani*" (man *dhurani*). While distinguishing them from mainstream men or *parikhs*, Bikash also displayed sexual interest in them: "You know, some *byatachhele dhuranis* are actually very good-looking!" Dilip's circle in nearby Kalyani used *dupli kothi* as an analogous term for *kothis* who were seen as more masculine or took both penetrative and receptive roles, paralleling the term *double-decker* discovered by NGOs in South India (Khan 2004). Both terms suggest Anglophone roots (duplicate, double) and imply a duality of gender/sexual roles. They are newer usages of uncertain provenance: Heena said she learned *dupli kothi* from well-traveled *lagan* dancers like Dilip in the early 2000s, whereas communities at Ranaghat, Murshidabad, and Coochbehar heard these terms only when NGO networks further spread such vocabularies in the 2000s.

Irrespective of terminological variations, people like Bikash and Dilip sometimes include potential partners within *dhurani* circles rather than strictly externalizing them as *parikhs*, thus recognizing a gendered spectrum wherein some *dhuranis* may take on masculinized roles. This extends to Bikash's own fluid, overlapping subject position. While Bikash does not use *byatachhele dhurani* for herself, she sometimes does describe herself as *meyeli chhele* (feminine boy/male) and is called both Bikash-*da* (elder brother) and Bikash-*mom* (mother) at Ranaghat. Her quotidian understanding of gender/sexual fluidity encompasses an understanding of diverse forms of desire—she told me about some women in her neighborhood who desired *dhuranis* and vice versa; she even nonjudgmentally (but surreptitiously) facilitated such connections. At Ranaghat, I also heard many stories of *chaparbazi* or *chaptabazi*—a secretive practice within *hijra gharanas* where *hijras* take other *hijras* as partners, sometimes even nonlegally marrying them. Once, when I was visiting Bikash, her *hijra* daughter Chhoti described one such wedding between two *nirvan* (castrated) *hijras*; as she said: "One of them wore a turban and the other dressed up as a bride!"

Thus, while idealized sexual roles within older communities anticipate later definitions of the *kothi*, a strict masculine–feminine binarism is not the only template of desire recognized within these networks. Even when this schema is followed, social scripts of femininity are often contravened—witness *dhunuri-dhurani* promiscuity, Bindiya fucking her *parikhs*, and *hijras* marrying as husband–wife. There are complex moral negotiations with such gender/sexual diversity. While Bindiya had faced disapprobation for her role-switching, within the Nadia community, Bikash is implicitly recognized as having a more ethical fluidity than Dilip, who is often criticized for ill-treating his wife. Contrastingly, Bikash is unmarried, and despite mostly wearing male attire, is respected as a mother-figure by feminine-attired *hijras* and *kothis*.

Such varied negotiations were often elided within an emergent institutional discourse on the *kothi*. While its arrival was presaged, *kothi* might have remained a more marginal term in West Bengal—for some, an infrequently used synonym for existing words, for others, altogether unknown—except for the emergence of metropolitan gay and HIV activism. Intergenerational and transregional community linkages were increasingly complicated by institutional mediations, resulting in both continuities and divergences between the *kothi* and preceding discourses.

Convergent Histories: The Institutional and Subcultural Dissemination of MSM

From the late 1980s, a growing number of middle-class, gay-identified men began forming the first support groups and activist collectives in Indian metropolises. In Mumbai, Ashok Row Kavi, a journalist commonly credited as the first Indian to come out to the media as a gay man in 1986, cofounded the *Bombay Dost* magazine in 1990, and later in 1994, the NGO Humsafar Trust (HST) (Singh et al. 2012). *Bombay Dost* followed several publications brought out by diasporic South Asians in Western metropolises, and urban Indian activists situate it within a West-to-rest teleology of LGBT activism: "Before the Internet, these publications informed Indian audiences about the happenings in the West . . . The ripples . . . finally reached Indian shores" (Singh et al. 2012: 51). In Kolkata, Pawan Dhall, a young aspiring journalist, made contacts with other activists by placing personal ads in Indian and diasporic LGBT publications (Dhall 2005). Moving beyond the secretive and sex-centric nature of previous gay men's groups in Kolkata, Dhall founded the newsletter *Pravartak* in 1991 and cofounded the support group Counsel Club (CC) in 1993 (Dhall 2005: 117–19). CC became associated with Humsafar: Row Kavi's coming out had inspired Dhall, and he functioned as the *Bombay Dost* representative in Kolkata (Singh et al. 2012: 55).

Even as Dhall was establishing CC, Debanuj DasGupta, then a student at an elite Kolkata college and later a prominent US-based academic-activist, was discovering the cruising sites of the city.[6] Educated in Anglophone terminology, Debanuj called themselves gay. But at the south Kolkata lake, they also learned words in Dhurani Bhasha. In a conversation in 2015, they told me: "These words percolated to us from the *kothis* . . . you had to actually go there to learn them . . . maybe someone would say, touch my *likam* (penis) . . . so I learnt what *likam* meant . . . we didn't know *kothi* yet, *dhurani* was the word in circulation." Debanuj also discovered CC and read the *Bombay Dost* magazine circulated at CC meetings. Through the magazine, they learned about a conference in Delhi organized by

Shivananda Khan, a UK-based activist who had just begun work on same-sex behavior and HIV prevention in South Asia. Debanuj met Khan in Delhi, who was setting up the Delhi office of his NGO Naz (later Naz Foundation International or NFI). Khan provided Debanuj with funding to establish the Naz Calcutta Project around 1993/4. This was part of a larger attempt by both Khan and Row Kavi to recruit affiliates and expand their respective networks (Cohen 2005: 292).

Parallel to such metropolitan networking, nonmetro and less elite people also entered spaces like CC. Debanuj noted, "suburban people first started contacting CC through letters sent to CC magazines . . . letters from suburban and rural areas also came." This was a time of increasing writing on sexuality and gender in the Bengali media. Bengali neologisms such as *samakami* (same-desiring, homosexual) and *rupantarkami* (transgender/transsexual) were being coined in the early 1990s by journalists and writers. In 1995, the Bengali daily *Anandabazar Patrika* carried an article on *Pravartak* titled "*Prakashye Bikri Hochhe Samakami Patrika*"—"homosexual magazine being sold openly"—public homosexuality being so scandalously sensational that it seems to exceed personhood and infuse the magazine itself (Anandabazar Desk 1995). Susanta discovered CC through this article, and soon took an active role in organizing CC meetings. He fostered more nonelite contact; as he said: "I used to take CC partners to cruising areas." Sarswata, a middle-class and dominant-caste activist from a Kolkata suburb who (like Susanta) discovered CC through the Bengali media, told me over several conversations that people like him, who had no prior contact with *dhurani–kothi* circles, learned intra-community languages after visiting cruising sites with people like Susanta.

These contacts gained importance with the expansion of HIV/AIDS activism when activists began surveying fields and mapping target groups for HIV prevention. With the emergence of AIDS as a public health concern and gay men as a vulnerable group in the 1980s, lobbying by Western and diasporic activists had led to alliances between LGBT NGOs and transnational development agencies. Aid agencies and bilateral or multilateral institutions such as DFID (Department for International Development, UK), WHO (World Health Organization), and UNAIDS (Joint United Nations Programme on HIV/AIDS), as well as large private foundations, were increasingly willing to fund research and intervention on HIV and male same-sex behavior (Cohen 2005: 283–4). Further, in the 1990s, India's economic liberalization made it easier for NGOs to obtain transnational funds for social work (Roy 2022). Indian gay activists picked up on HIV funding early. Row Kavi was allegedly the first Indian representative to attend the International AIDS Conference (IAC) in 1989 (Singh et al. 2012: 52). However, Humsafar started HIV-prevention work some years later. Arguably, the first Indian survey on HIV transmission through male-to-male sex was a study at Chennai in 1992/3 supported by WHO and partly conducted by Sunil Menon, an anthropologist who later became associated with Naz (Cohen 2005: 284). Soon after, the Naz Calcutta Project initiated the first mapping and outreach program in Kolkata in 1994–6 with funds from the Naz Project London. Debanuj described how they traveled to Kolkata suburbs to map cruising sites and met *dhurani* figures like the *"eksho-likam mashi"* (hundred-penis aunt—a humorously named senior community member who had apparently tasted a hundred penises). This outreach resulted in a paper on sexual networks that Debanuj presented at the IAC in 1996 (DasGupta 1996). Subsequently, the Naz Calcutta Project wrapped up due to funding issues, and members formed an NGO called Praajak, which undertook another "needs assessment" survey in 1996–7 for gauging the sexual health needs of males who had sex with males in Kolkata, jointly funded by DFID (UK) and the West Bengal government (Praajak 1997). Meanwhile, Humsafar diversified to encompass AIDS outreach and research; they performed advocacy with the Maharashtra state government for funding a survey to construct a "sex map" of Mumbai in 1998 and then started outreach around 2000 with a combination of state and foreign foundation funds (UNICEF 2002: 101–7).

Thus, across regions, the state increasingly entered the NGO–funder nexus— despite initial bureaucratic denial of the existence of homosexuality in India and the criminalization of same-sex behavior under the colonial-era Section 377 of the Indian Penal Code, which (until 2018) declared nonheterosexual penetrative intercourse as unnatural, although prosecutions were rare (Cohen 2005; Row Kavi 2008). The state's seemingly contradictory interest in working with sexual minority groups was propelled by the lure of foreign funds and the expansion of governmental apparatuses of disease control to HIV and AIDS. The Indian government's National AIDS Control Organization (NACO) began in 1992 with funding from the World Bank, and "sentinel surveys" by NACO and NGOs revealed HIV infection in India to be concentrated among "high-risk groups" like female sex workers and MSM, rather than generalized (Row Kavi 2008; UNDP 2008; Vijayakumar 2021). Thus, gradually, such groups became constituted as subjects of biopolitical power—a distinctive form of modern power that targets and manages populations, calibrates various characteristics of demographic groups, and aims to enhance their welfare (Foucault [1976] 1990; Lakkimsetti 2020). The state's juridical censure of same-sex behavior was contradicted by the increasing biopolitical interest that some sections of the same state took in preventing HIV transmission within groups who exhibited such behaviors and from such groups to larger society; this contradiction fostered ambiguities and openings in governance that activists could utilize (Lakkimsetti 2020; Vijayakumar 2021). Further, during India's economic liberalization, international financial institutions fostered neoliberal policies through which the state's developmental functions were increasingly shared with or shifted to private and nongovernmental actors (Roy 2022). The World Bank pushed the Indian state to involve NGOs in its AIDS response (Vijayakumar 2021). In this changing climate, CC members formed an NGO named Integration Society in 1999 (Joseph 2005). Integration undertook state-funded "needs assessment" surveys where intermediaries between metropolitan circles and less elite networks like Susanta played an important role. Sarswata narrated that his nonelite contacts increased further through "field visits." However, in informal conversations with other former CC members, I also heard that some middle-class gay participants were wary of including visibly feminine nonelite people in club meetings, fearing that their presence would expose members to stigma; they remained more as targets of intervention.

The issue of what terms to use to identify target groups came up in the surveys. Neither Anglophone terminology nor corresponding Bangla neologisms were much used in the surveyed sites; the Praajak survey report generalized this observation to remark, "words such as 'gay' . . . which imply an individualistic sense of identity based on same sex attraction do not describe the experience of most Indian males" (1997: 6). In that context, both Debanuj's 1996 presentation and the 1997 Praajak report used MSM. Tom Boellstorff notes that MSM was disseminated by US researchers through venues such as the IACs as a behavioral term both for males who participate in same-sex practices without forming a distinct sexual identity, and for those who use terms other than gay (2011: 292–5). The NFI network did not adopt MSM uncritically. Khan stated, "the term 'men' in MSM creates a generic category of MAN, ignoring local cultural constructions of what a 'man' is" (2004: 3). Praajak and Khan redefined MSM as "males who have sex with males" to avoid imposing conceptions of manhood and include variously gendered categories of "biological males" (Praajak 1997: 3; Khan 2004: 3). Khan further noted that MSM should not imply a common identity, bounded community, or "risk group" rigidly separated from heterosexuality as per the Western hetero/ homo binary, but rather, "male-to-male sexual behaviors" involved both self-identified sections like *kothis* and men (like those called *panthi* by *kothis*) who take part in MSM behavior without identifying distinctly from the "general male population" (2004: 3–4). But even as it was contested, MSM became increasingly hegemonic beyond NFI. In 2000, NACO, along with transnational funders like DFID and UNAIDS, funded a Humsafar-organized national conference for MSM (Infosem 2006). As Sarswata narrated, around 1999, an activist connected to the Humsafar network advised them to "use MSM instead of 'gay' or 'homosexual'" so that they would get state-funded projects for HIV prevention. Sarswata also mentioned how MSM, as a technical public health term, helped them avoid the stigma of homosexual demarcation—in his words, HIV prevention could act as a "*dhal*" (shield) for rights-based work.

The hegemonic legibility of MSM within emerging state–NGO–funder circuits meant that various terms were mapped under MSM. *Dhurani*, one of the self-designations found in the Kolkata surveys, was subsumed as "MSM slang" (Praajak 1997: 12). "MSM slang" suggests that despite caveats that MSM need not imply a community or group, it was yet transmuted from a term for individualized sexual behaviors to a population category or community with distinctive characteristics (Boellstorff 2011: 292–7). Concurrent Humsafar reports also evidence quick discursive shifts from "MSM activity" to "MSM community" to "MSM population" (2004a: 25–6), paralleling Praajak's construction of MSM as a "target population" (1997: 3). Thus, even as the universality of MSM was contested, its transmutation into a population meant that terms like *dhurani* were subsumed as colloquial, vernacular "slang" used by subsets of this newly constructed demographic.

Such vernacularization is multilayered. Though *dhurani* was noted in the Kolkata-based surveys, *kothi* had an edge over *dhurani*—it was found earlier in parts of Chennai in the aforementioned WHO-funded study, which posited a binary framework of *kothi* and *panthi* (Oostvogels and Menon 1993). *Kothi* was also mapped in other large surveys such as a 1997 NFI study in Bangladesh funded by the Ford Foundation, and soon, it gained precedence over similar terms in Praajak and NFI publications (Khan 1997). By 1999, Praajak staff, associated researchers, and communities were using *kothi* synonymously with *dhurani* (Joseph 2005). Gradually, *dhurani* is subsumed under *kothi* in NGO discourse. The publicity material for Manash, a documentary coproduced by Praajak, states that "'kothi' . . . is used across South Asia with local variations," and glosses *kothi* as a "feminine homosexual identity" (Praajak 2005). *Dhurani* is thus doubly vernacularized as a "local variation" of *kothi*, which is here subsumed as a regional version of the universalizing homosexual identity, and elsewhere as a subsection of the less identitarian (but still universalizing) MSM category. Such vernacularization extends to related terms. NGO and state documents increasingly cite *panthi* and *double-decker* as the standard terms for masculine partners and versatile males, respectively, based on reports from large, funded surveys in Chennai, Bangalore, and Bangladesh (Oostvogels and Menon 1993; Khan 1997; Khan 2004). Terms like *parikh* and *giriya*, corresponding to *panthi*, and *dupli kothi* corresponding to *double-decker*, are subsumed as "equivalent terms" used in different regions (HST 2007: 7; NACO 2007: 12).

The ascendance of *kothi* in NGO circles fostered its expanding usage through both dissemination and translation with extant terms. Susanta noted how NGO workers spread the term in the field (cruising areas like public parks): "New people in the field might be ambivalent about their orientation . . . then an outreach worker tells them, oh, you are a *kothi*! So, we give them a name, they try to fit within that . . . like this, they get segregated into a *label*." Susanta's description parallels scholarly observations of *kothi* being spread by fieldworkers and NGOs (Cohen 2005: 293; Boyce 2007: 181). This marks a shift from older processes of interpellating community members to a more institutionalized form of interpellation. Often, people inducted as *kothi* in the field would be subsequently taken to the offices of HIV-intervention projects where their names and newly mapped identities would be entered into written registers by project staff or new community members themselves (Khanna 2016: 109).

Further, unlike people like Bikash who referred to themselves as *dhurani* in intra-community contexts and not as a public identity—being called Bengali terms like *meyeli* publicly and asserting their visibility nonverbally through embodied expression—this newer generation also includes people who publicly designate themselves as *kothi*. In 2012, I attended a workshop on gender organized by a feminist NGO in Kolkata with Sushanto, one of Bikash's daughters, where we were asked to identify ourselves. Sushanto said: "I know what I am . . . I am *kothi*!" As Gowri Vijayakumar observes, HIV projects at Bangalore placed a high premium on being able to clearly know which sexual category one belonged to, and name oneself accordingly (2021: 100). This may suggest the influence of a gay/lesbian identity politics premised on coming out and claiming a fixed, stable identity (Katyal 2010). However, as we shall see, the narratives of self-identified *kothis* evidence variable interpretations of the term and continuities with older languages and communities. Indeed, while spreading in new ways, *kothi* was also a category into which extant words were incorporated. Raina, the Kolkata-based activist who did surveys for NGOs in the 2000s, told me: "Whatever terms like *dhurani* or *meti* we heard from people in the field, we wrote them down as *kothi!*"

The growth of small-scale community-based NGOs—known as CBOs in development parlance—across metro and nonmetro areas since the late 1990s further disseminated terms like *kothi* and bridged them with existing languages. The establishment of nonmetro groups is often traced to metropolitan organizations. CC is credited with organizing the "Network East" conferences that connected people across the state and with establishing "satellite groups" in smaller towns (Joseph 2005: 100). Metropolitan "organizations of broadly gay-identified men" are mapped as "the principal catalytic groups for community mobilization" (Boyce 2007: 182). In our conversations, Sarswata narrated that Dum Dum Swikriti Society, a CBO that he cofounded in a northern Kolkata suburb, evolved in the early 2000s from a suburban branch of CC.

Such metrocentric genealogies elide the agency of nonmetro people who sought out metropolitan resources and bridged them with existing networks and languages. In 2005, Nilimesh, a middle-class college student from Berhampore who did not know the older *dhunuri* circles of Murshidabad, read an interview of Sarswata in a Bengali magazine and found his way to Swikriti meetings, where he learned terms like *kothi*. Subsequently, Sarswata fortuitously shifted to Berhampore for a teaching job. Meanwhile, Nilimesh had discovered other young people like him and introduced them to Sarswata. One of them was Anik, who met Sarswata and Nilimesh before she encountered older *dhunuri* circles, and together, they cofounded a CBO, Madhya Banglar Sangram, in 2006. Swikriti and Sangram, along with several other CBOs, joined an organizational network named MANAS Bangla, headquartered in Kolkata. The MANAS network initially crystallized in 2003 in response to violence on gender-variant people in Kolkata's cruising areas, and went on to receive HIV-intervention projects from the West Bengal State AIDS Prevention and Control Society (WBSAPCS), the state subsidiary of NACO. Meanwhile in Nadia, Shyamoli-*ma*'s disciples proactively enabled organizational expansion. While seeking money (*chhalla*) in trains, they learned of CBOs in neighboring districts and helped connect them with Shyamoli-*ma*, whose *khol* (house, gathering place) became a field site for MANAS Bangla. In North Bengal, Sumi fled a hostile family environment in Coochbehar to Siliguri, where CC, and later MANAS Bangla, had established contacts. After working in a MANAS-administered HIV project there, she returned to Coochbehar and founded the CBO Moitrisanjog in 2009.

Many younger people like Anik or Sumi first learned terms like *kothi* mediated through metrocentric NGO activism. The emergence of *kothi* communities in some areas involved people from other places, like Sarswata, coming in and spreading intra-community language. People also traveled to cities like Kolkata for activist events and acquired language. Anik's friend Ahmed told me, "We heard how people in Kolkata spoke, and learnt more words from them." Indeed, Ulti—the name for the language used within Kolkata activist circles and the *hijra gharanas* of Bengal—increasingly replaced regionally varied names like Dhurani Bhasha or Dhunuri Bhasha. However, even as communities formed around new CBOs and related activist networks, their uptake of the *kothi* as a term for self-identification presumes *some* link with older languages and networks—rather than it simply spreading from HIV projects as some accounts suggest (Khanna 2016: 104). Sarswata could not have spread the language unless he had first learned it from the Kolkata cruising networks and intermediaries like Susanta. Further, newly crystallizing *kothi* communities often gradually linked up with older circles where these existed. In Murshidabad, while the metro activist Sarswata interpellated Anik as *kothi*, Anik was also subsequently discovered by Shyam, who already knew the term. The Dhunuri Bhasha of Shyam's generation was largely mutually intelligible with the Ulti that had arrived from Kolkata. Some younger community members, such as Anik's contemporary Soumen who was from a more working-class background, had also learned terms like *kothi* through *hijra* and *dhunuri* networks before NGOs arrived. Anik became Soumen's sister, and their generation claimed Shyam and Govinda as foremothers—naming the latter Govinda-*ma* or "Mother Govinda." This process restored a sense of intergenerational lineage: suturing the *kothi* with the *dhunuri*, and blending and sometimes replacing older language with newer terms. As Govinda noted, "Earlier, we used to say *dhunuri*, now, they say *kothi*!"

I witnessed a similar process of intergenerational linkage in Nadia. Sunita, a young community member who learned *kothi* from friends in the 2010s, once heard the word *dhurani* from Bikash and asked its meaning. One of Bikash's daughters explained: "What the *kothi* is, so is the *dhurani*!" However, despite this apparent equivalence, this generation largely did not use *dhurani* as a public self-designation, partly because of the greater currency of *kothi* in CBO networks, and partly because *dhurani*—despite its generic use for feminine male-assigned people in older circles—also specifically means a sex worker or a sexually promiscuous *kothi* in Ulti, being related to the verb *dhurano* (to have sex). Bikash told me how one of her *kothi* daughters once explained to her that *dhurani* could describe both *kothi* and female sex workers. Middle-class *kothis*, in particular, wanted to dissociate themselves from such imputations, suggesting emergent tensions around respectability among *kothis*, explored more in Chapter 3.[7] Some community members, particularly HIV project staff who interacted with funders, also identified themselves as "MSM," but overall, *kothi* became the most common self-designation in the wider communities connected to these CBOs.

Meanwhile, in Coochbehar, *kothi* was sutured not with older subcultural terms but with Bengali phrases like *meyeli bhaber chhele* that Sumi and Pintu had used before NGO expansion. Such uneven convergences between institutional and non-NGO networks foster the transregional standardization of subcultural language but also interrupt linguistic homogenization. In West Bengal, *parikh* rather than *panthi* has remained the more common term for masculine partners. *Dupli kothi* and *dupli* have spread to Coochbehar and Murshidabad as designations for sexually versatile people, rather than the officially recognized term *double-decker*—thus, not all emergent usages are institutionally disseminated.

Indeed, at Nadia, I observed how more experienced *kothis* saw new community members who only knew a few words like *kothi* or *parikh*—the ones most used in HIV-related discourse—as *kachchi* (unripe) *kothis*. Once, after a gathering at the CBO Swikriti in 2012, a young, relatively masculine-presenting community member, who was newly learning Ulti, interpreted the Ulti word *tonna* to mean boyfriend. An older *kothi* who had declared herself as his mother corrected him: "No—*tonna* is man!" To the other *kothis*, she explained: "He is *kachchi*, hasn't become *pakki* (ripe, mature) yet!" Thus, becoming a *pakki kothi* involved a more comprehensive initiation into larger intra-community vocabularies beyond institutional language.

The linear intergenerational transfer of language and the dissemination of terms from the HIV industry are thus *both* complicated by uneven flows and multidirectional mediations between languages. Institutional expansion converges with the uneven transregionalism of older networks; *kothi* is inserted into existing discourses through convergences between institutional and intergenerational interpellation and transregional translation between locally distinct vocabularies. In a 2011 interview, Agniva Lahiri, a Kolkata-based activist, told me that stronger *kothi* communities emerged precisely in locations where HIV projects connected with existing community networks, where communities sustained even after projects closed. Elsewhere, people typically dissipated once HIV projects ended.

Mapping MSM: The Kothi *as Local Knowledge for the Neoliberal HIV Industry*

However, despite the aforementioned continuities and sutures, the *kothi* was not a simple extension of *dhurani* networks but was also overdetermined by an evolving institutional discourse around the MSM rubric. There were well-known differences between Row Kavi, Khan, and their respective networks regarding the place of *kothi* within MSM, dubbed "the *kothi* wars" (Cohen 2005). Both activists mapped a wide array of sexual behaviors under the MSM rubric, modifying it to the South Asian context. Row Kavi constructed an "MSM Circle" with various subcategories, including self-identifying groups (gay men, *kothis*, *hijras*), non-self-identifying MSM, and occupational groups providing sexual services like massage boys (HST 2004a: 30). Khan meanwhile documented "a bewildering variety" of behaviors and identities, including self-identified *kothis* and *hijras* who desire men and "normative" men who do not adopt sexual identities but perform masculine penetrative roles with *kothis* and/or have sex among each other—usually for "*maasti*" (fun) or to release their "body heat" through "semen discharge" (2004: 3–4). However, Khan emphasized the *kothi* as the "primary and most visible framework of MSM behaviours," following from his assumption that "male-to-male" sex in India, despite its variety, was structured overall through "a gendered dynamic, rather than in terms of sexual orientation"—the same-sex behavior of normative males do not constitute identities distinct from heteronormativity; only the gender-variant identify as distinct categories; their gendered visibility makes them vulnerable to stigma (2004: 4). While MSM included gay men who identified as per sexuality, they were primarily "urban, English-speaking elite" (ibid.).

However, Row Kavi and Humsafar did not see *kothi* as so primary or gender as the predominant axis of identity and vulnerability, stressing the occupational vulnerability of groups like massage boys (HST 2004a: 30). They also de-emphasized penetration as an axis of gendered differentiation. As per Khan and affiliates, *kothis* generally "prefer to be sexually penetrated" due to their internalization of normative femininity; sexual fluidity is shameful and secretive (Khan 2004: 4–10; Praajak 1997). Row Kavi critiqued Khan's cultural generalization of the penetrator–penetrated binary (Cohen 2005). Humsafar depicted *kothis* as more fluid, citing the *dhoru kothi*, a usage found in Mumbai designating *kothis* who penetrate (HST 2004b; Row Kavi 2008). Neither was (homo)sexual identification seen as foreign. Row Kavi conceded the eliteness of gay-identified men, but saw gay identity as rooted in a long history of Hindu homoeroticism, and deemed it as more empowering than putatively indigenous terms: "to protect nonelite MSMs is to make them gay, to put them in the position of power" (Cohen 2005: 295). As Cohen notes, Row Kavi attacked Khan as orientalist, producing exotic difference for funders while disempowering MSM by denying them access to the globalizing gay construct (2005: 290–6).

However, I contend that certain fundamental similarities underpin the NFI and Humsafar discourses on MSM and *kothi*—while recasting MSM in South Asian terms, both subsume *kothi* as local and/or vernacular relative to MSM in parallel ways. Both strategically focus on gender/sexual identity (or lack thereof) as the primary axis for classifying people, subordinating other aspects such as knowledge traditions, language, or occupation that also characterize *hijra–kothi* communities (Reddy 2005). This renders gender and sexuality as universal rubrics for organizing personhood and collectivity. Further, while both map gendered differences among MSM, and Khan substitutes "male" for "man," their cartographies are overdetermined by the "biological essentialism at the core of the MSM category" (Boellstorff 2011: 296). Both essentialize *kothis* as males and gendered subject positions are classed as per male sexual behavior.

While the instrumental focus on sexual behavior is expected of HIV-prevention discourse, the subsumption of *kothi* within MSM has larger ramifications: the male–female sex binary becomes a universal biological *fact*, while *kothi/dhurani* discourses become localized cultural *constructs*. Khan glosses *kothi* as a "local sexuality" operating within "local cultural constructions" of "gendered sex roles" (2004: 3–4); "the *kothi* perceives himself and his desire for other males in the context of gender roles in South Asia" (2000). The positioning of *kothis* among "other males" establishes maleness as an underlying biological reality while *kothi* gender becomes a regional construct. Humsafar, meanwhile, describes *kothis* as "men" who are "allegedly effeminate" but actually situationally fluid (HST 2004b: 1). Khan prioritizes *kothi* femininity more but still sees it as contextually constructed, unlike maleness: "Males . . . feminise their behaviours" to "attract 'manly' male . . . and/or as part of their own gender construction" (2004: 4). Thus, both static and fluid understandings of *kothi* subjectivities subordinate aspects like femininity as less primary axes of categorization relative to their sex category (male), from which their sexual typology (MSM) follows. This subsumption of the *kothi* as a local MSM subtype reinforces the vernacularization of *kothi/dhurani* discourses by downplaying their spatial scale and subordinating *kothi* articulations of selfhood as localized cultural constructs of gender relative to a universalized, naturalized discourse of sex, effacing how the sex binary is *also* constructed.[8]

Humsafar's MSM circle further suggests an incipient attempt to distinguish gender from sexuality and separate gender identities from sexual ones: *hijras* are designated as a "transgender" group but *kothis* are not, though at this point "transgender" is still listed under MSM (HST 2004b: 1). Thus, unless *kothis* take up a *hijra* identity which is popularly predicated on consistent feminine visibility, they are depicted as essentially males who are "allegedly effeminate" (HST 2004b: 1), who "perceive" themselves as feminine (Khan 2000), or have "internalised" cultural femininity (Praajak 1997: 14). While some *kothis* do identify as feminine males, this precludes other articulations like *kothi–hijra* overlaps—*kothis* are relegated to sexual categories based on socially assigned maleness unless they consistently present as not-men.

Kothi–dhurani femininities are also often depicted as limiting and patriarchal: "A low level of self-esteem" characterizes "their feminine *dhurani* identity . . . patriarchal value systems which rundown 'femininity' have been internalised . . . (making them) indifferent about health risks during sex" (Praajak 1997: 14). *Kothis* apparently accept abuse from partners as they have internalized ideas of feminine weakness (Khan 2004: 11). Figures of promiscuous, agential femininity encountered in surveys—such as the aforementioned "hundred-penis aunt"— are marginalized in such descriptions, as are relatively masculine people within *dhurani* communities.

This tendency is linked to emerging discourses of gay identity in the urban middle-class circles to which many activists belonged. In West Bengal in the 2000s, both gay and its Bengali counterpart *samakami* were associated with femininity in popular imagination and community circles. In 2012, a young man, who had been the *parikh* of some *kothis* in Kalyani, opined during a conversation with local *kothis* that the "most extreme stage of being *gay* is becoming *hijra*"—placing gay within the same linear scale of femininity into which the *kothi* is often placed vis-à-vis the *hijra* (see Chapter 1). Meanwhile, I observed in Murshidabad that middle-class *kothis* like Anik and Ahmed, who were exposed to English terms, sometimes described *parikhs* as "straight" or "bisexual," while describing *kothis* as "gay" or *samakami*—suggesting that masculine men like *parikhs* were assumed to desire women either primarily or in addition to *kothis*, while exclusive desire for men and femininity were conflated in the gay/*kothi* figure. At Kolkata, Sonia, a *kothi* (later transgender-identified) CBO activist, told me in an interview in 2011: "We thought that what the *kothi* was, so was the *gay*, only in English—later, we realized that *gays* had a different thing going on!" Similarly, *kothis* in Mumbai mapped the gay as an anglicized version of the *kothi* (Gupta 2005). This suggests how the *kothi* may be transculturally generalized and cross-linguistically projected onto other categories at different scales, as discussed in the introduction.

However, Sonia's mention of "a different thing" suggests a contrasting emergent sense of the gay/*samakami* that disrupted its conflation with femininity and emphasized a more symmetric model of male–male desire where neither partner is necessarily feminized, paralleling transnational tendencies (Altman 2001; Reddy 2005). At a "gay party" in Kolkata in 2011, Rupesh, a middle-class gay man, complained to me frustratedly regarding some *kothis* he knew: "Why do so many gay men imagine themselves to be women?" He then averred that he found the idea that one had to be feminine to desire men to be regressive. Such viewpoints informed official reports such as an NFI-funded study from 2007, which—like Praajak's earlier reading of *dhurani*—interpreted *kothis* as having internalized patriarchal gender roles, resulting in unequal relations with dominating, penetrating men, unlike "egalitarian" gay relationships (Bondyopadhyay and Shah 2007: 36). The adoption of MSM, meant to prevent cultural universalism, could not thus prevent the elevation of gay identity as an idealized "egalitarian" referent to which the *kothi* was negatively compared. Rupesh's reading of *kothis* as regressively minded gay men extends the aforementioned subsumption of *kothi* as a local homosexual identity (Praajak 2005). MSM and gay—despite their differences—might thus be similarly used to not only subsume *kothi* and *dhurani* but also reduce them to "local identities based upon penetration" (Praajak 1997: 26). They thus represent distinct, yet sometimes convergent, processes of vernacularization.

State Cartographies: Linear Scales of Penetrability and Risk

The penetration-based understanding of the *kothi* was formalized through the state's increasing incorporation of MSM into its HIV-prevention apparatuses. Despite acknowledging MSM as a key affected population, NACO did not pay much attention to MSM till the third phase of its National AIDS Control Programme (NACP-III), 2007–12 (Row Kavi 2008). Responding to advocacy by NFI and Humsafar, NACP-III defined MSM as a core "high-risk group" (HRG), alongside female sex workers and intravenous drug users (NACO 2007). Despite their erstwhile differences, NFI and Humsafar representatives collaborated on the "technical resource group" for NACP-III, which mainly comprised representatives of well-connected metropolitan NGOs (NACO 2007: viii)—indicating a tiered hierarchy of expertise rather than democratic community consultations.

The sexual typology adopted by NACP-III combined elements of both NFI and Humsafar discourses on MSM. The definition of *kothi* in the NACP-III guidelines for MSM-focused projects directly quotes a DFID-funded Humsafar survey: "males who show varying degrees of 'femininity'" and are mostly but not always receptive (HST 2007: 7; NACO 2007: 12). This definition, while conceding sexual variations, explains the gendered diversity of *kothis* in terms of a linear metric ("varying degrees"); again, maleness remains uninterrogated while femininity is placed within scare quotes.[9] NACO then simplifies this further to a linear graph that correlates gendered identification and femininity with penetrability and risk. Self-identified *kothis* and *hijras* ("anal receptors") are most at risk for HIV, followed by "double-deckers" or *duplis* ("anal receptors and penetrators"), followed by the non-identifying *panthi* ("anal penetrators") at least risk (NACO 2007: 13). This reflects NFI's emphasis on *kothi* receptivity and on *kothi* as the primary MSM identity. Indeed, *panthis* were not counted as an HRG in NACP-III and excluded from the purview of projects (NACO 2007: 13). But like Humsafar's MSM circle, the typology also undermines *kothi* gender—*hijras* are listed as "TGs" or transgender (which is still placed under MSM) while *kothis* are not (ibid.). This suggests an incipient separation between MSM and transgender categories that gets formalized in later phases of the NACP, where *kothi* has remained an MSM subcategory while *hijras* are placed under separate transgender projects (see Chapter 6).

Such construction of "high-risk groups" happens within what Jason Hickel terms a neoliberal paradigm of HIV prevention propagated by donors like the World Bank and its partners, which places greater responsibility for HIV transmission on the unsafe sexual behaviors of individuals or groups than on socioeconomic drivers of HIV transmission such as rising economic inequality, labor migration, and survival sex—often fueled by the neoliberal economic policies promoted across the Global South by the same donors (Hickel 2012). The World Bank remained a significant, though not sole, funder for several phases of the NACP (Vijayakumar 2021). NACO (2017) acknowledges inequality as a structural driver for HIV but targets behavior change (e.g., condom usage) over structural transformation. In that context, despite NACO's advocacy against HIV-related social stigma, the construction of *kothi* as a feminized penetrable victim identity and a high-risk MSM subtype during NACP-III provided a target group for both locating the cause of HIV transmission and the responsibility for preventing its spread.

This happened in the guise of bolstering "community ownership" and incorporating "local" knowledge in HIV-prevention projects. In the 2000s, NFI advanced a model for a "rapid scaling up" of projects "based on community building" and "using *kothi*-identified males as service providers" (Khan 2004: 12). NACO accordingly recommended that CBOs should be deployed to reach target populations "in the local idiom" (Khan 2004: 11). MSM organizations would also ensure "community ownership" of the services being provided (NNACO 2007: 76). Accordingly, NACO awarded projects to CBOs through its state subsidiaries like WBSAPCS, and associated communities became hopeful of obtaining state-funded "targeted intervention" (TI) projects meant to reduce HIV prevalence and transmission among MSM. Between 2004 and 2012, the Kolkata-based MANAS Bangla network received and administered TIs in various districts of West Bengal. Swikriti and Sangram received their own short-lived projects in Nadia (2009–12) and Murshidabad (2011–12), respectively; Swikriti took over a previous MANAS field site at Ranaghat and recruited Bikash as a peer educator. While metropolitan activists had undertaken earlier surveys, NACP-III stipulated the recruitment of "local HRG communities" to map risk groups to get "results . . . closer to reality" (NACO 2007: 26). CBOs supplied workers "knowledgeable about the local context" (ibid., 63). These workers quantitatively mapped various details such as the number of people in particular field sites, their sexual typology (*kothi, dupli, hijra*), their frequency of sexual contact, and the number of condoms distributed to them—compiling such data into various "formats" and "registers" for reporting to the state (ibid., 60–90).

The Exploitation of "Local" Knowledges

Such mapping relied on *kothi–dhurani* spaces, networks, and knowledges in multiple ways. In Nadia, Bikash's and Dilip's *khols* (residences) became mapped as "hotspots" where HRGs congregated. Project staff acknowledged that no project could run in Ranaghat without Bikash's close knowledge of the area. In a 2012 conversation, Bikash boasted: "My house is itself a field!" Swapan in Kolkata noted that her generation had helped create gathering spaces in public areas like parks, which TIs later utilized: "Then, there were no organizations; the police would chase us with sticks—but we went again!" In Murshidabad, Shyam's aforementioned skill at intergenerational interpellation—as she said, "if we can't recognize others like us, who can!"—helped Sangram to find HRGs, facilitating the expansion of HIV projects into the district.

Community workers and their "local" knowledges, however, were poorly remunerated: Rs. 1,500 (less than $50) per month for the lowest post of "peer educator" during NACP-III (Aneka and KSMF 2011). During NACP-IV (2012–17), their monthly pay increased to Rs. 3,000—still less than $50. Higher posts typically require at least some English knowledge. At the Swikriti project in 2011, I saw peer educators memorizing English terms (e.g., MSM, HRG) for promotional tests for higher-paid posts like outreach worker.

Kothi–dhurani languages and knowledges thus become a relatively devalued vernacular within this stratified language economy. As Vijayakumar argues regarding female sex workers, "community mobilization" becomes "a strategy for placing responsibility for HIV prevention onto groups at risk" (2018: 173). The *kothi* becomes an exploitable, precarious labor pool serving as cheap public health workers, serving the World Bank's neoliberal agenda of reducing public spending on health (Hickel 2012). Such exploitation parallels the establishment of organizational hierarchies. NFI positioned itself as "an MSM CBO nodal agency" that oversaw "local level CBO providing services" (Khan 2004: 12). While NFI (2011) claimed to strengthen its local partners, "local" CBOs did not have direct say in NACP-III policy; community inputs were mediated through NFI and Humsafar, who served as national MSM representatives (NACO 2007: vii). NACO and WBSAPCS sometimes also defunded CBOs and closed HIV projects abruptly without adequate explanation, as happened to both the Sangram and Swikriti projects in 2012 (Dutta 2013).

Such power structures rely crucially on vernacularization and global/local hierarchies. The HIV industry seemingly valorized "local" communities and knowledges for providing results closer to reality (NACO 2007)—making them the substantive or particular counterpart to abstract predefined global paradigms of HIV control, but simultaneously limiting their ability to modify transnational policies and categories. If, as Khanna (2016) argues, the *kothi* was partly produced by the HIV industry, the *kothi* also performed the work of producing MSM into a *better* universal, giving it local concreteness and cultural truth—facilitating (in NFI's words) the "scaling up" of not just services, but also of the HIV industry and the MSM category as they expanded across South Asia. But the apparent valorization of the "local" disempowered communities positioned as local, who were strategically leveraged to provide representational "reality" but materially devalued. The valorization of *kothi* authenticity further reified it as a static local sexuality, eliding its spatial dynamicity and limiting access to (trans)national institutional discourse. The reified *kothi* provided a victim figure via which development capital was routed from funders to NGOs, and from which funders gained symbolic capital—during NACP-III, NACO and the World Bank proudly announced the reduction of HIV infections in India through community-based interventions (IDA 2009).

Institutional–Subcultural Translations: Hegemonic Cartographies and Ruptures

In Gidwani and Wainwright's theorization of capital-not-capital complexes, capitalist logics both parasitically rely on elided sociocultural logics like gender and caste and function as a "structure-in-dominance" in relation to them (2014: 44). Analogously, the state–NGO–funder nexus around HIV prevention selectively utilized and promoted certain aspects of *dhurani–dhunuri–kothi* communities, reifying tendencies like feminized penetrability into bounded identities to foster the biopolitical construction of HRGs as "domains and objects of knowledge" (Foucault 2007: 118). Capitalist logics of HIV prevention utilized preexisting subcultural formations—the network of *khols*, of *dhurani–dhunuri* languages. The constitution of HRG populations both depended on and modified extant logics of community formation via the collusion of community networks in constructing hegemonic categories, translating risk-based MSM cartographies into subcultural language and vice versa.

At a CBO-funder meeting in Kolkata in 2010, Susanta explained: "We now map MSM into the following sub-sections: *kothi*, feminine males; *parikh*, their *swami* (husbands); and *dupli*, versatile males." Susanta thus picked up the common husband–wife (*swami–stree*) idiom that we encountered in earlier narratives—where it signified particular relationships of *dhuranis*—and translated it into generalized population categories under the MSM rubric. If community workers serve to provide results closer to reality, "reality" itself is mediated through such translations between intra-community and official usages—flexibly varied *dhurani–kothi* usages become reified into a fixed cartography of groups differentiated by sexual behavior and risk.

As CBO networks expanded beyond metropolises in the 2000s, such translations bolstered the translocal standardization of subcultural discourse, reinforcing the association between femininity and penetrability. In 2009, I accompanied Anik to a village near Berhampore during a survey on MSM populations in Murshidabad, intended to demonstrate the need for a funded HIV project to WBSAPCS. At the house of her friend and sister Rahim, Anik inquired about her sexual role. Rahim hesitated: "I would take, I suppose?" Anik prompted, "Of course you would take, aren't you *kothi*?" Rahim embarrassedly replied, "yes, of course!" While Rahim had been unsure how to map her sexual behavior vis-à-vis her gender variance, the *kothi–parikh* schema provided a neat grid of identification—of course, *kothis* would also be penetrated. Such consolidations of identity align *kothi/dhurani* languages with the risk-based cartography of MSM subsections. Anik advised Rahim: "Sister, be careful, always make them (*parikhs*) wear condoms!" Wearing condoms becomes the naturalized function of the masculine, mainstream, penetrative *parikh*, while sexual risk and penetrability are conflated in the feminine, vulnerable *kothi*, who is also responsible for providing condoms. In her 2011 interview, Lahiri critiqued: "*Kothi* is reduced to a sexual identity, all *kothis* are assumed to be anally receptive; no one asks—do you also penetrate?" However, given HIV-related social stigma, activists like Anik did not usually represent *kothis* as a high-risk penetrated group in public advocacy on HIV and safer sex; it functioned more at the intra-community level.

The categorical divisions between *kothi*, *dupli*, and *parikh* were reinforced through practices such as the entry of clients' names in "registers" maintained in the DICs (drop-in centers) of HIV projects (a community space adjacent to the office). At Swikriti's DIC in Ranaghat, new entrants (including myself) were

Figure 2.2 Illustration of a *parikh* (left) and *kothi* (right) at Sangram's DIC in Berhampore, 2011, stating: "One shouldn't have sex without condoms as HIV may spread." Courtesy author.

instructed to write K, D, or P (*kothi, dupli, parikh*) in the register. At a MANAS Bangla project in Kolkata, I saw a peer educator shaming a community member for identifying as *dupli* but wearing feminine attire: "How can you still say you're *dupli*?" This paralleled and reinforced the linear correlation between femininity and penetrability in official discourse; apparently, someone so overtly feminine could not be sexually versatile. At another Kolkata DIC, I witnessed a debate between two project staff regarding whether *duplis* would ever wear *sarees*. While a young peer educator asserted that they could, a senior outreach worker insisted: "Your idea is wrong!" Apparently, only *kothis* would want to wear *sarees*.

Rather than entirely new or discontinuous, such cartographies that seek to strictly separate *kothi* from other categories might converge with older tendencies of feminine idealization to further consolidate hegemonic *kothi* identities. In a conversation in 2011, the older *dhunuri* Shyam mentioned her strictly receptive role to Anik, who exclaimed, "You are truly the ideal *kothi*!" Like the *akkhar* (ultimate) *dhurani* of earlier generations, Anik sometimes marked the exclusively penetrated *kothi* as the *arial kothi* (extreme/ultimate *kothi*). The process of intergenerational and transregional linkage between languages and communities converged with standardized institutional cartography to link and amplify behavioral ideals (*akkhar dhurani, arial kothi*), marking selective conjunctures between *dhurani* and *kothi* formations that potentially elided other possibilities like the *byatachhele* or "man" *dhurani*. People who breached idealized gender/sexual roles or transgressed categorical boundaries could attract censure.

For instance, Abinash, a male-presenting participant in the *kothi* circles associated with Sangram, sometimes designated himself as *dupli*. In 2008, he caused a minor scandal by having sex with another *kothi*. The Ulti idiom that Anik's *kothi* sisters used for such sex is *porota bela* or "kneading bread together," a metaphor that underplays penetration. Reactions varied from amused gossip to more serious expressions of disgust: "*Chhi* (shame) . . . *porota bela* between one *kothi* and another!" One *kothi* commented derisively about Abinash: "He's hardly a *parikh*, only a *dupli kothi*!" Here, the *dupli kothi* becomes an inferior kind of *kothi*— neither truly masculine, nor really *kothi*—derided within the community and elided by official cartographies that assume clear *kothi–dupli–parikh* boundaries, providing institutional sanction to the loose taboo against sex among *kothis*.

While Abinash was censured as a *kothi* who had transgressed her proper role, people regarded as more masculine may be shamed for breaching male gender and sexual roles. Dipa, a *kothi* in Raina's circle at Kolkata, once commented derisively about a person whom she perceived as a *dupli*: "He's a man—why does he take it in the ass? Shouldn't he only penetrate?" In another case, a young *kothi* in Berhampore had a *parikh* who puzzled her by avoiding penetrative sex. One day, she was mortified to discover him doing *bhel* (overtly feminine mannerisms) in the company of some other *kothis*. She shamed him—"you are really a *hijra magi* (*hijra* woman)!"—and left.

The convergence of institutional structures with intra-community ideals hardened the insider–outsider division of earlier *dhurani/dhunuri* circles into spatialized separations between *kothis* and more masculine MSM (*duplis, parikhs*).

Given the reliance on *kothis* as both clients and the primary labor pool, HIV project offices often became marked as *kothi* spaces. As Sarswata once joked about a MANAS Bangla DIC near Kolkata: "There are only *kothis* inside, no *parikhs!*" At the Ranaghat DIC, I met Sonu, a self-designated *dupli* who was also sometimes perceived as a *kothi* within the community, several times between 2010 and 2014. Arpan, a *kothi*, once complained in his absence: "Why will he do *dupligiri* (*dupli* behavior), being a *kothi*. . . don't let him enter the DIC!"

Sonu, meanwhile, told me that most *duplis* prefer to socialize with other *duplis* rather than with *kothis*. At Kalyani, Honey observed, "The *duplis* who cruise at the railway station like others like themselves—they don't like feminine people!" Such tendencies suggest the consolidation of the *dupli* as a separate subject position in contradistinction to the older usage *dupli kothi*, and the emergence of newer communities based on a symmetrically gendered model of attraction between masculine men, as elaborated in Chapter 6.

The *kothi* censure of the *dupli* partly derived from concerns around differences in gendered privilege. In conversations between 2007 and 2012, several *kothis* across Murshidabad and Nadia complained to me how many *duplis* avoid *kothis* in public, even if they know them in community spaces. A *kothi* in Berhampore attributed such behavior to *dupli* anxiety about masculinity: "*Duplis* are scared to be seen with us, lest people think they aren't *byatachhele* (men)!" Indeed, Abinash was repeatedly accused of such behavior.

Departures from Institutional Cartographies

However, not all people uphold status differences or neat behavioral divides. *Kothis* at Ranaghat observed that although Sonu did *moddapon* (masculine behavior) among men, he did not shy away from doing *kotipon* (*kothi* behavior, feminine mannerisms) when with them. Despite Arpan's objection, he was never really excluded from the DIC. Bikash's daughter Jolly defended Sonu's *dupligiri* to Arpan: "So what, he likes it—what about you doing *ladiespon* (behavior like "ladies") despite being a boy?"

In Berhampore, despite the scandal over Abinash's behavior in 2008, several newer entrants challenged idealized *kothi* roles and *kothi–dupli* divides. In 2012, at Sangram's DIC in Berhampore, I witnessed a debate where some *kothis* challenged the idea that *kothis* could not penetrate their partners. One *kothi* said: "Who says *kothis* can't fuck men? It's a matter of personal pleasure." Another replied hesitantly, "Yes . . . but there should be some distinction between *duplis* and *kothis!*" As Vijayakumar observes in HIV projects in Bangalore, DICs are not only sites where institutional categories are imposed, but also spaces where naming practices are contested (2021: 101). But such contestations are part of a much longer tendency in broader *kothi/dhurani* community spaces beyond HIV projects—recall Bindiya's contestation of *kothi/dhurani* sexual receptivity in the Kolkata *dhurani* circles. In Murshidabad, contestations around *kothi* behavior happened in public cruising spaces before and after Sangram's HIV project (2011–12). Barin, Binoy, and Sumon, three friends who entered *kothi* circles around 2009, were all sartorially male-presenting and maintained a public masculinity while undertaking working-class jobs as clerks, salespersons, and suchlike. Binoy was even married with children. Barin designated himself as *dupli*, and had a history of casual sex with *kothis*. While I heard many jokes to the effect that *kothis* should be cautious around him as he would establish a putative sisterhood only to later proposition them sexually, he also earned respect for his public alliance with visibly feminine *kothis*. Kanchana, a feminine-attired *kothi*, jokingly told me: "Careful, he's *dupli*, he might fuck you!" She added, "but he's actually very good . . . he goes around with us *kothis* freely!" During one public outing in 2012, Anik observed how Barin and Binoy hugged other *kothis* as sisters and performed the *hijra* clap. Anik wryly commented: "How are they less than any *kothi*? Sometimes, they say Ulti words that even I don't know!" Here, the multidimensional nature of community affiliation as *kothi* or *dhurani*—related to several aspects beyond erotic/sexual practice—troubles the linear cartography of *kothi* femininity and penetrability in HIV discourse; someone who is neither overtly feminine nor sexually receptive might be seen as equally *kothi* based on other qualities like knowledge of Ulti.

During the aforementioned gathering, Binoy discussed how *kothi* sisterhood endures more than relationships with mainstream men: "*Kothis* become *apon* (trusted kin) to each other, *parikhs* never become *apon*!" Binoy later adopted a younger *kothi* as his daughter after recognizing her at a public place through her *lachak* (feminine gait), much like how older *dhunuris* had found each other. However, while participating in *kothi* sisterliness with Barin, Binoy also confessed that he occasionally made Barin his *parikh*.

Such sexual alliances challenge *kothi* ideals of feminine desirability. In 2014, a *kothi* teased Sumon that due to his lack of overt femininity, he would need to lure *parikhs* with alcohol. Sumon disagreed that *parikhs* who desired feminine *kothis* were his only option: "Recently, a *kothi* saw me and fell in love . . . I said, I am *kothi* too, but he wouldn't listen!" Further, Barin and Sumon often described how they would pick up masculine men as *parikhs*, but such men exhibited *dupli* behavior, wanting to suck them off. Many *kothis* in Berhampore became increasingly appreciative of such sexual/romantic possibilities beyond the *kothi–parikh* schema. Guddu and Prem, both feminine-attired *kothis*, remarked how "*straight parikhs*" ultimately left *kothis* for women, but *duplis* like Barin made for better partners. Abinash defended his *dupli* behavior on similar grounds: "*Parikhs* will fuck and leave us . . . it's better to have relations within the community itself!" Further, he claimed to have successfully done "*behavior change*," inducing *kothis* to have sex with him rather than *parikhs*—thus appropriating the language of HIV prevention to subvert HIV-related cartographies of sexual behavior.

These people thus rearticulate the *kothi* beyond the *kothi–parikh* sexual binarism. Rather than separating *dupli* from *kothi*, they refashion *kothi* as a form of sisterly community that does not preclude flexible sexual arrangements— *duplis* shift from being scorned to being included among *kothis* as sisters in some contexts, or as better partners than *parikhs* in others.

Departures from the *kothi–parikh* schema are also bolstered through the dissemination of gay pornography, where sexual versatility is common, and the anal recipient ("bottom") is often masculinized. Such media has spread beyond metropolises in the 2010s with the proliferation of relatively cheap smartphones, though internet access remains uneven. Such porn largely depicts attraction between masculine men, but *kothis* may still perceive such media through a *kothi–parikh* framework. At Berhampore, I observed *kothis* watching gay porn on phones and mapping "bottoms," or men they perceived as more feminine, as *kothis*. However, Anik also once observed: "In *gay porn*, sometimes there is *parikh-parikh* sex!" Such porn thus fostered the realization that masculine men (*parikhs*) may switch roles and may desire masculine or sexually versatile partners. Indeed, *duplis* like Binoy averred that they preferred watching gay to straight porn.[10]

Challenges to *kothi–dupli* divides also derive from sources less connected to flows of media, technology, and capital—for instance, working-class or Dalit *kothis* in rural areas who maintain their expected social role as men to some extent, but play feminine roles in "folk" theater forms such as *monoshagaan* and *alkap*, which involve male performers of varying identities playing mythical female roles without being necessarily seen as gender nonconforming, providing a socially sanctioned space for feminine self-expression. While such role-switching may serve as a socioeconomic survival strategy, such performers may also take pleasure in gender/sexual versatility. Tanmoy, from a village near Berhampore, performs mythic female characters in *monoshagaan* but farms the land as a man. When I visited her in 2012 with Anik and Shyam, she expressed delight at having been gifted a *saree* by a *parikh* to wear in her next performance, but also proudly recounted how manly he appeared while working in the fields. Shyam confessed, "Well, when I first saw you, I was attracted to you!" Tanmoy flirtatiously replied, "Come then, let me fuck you!" He then narrated an incident when he'd orally penetrated a *parikh*. In Coochbehar, Subesh and Suresh live as married men while dressing as female during *monoshagaan* performances. They describe themselves as "*chhele-quality'r meti*" (metis of male quality) or "*gents hijra*" (gentlemen *hijra*), as contrasted with "*meye-quality'r meti*" (metis of female quality) like Sumi, and also sometimes call themselves *samakami*. In a conversation in 2014, Suresh narrated how some *parikhs* would suck them off, and averred that many *metis*, despite claiming to only be receptive, get pleasure from oral penetration. But Suresh also conceded that some *metis* or *kothis* were comfortable only in receptive roles: "They don't let partners even touch their penis!"

Meanwhile at Ranaghat, Bikash's appreciation of gender/sexual diversity influenced younger *kothis* as well. In 2012, Sudip, one of Bikash's daughters, fell in love with a *dupli*. Some *kothis* teased Sudip that her partner was really a *dhurani* who went around soliciting *parikhs* and took it in the ass, instead of fulfilling his husbandly duties. But Bikash encouraged the affair and even helped arrange a nonlegal wedding for them at the DIC, saying, "it's good that it's happening among ourselves . . . it's more fun and relaxed that way!" Meanwhile, Swikriti organized a community program at a nearby town where there was a discussion on relationships. An attendee commented: "We hear that love happens between men and women, and for us, between *kothis* and *parikhs* . . . but being a *kothi*, I have romanced another *kothi*, for which I've heard insults. Why can't love happen between *kothis*?" A *hijra* activist supported her: "Why not—even among *hijras* you have *chaparbazi* (intra-*hijra* sex)!"

Across regions, therefore, diverse sources foster the awareness of alternative configurations of desire beyond the *kothi–parikh* model. Thus, the *dupli kothi* and similar framings often return. In 2011, I accompanied project staff at Ranaghat to field sites like the railway station, where I observed outreach workers referring to certain clients as *dupli kothi* and even distributing condoms to *kothis* saying they could use it both for penetrating and being penetrated. Ajit, Bikash's daughter, explained the sexual preferences of one community member thus: "He likes *halka* (light) *kothis*, meaning *kothi* and *dupli* mixed." In Berhampore, Anik often referred to Binoy and Barin as "*kothi, dupli typer*" (*kothis* of the *dupli* type). Thus, while the MSM rubric separates *double-decker* from *kothi*, *dupli* may retain its older adjectival role, signifying variant *kothi* subjectivities and rendering *kothi* as a broad umbrella term (*halka kothi, dupli kothi*). *Dupli kothi* parallels Bikash's phrase *byatachhele dhurani*, indicating the continuing acknowledgment of gender/ sexual diversity across *dhurani/kothi* generations.

While *dupli* behavior is often associated with more masculine *kothis*, feminine-attired *kothis* (*bheli* or *bhelki kothis*) may also be *dupli*. In several conversations, Ajit critiqued how HIV-prevention models assumed that "*bhelki kothis* always take it in the butt." After Ajit transitioned sartorially, she told me: "I can still fuck *kothis*!" I also heard many anecdotes across districts about men whom *bhelki kothis* picked up as *parikhs* but who then asked to be fucked, prompting varying responses ranging from embarrassment to delight.

Apart from sexual versatility, *kothis* also articulate femininities that challenge cultural constructions of feminine sexual passivity. Much sexual slang in Indian languages stresses the phallic agency of the insertive partner (*ganr neowa* in Bengali—taking someone's ass, *chodna* in Hindi—fucking someone).[11] However, certain Ulti idioms such as *parikh khaowa* ("eating" or sexually consuming *parikhs*) and *parikh deowa* (giving or sharing *parikhs*) shift emphasis from phallic penetration to an agential consumption *of* the phallic male. Across districts, I often witnessed *kothis* asking each other how many *parikhs* they'd "eaten" lately, or if someone could share a *parikh* by facilitating access to him.[12] As intra-community idioms, such discursive acts may not publicly subvert social gender hierarchies, but do signal expressions of agency unavailable in standard language.

Given such departures from hegemonic cartographies, the practice of surveying and mapping people in field sites into population categories might be subverted. Experienced CBO staff often take very strategic approaches to mapping. During NACP-III, given the pressure of reaching high target populations combined with low salaries, staff often performed the entry of clients into the registers on their own, without directly soliciting input on which categories the clients identify with. Outreach workers in a project in South Bengal explained to me: "Sometimes we talk to them and verify . . . but often, we just guess based on their behavior or dress and fill in the *typology*!" This process of assessing typology continues *dhurani/kothi* practices of recognizing community members through gendered traits, but without necessarily interpellating the client into institutional categories directly. Further, the cartographic data itself was hardly seen as sacrosanct: I heard several accounts of fudging or changing client categories on registers to maintain population targets. For instance, MANAS Bangla projects initially included *parikhs* within project registers, but around 2009, NACO reminded them that *parikhs* should be excluded from HRGs. Sumi laughingly recollected the ensuing incident at the Siliguri MANAS project: "we sat overnight and changed all the Ps (*parikhs*) to Ds (*duplis*)! We joked, oh, we thought that guy was a *parikh*—but you know, he's really a *dupli*!" They thus satirized the whole process of mapping through which *kothi* workers are expected to provide "reality" and authenticity. No consultation was sought with clients, whose subjectivities were not brought into the process.

Conclusion

We have seen how subcultural languages and networks both converge with and disrupt institutional cartographies, complicating attempts to establish a standardized schema of MSM subgroups. Categorical ideals and transgressions are negotiated variably across time and space, and even among different individuals within the same community. More accepting *dhurani* seniors like Bikash, for instance, make for more inclusive *kothi* communities. Overall, given its ties to long-standing and diverse community networks, the *kothi* has remained irreducible to the penetrated, victimized subject of development that was sought to be mobilized to facilitate transnational capital, posing a contradiction within the capital–noncapital complex of the HIV industry, and challenging the biopolitics of the MSM.

Such contradictions may be contained through vernacularizing processes. During a discussion on *kothi-dupli* overlaps in 2011, Anik wryly remarked, "That's another story—we are not going to tell them (funders) that!" Given the highly hierarchical structure of funding, CBO activists feared to openly challenge institutional categories; quotidian language and practices may remain strategically hidden from official discourse. This retained the facade of neatly separate populations, and bolstered the positioning of *kothi–dhurani* discourse as an unofficial and private vernacular relative to the MSM rubric. Such vernacularization was reinforced by higher levels of institutional discourse that perpetuated a homogenized *kothi* archetype, such as this 2007 report sponsored by NFI and DFID:

> In the kothi context, a biological male who is penetrated becomes . . . 'like a woman' . . . (he) internalises a stereotypical . . . image of the woman, and looks upon victimisation . . . as an integral part of existence . . . The gay identity . . . linked to egalitarian relationships between 'men' does not find a very strong footing in India. (Bondyopadhyay and Shah 2007: 35–6)

Besides eliding sexual variations, this renders the agency involved in *kothi* femininities and receptive roles illegible within the teleology of political progress exemplified by putatively egalitarian gay relationships; their association with a stereotypical, backward heteronormativity obscures the dynamicity of *kothi–dhurani* negotiations with power. Elsewhere, urban Anglophone gay activists are described as the politically aware "intellectual(s)" of the movement while "vernacular speaking" *kothis* are positioned as targets of empowerment, implicitly undergirding a metrocentric hierarchy of progress (Singh et al. 2012: 80–116). *Kothi–dhurani* expressions that contravene patriarchal ideals, like "eating" men, thus may become effaced and/or positioned as part of a devalued vernacular. Such vernacularization parallels or presages other processes of hierarchization studied over the subsequent chapters.

Chapter 3

VERNACULARIZATION AND NON/ LINEAR GENDER AMONG *KOTHIS*

"From my childhood, my *mon* was soft, like women. I wanted to become a girl."
Thus said Shyamoli, a *hijra* interviewed in a Bengali media article from the 1990s
(Ahmed 1995). *Mon*, also transliterated as *mana*, "means both mind and heart" in
several South Asian languages (McDaniel 1995: 43). In Shyamoli's narrative, the
mon harbors a likeness to women and culturally archetypal feminine attributes
like softness. *Hijras* in Hyderabad similarly describe themselves as "like women"
(Reddy 2005: 134). But this likeness means different things to different people. For
people like Shyamoli, being "like" women implies a transitional tendency toward
embodied womanhood: a desire to "become" and/or be socially perceived as a
woman. One evening in 2014, at the DIC in Ranaghat which had recently been
reopened by a new CBO, Sampriti, after the closure of Swikriti's HIV project in
2012, some *kothis* and *hijras* from the area gathered and conversed on various
topics, including transition and emasculation. Nita, a local *hijra guru*, remarked:
"We *kothis* have a *niharinipon* (womanliness, woman-like quality) in our *mon*."
She averred, "it is for this *niharinipon* that we do all this"—wear feminine attire,
undergo *chhibrano* (emasculation). She said she had undergone *chhibrano* to
gain *shanti* (peace) and described feeling pleased when publicly perceived as a
woman. Unlike Shyamoli, though, Nita did not seem to understand *niharinipon* as
"soft," and later described giving *bila* (aggressive insults) to men who treated her
disrespectfully.

Other *kothis*, *dhuranis* or *hijras* use the idea of likeness to connote a femininity or
similitude to women that remains distinct from social or embodied womanhood.
Bikash of Ranaghat, as mentioned earlier, described herself as *meyeli chhele*
(feminine male) and *meyeder moton* (like girls/women). But despite occasionally
wearing feminine attire, she never articulated the desire to "become" a woman,
while positioning herself as feminine in terms of her erotic role relative to her
swamis (husbands) and her kinship role as a *kothi/dhurani* mother. Even *kothis/
hijras* who transition physically may distinguish themselves from women for
various reasons explored in previous literature and later in this chapter.[1]

Given these shifting interpretations of femininity, *kothis* and *hijras* use diverse
words and idioms, drawn from both colloquial Bengali and Ulti, to distinguish
between their varied expressions of femininity or womanliness. Whereas the

previous chapter studied the sexual cartography of MSM, here, I delve into intra-community distinctions based on gendered attire, embodiment, and behavior, and explore their relation to processes of vernacularization. This necessitates a closer look at Ulti terms like *bheli* that we briefly encountered earlier. At a community gathering in Kolkata in 2011, two *kothis* in feminine attire, one from Murshidabad and the other from Nadia, discussed the male-attired people around them: "They are also *kothis*, but you can't tell easily because they are *kodi* . . . they are not *bheli* like us!" *Kodi* and *bheli* are thus translocal terms, used in several districts of West Bengal, which describe differences in gender presentation.[2] Being *kodi* (where "d" is pronounced as ɽ) means wearing male attire and/or performing masculine behaviors or mannerisms. *Kodi* corresponds to *kada* in Hyderabad and *kade* in North India—terms that broadly describe *kothis* or *jananas* who are closer to social masculinity relative to overtly feminine or *hijra*-like *kothis* (Reddy 2005: 63; Nagar 2019: 42). The aforementioned *kothis* contrast *kodi kothis* with *bheli kothis*. *Bheli* is the adjectival form of *bhel*, an Ulti word signifying various forms of feminine expression that I unpack later. While *bhel* does not seem to have a direct transregional counterpart, the *kodi–bheli* distinction parallels some aspects of the subdivisions within *kothi* and *janana* communities in other regions (Reddy 2005; Nagar 2019).

Exploring some ways in which *kothi* communities in West Bengal distinguish among their differing femininities, this chapter explores how these distinctions crystallize into hierarchical divides between different kinds of *kothis*, or conversely, are destabilized or undone. Processes of vernacularization fostered by NGOs and elite activists reinforce varying forms of linear gradation and hierarchization between "more" and "less" feminine people, even as diverse usages of Ulti terms and resignifications of categories like MSM contravene linear hierarchies. I draw on analyses of fluidity across different subcategories of the *kothi* or *janana* spectrum (Reddy 2005; Nagar 2019). Nagar notes that though *kade taal jananas* regard themselves as having more social prestige than *hijras*, some shift to being *pacci jananas* who wear feminine attire like *hijras* (2019: 42). Reddy observes "constant movement . . . between the various koti 'identities,'" though such fluidity may attract disapprobation from senior *hijras* (2005: 207). Broadly, these studies explore fluidity across a given schema of identity: "Most . . . recognize differences among these identities, but that does not . . . preclude the enactment of two or more of them" (Reddy 2005: 76).

During my fieldwork, I observed how terms like *kodi* and *bheli* are not only used to distinguish between different kinds of *kothis* but also in ways that contravene such categorization—for example, to denote different modes of dress or behavior deployed by the same person. In that context, I explore not so much fluidity across a given schema, but the non/linear making and unmaking of categorical boundaries themselves, extending the study of non/linear distinctions between *kothi/hijra* and *kothi/parikh* categories in earlier chapters. The establishment of divides between different kinds of *kothis* is often based on linear gradations of their supposedly lesser or greater femininity and connected to caste and gender hierarchies that distinguish between appropriate and inappropriate forms of femininity. However, various practices trouble or undo such linearities: people switch between multiple subject positions and blend different modes of dress or behavior, demarcations between positions shift contextually, and cartographies are charted contradictorily—for instance, the same person may be charted as *kodi* and *bheli* by different people. As we shall see, such tendencies not only destabilize linear gradations of *kothi* femininity, but also show how linear metaphors can be used in nonlinear ways, thus exceeding critiques of linear spectra of identity in Western queer/trans scholarship, which tend to favor alternative nonlinear frameworks (Halberstam 1998; Castleberry 2019).

The following sections map these varied non/linear (both linear and nonlinear) processes of differentiation and chart their relation to multiple forms of vernacularization. While we have seen how *kothi/hijra* discourses are subordinated as vernacular relative to biopolitical categories like MSM, this chapter studies how activist articulations of MSM and homosexual identity intersect with discourses of LGBT rights that, despite liberatory possibilities, may reinforce dominant-caste constructs of nationalism and culture. This intersection results in compounded processes of vernacularization that reinforce caste and gender norms and related linear hierarchies within *kothi* communities and CBOs, delegitimizing femininities seen as too sexual or aggressive relative to sanctioned models of feminine maleness.[3] However, diverse *kothi* practices contravene hierarchical divides; further, *kothis* contest activist discourse, take advantage of ambiguities therein, and resignify dominant categories, troubling linear hierarchies.

Bhel, Pon, Bila: *Non/linear Gender in* Kothi–Hijra *Communities*

We *kothis* survive through *bhel*—look how we expand our breasts with bras stuffed with rags!

—Kanchana, Murshidabad

Kanchana, a *kothi* dance teacher from a small town in Murshidabad, made this remark in a conversation in 2016. A multivalent word with contextually shifting connotations, *bhel* broadly signifies various forms of sartorial or behavioral expression socially coded as feminine. *Bhel* and related phrasal verbs like *bhel dewa* (giving *bhel*), *bhele thaka* (being in *bhel*), and *bheli howa* (becoming *bheli*) may refer to the act of wearing feminine attire and/or makeup—especially in flashy or flamboyant ways. Heena from Nadia explained to me: "If someone puts on a lot of makeup, we say, you have so much *bhel!*" In the behavioral sense, *bhel kora* (doing *bhel*) or *bhel dewa* (giving *bhel*) may signify various acts, mannerisms, and affectations associated with femininity—for example, swaying hips or moving hands gracefully. At Ranaghat in 2012, Bikash described how she and her friends seduced men: "We take money from *parikhs* by doing *bhel*, by waving our hands!" Her description and accompanying gestures suggested a conscious accentuation of coquettish femininity, similar to the intentionally exaggerated "feminine wiles" of *kothi* dancers in North India where the term *bhel* seems absent (Morcom

2013: 106). *Kothis* "do *bhel*" in both female and male attire in various contexts—including but not limited to flirtation with men—and across diverse spaces, from public cruising spots like parks to intra-community spaces like DICs and houses of community members. While Bikash did *bhel* publicly in male attire, other *kodi* (male-attired) *kothis* may conceal their *bhel* to avoid exposure and stigma. Once, in 2014, I was on a commuter train with Trisha, a *kothi* from the Nadia circles, when we met a male-attired *kothi* who was waving his hand in dance-like gestures while listening to music on headphones, but also tried to hide from acquaintances nearby to whom he presented a masculine front. Trisha wryly remarked: "Look, how he's covering his face with a handkerchief while doing *bhel* . . . as if no one will see!"

These examples show how quite different practices are mapped as *bhel* and differences in how openly such behaviors are performed. A common idiom I heard from older *kothis* and *hijras* states that "*kothis* have thirty-six kinds of *bhel*," where "thirty-six" is not meant literally but connotes the multiplicity of *bhel*. *Bhel* may describe both consciously stylized, flamboyant, or sexualized expressions of femininity and involuntary mannerisms. In a 2015 conversation, Bikash remarked: "I love watching the *bhel* of *kothis*; when Anita (a local *kothi*) talks, she makes her fingers dance in such a way!" Such consciously performative forms of *bhel* parallel some aspects of camp in Western queer/trans subcultures, such as stylized gender expression, self-conscious eroticism, and pleasure in exaggeration, theatricality, or artifice (Martinez 2012: 139). Jhilik, a *kothi* from Nadia who stayed in male attire at home but performed *hijra* professions in female attire elsewhere, once described to me how she would cry and exaggerate her penury, performing a feminized helplessness, so that *hijra gurus* sympathetically allowed her into their groups. She laughed and added, "You know the *bhel* of *kothis*!" Heena told me that *bhel* might be related to the Bengali term *bhelki*, which means magic or trickery: something deceptive or illusionary, but also fantastic and magical. *Kothis* sometimes use *bhel* and *bhelki* to explicitly designate artifice—*bheler* or *bhelkir jok* (hair of *bhel/bhelki*) denotes a wig; doing *bhelki* might refer to lying or creating drama.

However, *kothis* also use *bhel* to describe mannerisms or behaviors that are not consciously performed. Bela, a *kothi* from North 24 Parganas who had to remain in male attire in her job, told me how her coworkers could tell that something about her was different because however much she tried, she could not hide her "*chokher bhel*"—the demure, feminine expressions of her eyes. Another *kothi* from Nadia told me that though his family forced him to keep a beard, his walk and hand movements gave him away: "My *bhel* shows that I am a *kothi*!"

While unpacking the similarities and differences between *bhel* and camp is beyond my purview, the possibility of such a comparison suggests the translocal resonances of *bhel* with practices elsewhere. Though the term *bhel* seems specific to West Bengal, its usages exceed a local referential frame, exemplifying a form of situated non-locality. Heena, who also speaks Hindi, told me: "*Bhel* is not used in Hindi, Bengali *kothis* say *bhel*; they (Hindi-speaking *kothis*) use words like *lachak matak karna*." *Lachak matak karna* denotes moving the body in a supple way and connotes a coquettishly feminine way of walking or dancing, which corresponds to some aforementioned forms of *bhel*.[4] Thus, *bhel* is seen as translatable into other languages, even if partially. Further, *kothis* see the behaviors and embodiments associated with *bhel* as being legible to people from other regions. In 2012, Srijan from Berhampore narrated how she encountered a group of foreign tourists in Kolkata who, upon seeing her, exclaimed "Indian gay! Indian gay!" Srijan thought this happened because she was "walking with *bhel*"—a pronouncedly feminine gait. Just as foreigners may read *kothis* as gay based on their *bhel*, *kothis* read *bhel* into queer/trans people elsewhere and recognize *bhel* as a sign of their commonality. In a 2021 conversation, Tara, a *kothi* from Nadia, told me excitedly after watching some American shows featuring queer/trans people: "You know, foreign *kothis* have *bhel* too!" Much like *kothi* itself, *bhel* may be projected onto transregional and transnational scales and seen as translatable with other terms, practices, and embodiments.

Bhel is related to various other intra-community terms in West Bengal. *Kothis* who wear feminine attire and/or do behavioral *bhel* are called *bheli kothis*, or alternatively *bhelki*, *bhorokti*, or *lahari kothis*, with local variations in which terms are used and their exact meaning.[5] Phrases like *bheli kothi*, *bhorokti kothi*, and *kodi kothi* may mark different kinds of *kothis*, paralleling similar usages elsewhere—*kothis* like Heena who knew Hindi treated *kade taal janana*, a term noted in Nagar (2019), as synonymous with *kodi kothi*. However, such terms may also mark transitional stages for *kothi/hijra* individuals—for instance, becoming *bheli* from *kodi*—or different sartorial or behavioral modes adopted by the same person. In such cases, words like *bheli* and *kodi* may be combined with the suffix *pon* or *pona*, which denotes way or manner in Bengali—for example, *meyelipona* means behaving in a girlish way. Adding this Bengali suffix to Ulti words, *kothis* may describe themselves or others as *bhelipon* or *kodipon* (*bheli* or *kodi* in dress or behavior), *niharinipon* or *laharanpon* (womanly), *tonnapon* or *moddapon* (manly), *chhibripon* (*hijra*-like), and so on.[6] As a *kothi* told me during a conversation at Ranaghat in 2011: "I like doing a little *niharinipon*, putting on a little makeup." Another *kothi* asked me self-consciously during a community gathering at Kolkata: "Am I looking too *moddapon* today?" Interestingly, Pushpesh Kumar notes that *kothis* in western India use *kothpan*—roughly, *kothi*-ness—to mean "the essence of being *kothi*" (2016: 194). Nita's aforementioned description of *niharinipon* (womanliness) in the *mon* suggests that *pon* may be used similarly to indicate essential, interiorized attributes. However, as we will see, *kothis* also switch between or mix *niharinipon*, *tonnapon*, *bhelipon*, and *kodipon* in contextually varied ways. Thus, *pon* may mark both stable gendered subjectivities and sartorial or behavioral modes that are variously combined.

This multivalence of *bhel* and *pon* means that they may express varied assemblages of attire, behavior, erotic role, and subjectivity—including strong identification with womanhood, femininities distinct from womanhood, and contextually changing levels of (dis)identification with womanhood or femininity. While *kothis* and *hijras* sometimes understand these variations as a gradation between "more" and "less" feminine people, these words are also used in ways that contravene linear gradations—people may be *kodi* in attire but behaviorally *bheli*, or a stable binary femininity in one aspect such as sexual role may be combined with fluidity in aspects like attire.

I explore the linear usages of these terms first. *Kothis* who sartorially transition from *kodi* to *bheli* or *bhorokti* may articulate this transition as a unidirectional, irreversible process. Sonia, a *kothi* (later trans-identified) activist from Kolkata, gradually began wearing socially feminine attire from 2010 onward, starting with androgynous *fatuas* (loose, flowing shirts) and eventually wearing *sarees*. In a 2014 conversation, she said: "A *kothi* who has once worn *satra* (dress), come into *bhel*, she can never give everything up and go back to being *kodi* again! I can never become *kodi* again—I would go crazy!" She further explained, "*kothis* love to imagine themselves as women!" Sonia thus saw the transition from *kodi* to *bheli* as a temporally linear, irreversible expression of their self-imagination as women, paralleling trans narratives explored in subsequent chapters.

Kothis may also articulate a similar trajectory from *tonnapon* to *laharanpon*. Kanchana, who comes from a small-town Muslim family, began dressing in feminine attire soon after moving to Berhampore as a college student and reverted to *kodi* clothes only while visiting family. During a brief outing in male clothes in 2011, she told me: "I am feeling such discomfort in *tonnapon*!" She particularly disliked how male trousers accentuated the crotch area: "*Tonnas* (men) like making their penises prominent—but we *kothis* want to hide our penises!" She preferred clothes she described as *laharanpon* or *chhibripon* (womanly, *hijra*-like). As noted earlier, she said such *bhel* enabled *kothis* to survive.

Kanchana's increasing sartorial *bhel* led to her eventual *chhibrano* (emasculation), which she did without permanently joining a *hijra gharana*. Bibi, a teenaged *kothi* from a Kolkata slum who did join a *gharana*, once told me that she planned to undergo *chhibrano* before full puberty hit so that her "*tunnipon* (girl-ness) would be good," suggesting how *chhibrano* served as a way of realizing a desirable feminine embodiment (*tunnipon*), in addition to reinforcing one's *hijra* status.

Chhibripon, Bhel, *and* Bila *versus Social Womanhood*

However, a linear *kodi* to *bheli* trajectory does not necessarily imply transition to womanhood. Even for those desiring it, womanhood per se may be regarded as impossible. *Hijras* in Reddy's ethnography assert that they are "like women" and take care to appear like cisgender women as much as possible, but also declare that they are not women with variable regret or pride, one reason being that they cannot give birth (Reddy 2005: 127–35).

Yet, some of my *hijras* interlocutors did see emasculation as making them women. Bindiya, the *hijra* from Kolkata we met earlier, told me casually during a conversation in 2012, "I got cut and became a *magi* (woman)." She later added that she had become mellow after *chhibrano*—just like a "*ghorer bou*" (housewife)— despite her previous masculinity. More commonly, though, *hijras* are clearly distinguished from women. As a *kothi* remarked during a conversation at the Ranaghat DIC in 2013: "At night, you can't always tell if someone is a *magi* or a *hijra!*" Another *kothi* at Ranaghat once remarked, "You don't become a woman just because you cut off the penis—you become a *hijra* only!" As Cohen notes, *hijras* might see emasculation as becoming a mixed or intermediate gender—"Through the bleeding, maleness flows out, femaleness flows in; mixture results" (1995: 285). Such understandings, in which the body permits partial feminine embodiment but not unequivocal womanhood, are not simply biologically essentialist. In the Ulti lexicon, both castrated and *akua* (non-emasculated) *hijras* and *kothis* are distinguished from *tonna* or men—which suggests that the body is not the sole determinant of selfhood, but bodily change has limits.

Social legibility reinforces this limit. Many of my interlocutors were keenly aware that they are not seen as women even if they transition sartorially and/or anatomically. During a conversation in 2012, Bapi, a *kothi* from Nadia, told me rather despairingly: "However good you look when you dress up, people won't see you as a woman . . . they see you as a *launda* (feminine boy) only!" However, the position of feminine presentation yet non-womanhood may also be articulated affirmatively. Kash, a female-attired *kothi* and dancer from Nadia, told me in a conversation in 2014: "Women are women . . . we are separate!" She added: "I feel I am no less than any woman . . . even if they're with women, men still turn and look at me!"

In this context, expressions like *pon* and *bhel* enable the articulation of femininities that are not only distinct from social womanhood but even permit certain liberties relative to it. Honey, a *kothi* from a Dalit family in Kalyani whom we met in Chapter 1, told me over several conversations between 2011 and 2013 that she was *meyeli* from childhood and desired to wear *niharinipon* (womanlike) dress occasionally. While she dressed in female attire while doing *chhalla* away from home, her sartorial *niharinipon* did not mean she wanted to present as a woman. During a 2012 trip, I accompanied her to a seaside tourist spot in South Bengal where she went out in a *saree* one evening, but remarked that it was "more *moja* (fun) to do *chhibripon* (*hijra* mode)" than try to be perceived as a woman. As I observed over the evening, this "fun" entailed doing *bhel* by openly flirting with multiple men and behaving in flamboyantly seductive ways on one hand, and retaliating aggressively when harassed on the other. Honey and her friends referred to the latter as *bila kora* (doing *bila*). Like *bhel*, *bila* is a broad term for a complex set of behaviors, gestures, and expressions—particularly aggressive, rude, or threatening behavior, including sexual insults, which may be performed nonseriously during mutual teasing among *kothis* or more seriously during actual confrontations outside or within the community.

Chhibripon, *bhel*, and *bila* all contravene ideals of womanly conduct based on intersecting caste and gender norms. South Asian women are subject to widespread patriarchal norms that connect the honor of the family and community to the maintenance of feminine chastity, though specifics vary by caste, region, and period (Still 2011; Abraham 2014). Dalit movements and scholarship, building on the work of the revolutionary Dalit leader B. R. Ambedkar, have powerfully demonstrated how caste and patriarchy are co-constituted; the hierarchical and exploitative division between castes is maintained through endogamy and control over female sexuality

(Paik 2022: 9–10). Dalit feminist critique shows how "society's moral hierarchy of respect and decency" stigmatizes oppressed-caste women who become associated with sexual excess and vulgarity, while dominant-caste women are associated with sexual modesty and social respectability (Paik 2022: 1–2). Dalit trans activist Grace Banu points out the intersection between transphobia and dominant-caste morality, which hypocritically stigmatizes sex work as taboo while compelling trans people to adopt such professions through social exclusion (Banu 2018).

In Bengal, norms of sexual modesty were historically contested by oppressed-caste women singers in the early colonial period who performed eroticized forms of popular culture replete with sexual innuendos; however, nineteenth-century nationalist and reformist movements derided women's popular culture as obscene (Banerjee 1989). Such movements constructed an idealized national culture that positioned Bengali middle-class, dominant-caste women—the *bhadramohila* (genteel woman)—as sustainers of cultural tradition through their nurturing roles in the private sphere, offering them limited educational and professional opportunities contingent on fulfilling this symbolic role (Chatterjee 1989). Some elite-led social movements also extended such ideals to subaltern women (Sangari and Vaid 1989). Overall, intersecting ideologies of caste, patriarchy, and modern nationalism have reinforced some version of sexual modesty, demureness, and sartorial restraint for women across socioeconomic backgrounds and regions— female sexual expression in public risks social disrepute and sexual violence (Lukose 2009; Gilbertson 2014). In Bengal, families across classes, castes, and religions may evoke *shomman* (social respectability, honor) to enforce variable restrictions over women's public mobility and interactions with men (Naved et al. 2007). Following economic liberalization in the 1990s, some forms of fashionable dress, romance, and consumerism may become more acceptable for middle-class women as part of newly desirable cosmopolitan lifestyles, but such women continue to face pressures to maintain a balance between newer markers of status and norms of respectability (Gilbertson 2014).

In that context, *bhel* allows the articulation of femininities distinct from normative social womanhood. At Berhampore, Kanchana avowed a consistent femininity through her sartorial *bhel*, but her behavioral *bhel*, like Honey's *chhibripon*, contravened womanly modesty. *Kothis* often remarked on her flamboyantly feminine mannerisms in public, including flirting with potential *parikhs*, which they saw as typical forms of *bhel*. As Anik described: "Kanchana keeps dancing, walking flamboyantly on the street . . . if she sees a guy, she'll twirl, she'll adjust her bra, she'll expand out her butt!" One morning in 2011 when we were walking together, Kanchana loudly proclaimed as we entered her neighborhood: "Here, I am entering my area! Now, I will eat men!" Such behavior made her a target of gossip, notoriety, and admiration among *kothis* and beyond. Notwithstanding her female attire, other *kothis* often remarked that women— especially *bhadramohilas* from respectable families—never behaved like this. They sometimes marked her actions as like low-caste women, sometimes as unlike women altogether. In a 2007 conversation, Kanchana told me that she did not want to "become a woman"; she was fine doing "*bhel* in this way."

Similarly, *chhibripon* implies the assumption of *hijra*-like behaviors that, as noted in Chapter 1, transgress social norms governing womanly behavior. *Kothis* with varying levels of identification with *hijras* may adopt such practices. Sunita, a *kothi* from Nadia who said she wanted to "become a woman," nevertheless conceded that doing *hijrepon* was more advantageous than attempting womanhood when threatened in public spaces; she meant the behaviors *hijras* deploy when asking for money, such as clapping and abusing aggressively. At Berhampore, one of Kanchana's behaviors that other *kothis* perceived as like *hijras* and unlike women was that she publicly reacted against harassment using sexualized insults—once, in 2011, she retaliated against a young man who verbally harassed her saying, "How many fuck your mother?" In a 2007 interview, she attributed these behaviors to her long history of being abused: "They have dragged me down to the mud—I'll drag them down further!" This lowered social status ("mud") also paradoxically brings power through the ability to transgress bounds of decency ("drag them down"). While such behavior could lead to the loss of respectable status for women, with *chhibripon* there is less to lose.

Chhibripon or *hijrepon* delinks such behaviors from their association with lineage-based *hijras*, enabling *kothis* and non-*gharana hijras* to deploy them situationally or strategically while defying authenticity criteria like emasculation or initiation. In 2011, at a community gathering in Kolkata, Deblina, a *bheli kothi*, described how, during a holiday with *kothi* friends, she had scandalized a shopkeeper who was refusing to bargain by threatening to untie her wrapped skirt, although she was not emasculated—the recollection of his shock at her threat prompted peals of laughter from other *kothis*. Kira Hall describes *kothis* in Delhi doing "hijra-acting" as parody—mocking *hijra* pretenses to authenticity and celibacy while valorizing *kothi* identity as less hypocritical (2005: 126). However, for *kothis* like Deblina and Honey, *chhibripon* implies having "fun" not by parodying *hijras* but by scandalizing the public through *hijra*-like transgressive behavior, while Sunita suggests that it may be deployed to navigate real-life hostile situations. As we saw in Chapter 1, Honey sometimes actually assumed *hijra* identity and professions outside *gharanas*. Her combination of sartorial *niharinipon* (womanly attire) and behavioral *chhibripon* suggests how *kothis* combine different modes of expression to claim femininity while contravening both respectable womanhood and *hijra* hierarchies of authenticity.

Departures from social womanhood are not only evident in public interactions. Practices like *bhel* and *bila* also strengthen bonding and kinship among *kothis* through shared pleasure or fun in discussing and performing scandalously erotic forms of femininity in community spaces. Across several districts, I commonly observed how *kothis* would share stories about each other's *bhel* in gathering spaces like DICs and cruising spots. In Dinajpur, North Bengal in 2014, Krishna, a *kothi/meti* community member, laughed while narrating to her *meti* sisters how one of them, Kiron, had recently behaved at a fair: "She was doing such *bhel*, she was almost falling over *parikhs*!" Krishna's tone manifested amusement at the excessiveness of Kiron's gestures, suggestive of her unrestrained sexual desires, but also delight in the public scandal of such behavior. In Murshidabad in 2011, *kothis* discussed in similarly scandalized yet delighted tones how Ranu, a male-attired *kothi*, adopted an extremely coquettish and sultry voice during public conversations with men: "Ranu has such *bhel*... must she talk with her *parikh* like that?" These comments suggest a conscious pleasure in the performative excess of *bhel*—the intensification and display of eroticized or hyperfeminine mannerisms in certain kinds of *bhel*. Such *bhel* evokes parallels with performances of drag and camp in quite different contexts such as queer nightlife in Indian metropolises and US drag subcultures (Khubchandani 2020; Newton 1972). Like drag queens, *kothis/dhuranis* may flaunt their prowess at erotic performance and consciously assume glamorous, sexy, diva-like personae while doing *bhel*, but in more quotidian contexts. During a shopping trip in 2011, Bikash successfully bargained with a shopkeeper by calling him *shona* (roughly, darling) and flirting with him. She then boasted to other *kothis*: "See Bikash-*rani*'s (Bikash-queen's) *bhel*!" In Murshidabad, Kanchana sometimes referred to herself as *bhelkirani* Kanchana—the queen of *bhelki* or *bhel*.

Besnier notes how trans feminine *fakaleiti* in Tonga "take on a ludic role reminiscent of camp ... assuming the part of outrageously promiscuous creatures, particularly for ... audiences of *leiti* and women friends" (1997: 17). Similarly, *kothis* not only discuss or flaunt their *bhel* with men but also perform *bhel* for each other. Srabonti, Bikash's granddaughter in the terms of *kothi* kinship at Ranaghat, remarked during a conversation in 2021 that "*bhel diye kotha bola*" (speaking with *bhel*) has become her habit while talking to *kothis* more than in interactions with men. This entails speaking in a consciously intensified sultry or mock-seductive voice or using exaggeratedly sexualized gestures and vocalizations—not usually to flirt with other *kothis*, but rather to allude to each other's promiscuity, perform scandalous behaviors, and assume eroticized personae. During a gathering in 2021, Srabonti's friend Rajkumari asked their group, "How many dicks did you all suck today?" She added in a quasi-orgasmic tone: "Ahh, *khub moja* (lots of fun)!" A *kothi* replied, appreciating her *bhel*, "You are the best *bhelki kothi* in our group!" On another occasion, a *kothi* complimented Srabonti's makeup, saying she was a "*nayika*" (film heroine). Srabonti replied mock-flirtatiously: "Ahh, ahh, *swami* (husband), ahh, *khub moja*!" But the erotic behaviors and personae associated with *bhel* may also be teasingly derided or shamed. During another conversation at Ranaghat, one *kothi* mocked another for speaking with excessive *bhel*, seen as symptomatic of her excessive sexual desires: "Hey you *bheli magi* (*bheli* woman), you've come to show *bhel* here, do you have no work? Let's shove some bananas up your ass!" Srabonti and Rajkumari were both often teased as *bajari magi* (marketplace woman, slut), *dhurani*, or *barkha* (prostitute). In turn, they claimed their detractors were just jealous of how much sex they had.

Such behaviors evidence how *kothis* not only express femininities distinct from womanhood but may also manifest an ambiguous affinity with socially derided forms of womanhood. In a conversation in 2010, a *kothi* at Berhampore remarked how "*kothis* do so much *bila*" with each other, referring to interactions where *kothis* insult each other humorously or seriously. Common insults used during such *bila* include *beshya* (prostitute) or *magi* (woman in colloquial Bengali, often implying

Figure 3.1 *Kothis* at a community gathering in Kalyani, 2023. Courtesy author.

a woman of lower-class status or loose morals). At the DIC in Ranaghat in 2012, I observed one such mock-fight between two male-attired *kothis* regarding who lived in a more disreputable area. One *kothi* said, "your neighborhood is more slutty, *magi*," and clapped vigorously toward the other. The other clapped back: "No yours is, you *beshya!*" In 2010 at Berhampore, Kanchana humorously insulted me for refusing to settle with one man, calling me *"benarosher beshya"*—a slut from Benaras or Varanasi, a North Indian city known for its courtesans—even as she flaunted her own promiscuity on other occasions.

Such *bila* invokes promiscuous womanhood to insult but also to indulge in humorous imputations of scandal, playfully replicating and parodying the stigma around female promiscuity. Indeed, *kothis* might retaliate against such insults by mocking claims to sexual purity. During an exchange at Ranaghat in 2021, Srabonti called her friend Rajkumari *"noshto meyemanush"* (spoiled woman), to which Rajkumari retaliated—"Why, are you a *sati* (chaste, virtuous woman)? Just a while ago, you said you had lots of fun taking it in the ass!" A *kothi* in the Berhampore circle was mockingly named "Ijjotwali" (the one with *ijjot* or honor) for claiming sexual chastity. A *kothi* laughingly narrated to me: "She used to say I'll sacrifice everything but my *ijjot*—now, she has entered the market herself!"

Countering claims of sexual virtue, some *kothis* explicitly reclaim the prostitute figure. During another exchange at Ranaghat in 2021, Rajkumari insulted Rakhi, another *kothi*, saying: "You just lost your husband, now you've gone to get fucked, you *rendi* (slut)!" Rakhi replied: "Listen *magi*, I am a pure slut from Sonagachhi (a famous red-light area in Kolkata), understood? Don't you take dicks in your ass? I do it—I admit it!" At a gathering in Kolkata in 2017, a mock-fight among some male-attired *kothis* insulting each other as sluts was resolved by an older *kothi* who asserted with relish: "We are all *khanki* (sluts)!" Such enactments are not only humorous or parodic. Sumi in Coochbehar once remarked that *kothis* could be much more free and friendly with female sex workers than conventional middle-class women. Of course, some *kothis* do sex work themselves—ironically enough, Ijjotwali of Berhampore eventually became a sex worker.

Kodi–Bheli *Divides and Hierarchies*

While the scandalous pleasures of behavioral *bhel* may strengthen bonding among female- and male-attired *kothis*, the socially transgressive aspects of *bhel*, *bila*, and *chhibripon* evoke anxieties among some *kodi kothis* who distance themselves from publicly *bheli kothis* even if they do *bhel* in private intra-community spaces. Such tendencies may reinforce distinctions and hierarchies between *kodi* and *bheli kothis* that extend the linear sense of *kodi* to *bheli* transition to a comparative gradation of *kothis* based on their degree of overt femininity.

Abinash, who hailed from a middle-class, dominant-caste family in Berhampore, privately assumed some feminized roles, such as being called sister by other *kothis* and adopting a *bheli naam* (feminine name) in intra-community circles. Once, when he accidentally split his trousers while trying to sit astride a chair, he exclaimed with mock horror, "Oh no, my vagina is now exposed," as *kothis* laughed. While this humorous evocation of scandalous exposure is reminiscent of *bhel*, publicly, Abinash maintained a masculine front. In a conversation in 2012, a *kothi* complimented Abinash that he looked good in *tonnapon* (male attire). Pleased, he distinguished *kodi kothis* like himself from *bheli kothis* like Kanchana: "Although we do *kothipon* (*kothi*-like behavior), we are not that much *kothi* in the way Kanchana is *arial* (extreme) *kothi!*"

As the previous chapter noted, Abinash was also sexually *dupli* and had sex with *kothis*. Kanchana, meanwhile, said she could never imagine taking a penetrative role. Thus, Abinash and Kanchana presented a strong contrast between the *bheli* and *kodi* types which, for them, also aligned with the *kothi–dupli* divide. Feminine attire, bodily transition, feminine sexual role, and public *bheli* behavior all aligned for Kanchana, while Abinash's male attire aligned with his relatively masculine sexual role and socially *kodi* behavior. However, this *bheli–kodi* separation across several registers of subjectivity and practice may be seen as a difference of degree, not a rigid binary—Abinash positioned *bheli kothis* as more "extreme" *kothis* than *kodi kothis*. This linear divide widened with time. Eventually, Abinash married heterosexually to honor his family's wishes and minimized community contact; Kanchana transitioned and became estranged from family.

Kodi kothis like Abinash not only distinguish themselves from *bheli kothis* but may also deride *bheli kothis* for acting in disreputable ways, while *bheli kothis* may deride *kodi* ones based on ideals of consistent femininity and authenticity, resulting in contextually variable hierarchies between *kodi* and *bheli* positions pivoting around public femininity.

These tensions are informed by models of caste and gender respectability in Bengali and Indian society. Notions of *shomman*—social and familial honor as well as caste/class respectability—are not just tied with feminine sexuality. The breach of heteronormative male gender/sexual roles (marrying, being a good son) may be seen as detrimental to family honor or social respect (Hall 1997). The previous chapter noted how some *kodi* and *dupli kothis* avoid public exposure with overtly feminine *kothis* for fear of loss of social standing. Some further attempt to castigate and control *bheli* behavior. At Berhampore in 2015, Ranu, a *bheli kothi*, complained about a *kodi kothi* thus: "He is not comfortable with *bhelis*, he keeps saying, *kodi kor*!" *Kodi kor* translates as "do *kodi*" and connotes hiding femininity or acting in socially masculine ways.[7]

Castigations are particularly directed toward behaviors associated with *bheli kothis*—especially sexualized *bhel* and aggressive *bila*—and sometimes even toward wearing feminine attire. In 2008, Anik complained to me how Kanchana sashayed and preened herself in public to attract men: "She has no sense of *shomman* (respect)! We can't ever do things like that . . . don't we have *shomman*? Everyone in Berhampore sees her in that dirty way!" The "we" are *kodi kothis* who have *shomman*, which *bheli kothis* supposedly lack. Years later in 2015, Anik told me that *kodi* and *bheli kothis* were "getting divided" at the local cruising site: "The *kodi kothis* sit on one side of the field, the *bheli* ones on another. . . . The *kodis* say, what is the image that is being created of us in society? For these people, we are not able to retain any *shomman*!" Such attacks may conflate various contextually distinct forms of *bhel* and *bila*. In a community gathering at Berhampore in 2014, Kajol, a male-attired, middle-class *kothi*, complained to other *kodi kothis* about *bheli kothis* associated with the CBO Sangram: "People are coming to know Sangram as a place of ass-fuckers . . . the way that they express themselves, people are realizing that these people take it in the ass!" Besides targeting sexualized behaviors, he also complained how they interacted among themselves or with others using the *thikri* (clap) and supposedly vulgar language: "The way they behave, one can't go anywhere with them. . . . Giving claps everywhere, saying language like 'hey *magi*' in every sentence to each other!" *Magi*—the aforementioned colloquialism for "woman," implying loose morals—marks the sexualized designations used by *kothis*, while claps mark characteristically *hijra* forms of social interaction, including real or humorous aggression. Thus, various behaviors are lumped together as contravening social norms related to *shomman*.

The *kodi–bheli* hierarchy is not only an "us" versus "them" binary but may also invoke a linear gradation between acceptable femininity and excessive, unacceptable forms. In a 2007 interview, Abinash launched into a rant against *bheli kothis*: "Wearing *sarees* and bangles is not acceptable in society; we should do that which increases our *shomman*. I am not saying that one shouldn't be feminine at all . . . Why shouldn't one be sensitive, cry at seeing suffering? But that doesn't mean one need be entirely *bheli* . . . that one must always go out in *sarees*!" Abinash constructs a linear gendered hierarchy—some femininity (like emotional sensitivity) is fine; being "entirely *bheli*" is not. In another conversation, Sujit, a *kodi kothi* at Ranaghat, said:

> Our hips also sway when we walk . . . but we don't give people the opportunity to say anything! If I walk holding hands with a guy, no one thinks much of it . . . most think, they're just good friends! But when someone's dressing up as a woman and taking some guy inside her room, then it becomes clearer to people. . . . What's the need to show so much?

Again, some embodied femininity is fine, "so much" is bad. However, the line demarcating acceptable and excessive femininity differs. While Abinash and Sujit targeted both feminine dress and behavior, Kajol exempted attire: "There's no need for them to be *tonnapon* (male-attired), let them just correct their behavior!"

While *bheli kothis* are censured for their excess relative to more contained forms of feminine maleness, they may also be condemned for breaching norms of womanhood. On several occasions between 2007 and 2012, Anik rebuked Kanchana in my presence—"Does any woman from a *bhadra* (genteel/respectable) family behave like that?" Or, "We are like women. . . . Do women give *thikris* (claps) on the road, do they do *bila*?" Once, when Kanchana had temporarily joined a *hijra* house, she replied: "Why will I try to be a woman—we are *hijras*, we'll stay like *hijras*!" Unlike Abinash, Anik did not target attire but rather Kanchana's sexualized, aggressive femininity, which contravened middle-class, *bhadra* ideals of womanhood. Thus, *bheli kothis* may be condemned as both too feminine and yet not womanly enough, breaching both male and female forms of *bhadrata* (genteelness) and *shomman* (respectability).

On the other side, *hijra* critiques of the inauthenticity or inconsistency of *kothi* femininity and suspicion of *kothi* opportunism may be displaced onto the *bheli–kodi* divide, evidenced in the reactions of publicly *bheli kothis* to *kodi kothis*. At Berhampore, Abinash was sometimes castigated by *bheli kothis* as *shubidhebadi* (opportunistic) for trying to preserve a socially masculine front. During a conversation among some *kothis* at Berhampore in 2010, a *bheli kothi* castigated *kodi kothis*, saying, "You are all *bhekdhari* (pretenders)!" She alleged that they pretended to be men for social status and were not "*ashol*" (authentic) *kothis*. Meanwhile, in 2014 at the Ranaghat DIC, a lighthearted fight broke out between a *kodi kothi* with a mustache and another male-attired but clean-shaven *kothi*. Nita, the local *hijra guru*, said: "A mustachioed person giving *bila*—what daring! Don't allow any *kothi* with a mustache in the DIC!" Another *kothi* laughed and said: "These people are opportunistic; they take advantage of both sides!" While lighthearted, the *hijra guru*'s support of the clean-shaven person suggests a linear hierarchy where greater embodied maleness is derided, reversing the aforementioned *kodi–bheli* hierarchies. *Bheli kothis* may also see themselves as more beautiful and naturally desirable to *parikhs* due to their embodied femininity, and mock *kodi kothis* who deride them as being jealous.

While ideals of authenticity based on consistent public femininity are deployed by *bheli kothis* against *kodi kothis*, we saw in Chapter 1 that *bheli kothis* may also be regarded as inauthentic by *hijras*, showing the shifting nature of authenticity ideals (Saria 2021: 101). As we saw, *gharana*-based *hijras* may also prefer *kodi kothis* as they are not seen as socially exposing *hijras* in ways that *bheli kothis* might. The unstable access of *bheli kothis* to *hijra* status weakens the attempted use of authenticity ideals and linear hierarchies against *kodi kothis*. However, *kodi* condemnations of *bhel* may be reinforced by institutional activism, as explored below.

Activist Discourse and Bhel/Bila

Alongside lay community members who feared social disrepute, senior activists and NGO staff also censured *bhel* and *bila* and reinforced linear *kodi–bheli* hierarchies, signaling tensions and ambiguities within activist discourse. As noted earlier, "LGBT" had been circulating in Anglophone activist circles as a putatively inclusive rubric for diverse sexual and gender identities since the 1990s. A "national gay conference" titled Yaarian held in Hyderabad in February 1999 resulted in the founding of the LGBT India "communication collective" that organized a "friendship walk" in Kolkata in July 1999, commonly seen as the first South Asian pride walk (LGBT India 1999). In this period, a discourse of LGBT rights developed among urban Indian activists that drew upon and translated between diverse influences, including transnationally circulating frameworks of gender/sexual rights, humanist and egalitarian strains in Indian and Bengali postcolonial thought, and Indian constitutional liberalism which promises fundamental rights to all citizens (Dutta 2012b). Through the 2000s, NGO–CBO networks and small-town activists also increasingly participated in such LGBT rights activism, generating discourse in both English and Bengali that went beyond HIV and sexual health. CBOs within the MANAS Bangla network helped organize the Kolkata Rainbow Pride Walks (KRPW) between 2006 and 2009. Leaflets distributed during pride demanded human rights for communities that they termed as LGBT or "sexual minorities" (*jounoshonkhaloghu*), decried stigma against such groups, and sought to foster social visibility and acceptance of gender/sexual diversity in general, including and beyond particular identities.

Advocacy material for public circulation, typically authored by NGO staff and volunteers (including me on occasion) under the guidance of senior activists, affirmed an ambitiously broad discourse of equality, diversity, and rights. The Bengali pamphlet of Swikriti, formulated around 2008, states: "We have not yet learnt to accept human beings as human, we have kept their physical, mental, and above all, sexuality-based differences . . . caged" (DDSS 2008). Drawing from such broad humanist impulses, the pamphlets urge the acceptance of gender/ sexual difference and rights for all. Going beyond specific identities, Sangram's contemporaneous Bengali pamphlet "demand(s) the human rights" of "all those who are marginalized for . . . sexual preference and social gender construction" (MBS 2009). The 2007 KRPW's English pamphlet states that the "rainbow stands for diversity in gender and sexual expressions," all "equally worthy of pride"; it demands "freedom from abuse and violence based on people's sexuality and gender expression" and advocates "freedom of expression" and "equality" for all (KRPW 2007).

Yet, two tendencies limit such inclusive advocacy for diverse gender/sexual expressions and reinforce processes of vernacularization. First, till the late 2000s, this activist discourse prioritized sexual identity and rights, often subsuming *kothis* and *hijras* under MSM and/or homosexual (*samakami*), despite emergent critiques of such subsumption by trans activists (UNDP 2008). The news release of the 1999 "friendship walk" claims to represent "lesbian, gay, bisexual and transgender groups of India" and demands their rights, but concretely mentions only the "right" of "men and women with same-sex attraction . . . to love each other" (LGBT India 1999). This tendency continued even after *kothis* became vital participants in pride walks as CBOs within the MANAS Bangla network took an active role in organizing pride in the 2006–9 period. While the 2008 pride leaflet celebrates "diversity in gender and sexual expressions" and mentions "transgender" a few times, it devotes more space to legitimizing "same-sex love" (KRPW 2008). Further, following HIV discourse, it positions "*kothis, hijras*" among "males who have sex with males," while LGBT people are collectively described as "sexually marginalized" (ibid.). Violence based on "gender identity" is mentioned but evoked primarily to protest the antisodomy Section 377 of the Indian penal code and to support the demand for decriminalizing "same-sex relations," positing the criminalization of same-sex activity as the primary cause of such violence and eliding other sociolegal factors (ibid.).[8] Thus, gender/sexual "diversity" is collapsed into "same-sex" behavior and associated marginality. Meanwhile, the Sangram pamphlet states that "to be different from the majority is not to be 'abnormal'" but immediately follows this with "*samaprem* (same-sex love) . . . is not abnormal" (MBS 2009).

In effect, the *kothi–hijra* spectrum is viewed through the optic of same-sex desire, whether as MSM or homosexual, which both—notwithstanding the behavior/identity distinction—biologically essentialize all *kothis/hijras* as primarily male. The intersection of gender and sexuality in this literature is not inherently problematic, since there is no strict gender/sexuality distinction in *kothi/hijra* discourse and erotic roles intersect variably with gendered ideas of selfhood, and some *kothis* (as noted in Chapter 2) overlap with gay/*samakami* identity. However, the generalizing subsumption of all *kothis* and *hijras* under homosexual/MSM fosters the prioritization of "same-sex" sexual expression and rights over aspects of subjectivity and behavior irreducible to same-sex desire.

Second, the advocacy of rights and freedom of expression is limited by an attempt to justify and normalize LGBT identities in terms of elite nationalist constructs of Indian culture, in keeping with assimilationist and (homo)nationalist tendencies within Indian LGBTQ activism critiqued by many scholars (Upadhyay 2020; Sircar 2021). Since the late 1990s, an ascendant Hindu Right attacked LGBT identities as foreign, morally corrupt, and threatening Indian culture (Kapur 1999). In that context, activists went beyond the strategy of using MSM discourse as a medicalized shield for LGBT activism. On one hand, elite activists associated liberal democratic rights with Western "developed" nations and saw "developing" countries like India as slowly catching up, marking an internalization of developmentalist and civilizational hierarchies of progress by Indian elites (LGBT India 1999).[9] On the other, activists also countered queerphobic Hindu nationalism by reclaiming cultural history, evoking same-sex desire and gender variance in South Asian myth, religion, and literature to disprove their presumed incompatibility with Indian society (Kapur 1999; Dutta 2012b). With the incorporation of the Hindu Right into the government under the aegis of the Bharatiya Janata Party (BJP) and its increasing embrace of neoliberalism and developmentalism since the 2000s, Hindu nationalism has selectively opened up to LGBT rights, conditionally including dominant-caste Hindu LGBTQ people while continuing to marginalize other minorities, particularly Muslims (Upadhyay 2020; Sircar 2021). In that context, queer reclamations of Hindu cultural history may bolster an Islamophobic "homohindunationalism" that idealizes the supposed precolonial Hindu tolerance of gender/sexual difference, effacing the constitutive link between Hinduism and caste patriarchy and blaming Islam (alongside British colonialism) for homophobia in postcolonial India (Upadhyay 2020; Sircar 2021).

In the aforementioned activist literature, the reclamation of Hindu histories was tempered by a liberal, secular, and reformist self-critical gaze that questioned majoritarian views (particularly regarding gender/sexuality), and yet ultimately reinforced dominant-caste norms. The LGBT India collective, which included both the Hindu right-leaning activist Ashok Row Kavi and the Muslim-origin activist Owais Khan, cited the nineteenth-century "Bengal renaissance" to explain their choice of Kolkata for the first pride walk (LGBT India 1999). The "renaissance" drew upon Enlightenment ideals and egalitarian strains in South Asian history to launch reformist critiques of dominant-caste Hindu practices such as *sati* (widow-burning) (Dasgupta 2009). Later activism evokes this reformist legacy. Sangram's pamphlet states: "Social gender construction has divided men and women into two rigidly separated categories . . . this division is false" (MBS 2009). The Swikriti pamphlet "questions wrong ideas about gender, sexuality and sexuality-based differences" (DDSS 2008).

But the critique of social gender/sexual constructs contrasts with the lack of critique of caste, which, in intersection with gender, underlies the censure of nonnormative femininity and *bhel*. Rather than *kothi–hijra* practices, affirmative examples of gender/sexual diversity are drawn from Sanskrit texts that, since the colonial period, have been used by dominant-caste elites to fashion a Hindu nationalist identity (Lothspeich 2008). The Sangram pamphlet cites gender fluidity in Sanskrit scriptures and epics like the *Mahabharata*, mentioning, among other examples, that Vishnu, a Hindu god, "took on a Mohini (female) *roop*" (MBS 2009). Gods changing between various *roops* (forms), sometimes across gender, is common in South Asian myths (Pattanaik 2012). The 2009 Kolkata Pride leaflet cites examples of same-sex love in Hindu temple art and Sanskrit texts like *Kama Sutra* to decry the social intolerance of gender/sexual variance as hypocritical (KRPW 2009). These evocations elide the historical exclusivity of Sanksrit and its relation to caste hierarchy (Sawhney 2008: 6). They further reinforce a broader pattern wherein Hindu dominant-caste culture becomes encoded as Indian culture across both liberal and right-wing nationalist discourses (Upadhyay 2020: 468).

Strengthening Linear Hierarchies

In effect, these strategies resulted in a gradation of acceptable difference that reinforced *kodi–bheli* hierarchies within *kothi* communities. The first tendency of prioritizing sexual identity and rights meant that feminized expressions like *bhel* were seen as less essential components of identity than same-sex desire. The second tendency of assimilation within dominant-caste ideas of Indian culture reinforced the condemnation of *bhel/bila* as harmful to respectable social image and inclusion, while certain forms of feminine maleness were condoned. These tendencies correspond to distinct but intersecting forms of vernacularization. The first continues the positioning of *kothi–hijra* communities as local and vernacular relative to MSM and homosexual categories. Corresponding to the second tendency, activist discourse in West Bengal evokes Sanskrit-origin Bengali words like *shomman* (honor, respectability) and related caste/gender ideals to deride *bhel/bila*. Such practices are sought to be contained within private spaces and related Ulti terms are, in effect, positioned within a subordinated vernacular register of speech relative to formal, public activist discourse in Sanskritic Bengali and English. Both tendencies are evident in activist attempts to discipline people within organizations, HIV projects, and events like pride walks.

In a 1997 report that understands *kothis* as MSM, the activist Shivananda Khan states: "*Kotis* are characterised by 'feminised' behaviours (often exaggerated), particularly in specific spaces . . . [that] make them visible in a public arena and is used . . . to attract *panthi* males for sex" (Khan 1997: 44). The primary impetus for such behaviors is cast as sexual, eliding their aforementioned uses for self-expression or intra-community bonding. This tendency is later reinforced by elites connected to metropolitan LGBT activism, and together with assimilationist tendencies, used to condemn *bhel* and *bila*.

Ahmed, a dancer trained in Indian classical dance from an upper-middle class Muslim family with residences across Berhampore and Kolkata, was a rising *kothi* leader within the CBO Sangram. In a 2007 interview, he told me that his friend circle encountered "homosexual" before *kothi*: "We knew ourselves as homosexual first, we learnt *kothi-parikh* later, after coming to the DIC." Referring to male masturbation, he stated that all men had homosexual potential, "because while being male himself, he has sex with himself." To a white gay man visiting Berhampore in 2009, he explained that both *kothi* and *parikh* were "local language words" for "homosexual," eliding the distinction from men claimed by many *kothis*. Further, reversing the aforementioned transregional scalar projections of the *kothi*, Ahmed's explanation rescaled and subsumed the *kothi* as a localized vernacular equivalent of the transnational homosexual.

Such vernacularizing subsumption meant that *kothi* femininity and *bhel* were acknowledged but delegitimized relative to homosexual maleness. In an organizational meeting in 2008, Ahmed condemned public *bhel*, reminding his peers: "We are men only, feminine men (*meyeli purush*)!" In another meeting, Ahmed said, "What's the bad thing about *kothis* from society's perspective? *Bhel*! So, it's best not to reinforce ideas like *kothis* necessarily have long hair . . . or that all *kothis* wear *sarees* and bangles!" In a 2007 meeting, he castigated some *bheli kothis* for seducing men by suggestively undulating their breasts: "What they did wearing padded bras yesterday, that's what looks bad!" Given that Ahmed understood *kothis* as feminine homosexual men and believed all men have homosexual potential, such *bheli* behavior seemed superfluous: as he said, "We, too, have sex with *parikhs*, we don't need to behave like that!" His castigation of *bheli* display while condoning less overt forms of courting *parikhs* implicitly reinforced a linear hierarchy of *kothi* femininity. As a figure bridging Kolkata with Berhampore, Ahmed's propagation of the idea of *kothis* as feminine homosexual men helps translate and expand the homosexual beyond the metropolis, and simultaneously recasts the *kothi* as primarily male: once *kothi* femininity breaches respectable maleness, it is condemned.

Hindu dominant-caste activists, who often led CBOs, further reinforced such tendencies. For instance, Arnab, a Brahmin gay and *kothi*-identified activist who had a well-paid government job at Berhampore and volunteered with Sangram, helped author Sangram's pamphlet in Sanskritic Bengali. The pamphlet cited examples of gender fluidity in Sanskrit texts to state ruefully: "Despite so many examples, we can't accept a little gracefulness (*shamanyo komonio byabohar*) in men" (MBS 2009). Yet, in contrast with "a little" gracefulness, Arnab evoked *shomman* to condemn overtly sexualized or assertive femininities. In the aforementioned 2008 meeting, Arnab reprimanded some *kothis* for various behaviors characteristic of *bhel* and *bila*, including flirtation, cracking sexual jokes or gossiping in public, and using the *hijra* clap:

> You people imitate women, but don't do it thoughtfully . . . you don't take the good things from them . . . the way you behave on streets . . . the way you do *bila* . . . wearing *sarees* and bangles, doing *haha-hihi*, giving *thikri* (the clap) . . . how does it look in society? This only means that you have no *atmo-shomman* (self-respect)! No one here has any *shomman* in society except Ahmed!

Arnab's diatribe was not very effective—the assembled *kothis* listened contritely, but later resumed such behaviors—but it indicates several salient tendencies within activist discourse. Arnab casts the complex dis/identification with womanhood and femininity evident in *bhel* and *bila* as a thoughtless copy of womanhood rather than legitimate expressions of subjective femininity. His reference to "the way you behave on streets" links this imitation with sexual solicitation. The imitative model belies both the strongly interiorized femininity evident for some *kothis* and the conscious ways in which *kothis* perform feminine gestures or personae for bonding and pleasure, such as the aforementioned enactments of sexually transgressive femininity. Arnab's derision of the *hijra* clap while he positions Ahmed as the only *kothi* with *shomman* suggests that *kothi* femininities that evoke *hijra* strategies of *bila* are problematic, but some kinds of feminine maleness and androgyny that fit dominant-caste culture, particularly in devotional, sacred, or artistic contexts, are acceptable. As a classical dancer, Ahmed wore ornaments and makeup during performances and occasionally enacted androgynous religious figures like the *Ardhanariswar*, a half-male, half-female deity combining the Hindu god Shiva and his consort Parvati (see Figure 3.2).

Arnab's defense of "a little gracefulness" but castigation of public *bhel* parallel and reinforce the aforementioned linear hierarchies between permissible and excessive femininity. But his diatribe also conflated sartorial *bhel* with behavioral *bhel* or *bila* (wearing sarees, doing *haha-hihi*, etc.). While Arnab sometimes castigated male-attired *kothis* for public *bhel* and *bila*, he particularly associated sartorially *bheli kothis* with such behavior. During another meeting, he described how female-attired *kothi* sex workers boldly flirted with policemen, and then generalized: "You know how *bheli kothis* are!" This simplifies the idea of a linear range of *kothi* femininities into a binary *kodi–bheli* divide. In a 2014 conversation, Kanchana told me that she felt Arnab had helped strengthen *kodi–bheli* divides in Berhampore.

Further, Arnab's suggestion that contravening social respectability (*shomman*) implies a lack of self-respect (*atmo-shomman*) seeks to internalize the hegemony of *shomman* and negate the possibility of an affirmative sense of selfhood beyond such norms. In a community gathering in 2010, Arnab posited that promiscuity and unsafe sex among *kothis* stemmed from an internalized lack of self-worth due to social stigma: "They feel their life has no worth, so don't care if they contract a sexual disease!" This evokes the tendency of seeing *kothis* as at-risk victim figures in HIV-related discourse on MSM, as discussed in Chapter 2. The *kothi*, particularly the *bheli kothi*, thus becomes positioned as both a victim lacking self-esteem and a figure of sexual excess lacking self-respect—the transgression of caste/gender ideals in *kothi–hijra* practices is rendered illegible. Anglophone and Bengali discourse on MSM that positions *kothis* as sexually feminized men and Sanskritic Bengali discourse on *shomman* coalesce in the devaluation of *bhel*.

The activist devaluation and disciplining of *bhel* and *bila* were bolstered by the organizational hierarchies within HIV projects run by the MANAS Bangla network and other CBOs during the third phase of the NACP (2007–12). Activists and scholars have noted how the tiered structure of targeted intervention projects for HIV prevention bolstered intra-community hierarchies in some cases (Aneka and KSMF 2011; Vijayakumar 2021). In several HIV projects funded by WBSAPCS,

Figure 3.2 Portrait of Ardhanariswar by trans/*kothi* artist Honey Halder; the caption reads: "Woman and man in the same body." Courtesy of the artist.

I observed how relatively senior staff like counselors or outreach workers, who supervised lower-ranking staff like peer educators, policed their *bhel*. In 2011, WBSAPCS awarded Sangram with a short-lived HIV-prevention project for MSM in Murshidabad. Relatively educated, middle-class community members obtained higher posts. Anik, who became the counselor, told me she did not want to recruit *bheli kothis* as staff: "*Bheli kothis* never work properly ... they only do *bhel!*" Some MANAS Bangla projects at Kolkata even had temporary restrictions against *bheli kothis* coming to their DICs; as Anik told me, such *kothis* were apparently associated with sexual flirting and picking up men around the DIC area.[10] CBOs needed to rent rooms or apartments in middle-class or mixed-class neighborhoods for project offices and DICs, so there were concerns about objections from neighbors and loss of rental space. However, such bans were not consistently enforced since projects also needed to draw *kothis* to meet numerical targets set by funders regarding the number of MSM to be reached. At Murshidabad, some *kodi kothis* who were afraid to mix with openly feminine *kothis* could not work effectively to find more *kothis* in the field. Thus, despite Anik's reservations, Sangram had to rely on *bheli kothis* to draw *kothis* to the project. The contradictory needs of CBOs—maintaining social respectability in middle-class neighborhoods versus incorporating more MSM—weakened disciplinary attempts.

Further, injunctions against *bhel* were spatially uneven and contested. In Coochbehar, North Bengal, injunctions against *bhel* were noticeably absent— the CBO Moitrisanjog Coochbehar was founded in 2009 by the oppressed-caste activist, Sumi, who was herself sartorially and occasionally behaviorally *bheli*, and had experienced discrimination while working in a MANAS Bangla office in North Bengal. Meanwhile, at Kolkata, Raina, the trans/*kothi* activist who worked temporarily in MANAS Bangla, told me how senior activists had berated her friends when they changed into feminine attire and did *bhel* with men during a trip to Delhi to attend a meeting of NGOs: "*Kothis* went out in the evening in *thoshok* (flamboyant makeup, dress); seniors said, aren't you leaders, how can you do something like this? One of us replied—you are jealous because you do not get *parikhs* like we do!" This shows how idealized models of activism and leadership reinforced gendered and class/caste respectability, but also how existing intra-community tendencies served to contest such norms—as mentioned earlier, *bheli kothis* often accuse *kodi kothis* of being jealous of their desirability to men.

Contestations regarding *kothi* dress and behavior became especially intense at pride walks in Kolkata in the late 2000s, since these were public events where metropolitan and district-based activists congregated. There was a relative paucity of middle-class, openly gay/lesbian people beyond leading activists till the late 2000s (Gupta 2005). Thus, the Kolkata pride walks relied heavily on *kothi* volunteers from the CBOs of the MANAS Bangla network for purposes ranging from obtaining police permission to bringing participants to pride; while MANAS Bangla did not directly participate in pride, planning meetings were sometimes held in its offices. In a meeting I attended in June 2009, some activists expressed concern about the declining numbers of active *kothi* members in some CBOs, reflecting their reliance on *kothi* communities. But this participation also evoked anxieties regarding how *bhel* or *bila* might affect the image of the community and calls for rules and discipline. In a meeting in 2007, a Kolkata-based *kothi* activist stated that the way some people dressed during the last walk "was indecent and lowered the dignity of the walk." Another activist stated outright that "suggestive dress shouldn't be allowed in the rally" while another supported the "need for disciplining." At another meeting in June 2009, an activist suggested that each CBO should order their *kothi* members to leave after the walk and not stick around the area to "do *bhel* and *bajar*," where *bajar* refers to soliciting (literally, shopping for) men. One activist rued that in past walks, *kothis* "did like this and this in front of media"—physically demonstrating an erotically suggestive undulation of the breasts. Another activist lamented the futility of disciplining efforts: "Every year there is *bila* . . . good *kothis* come but *bila kothis* also come!" Given the behaviors targeted, the good versus *bila kothi* divide aligned with the *kodi–bheli* divide.

Concerns about dress were sometimes justified through a graded teleology of social acceptance that reinforced linear hierarchies targeting excessive femininity. Pratyush, a young, middle-class gay man in Kolkata involved with organizing pride, told me in a 2007 interview: "People come dressed in gaudy clothes, this gives the general populace a negative impression . . . first, we must try to show that we are not different from them!" He contended this drove away middle-class gay people from pride. This signals respectability hierarchies between gay and *kothi* categories (Gupta 2005; Khubchandani 2020). But some *kothis* echoed such stances too. Abinash, the *kodi kothi* from Berhampore, told me during another conversation that year: "Will society accept us in *sarees* outright? Society is like a baby; we have to feed it bit by bit." Neither of them saw sartorial freedom as an essential part of the rights they otherwise espoused; the linear teleology of society progressing "bit by bit" postponed such freedom to a more tolerant future.[11]

Like Arnab, activists at pride also targeted *hijra*-like behavior. At the 2006 pride, I noticed Mondira, a dominant-caste, Kolkata-based CBO activist, reprimanding some *kothis* for clapping while talking among each other. When I asked, Mondira explained that in prior meetings concerns had arisen from the community itself that giving *thikri* didn't look good and harmed the image of the community. While seeking to distance *kothis* from *hijras*, this did not translate into a rigid respectability hierarchy between *kothis* and *hijras*. Arnab condemned *bheli* behavior as worse than *hijra* practices: in a 2007 Sangram meeting, he argued that *gharana*-based *hijras* flirt with men or use sexualized insults only in specific occupational contexts, rather than recreationally in public spaces—"When they walk on the street, they just walk as usual!" At a Sangram event in 2010, I heard a conversation between Abinash and Annapurna, the local *hijra guru*, on *bhel* and *bila*. Abinash felt such practices were better left to *hijras*; Annapurna agreed that *kothis* should remain *kodi*. Eroticized *bhel* contravenes the ideal of *hijra* asceticism espoused by senior *gharana hijras*, though junior *hijras/kothis* routinely deploy such behaviors. Sangram's board members invited *hijra gurus* to some Sangram events, especially those like Annapurna who—as noted in Chapter 1—strove to appear more respectable than lower-ranking *hijras*. In the 2010s, *hijra gurus* were also invited to Kolkata prides given the rising visibility of transgender activism, detailed in subsequent chapters. Thus, rather than *hijras* being wholly abjected by gay/*kothi* activists, respectability hierarchies were contingent, and at least some *hijras* were positioned above *bheli* or *bila kothis*, who bore the brunt of activist policing.[12]

Besides these unstably shifting hierarchies, there were tensions between the aforementioned "need for disciplining" and commonly evoked ideals of personal freedom. The minutes of a pride planning meeting in March 2007 noted that after much debate, ultimately, it was agreed that there should be no strict dress code that would infringe on individual freedom, but given the political advocacy nature of the walk, it would be better if the participants dressed strategically . . . if the theme of the walk was "peace", then white could be emphasized . . . (for) a theme of protest . . . "black" might make sense.[13]

Some *kothis* also protested the censure of dress. As one person in a 2009 pride meeting said: "Shouldn't we have the desire to dress up?" Given such contestations and the difficulty of enforcing strict interdictions, activists sometimes gave in partially. In a 2009 meeting of Sangram preceding the Kolkata pride walk, Arnab disdainfully stated: "If they want to dress like *hijras*, let them—but they shouldn't spoil the image of the organization by flirting with men!" The aforementioned trope of victimhood could also be evoked to garner sympathy for *kothis*. At the 2008 pride walk, a gay activist stated in his speech: "We laugh at the gaudy makeup (*rong makha*) of *kothis*, but has anyone tried to understand their inner pain?"

Given these contradictory tendencies, attempts to impose dress codes were unsuccessful, but the injunction against *thikri* (clapping) was enforced more regularly. I saw activists asking *kothis* not to clap in several Kolkata pride walks. During the 2006 walk, the aforementioned activist Mondira ordered a volunteer: "Go, see who is clapping there, ask them to stop!" Overall, a graded acceptance is again apparent: sartorial *bhel* was reluctantly permitted, indulged, or tolerated; behavioral *bhel* and *bila* (flirting, clapping) attracted more censure.

The censure of public *bhel* and *bila* is also contradicted by their private allure. In private, Arnab and Ahmed positioned themselves as mothers or sisters to other *kothis* and indulged in *bhel* and *bila*. During a gathering at his home in 2009, Arnab admitted his desire for sartorial *bhel*: "Even I want to do *bhel* sometimes, I've never done it . . . one day, I'll go out in female dress!" Another day, Arnab told me in a tone of scandalous delight how he and some *kothis* had coquettishly flirted with another *kothi's parikh*: "You know what we did for two hours? We called up Srijan's *parikh* . . . he thought it was Srijan . . . we took turns with him, did such *bhel!*" Ahmed also indulged in behavior typical of *bila*. One evening in 2009, he observed a *kothi* shopping extravagantly and later teased her: "It seems you have a lot of money; did you earn it through sex work?"—punctuating the sentence with emphatic claps. While undertaken for fun, their *bhel* also served for self-expression. Ahmed privately assumed a *bheli naam* (feminine name), Ahmedi Mata (Mother Ahmedi), which expressed a humorously exaggerated diva-like and motherly role, but I observed how he also genuinely enjoyed taking younger *kothis* under his wing and maternally grooming them. Thus, *kodi kothis* and gay men who censure overtly *bheli kothis* may partake in the transgressive femininities of *bhel* and *bila* for private fun and self-expression, while publicly maintaining a respectable feminine maleness or androgyny (e.g., Ahmed as a classical dancer).

Overall, given the multiple tensions within the activist policing of *bhel* and *bila*, these behaviors were not entirely erased or abjected, but strategically privatized and censured when too public or excessive. The subsumption of *kothi* as a vernacular equivalent of Anglophone categories like MSM or homosexual (and their translated

Bengali counterparts) functioned alongside Sanskritic Bengali activist discourse (e.g., ideals of *shomman*) to delegitimize affirmative senses of *bhel* and *bila* in *kothi–hijra* language. Sometimes, Ulti terms like *bhel* were themselves seen as inappropriate. During a meeting in Kolkata before the 2013 pride walk, some *kothis* and I were gossiping about incidents of *bheli* behavior when a young gay volunteer objected: "What *asleel* (vulgar) words are you saying . . . '*bhelki kothi!*'" Such censure of even the mention of *bhel* in public was rare, and rather ineffective—we just ignored him and continued. However, it falls within a broader pattern wherein *bhel* and *bila* are sought to be contained within informal, private spaces while activist discourse in formal, public contexts uses Sanskritic Bengali to censure such practices— *asleel*, like *shomman*, is a Sanskrit-origin word denoting vulgarity that has been used to stigmatize Dalit women's sexuality (Paik 2022: 1). Ulti terms are implicitly positioned within a vernacular linguistic register relegated only to nonserious fun and associated with vulgarity. While Ulti is an intra-community language and *kothis* do not usually teach words like *bhel* to outsiders except trusted allies, Sanskritic activist discourse additionally restrains the public behaviors associated with *bhel* and *bila* and elides their positive valuations in Ulti. In seeking to contain *kothi–hijra* discourses and practices, this vernacularizing process attempts to manage multiple contradictions—between the assimilationist tendencies of elite activism and *kothi– hijra* transgression of caste/gender ideals, and between the reliance of pride on *kothi* participants and their potential disruption of activist agendas.

This process of containment through vernacularization was paralleled within HIV projects, which, as noted earlier, needed *bheli kothis* to increase the ranks of MSM. Projects even used *bhel* as labor. At Sangram's DIC, I observed that senior staff often disciplined *kothi* peer educators with statements like, "don't do *bhel*, do *kaaj* (work)!" Doing *bhel*—which could refer to dressing up in office time, gossiping in the DIC, or flirting with men in the field—was seen as a frivolous distraction from the real work of HIV prevention and (when outdoors) as attracting disrepute to the CBO. However, *bhel* also served as a strategy for meeting project-related targets. On Human Rights Day in 2010, Swikriti organized a WBSAPCS-funded stall for distributing informational literature on HIV to the public beside a rail station in Nadia. A senior staff member deployed Nina, a female-attired *kothi* known for her *bhel*, to lure male clients to the stall: "*Madam*, why are you standing and posing here? Go seduce those *parikhs*, bring them here!" On another occasion in 2009, I accompanied Roshni, a *kothi* who worked in one of MANAS Bangla's HIV projects and alternated between *kodi* and *bheli* attire, to a crowded rural fair south of Kolkata where MANAS Bangla had set up a stall featuring literature on HIV and LGBT rights. Roshni flirted with many men at the fair but mixed in various messages with her advances: "It's fine if you guys want to have sex with us, but you must treat every human being with respect!" Later, Roshni told me how she was repeatedly disciplined by seniors: "They say I pick up *parikhs* in the field instead of working . . . maybe I've done it occasionally, but they should actually look at the work that I have done!"

Bhel was thus simultaneously exploited and denied legibility as labor, in keeping with the broader devaluation and invisibilization of feminized labor in capitalist economies (Oksala 2016; Ramamurthy 2004). This was undergirded by linguistic hierarchies. As noted in Chapter 2, English knowledge is a valued skill for senior posts like program manager in HIV projects. Meanwhile, *kothi* field workers who deployed *bhel* usually occupied lower positions; the derision of *bhel* as unproductive suggested the devaluation of their knowledge of *kothi–hijra* languages and practices. The positioning of *kothi–hijra* language as a subordinated vernacular relative to Anglophone and Sanskritic Bengali activist discourse enabled the simultaneous exploitation and containment of practices like *bhel*: concurrently utilized, devalued, and disciplined.

The vernacularization of *kothi–hijra* discourses of *bhel* thus spanned diverse sites (pride walks, HIV projects) and demonstrated the intersection of multiple tendencies spanning different levels within multilayered constructions of scale—from the biological essentialism of transnational MSM discourse to elite articulations of *shomman* in Bengali, the "regional" language. The compounded effect of these discourses was to reinforce certain intra-community tendencies, like *kodi–bheli* divides, but elide others, like bonding over the transgressive pleasures of *bhel*. While the *bheli* behaviors of male-attired activists indicate a privatized form of *kodi/bheli* overlap, their censure of public *bhel/bila* strengthened linear hierarchies and binary divides between *kodi* and *bheli kothis*. However, the intersection of multiple dominant discourses also held ambiguities and tensions (e.g., around ideals of freedom) that destabilized the subordination of transgressive *kothi/hijra* practices.

Non/linear Bhel: Disrupting Kodi/Bheli Divides

Despite the aforementioned respectability-based divides, *kothis* and *hijras*—especially those from nondominant class or caste backgrounds—manifest diverse forms of switching and blending between *kodi/bheli* modes of expression in public spaces, informed by both social pressures and subjective desires. This section explores how such tendencies disrupt hierarchical separations and linear gradations between *kodi* and *bheli*, good and *bila*, masculine and feminine *kothis*. *Kothis* who switch between or blend *kodi/bheli* modes may also reclaim activist discourse and resignify dominant categories like MSM, countering the effects of vernacularization.

Situational Shifts: Negotiating Social Pressures

Some shifts between *kodi* and *bheli* behaviors indicate adaptations to social situations, such as staying in *kodi* or male attire near home but publicly adopting *bheli* attire/behavior elsewhere. Such switching may or may not correspond to subjective overlaps with masculine gender/sexual roles: Jhilik and Khushi provide contrasting cases. An orphan from a lower middle-class family, Jhilik was raised by an unmarried aunt in a village in Nadia. In a 2014 interview, he described his childhood liking for makeup and dresses, but unlike some *kothis*, Jhilik evidenced no discomfort with genitalia. In high school, he had surreptitious sex with both boys and girls, taking both receptive and penetrative roles. Today, he prefers *parikhs* who are somewhat *dupli* (versatile): "I've had *parikhs* suck my dick!" In adolescence, he met some *chhallawali hijras* through a local *kothi* and intermittently did *chhalla* in female attire in North India; his aunt appreciated the income and did not object. Jhilik narrated with relish how he did "*bhel-bharki*" (behavioral *bhel*) during trips with *chhallawali hijra* friends—even while being in male attire himself—like flirting with policemen to escape harassment. His neighbors did not know his occupation but occasionally saw him in feminine clothes: "I never got harassed, people here know me since my childhood and love me!" But he did tone down his attire before returning home, changing out of *sarees* and wearing clothes like *patialas*, trousers worn by women that also have unisex versions: "If I wore *sarees* and bangles, I'd lose whatever *shomman* I have!" After joining university on his savings, he now mostly dresses male; he fears being harassed in "sophisticated" spaces like his college. This signals both situational pressure and shifting desires: "I don't desire *satra* (female attire) so much anymore. . . . I like wearing *simple* (male) clothes in public, but I am not *gupti* (hidden)."

Jhilik's sexual versatility and situational switching contravened the *bheli-kodi* divide, conforming neither to the figure of the *kodi kothi* whose femininity is hidden or respectably contained nor to the consistently feminine *bheli kothi* who is also sexually receptive. However, his switching adapted to social norms of *shomman*, publicly breaching them only when away from home or university.

Khushi, from a working-class family in Murshidabad, similarly described herself as "neither *gupti* (hidden) nor *bheli*," thus locating herself beyond a rigid *kodi–bheli* divide. But she was more uncomfortable with male dress. In a 2015 interview, she said: "When I go (outside Murshidabad) I wear *sarees*; (here) I want to pluck my eyebrow, grow my hair, (but) I fear, what will neighbors say? My family might be insulted." While fully male attire felt forced, she did not desire consistent female attire either: "I am fine with *kodi* attire like jeans and t-shirts, I wear them like how girls do, a *kothi-bhab* (sense of being *kothi*) remains. . . . I want to alternate, sometimes wearing dress like men, sometimes women. I am neither *gupti* nor *bheli*." She thus desired a more voluntary alternation than her situationally constrained switches.

Beyond Situational Switching

Other cases of switching are less influenced by the social pressure of *shomman*. *Pon* or *taal* (mode/style)—*kodipon* or *kodi* mode, *bhelipon* or *bheli* mode—may be used to express an agential alternation between styles that disrupts the sense of *kodi* and *bheli* as separate *kothi* types. Srijan, a theater actor from a middle-class family of Murshidabad, sometimes adapted her attire socially, such as staying *kodi* in theater troupes where she sought work. But she also switched to get different kinds of *parikhs*. Unlike Jhilik, Srijan was strictly sexually receptive and was somewhat disapproving of *dupli* behavior by *kothis*. Once, she was shocked to learn that I had erections while being anally penetrated, and asked me, "Are you even a *kothi*?" But unlike Kanchana, her feminized erotic role did not correspond to consistent feminine attire. In a conversation in 2007, Srijan averred that "though we are *meyeli* (feminine), we are not women." In 2011, I visited the *hijra guru* Annapurna's house with her, where a *hijra* noticed her body hair and recommended emerging hair removal treatments. Srijan breezily replied, "What use is it to us? We are not going to join *hijra* houses . . . we are *kothi*, we'll remain *kothi* only!" This subject position meant that while adopting a feminized position vis-à-vis *parikhs*, she flexibly performed this role in both male and female attire as per what different *parikhs* desired. As she explained to the *hijras*: "Some want me in *koditaal* (*kodi*-mode), while some *parikhs* want me in *bhelipon* . . . and *duplis* don't want me in *niharinipon* (woman-mode) at all! There is a demand for *bhelipon* also, for *koditaal* also . . . but the markets are different!" Some *parikhs* wanted her in "normal" male dress because of fear of social exposure: "One *parikh* said he'd love me like a woman, but would feel comfortable if I visited him in *normal* [*sic*] dress." However, others actively desired her in *kodipon*: "It seems I have more demand in *kodi* attire . . . somehow people still realize I am *kothi* . . . so many checked me out today!" Her pleasure at being desired in *kodipon* contrasted with Kanchana's discomfort in male dress.

Kothis not only switch between *kodi* and *bheli* as distinct modes, but also blend *kodi* and *bheli* modes. Sushanto, a *kothi* who worked at the HIV project at Ranaghat run by the Kolkata-based CBO Swikriti, told me in a conversation in 2012: "I like to do a little *kothipon*, a little *niharinipon*, to put on a little makeup and do *bhel* and *bajar* (shopping) for men, but I don't have so much desire for full female attire." Sushanto used words like *kothipon* in a linear fashion to claim a "little" versus "full" feminine presentation, but here, this did not imply an opposition to public *bhel* and *bajar*—behaviors often derided by activists.

While Sushanto publicly adopted some *bheli* adornments and behaviors while staying in *kodi* attire, other *kothis* both switch between attires and blend *kodi* dress with behavioral or sartorial *bhel*. From oppressed-caste backgrounds, Joy and Golu at Berhampore switched between *tonnapon* and *maiggapon* (male and female attire) occupationally, growing their hair when seasonally dancing at weddings in North India (*lagan*), but wearing male attire back home, where they sometimes undertook temporary jobs like cooking in people's houses. Occasionally, they wore *satra* (feminine dress) in their hometown too, since their families had gradually come to accept them in such attire. In a conversation in 2012, Golu told me:

> See, we dress up *puro* (fully) in *maiggapon* (woman-mode) on festival days, we go around town and have a lot of fun, but the very next day, we wear usual male dress. But we don't become entirely *tonnapon* (male-mode), some *bhel* always remains in our face and eye movements, in our gait! And you know, we *kothis* look feminine if we just wear a *top* (feminine shirt) with *jeans*!

Here, the *bhel* of feminine bodily movements is combined with *tonnapon* dress and sometimes with somewhat feminine clothing like tops, to make for a look that is neither "fully" *maiggapon*—reserved for festive occasions—nor entirely *tonnapon*. While increasing access to commercial casual wear like tops and jeans facilitates such blending, there may be blending within older forms of dress as well. In Dinajpur in North Bengal, I observed how *kothis* (or *khaptis* as they are also known there) often wear a *gamchha* (towel) across their shoulders like the *orna* or feminine scarf while wearing the male *lungi* (wraparound) in their lower half.[14]

While these *kothis* see themselves as combining a "little" or "some" *bhel* with male attire, Ajit, one of Bikash's daughters at Ranaghat, described her presentation as exactly midway between *kodi* and *bheli*: "*adha* (half) *kodi, adha bheli.*" Raised by a supportive mother who protected her from hostile family and neighbors, Ajit was marked out as feminine from her childhood. As she said in one conversation, "Anyone can tell I am *kothi* just by looking at me!" But she also conceded her sexually *dupli* behavior, and like Abinash, said she was not like those *arial* (extreme) *kothis* who were only receptive. However, her *dupli* position corresponded neither with *kodi* presentation nor binary switching. One evening in 2012 at the Ranaghat DIC, she was planning an outing with a *bheli* friend who offered to dress her in *satra* (female clothes). Ajit instructed: "No, dress me up neither as a man nor as a woman, but as a *kothi!*" Another day, she discussed her dress options with her friend Sushanto for a shopping trip. Sushanto speculated, "Shall we wear *satra*?" Ajit replied, "No, why? We'll go dressed *adha-adha* (half-half) only!" She thus saw her "half" presentation as no less legitimate than "full" masculine or feminine attire, suggesting a nonhierarchical linearity. In practice, this meant wearing makeup and feminine tops with jeans, but not usually the padded bras or *sarees* worn by *bheli kothis* like Kanchana.

Contravening Hierarchical Divides

While expressions like "little *kothipon*" or "half *bheli*" evoke a linear gradation of femininity, they are distinct from the aforementioned linear hierarchies and rather express diverse forms of switching and blending that the aforementioned *kothis* undertake without distancing themselves from "more" feminine *kothis*, often while maintaining a socially visible femininity across switches. Thus, such *kothis* may be perceived as intermediaries between *kodi* and *bheli* camps. As Anik at Berhampore told me in a 2015 conversation: "Some *kothis*, like Srijan, cross both sides, pass messages from one side to the other!"

Further, such *kothis* may repurpose activist discourse to challenge respectability-based *kodi–bheli* divides. One summer night in 2009, Srijan entered the central square field in Berhampore, where *kothis* commonly congregated, in *kodi* dress but sashaying and dancing by herself. Some *kodi kothis* confronted her: "Hey, why are you acting like this?" Sujoy simply gave *thikri* (clapped) at them. One replied: "Why do you do that—not good!" Srijan rallied back: "One can't decide good and bad like that . . . everyone has a distinct *choritro* (character). Just like you like sitting in the field, I like doing *chhibripon* (*hijra*-mode) . . . saying good and bad is foolish, the way we take it in our ass looks bad to society, but we still like it!" One of them responded with the familiar critique of excess: "But why *so much?*" Srijan countered: "Well, *kothis* will do *kothipon* (*kothi*-like behavior) when they come into the *kothimahal* (*kothi* world)!" Srijan's phrase "everyone has a distinct character" echoes the rhetoric of diverse identities and freedom of expression advocated in pride walks—she had attended several by then—but takes such discourse beyond the graded acceptance practiced by activists, using it to defend behaviors derided in NGO spaces. Such defenses show the instability of the politics of pride and visibility, suggesting how related discourses may be reclaimed and resignified as they intersect with *kothi* practices such as *bheli–kodi* overlaps.

Sometimes, frameworks like MSM became imbued with meanings that contravened activist discourse. At a gathering in Berhampore in 2014, Shundori, a *kothi* who switched between *kodipon* and *bhelipon*, countered the *kodi kothi* Kajol's aforementioned complaint that *bheli kothis* were defaming Sangram as a place of "ass-fuckers." Shundori said:

> We're all MSM, we all take it in the ass, that's why funded projects are coming, that's why third gender people are getting recognition . . . These people take advantage of the recognition of third gender people but then won't go out publicly with them, they'll take it in the butt secretly and mingle indoors with the same people they criticize!

While critiquing the hypocrisy of *kodi kothis* who condemn public *bhel* and eroticism but partake in feminine kinship and sexual roles privately, Shundori emphasized the erotic feminization of MSM rather than subordinating femininity to maleness as seen earlier. MSM was conflated with "third gender," a typical description of *hijras* in media discourse. Shundori thus placed MSM in relation to another superseding scalar and discursive framework, dissociating it from masculinized homosexuality. This suggests that the plurality of superseding categories and vernacularizing processes potentially creates contrary possibilities within representational frameworks; *kothis* may counteract or resignify one dominant category by evoking another.

Apart from *kodi* respectability, *kothis* who switch between *pons* also contravene *hijra* ideals of authenticity and consistency. During a group trip to a seaside town in 2012, Bibi, a *bheli kothi* who planned to join a *hijra gharana*, criticized Priyanka, a *kothi* from Berhampore, for alternating between *niharinipon* and *tonnapon* over the trip. Echoing *hijra* critiques of *kothi* fluidity, Bibi said: "You go out as a woman and then become a man! There is no certainty to these people, one can't trust them!" Priyanka countered: "How does it matter to you if I go back to *tonnapon?*" Priyanka, a frequent participant in pride walks, thus implicitly evoked the framework of individual freedom and choice, common in activist discourse, to contest intra-community norms.

Non/Linear Bhel

While public forms of switching and blending that evoke linear conceptions of the *kodi–bheli* schema may disrupt graded hierarchies, the scenario is complicated further by the shifting nature of the *kodi–bheli* distinction itself, which not only de-hierarchizes but destabilizes the distinction altogether. Since *bhel* designates varied forms of sartorial and behavioral femininity, *bheli* and similar terms like *bhorokti* have shifting meanings—a sartorially *kodi* person may be designated as behaviorally *bheli*. During a conversation in 2014, a feminine-attired *kothi* in Shantipur, Nadia, referred to some local *kothis* as *kodi* due to their male attire. However, when I asked them later if they were *kodi*, one of them exclaimed, "No, we are *bhorokti kothis!*" Hanging out with them at the local railway station, I observed how they swayed their hips, performed the *hijra* clap, and seduced *parikhs* in public. Such behaviors, rather than attire, underlay their claim to being *bhorokti*. Indeed, some sartorially *bheli kothis* recognize that male-attired people may be equally *bheli*. In Kolkata, Raina described certain *kothis* to me as "not *bheli*, but then also very *bheli*," while in Nadia, a *bheli kothi* once referred to a male-attired friend as "not *bhorokti*, but no less than *bhorokti*." Such statements recognize that being *bheli* or *bhorokti* takes different forms, complicating a singular linear axis ranging from lesser to greater femininity.

Equal claims to *bhel* were especially evident at Ranaghat. In 2011, I went on a shopping trip with Bikash and her *kothi* daughters, comprising people in both male and female attire. Yet, after we successfully flirted with male shopkeepers to bring prices down, Bikash remarked delightedly: "All of us here are *bhorokti!*" Here, *bhorokti* designates a public behavioral femininity that does not depend on attire, enabling commonality and bonding between differently dressed *kothis*. Later, while shopping for shoes, Bikash advised her daughters: "Wear this shoe in *tonnapon* (male mode), that one in *laharanpon* (female mode)!" Bikash's usage of *pon* encouraged switching or blending while her recognition of male-attired *kodi kothis* as *bhorokti* contradicted the linear forms of the *kodi–bheli* divide and related respectability hierarchies. Since the CBO Swikriti's HIV project in Ranaghat relied heavily on Bikash, her support of *bhel* meant that *kodi–bheli* hierarchies did not gain much footing there. Silk, one of Bikash's daughters, once described how Bikash united different kinds of *kothis* through her motherly love: "Bikash loves both her *kodi* and *bheli* daughters!"

Some *kothis* go further and map *kodi kothis* as more *bheli* or *arial* (extreme) *kothis* than female-attired people. At Coochbehar, Sumi—who publicly wears feminine attire—described Suresh and Subesh, male-attired and heterosexually married *kothis*, as being more *bheli* than herself due to their flamboyant femininity and behavior with men in public. In a conversation in 2014, she remarked: "The kind of *bhel* that they do, many *bheli kothis*—even *hijras*—won't be able to do that!" Meanwhile, during a conversation at Ranaghat, Sushanto remarked that *kodi kothis* sometimes exhibited more feminine sexual behavior than *bheli* ones: "Sometimes, those in *tonnapon* (male-mode) turn out to be *arial kothis* during sex . . . and those who are more *bhelki*, they don't care, they do *dupli* (sexually versatile) behavior!" This contradicted the aforementioned construction of sartorially *bheli kothis* as more "extreme" *kothis* than *kodi kothis* and their greater association with feminized sexual roles.

Thus, *kothis* may deploy linear idioms (more *bheli*, more extreme *kothi*, etc.) to recognize an unpredictable nonlinearity to feminine expression—someone sartorially *kodi* may be more behaviorally *bheli* than sartorially *bheli kothis*; someone who is outwardly more feminine may be less typically feminine otherwise. The contextually multivalent usages of *bhel* and *pon*, which can refer to varied forms of gender/sexual expression, disrupt a linear gradation of *kothis* along any singular axis of femininity—not rejecting linear metaphors but using them in nonlinear ways. Such non/linearity (simultaneous linearity and nonlinearity) exceeds queer/trans critiques of linear arrangements or spectra of identities, such as Halberstam's critique of the "masculine continuum" (1998: 151), Thomas and Boellstorff's critique of the autism spectrum (2017: 9), or Castleberry's critique of a linear gender spectrum (2019: 404), all of which seek alternative frameworks beyond linearity. If transposed to this context, such critiques might undermine the non/linear suppleness of *kothi* discourses and practices.

The shifting, non/linear nature of the *kodi–bheli* divide may destabilize hierarchies related to *shomman*. Shaunak, a male-attired but *bheli kothi*, was once accosted in the Ranaghat DIC by another male-attired *kothi* for clapping like *hijras*. The *kothi*, who had known Shaunak in a more masculine avatar, said: "Why are you behaving like this? You have become so strange!" Shaunak responded, punctuating her statement with loud claps: "Are we *kodi* like you (clap)? Are we fearful like you (clap)?" Her friend laughed and went silent. Such instances destabilize the poles of the *kodi–bheli* divide. *Kothis* who are sartorially *kodi* but do behavioral *bhel* and *bila* and apply the *kodi* label to other male-attired *kothis* interrupt the consolidation of a clear binarized divide between *kodi* and *bheli kothis*, as attempted by activists like Arnab.

However, practices like behavioral *bhel* and non/linear *kodi–bheli* overlaps were also censured in CBOs and HIV projects, suggesting their potential threat to dominant activist discourses. Besides sartorially *bheli kothis*, male-attired *kothis* were also derided for doing *bhel*, and there were attempts to prevent *kothis* from switching between attires. Sumi told me that while working at MANAS Bangla's HIV project in North Bengal, they had received a directive from senior activists: "*Kothis* who are *kodi* should not change in the DIC and go out in *bhel*, and *kothis* who come in *bheli* dress should stay in *bhel*!" The concern, as Sumi gauged informally, seemed to be that neighbors might be shocked by such switches, and *kothis* changing into female attire and doing *bhel* with men might create trouble in the neighborhood. While this ban was ultimately not strongly enforced, anxieties about *kothis* switching from *kodi* to *bheli* or performing behavioral *bhel* were recurrent. Toufik, a male-attired *kothi* who was behaviorally and sometimes sartorially *bheli*, told me how both her attire and behavior were policed when she worked in MANAS Bangla in Kolkata: "You can't behave like this, you can't dress like that . . . after I left, I felt I became free!"

Conclusion

This chapter has surveyed how both distinctions and overlaps emerge in *kothi* communities in relation to transgressive practices like *bhel* and *bila*.

The strengthening of linear *kodi–bheli* divides through intersecting processes of vernacularization parallels and extends the elision of overlapping identity categories evidenced in the attempted standardization of *hijra–kothi* and *kothi–dupli* divides studied in preceding chapters. However, the superseding tiers of Anglophone and Bengali activist discourse within the multilayered hierarchies of vernacularization are neither monolithic nor uncontested; given the ambiguities and tensions within such discourse, *kothis* like Srijan may evoke activist ideals to reclaim derided embodiments and practices. While organizational hierarchies within HIV projects further the vernacularization of *kothi–hijra* discourse and the exploitation of *kothi* labor, HIV-related categories like MSM can also be reappropriated, as Shundori shows.

Overall, processes of vernacularization attempt to contain the diverse, messy practices of *kothi–hijra* communities, such as *kodi–bheli* overlaps, and relegate them to private and intra-community spaces, but forms of non/linearity or nonhierarchical linearity within *kothi–hijra* communities, and the contravention of respectability ideals and hierarchies, cannot be erased or entirely subsumed. This contested, contradictory terrain is complicated further with the increasing prominence of the transgender category within NGO and activist networks from the late 2000s onward, as I explore in the next chapter.

Chapter 4

RUPANTARKAMI NARRATIVES AND THE ATTEMPTED STANDARDIZATION OF TRANS INTERIORITY

In 2018, Surashree Bose, an accomplished dancer who had previously performed as male, came out as transgender in an interview to a Bengali webzine. She said:

> We do this *kaaj* (act/work) of becoming a woman from a man because the body is a man's but the *atma* (soul) is a woman's . . . One can't kill one's soul . . . but one can change one's body . . . Some nurture their *nari shotta* (woman's being) in their *monon* (thinking, subjectivity) while remaining in a man's body . . . others have the courage to change it. ("15 April Ashe" 2018)

The article described her both as transgender and its translated Bengali counterpart, *rupantarkami*—literally, someone who desires transformation (*antar*) in *roop* (form)—and lamented that such "normal, healthy" people were still pejoratively called *hijra* by ignorant people ("15 April Ashe" 2018). Bose's narrative marks the increasing visibility of transgender and/or transsexual identities in the Indian and Bengali media. Since the 2000s and especially in the 2010s, several public figures such as the academic Manobi Bandyopadhyay and the Bollywood scriptwriter Gazal Dhaliwal have come out as transgender or transsexual (Chaudhuri 2006; Dhaliwal n.d.). In that context, *kothi–hijra* communities and discourses come into increasing mediation with not only MSM and gay categories but also discourses of transgender and transsexual identity in English and Sanskritic Bengali, which gain increasing prominence in the NGO and activist sector in the 2010s.

For trans women like Bose and Bandyopadhyay, the interiorized *nari shotta* (woman's being or self) and the "man's body" are inherently irreconcilable—the two may coexist only due to social pressure and their contradiction is ideally resolved through transition to embodied womanhood ("15 April Ashe" 2018; Chattopadhyay 2014). Their narrative of an interiorized selfhood in conflict with the wrong body closely parallels Western biomedical descriptions of transsexuality (Stone [1987] 2014). However, while some of my *kothi* and *hijra* interlocutors who experienced discomfort with their bodies did describe themselves in similar ways, others saw themselves as different from women even as they avowed a stable interiorized femininity "like" women, and some expressed contextually changing senses of interiority, including overlaps with maleness—a diversity that suggests the coexistence of models of selfhood that are strongly contrasted in some queer and trans studies scholarship (Najmabadi 2013; Khanna 2016). As we shall see in subsequent chapters, some people even combine or alternate between identification as transgender women and the sense of being a separate gender, rather than affirming a singular selfhood. In that context, this chapter examines emerging mediations, hierarchies, and translations between dominant discourses of transgender identity in India and West Bengal and diverse *kothi–hijra* narratives of interiority, embodiment, and selfhood.

Rich scholarly and activist conversations have revolved around the expansion of transgender identity and politics through transnational circuits of media, activism, and development funding, exploring both empowering and hierarchical, even colonizing, aspects (Billard and Nesfield 2020; Boellstorff et al. 2014). While it is impossible to adequately survey this literature here, it has noted at least two distinct but overlapping logics of hierarchization related to transgender—one based on distinction, another on subsumption. Given its emergence in the United States, transgender might be associated with Western-origin or Anglophone discourses of gender that clearly separate gender identity from sexual orientation, which become established as correct or proper while other understandings that blur such divides become subordinated or delegitimized as incorrect or even offensive (Valentine 2007: 4; Leung 2016: 434). Transgender may also mark an elite or aspirational form of identification relative to which other identities, such as *hijra* in India, are cast as backward or not respectable (Mount 2020: 623; Dutta and Roy 2014: 331). While it may be hierarchically distinguished from other identities or discourses, transgender may also function as a universalizing category that subsumes culturally varied forms of gender variance under a homogenizing model of identity, based on dominant Euro-American and colonial logics of binary gender and unchanging selfhood, which becomes positioned as culturally nonspecific even as other discourses are cast as relatively particular and/or as local versions of transgender identity (Boellstorff et al. 2014: 434; Dutta and Roy 2014: 328; Chatterjee 2018: 316).

But while potentially reinforcing global/local and universal/particular hierarchies, the globalization of transgender is not a simple diffusion from the "West" to the rest (Jarrin 2016: 360). The category may be adapted, translated, or creolized in ways that variably converge with or diverge from Western senses (Hegarty 2022: 5; Mohan 2013: 30; Chiang 2021: 173). Indeed, many outside the West may not find transgender to be a culturally incommensurable category and adopt it as an appropriate name for preexisting subjectivities (Dutta and Roy 2014: 323). Non-Western activists also utilize transgender to access or build transnational networks of solidarity and mobilize support for domestic change (Billard and Nesfield 2020: 81). But while transgender is neither indubitably Western nor unidirectionally imposed, its adoptions or translations in non-Western locations are not always liberating. Transgender or transsexual identification might be mobilized to reinforce social hierarchies, such as those between middle-class transsexual women and working-class *travestis* in Brazil (Jarrin 2016), or between working-class Indian trans women who seek respectable office jobs and *hijra* beggars and sex workers from whom they dissociate themselves (Mount 2020).

In this context, this chapter, along with the next two, examines three dominant discourses of transgender identity that gain varying degrees of media, activist, and state recognition in India—the transsexual model associated with linear male-to-female transition, transgender as a third gender, and transgender as an inclusive umbrella term for diverse gender nonconforming identities that are yet sought to be clearly distinguished from sexual identities. This chapter particularly focuses on Bengali and Indian discourses of transsexuality and versions of the transgender umbrella that prioritize transsexuality as the default transgender identity. I see these as not just regional adaptations or transformative translations of a discourse of Euro-American origin, but as forms of universalism located outside the West that reinforce their own universal/particular hierarchies, such that *hijra* and *kothi* might be seen as particular, localized versions of a universal scientific ontology of transsexual or *rupantarkami* identity. Both distinct from and partly convergent with Euro-American forms of universalism, Indian interpretations of transsexual and non-English terms like *rupantarkami* are articulated as legitimate descriptors of a universal identity or state of being—even as they shift transsexual and transgender from Western histories and meanings by utilizing culturally specific conceptualizations of interiority, womanhood, and respectability, thus reimagining the universal. Simultaneously, such discourses also reference transnational Anglophone terminology such as "gender identity disorder" and foster the globalization of related ideas such as the concept of an innate, biologically rooted gender. While this process decenters trans universalism from an exclusively Western frame of reference, it also produces shifting hierarchies of vernacularization that reinforce the linguistically less prestigious, socially less respectable, scientifically less legitimate, and culturally more particular status of *kothi* and *hijra* discourses. Further, dominant forms of transsexual discourse tend to reinforce a model of stable interiorized identity and linear male-to-female transition (Stone [1987] 2014; Ewing and Taylor 2018). This elides diverse understandings of interiority and non/linear gender expression in *kothi–hijra* communities that encompass both stable and fluid senses of selfhood. Meanwhile, *kothis* and *hijras* may contest, adapt, or modify transsexual discourse. Overall, my focus is thus on mediations between non-Western forms of universalism and vernacularized (trans)regional discourses, rather than between the non-West and a singular Western "idea of transgender" (Boellstorff et al. 2014: 434).

The Emergence of Transgender

The word "transgender" is rare in Indian media and NGO documents before 2000. It is absent in several reports by Praajak, HST, and NFI between 1997 and 2004 that position *kothis*—and sometimes *hijras* or "eunuchs"—under the MSM umbrella (Praajak 1997; HST 2000; Khan 2004).

However, two categories circulate before "transgender" that influence its later articulations. One is the figure of the third sex or gender, typically equated with *hijras*, while the other is the transsexual person who transitions from "male" to "female" or vice versa. While we have seen how media and *gharana* articulations of the "third gender" restrict overlaps with manhood, this discourse does not typically permit transition to womanhood either. In one Bengali newspaper article, a *hijra* community member says she underwent emasculation to "become a woman," but is depicted as transitioning from "*purush* (man) to *brihannala*" (Ahmed 1995). *Brihannala* is a Sanskritic term used in Bengali for *hijras* and often treated as synonymous with third (*tritiyo*) gender (Bhaduri 2014). In some cases, the Indian state has also excluded *hijras* from legal womanhood on biologically essentialist grounds. In 2003, an Indian court disqualified Kamla Jaan, a *hijra* politician who identified as a woman, from a seat reserved for women since it saw her as a "eunuch," a castrated male lacking reproductive capacity (Jain and Rhoten 2020).

However, a medically inflected discourse of transsexuality also starts circulating in the Bengali media since the late 1980s, about a decade before "transgender" arrives through activist circuits. Rather than thirdness, this model emphasizes the inner psychological gender of transsexual persons that prompts anatomical transition to their desired gender. In separate conversations, the activists Susanta and Raina both recalled first encountering the word *rupantarkami* in issues of *Sananda*, a Bengali magazine for urban women, roughly between 1988 and 1990. In a 2013 conversation, Raina recalled: "*Rupantarkami* was translated by the journalists of Sananda from 'transsexual' . . . that's when I first came across the word; they said such people should be understood sympathetically from a psychological perspective." Years later, academics Ajoy Majumdar and Niloy Basu, in their pioneering Bengali study of *hijras*, translated "transsexual" as *lingorupantarkami*—someone desiring transformation in *lingo* or gender—and categorized some *hijras* as being psychologically *lingorupantarkami* (1997: 39). Their 2005 book *Samaprem* ("Same-sex love") reverted to *rupantarkami* as the equivalent of transsexual and categorized *kothis* as *rupantarkami* (Majumdar and Basu 2005: 156).

The earlier Bengali translation of transsexual relative to transgender reflects its older lineage in Anglophone psychiatric and biomedical discourse (Williams 2014). International media coverage of the transition of pioneering transsexual women such as Christine Jorgensen facilitated the transnational circulation of ideas about transsexuality from the 1950s onward and fostered discourse on transsexuality in Asia (Stryker 2009; Chiang 2021). Meanwhile "transgender," emerging from multiple sources among US communities, media, and doctors, took on meanings distinct from transsexual as describing people who do not anatomically transition or alternatively as an umbrella term for diverse gender-variant persons, and gained popularity in the United States by the 1990s (Williams 2014).

Unlike the West, both transsexual and transgender arrive in India through the media, NGOs, or elite activist discourse rather than grassroots communities. As Raina suggests, words like *rupantarkami* were initially used more as etic (external) descriptors by non-trans journalists than as self-designations. An NFI-sponsored report notes that these terms were largely unknown among *kothi* communities in Bengal in 1997 (Khan 1997: 44). In the 2000s, these words gradually became emic usages through middle-class people who adopted transsexual, transgender, *rupantarkami*, and *lingantarkami* (a variant of *lingorupantarkami*) as self-identities—particularly Manobi Bandyopadhyay and Tista Das, among the first Bengali transsexual women who went public with their identities and transitions (Chaudhuri 2006; Das 2009).

Bandyopadhyay, an academic who became the first openly trans college principal in India, hails from a dominant-caste Brahmin family; echoing a common trope of transsexualism, she says she realized early that she was a woman in her *mon* (heart/mind) and sought freedom from her wrongly male body through a "sex change" operation (Chowdhury 2015; Bandyopadhyay S. 2019). Her femininity and transition met with stigma and ridicule in middle-class spaces—she was derisively called *hijra* in college and classmates mockingly performed the *hijra* clap behind her back (Bandyopadhyay and Pandey 2017: 40). Such otherization prompted trans women like Bandyopadhyay to distinguish themselves from *hijra* communities, who, as Bandyopadhyay notes, are considered "*bibhotsho*" (monstrous) by "*shobhan samaj*" (decent society) (Chattopadhyay 2014: 20). In a public Facebook post, Bandyopadhyay regards *hijra* community members sympathetically as victims forced to adopt a "*bidghute pesha*" (grotesque profession) due to social exclusion, but does not acknowledge that *hijra* might also be an agentially professed identity (Bandyopadhyay 2022). In a 2009 essay, Das regards *hijra* as a "*bijatiyo shobdo*" (outlandish/freakish word), a derogatory label (*takma*) through which society stigmatizes transsexuals—not mentioning that it might also be a valid self-identification (2009: 9).

Transsexual seems to provide a more respectable option—in the 2000s, Bandyopadhyay came out publicly as a "postoperative transsexual" and demanded state recognition as a woman (Chaudhuri 2006). Unlike third gender discourse, transsexualism permits Das and Bandyopadhyay to claim transition to what they term a "complete" (*shompurno*) womanhood (Das 2013; Bandyopadhyay S. 2019). This signals an emergent distinction between transsexual women who claim socially respectable womanhood as well as access to middle-class spaces and other forms of gender variance denied such status—a tendency with transnational parallels. Carmen Jarrin notes the greater respect and access to medical care accorded to middle-class transsexual women than to working-class *travestis* in Brazil (2016: 360). In India, the transsexual–*hijra* divide presages the distinction claimed by some transgender women relative to *hijras* in the 2010s (Mount 2020). But as suggested by the aforementioned categorization of *hijras* as transsexual, it may also subsume *hijra* rather than remaining distinct—suggesting complex, conflicted forms of intersection.

Unlike the media circulation of transsexual, "transgender" initially gained currency through the NGO sector in the early 2000s. The activist Susanta recalled he first heard someone identify themselves as transgender in a workshop organized by HST in Mumbai in 2000. Madhuri, the *hijra* activist, recounted that she encountered the term in the early 2000s at an international HIV-related conference where she used "gay" to identify herself to the Anglophone audience, prompting a corrective from a senior activist: "He told me, '*beti* (daughter), you are not gay, you are transgender!' I was already dressing in women's clothes, but did not know the term. Later, I started calling myself *transgender*." This exchange suggests both early overlaps between gay and transgender identifications and gradual processes of distinction. In *Samaprem*, Majumdar and Basu distinguish between a general (*shadharon*) sense of male homosexuality (*samakamita*) that can include relationships between *rupantarkami* people and men, and a specific sense describing relations between men without any overt gender variance (2005: 43). Bandyopadhyay evinces changing stances. In a 2018 article, she says: "When two *samakami* (homosexual) people have sex, one of them becomes a man, the other a woman . . . though externally a man, one may be a woman in their internal gender" (Bandyopadhyay 2018). However, in a later interview, she states that if a "bodily male" person is a woman in their *mon* (heart/mind), their relationships with men cannot be seen as *samakami* relationships (Bandyopadhyay S. 2019).

Even as activists began to distinguish transgender from gay, early NGO discourse often treated "transgender" as a synonym for *hijra* and subsumed both under MSM in biologically essentialist terms. A 2002 report on HST's HIV intervention activities described its target group as "men having sex with men (MSM), including transgenders (*hijras*)" (UNICEF 2002: 99). Later, the guidelines for the third phase of the NACP (2007–12), authored by non-*hijra* activists from prominent NGOs like HST, positioned *hijras* as a subgroup of MSM who were "covered under the term 'transgenders' or TGs" and further defined *hijras* as a "cultural group, a 'third gender' (apart from male and female)," not clarifying whether this thirdness is anatomical or self-determined (NACO 2007: 12). The guidelines mentioned no other transgender identity and referred to "Hijras/TGs" as a combined phrase, effectively conflating these terms (NACO 2007: 13). The state initially conflated even transsexual with a third or separate sex/gender category, evident in the Election Commission's move in 2009 to allow "eunuchs and transsexuals" to register as "other" rather than male or female in voters' lists, with no mention of transgender ("Indian Eunuchs" 2009). This extended the previous recognition of "eunuch" as a third option on passports in 2005, suggesting the state's rather cursory attempts at recognizing a third gender in the 2000s.[1]

However, some emergent non-HIV activism articulated a broader sense of transgender, particularly a pioneering report on "human rights violations against the transgender community" in Bangalore by a civil rights NGO in collaboration with LGBT activists (PUCL-K 2003). This report included both *kothis* and *hijras* as transgender and voiced a prescient demand for gender self-determination: "Every person must have the right to decide their gender expression and identity . . . (including) the demand for *hijras* to be considered female as well as a third sex" (PUCL-K 2003: 76). The team behind this report included Famila, a tragically short-lived *hijra* activist who had some English education and was among the first *hijras* to work in NGOs (Revathi 2010). While espousing transgender–*hijra* solidarity and organizing under the transgender label, Famila pointed out that transsexual or transgender-identified people typically had more "class privilege" than *hijras*, many of whom were "not English-speaking," could not access expensive surgeries and pass socially as women, and sought recognition as a "third gender" instead (Sukthankar 2005: 165–9). Most *hijras* in West Bengal initially treated transgender as a foreign term. In a 2009 interview, the Kolkata-based trans activist Sonia told me: "Many *hijras* prefer to be called *hijra* as per their customs and professions."

Meanwhile, in the 2000s, several middle-class NGO activists started identifying as "transgender," using it to denote a subjectivity closer to transsexual womanhood, distinct from *hijra* and third gender. They formed mailing lists such as *transgender _sisters@yahoogroups.com* and Facebook groups such as Transgender India, which helped disseminate these terms and expand transgender community networks. People like Das served as inspirational figures. Amrita Sarkar, an activist who founded *transgender_sisters*, directed a 2008 film, *Rupantar* (transformation), featuring Das as a successful trans woman (Rupantar 2008). Das, playing herself, is complimented by the film's protagonist, a young trans girl, for being indistinguishable from cis women, and inspires her to study rather than join *kothi–hijra* professions.

While some aforementioned usages conflate transgender with *hijra* and third gender, others conflate transgender and transsexual. A 2004 article in the community magazine *Swikriti Patrika* alternates between "transsexual" and "transgender" interchangeably (Chakrabarty 2004). *Rupantarkami* stands for both—initially translated from "transsexual," it is later equated with "transgender" in the film *Rupantar* (2008), which describes its protagonists as "transgender people."

Such conflations suggest how globalizing transsexual discourse informs both the Bengali neologisms and early usages of transgender. The English description of *Rupantar* positions its subjects as "male-to-female transgender people," which equates *rupantar* or transformation with a linear "male-to-female" transition (Rupantar 2008). Biomedical discourses of transsexuality have been much critiqued for reinforcing a binary sex/gender model that sees "man" and "woman" as oppositional categories, permitting transition between them but often precluding mixture, ambiguity, and positions beyond the binary (Stone [1987] 2014; Ewing and Taylor 2018). In her pioneering critique, Sandy Stone shows how US transsexual women were expected to demonstrate a deep-rooted unease with their "wrong body," disavow any pleasure from their preoperative genitalia, and conform to feminine stereotypes to access gender-affirmative care—although actual transsexual narratives defy such straightjacketing ([1987] 2014: 6). The idea of a deep gender identity at odds with bodily sex rests on the modern construction of gender/sexual identities as interiorized, singular essences, which potentially elides other cultural discourses, such as certain Hindu devotional traditions, that see gender as not innately fixed but as fluidly changeable through practice (Ewing and Taylor 2018). Further, the common metaphor of being "trapped in the wrong body" has been critiqued for biologically essentializing trans bodies as (wrongly) male or female, making gender identity contingent on sexed transition (Asher 2010). Recent trans of color critique expansively reimagines transness from being necessarily imbricated in a linear temporal trajectory "from one location to another" to "a multidirectional movement in an open field of possibility," encompassing multiple temporalities (Chen and Cárdenas 2019: 473). But trans theorists also point out that the desire of some transsexuals for a seemingly linear transition to a stable embodiment and their nonnormative transgression of the sex binary to attain apparently normative genders challenge simplistic valorizations of resistance, performativity, and fluidity in queer studies (Chu and Drager 2019). In that context, my point is not to scapegoat transsexuals for perpetuating binary gender norms, even as cisgender people are let off (Valentine 2012). Rather, narratives of binary transsexuality may be simultaneously empowering for some but restrictive if adopted as a generalized model of trans/*kothi/hijra* subjectivity.

Interiority in Rupantarkami *Discourse*

Writing on the transsexual in Brazil, Carmen Alvaro Jarrin argues that the spread of transsexual discourse is not the diffusion or unidirectional transfer of an Anglophone "hegemonic category" that misses local complexities; rather, transsexual is modulated and transformed through translation by "local actors" (2016: 359–60). Transsexual is indeed adaptively transformed in its translation as *rupantarkami* or *lingantarkami*—activists like Das (2009) translate the transsexual ontology of gender by adapting older concepts of interior subjectivity in Sanskritic registers of Bengali. However, significantly, the actors of this process do not see these terms as localized articulations but rather as scientific and generalizable names describing a universal identity (Das 2009: 9; Majumdar and Basu 1997: 39). Thus, they shift the universal inasmuch as they advance their own conceptualization of a universal transsexual identity that parallels yet subtly differs from Western Anglophone articulations.

Rupantarkami narratives deploy words like *roop* (form) and *mon* (mind, psyche) that have Sanskrit roots and are common in both literary and colloquial Bengali. In a study of emotion in Bengal, June McDaniel notes how *mon* (also spelled *mana*) interweaves concepts that are distinct in English: "emotion and thought . . . are not opposed . . . *mana*, means both mind and heart, as well as mood, feeling, mental state, memory, desire, attachment, interest, attention, devotion, and decision" (1995: 43). Dominant *rupantarkami* narratives tend to reduce this rich plurality of *mon* into a standardized biomedical ontology, treating *mon* as the locus of a fixed inner selfhood and gender, though the inherent multivalence of *mon* also opens up *rupantarkami* discourse to contrary significations explored later.

The evocation of *mon* as a locus of inner selfhood draws from postcolonial Bengali literature and culture. As Sudipta Kaviraj argues, a distinctive theme of "modern literature is the exploration of the self . . . its individuality, its mentalism, its interiority" (2015: 190). The exploration of interiority is not new; medieval Bengali poetry explored the "inner mental states" of mythic or divine figures (Kaviraj 2015: 64–5). However, paralleling transnational tendencies, modern Bengali authors such as Rabindranath Tagore (1861–1941) shift to exploring the variable interiorities of ordinary social individuals, transforming older idioms of interiority to chart relations and conflicts between interiorized subjects and social structures (Kaviraj 2015: 192). In some of Tagore's songs such as *Keno tomra amay dako*, the *mon* is a site of imaginative freedom that comes into tension with social duties and expectations—the first line may be roughly translated as "why do you call upon me, my *mon* does not obey" (Tagore [1914] 2008).

For Das, too, the *mon* conflicts with social shackles, but is fixed in its gendered essence, containing one's inalienable selfhood as a woman. In her 2009 essay, she narrates her struggle against social barriers to resolve the conflict (*boishomyo*) between the "wrong body" (*bhool shorir*) of a man and the *mon* of a woman, seen as characteristic of all *lingantarkami* or transsexual people (Das 2009: 10–11). Resolution comes through transformation (*rupantar*) via "precise surgical procedures" that render her "*shompurno*" or complete as a woman (Das 2013). Bandyopadhyay, meanwhile, generalizes this personal understanding of completeness into a rubric for classifying trans people as per degree of transition. Some media articles use "*rupantarkami*" and "transgender" generically irrespective of operative status ("15 April Ashe" 2018). However, Bandyopadhyay and some journalists distinguish between *rupantorito* (transformed) people who have "become" women after completing transition and *rupantarkami* people, those desiring transformation (Chowdhury 2015; Bandyopadhyay M. 2019). In 2019, Bandyopadhyay publicly objected to a media article calling her *rupantarkami*: "I am not *rupantarkami*, I am a *rupantorito nari* (transformed woman)" (Bandyopadhyay M. 2019). *Rupantorito nari* adaptively translates the English "trans woman," marking anatomical status more clearly. Relative to the various forms of feminine expression articulated through the idioms of *bhel* and *pon* that, as the previous chapter showed, might describe both linear transition and non/ linear forms of gender expression, the *rupantarkami–rupantorito* distinction in formal, Sanskritic registers of Bengali establishes a generalized model of linear transition.

Das sometimes offers less biologically essentialist perspectives. In one Bengali article, Das (2014) states that "a *rupantarkami* person's identity cannot just be based on their body, it is a psychological position," although the article then assumes that all *rupantarkami* people will desire transition. At one point in her 2009 essay, Das writes that trans women's bodies are socially marked (*chihnito*) as male (2009: 10). This phrasing echoes the deconstructive critique of sex in US trans scholarship, which posits that body parts are not innately male or female but produced as such through socio-medical categorization (Spade 2011). However, she then reinscribes sex as an innate biological characteristic, albeit at odds with the trans person's socially assigned sex/gender. Quoting the biomedical term "gender identity disorder," she describes how some children with XY chromosomes do not adequately respond to testosterone during fetal development, causing their brains to remain "like women" and prompting a disjuncture between *shorir* (body) and *mon* (2009: 11–12).

The *mon* is thus understood through the deterministic idea of "brain sex," a common trope of biomedical trans discourse (Tannehill 2013). This marks a specifically transgender iteration of the modern concept of sexuality as expressing an inner truth of the self (Foucault 1988). Further, womanhood is both an interiorized essence and an external attribute to be realized through embodied transition—a narrative that suggests a metaphysical circularity linking essence and manifestation, being and becoming, or depth and surface, wherein the former supposedly preexists and determines the latter, but crucially depends on the latter for its actualization (Derrida 2004). The pressure to actualize essence falls more on trans women whose claim to womanhood is much more socially precarious than cisgender women—though Das was already a woman in her *mon*, she also had to attain (*utteerno kora*) her womanhood (Das 2013).

Even so, this narrative helps shift the locus of truth from the body in some older mainstream perspectives—such as the real–fake *hijra* distinction—toward an increasing recognition of interiority in public discourses on gender. Given its support within Western biomedicine, the model of (trans)gender identity based on a consistent inner essence has gained gradual acceptance within medical and psychiatric institutions in eastern India. Das initially faced suspicion from doctors who pruriently examined her body and dismissed her desire to transition due to her "functional" male anatomy, showing the newness and lack of acceptance of the biomedical transsexual discourse in the 2000s (Das 2009: 12). However, she eventually found doctors better versed in transitional surgeries, and by the 2010s, some government hospitals in Kolkata even began offering free gender affirmation procedures parallel to the increasing state recognition of trans identities (Chatterjee 2017). While such developments owe much to the struggles of pioneers like Das, access to such state-provided healthcare typically rests on gatekeepers like psychiatrists who issue "gender identity disorder" or "gender dysphoria" certificates required before treatment. Arpita, a trans woman from Nadia who accessed free hormone replacement therapy from a government hospital in Kolkata in 2022, shared with me that she was not only subjected to a humiliating strip-down test to verify her anatomical attributes but also underwent multiple psychiatric evaluations where she was repeatedly questioned regarding since when she had felt herself to be a woman in her *mon*, and since when she started liking "feminine things"—suggesting that affirming a consistent interiorized gender identity legible in conventional terms often determines access to transition-related healthcare.

Interiority in Kothi–Hijra Narratives

Evincing both divergences from and parallels with transsexual or *rupantarkami* discourse, *kothi–hijra* narratives articulate interiority variably as stable or changeable. Rather than a woman in a wrong body, the *mon* or interior is often described as feminine or "like women," which corresponds to varied trajectories of embodied transition or non-transition. Shyamoli, the *hijra* community member who (as previously mentioned) was interviewed in a Bengali newspaper article in 1995, said that her *mon* was "*meyeder moton*" (like girls) from childhood and that she "wished to become a woman" (Ahmed 1995). Though articulated differently from *rupantarkami* narratives, this suggests a stable interiority corresponding to a desired male-to-female transition. Ranu, a Dalit *kothi* whom I met at Murshidabad, spoke of her *mon* similarly but without desiring such transition. One evening in 2015, Ranu and her *kothi* friends had congregated at the square field in Berhampore, and the conversation turned to whether *kothis* should sit in a section usually occupied by men in the local stadium. At one point, Ranu explained their difference from men thus: "Yes, we have a penis underneath our pants, but our *mon* is like women (*meyeder moton*)." Subsequently, she narrated how a male friend had asked her why she sometimes dressed in feminine attire, and she had explained through an analogy with Shaktiman, a popular Hindi television superhero, who (like Hindu gods and some Western superheroes) has the power to change form: "I told him, you know how Shaktiman has two *roops*? We also have two *roops*. . . . Shaktiman switches between *roops* to destroy enemies, we do it to get our freedom!" While for Ranu "freedom" entailed the ability to wear feminine attire as desired—for example, during festivals, or while working temporarily in *hijra* houses—she also seemed comfortable in alternating between two *roops*, rather than wishing to realize one true *roop*. This was apparent in her comfort with both masculine and feminine names. As she added later: "since we have two *roops*, isn't it only fair that we also have two names?" Other *kothis* often remarked how Ranu switched between *magipon* (woman style or mode) and *tonnapon* (man mode), wearing male clothes in the daytime and then doing *khajra* (sex work) in female attire at night. Ranu's narrative thus suggests the combination of a stable interiority (*mon*) similar to but distinct from women and an alternation of *roops* that parallels the practice of switching between *pons* discussed earlier, rather than linear *rupantar*.

Another common way of speaking about the *mon* locates it as a site of desire. In a conversation in 2011, Honey from Nadia described to me the tussle between the social pressure to present as male and the desires of *kothis*: "If we always have to stay in *tonnapon* (male mode/attire), if we can't do *dhuranipon* or *laharanpon* (womanly or *dhurani*-like dress or behavior), then how will we meet our *moner shadh* (desire of the *mon*)?" This desire, while emanating from the *mon*, is articulated as a desire for behavioral or sartorial expression *like* women (*laharanpon*), rather than an interiorized essence *as* a woman or a wish to become a *laharan* per se. This feminine likeness gets further removed from the referent of womanhood through the word *dhuranipon*—dressing or acting like *dhuranis* rather than women themselves.

Understandings of interiority associated with a stable femininity may correspond to a subject position that is not only distinct from women but also understood as a lack or excess relative to women, which is not necessarily perceived negatively but often articulated in affirming ways. Durga, one of Bikash's daughters at Ranaghat, described a strong womanlike *bhab*—feeling or mental/emotional state—inside herself, but claimed a separate gendered position.[2] During a conversation among several *kothis* at the Ranaghat DIC in 2014, she said, "my brother tells me to become more masculine . . . but how will I change? Even if I cut off my hair, will the woman-like feeling (*meye-meye bhab*) inside me go away?" However, in a later conversation about her *parikh*, she laughingly said, "of course, a *parikh* will eventually marry; I am not a woman, after all—if he asks me for a child, will I get it out through my anus?" Her acceptance of her *parikh*'s probable marriage evokes a biologically essentialized notion of reproductive lack relative to cisgender women, but she also defiantly and humorously reclaims her apparent inadequacy, perhaps to minimize any potentially hurtful emotional investment in her *parikh* and to avert (even mock) the normative expectation of childbearing. She later contradicted a *hijra* who told her she should go in for *chhibrano* (emasculation) to become more womanly: "I'll stay just as I am! Maybe I'll just get bigger breasts . . . what huge status have you gained after *chhibrano*?"

Contrastingly, Nita, the *hijra guru* from Ranaghat who, as mentioned in the last chapter, described that *kothis* had a *niharinipon* (womanliness, womanlike quality) in their *mon*, elaborated in the same conversation that this *niharinipon* prompted *kothis* to not only imitate but even exceed women in feminine attributes: "If women show off their breasts, we'll make even bigger ones, if women wear short dresses, we'll wear even shorter ones!" Her statement, said slightly mockingly yet with relish, articulated a subject position that is in excess of womanhood, rather than simply derivative. This idea of the greater femininity of *hijras* or *kothis* relative to women evokes both the exaggeration of feminine behaviors like coquettishness in some kinds of *bhel* and the non/linearity of *kodi–bheli* distinctions discussed in the last chapter—as we saw, male-attired *kothis* may be seen as more *bheli* than feminine-attired *kothis*.

Further, desire and/or interiority may be understood as situationally changeable rather than fixed—the wish for feminization (sartorial, behavioral, or anatomical) might intensify or decline. In 2014, Ajit, the *kothi* daughter of Bikash we met in previous chapters, was growing out her hair, which she saw as becoming more *bheli* relative to her previously half-*kodi*, half-*bheli* presentation. Raised by a working mother and exposed to diverse women staff and activists in the NGO sector, Ajit was critical of the concept of being "like women," although she later went on to adopt a conventionally feminine name and attire. In one conversation, she explained, "I have never understood this concept of feeling like a woman . . . all women don't have a similar *mon*! I never say I'm like a woman, I'm like myself!" Rather than an interiorized womanliness, she attributed her hairstyle to *shokh* (fancy, interest). As she once explained to her *kothi* friends: "Now I have the *shokh* to grow my hair, so let me do it—maybe I'll cut it off some day!"

Such changes are also attributed to a variety of influences, enticements, or pressures. Rima, a *kothi* from a Dalit family in a Kolkata slum, narrated in a 2014 interview that during her childhood, some boys in her school "became" *kothi* by seeing overtly feminine *kothis* like her—"being *kothi* is *chhowache* (infectious) . . . seeing us, they became *kothi*!" Rima mused that seeing other *kothis* might have inspired them to express their inner selves: "what they already had inside them may have become more expressed!" While this recalls the preexisting interiorized essence of *rupantarkami* narratives, this was not her only explanation—Rima also speculated that since her *kothi* friends were good in studies, other classmates might have felt enticed to join them and adopt their behaviors. In a village of Coochbehar, Sonali, a *kothi* or *meti* dancer, narrated her life in terms that suggest such feminization through influence. In an interview in 2015, she told me: "In my childhood, I had little feminine mannerisms (*alpo meyeli bhab*), but I did not realize this myself, neighbors pointed it out." Raised by a single mother in a poor Dalit household, she was compelled to seek out income as an adolescent. Through contacts with local *kothis*, she started dancing in female attire in both Coochbehar and Bihar at weddings, fairs, and festivals—spaces where cross-dressed performance by feminine males has limited social sanction (Morcom 2013). This experience changed her: "I became like this after going to dance programs; my gait changed . . . my friends kept long hair, so seeing them, I also started growing my hair; gradually, I started having sex with men . . . mixing with *kothis*, habits (*obhyesh*) like theirs also entered me."

Sonali thus described both her sexual behavior and gender presentation as *obhyesh* or habits that "enter" her, suggesting an interiority that changed as externally she became part of a social group. Akhil Katyal shows how North Indian discourses of same-sex desire may conceive it as a habit (*laundebaazi*) rather than as an identity clearly distinct from heterosexuality (2016: 68). Nagar notes that *jananas* in Lucknow might see their desire for men as an acquired habit, though it is unclear if they also perceive their feminine gender expression likewise (2019: 88–126). While Sonali did not indicate any specific source for her articulation of "habit," the Bengal region evidences several cultural discourses regarding femininity acquired through practice. In some Hindu devotional traditions, particularly Bengali Vaishnavism, men may adopt devotional stances or *bhavas* where they worship male gods (particularly Krishna) in a female role, which does not usually exempt them from social expectations like marriage, but permits limited feminization, such as wearing feminine attire, within a ritual space (Ewing and Taylor 2018). Closer to Sonali's context, theater forms such as *jatra* and *pala* prevalent in Coochbehar and rural Bengal may feature male actors performing female roles, in keeping with sanctioned traditions of "female impersonation" in several theatrical genres across India (Morcom 2013: 87). Arnab Mukherji, a director working with such theater forms in Coochbehar, describes in a documentary how male actors change through performance: "Men who play female roles become women in their *mon* and *pran* (soul) by acting repeatedly as women" (Alpo Jana Golpogulo 2019).

Given the wider prevalence of such varied ideas regarding externally induced feminization, it is not surprising that some *kothis* and *hijras* explicitly articulate the *mon* as susceptible to influences. In 2013, I attended a customary ceremony held forty days after a *hijra*'s emasculation (*chhibrano*) with some *kothis* from Kalyani. After the ceremony, some attendees discussed how eating the *prasad*—the food offered to the mother goddess of *hijras* (*Murga Mata* or *Bahuchara Mata*) during the ceremony—could induce the desire for *chhibrano*. This led to a discussion between Mithu, a *hijra*, and Gopal, a *kothi*:

Mithu: Eat this, then the desire for *chhibrano* will also arise in your *mon*!

Gopal: Yes, after eating at another *hijra*'s ceremony, even my *mon* is acting strangely!

Later, they joked that it would be a pity if Gopal indeed got emasculated, as she supposedly had a huge penis. Gopal joked that she wanted to fuck someone before the operation; another *kothi* jokingly volunteered to be her partner. Here, the desire for feminization is located in the *mon* just like *rupantarkami* narratives, but as the joke suggests, it does not correspond to a prefixed femininity. *Hijras* may also cite economic reasons for undergoing castration–penectomy (Nanda 1999: 118). In 2011 at Berhampore, the *hijra guru* Annapurna told me that though she had been *meyeli* from her childhood, her *chhibrano* was economically motivated: "I saw all the wealth in *hijra* houses . . . it went to my head—suddenly, one day, I got myself emasculated!"

Further, *kothis* and *hijras* may understand the *mon* as not only susceptible to influences that prompt transition, but as a site of plural desires that contravene linear trajectories. In 2016, Silk, one of the *kothis* from Kalyani, took me to visit Bablu, an older *kothi*. Bablu had recently undergone emasculation without joining a *hijra gharana* but maintained good relations with local *hijras*. Despite her transition and conventionally feminine presentation, she did not evidence any discomfort when, during our conversation on a street near her house, an old acquaintance called out to her as "Bablu-*da*" (elder brother). Silk asked her if she'd be interested in going to a *hijra* function. She replied, "Why not? Sometimes I have the desire (*ichhe*) to be a *hijra*, but then I also desire to be a woman! And then I also desire to be a man!" Laughing, she added: "The *mon* of a *kothi* is like a *bohurupi* (chameleon, having multiple *roops*)!" Bablu here reclaimed the pejorative metaphor of the *bohurupi*—used by *hijras* to deride *kothis* who shift between attires—to articulate the *mon* itself as polymorphous, desiring a plurality of *roops*. Bablu's articulation of the *mon* as *bohurupi* disrupts *hijra* ideals of emasculation and contradicts the interiorized essence and linear transition narrative of *rupantarkami* discourse, even as her embodiment seemingly follows a linear pathway.

Thus, rather than simply providing a fluid or nonlinear counter to *rupantarkami* linearity, such understandings of interiority permit contingently varied combinations of linear and nonlinear tendencies. Bindiya, the *hijra* from Kolkata whom we encountered in previous chapters, told me over several conversations in 2011 that while she had become a *magi* (woman) after *chhibrano*, sometimes she wished to revert to *tonnapon* (man-mode). While she liked imagining herself as a woman—even a *ghorer bou* (housewife)—in relation to her *parikhs*, sometimes she felt her old desires returning when having sex with men, and wanted to act as the *parikh* herself. Further, when out doing *badhai* with *hijras*, she sometimes started behaving in *tonnapon* when challenged by local goons—"with men, I can become an *arial tonna* (extreme man)!" Thus, her womanhood was situational and relational rather than a teleological end, and permitted contextual reversions to *tonnapon*.

While such linear/nonlinear combinations—*tonnapon* returning after *chhibrano*—potentially disrupt linear gradations and hierarchies between male-presenting *kothis* and castrated *hijras*, overlaps between *hijra* and male identities may be hidden. Bindiya sometimes bragged about her recurrent *tonnapon* to junior *kothis* in private, but chided them if they called her publicly by male monikers like *da* (elder brother), thus preserving her image as a *nirvan* (emasculated) *hijra*—as noted earlier, she had been stigmatized by some *kothi–hijra* friends for her role-switching.

In sum, then, *kothi–hijra* narratives encompass both stable and variable senses of interiority, as well as situationally contingent combinations of linear and nonlinear transition. Scholars such as Afsaneh Najmabadi and Akshay Khanna question the dominance of notions of gendered or sexual selfhood based on an interiorized essence, a deep inner truth about oneself, which they, following Michel Foucault, associate with the rise of sexuality as a distinct domain of identity in nineteenth-century Europe and the subsequent transnational translations of such discourse (Najmabadi 2013: 293–7; Khanna 2016: 10–28). In different ways, both study non-Western sites to demonstrate context-dependent, relational concepts of selfhood that belie the notion of an interiorized deep self (Najmabadi 2013: 297; Khanna 2016: 343). However, *kothi–hijra* narratives variously evidence both notions of deeply interiorized selfhood (e.g., the *meye-meye bhab* in the *mon* that refuses to go away), and senses of the self that arise in relation to context rather than from a preexisting inner essence—indeed, the same individual (like Rima) may reference both senses. Accounts of interiorized femininity use concepts like *bhab* and *mon* that are not reducible to contemporary transsexual discourse and have much older, broader usages (McDaniel 1995: 43). Of course, the diffuse influence of postcolonial notions of selfhood or emergent ideas of gender/sexual identity cannot be ruled out even though the narratives above do not explicitly cite trans discourse. However, ascertaining the precise genealogies of the ideas deployed in these narratives is less important for my purposes than noting how *kothis* and *hijras* articulate plural, individually variable configurations of interiority and embodiment by flexibly adapting common concepts like *mon* and how their narratives may hold together apparently contrasting phenomena such as linear transition and fluid nonlinearity.

The Scalar and Ontological Ascendance of Transgender

Transsexual or *rupantarkami* narratives add to the conceptual resources available to people in *kothi–hijra* communities and women like Bandyopadhyay and Das serve as inspirational figures, especially to those with greater access to the media or metropolitan activist communities. At Berhampore in 2014, Anik, the middle-class *kothi* we met in previous chapters, shared with me in a conversation that she was considering gender affirmation procedures as she approached her thirties: "I want to first take hormones, then do breast surgery, and then SRS (sex reassignment surgery). I had the desire to do this from early on; when I was younger, I became inspired by Manobi (Bandyopadhyay); seeing her, I thought that I would become a woman." As previously mentioned, many *kothis* and *hijras* see emasculation as making them more womanlike, but womanhood itself may be seen as inherently impossible (Reddy 2005: 134). *Rupantarkami* narratives mark a departure from such ideas and suggest the increasing conceptual possibility of identifying as a woman. As Anik said: "I won't have any regrets in living my life as a woman!"

However, such inspirational implications are offset by multiple forms of hierarchization and vernacularization evident in transsexual or *lingantarkami/ rupantarkami* discourses, which may position *kothi–hijra* forms of identification as socially and linguistically less respectable and culturally more particular relative to the universal, scientific narrative of transsexuality. This happens even as transsexual activists critique existing norms of social respectability—Das, for instance, questions the veneer of respectability claimed by Bengali *bhadra* (genteel) society even as it violently denies human rights to trans people and subjects trans bodies to prurient curiosity (2009: 9–10). Bandyopadhyay, meanwhile, critiques social norms around womanhood such as their reduced familial rights and expectations that they will be physically petite or younger than their husbands (Bandyopadhyay 2021a). However, while contesting older patriarchal norms of respectable womanhood, middle-class transsexual women might establish newer distinctions between their identities and *kothi–hijra* subject positions that do not conform to womanhood—shifting rather than fully dismantling respectability hierarchies. In Das's 2009 essay, she positions *lingantarkami* as a more scientific, decent, and respectable word compared to *kothi–hijra* terminology:

> *Chhakka, moga, dhurani* are neither decent (*shobhan*) nor scientific words . . . such indecent words . . . (are) not respectable (*shommanio*) to any self-conscious (*atma-sachetan*) person . . . there is no usage of the word *lingantarkami* anywhere in Indian society or history. Everywhere, *bijatiyo* (outlandish) words like *chhakka, moga* or *hijra* are used. (Das 2009: 9)

This excerpt conflates pejorative ascriptions like *chhakka* (roughly, fag/sissy) with self-designations such as *dhurani* and *hijra*, paralleling the gay dismissal of these idioms as vulgar slang seen previously. It reads the historical absence of *lingantarkami* identity in India as a sociocultural lack, eliding *kothi–hijra* histories and effectively consigning them to a lack of "self-consciousness" for using supposedly pejorative designations. Simultaneously, the Sanskritic Bengali word *lingantarkami* is positioned as more respectable. This presages the tendency of transgender women dissociating from the stigma of *hijra* identity in the 2010s (Mount 2020).

But this is not only a respectability hierarchy. In contrast to *hijra* or *dhurani*, Das implicitly positions *lingantarkami* as a more "scientific" term befitting a "self-conscious" person (2009: 9). This suggests an ontological hierarchy wherein transsexual or *lingantarkami* putatively describes one's state of being more scientifically than *hijra* or *dhurani*. This idea converges with a contrasting tendency. While Das distinguishes the *lingantarkami* from the *hijra*, others subsume *hijras* under the transsexual category, seeing transsexuality as a deeper ontological reality that *hijras* or *kothis* express in culturally contingent ways. In Majumdar and Basu's text, *hijras* who elect emasculation are seen as transsexuals who "dream of becoming complete females" but cannot express their underlying femaleness as fully as transsexuals in "developed countries" with better surgical options (1997: 43). The gloss of some *hijras* as psychologically transsexual universalizes the biomedical transition narrative as a neutral, scientific reference frame as per which they are seen as unfulfilled transsexual women—combining logics of distinction and subsumption by placing *hijras* within the transsexual category but seeing them as less fully realized transsexuals.

Unlike the overt valuation of social respect in *kodi–bheli* hierarchies, the hierarchy of *shomman* (respect) thus may be refigured in *lingantarkami* or *rupantarkami* discourse in terms of an abstract "scientific" ontology and buttressed by linguistic hierarchy (Sanskritic Bengali words like *lingantarkami* vs. *dhurani* or *hijra*). While we saw in Chapter 3 how *hijras* and *kothis* understand womanhood as circumscribed by codes of *shomman* and hence as a *social* category, here, womanhood assumes a neutral ontological character rooted in psychology or brain sex, but is implicitly positioned within culturally specific hierarchies in being more *shommanio* (respectable) than *hijra* or *dhurani*. The scientific ontology of transsexualism thus serves as a universalized framework that facilitates—by scientifically justifying—identification with culturally located forms of womanhood. Transsexual discourse in Bengali, a "regional" language, aids trans globalization not only by recasting the Western transsexual in regionally meaningful (albeit hierarchical) terms but by seeking to universalize its particular ontology of the transsexual (*lingantarkami* or *rupantarkami*) as scientific. This is thus a multicentered form of transnationalism that, while universalizing the transsexual and *lingantarkami*, vernacularizes *hijra–kothi* discourses as culturally particular and/or linguistically less respectable forms of articulation relative to the formal, scientific discourse of transsexuality—rather than just a universalization of "first world" categories that several scholars critique (Billard and Nesfield 2020; Chatterjee 2018).

Meanwhile, Anglophone NGO discourse, following transnational tendencies, gradually starts using transgender (rather than transsexual) as an umbrella term. Initial descriptions of the transgender as an "umbrella" in some HST documents serve to widen it from just a moniker for *hijras* to include female-attired *kothis*, without any mention of non-*hijra* trans women or men (HST 2004b). A media article on trans activism similarly states: "The transgender community in India (is) represented largely by *hijras* and *kothis*" (Venkat 2008). Later, however, the "umbrella" shifts from this referential anchoring in *hijra–kothi* communities to not only include binary trans people but even prioritize transsexuality as the default model of transgender identity. A 2007 HST report commissioned by DFID (UK) and authored by non-trans health experts defines transgender thus:

> An umbrella term to mean those who defy rigid, binary gender constructions. . . . Transgender persons usually live full or part time in the gender role opposite to the one in which they were born. In contemporary usage, "transgender" has become an umbrella term . . . (for) a wide range of identities . . . including . . . pre-operative, post-operative and non-operative transsexual people; and male or female cross-dressers. . . . A male-to-female

transgender person is referred to as "transgender woman" and a female-to-male transgender person is referred to as "transgender man." (HST 2007: 8)

Despite referencing a "range" of identities beyond "rigid, binary gender constructions," the default ("usual") is established as binary identification with the "opposite" gender. The same page later describes transsexual as encompassing "male-to-female and female-to-male transsexuals," thus evincing a close parallel between the definition of trans women and men and the linear transition narrative of transsexuality, although the fleeting mention of "non-operative" transsexuals briefly suggests the possibility of trans identification without physical transition. Further, while the aforementioned *hijra* activist Famila had cautioned against equating all *hijras* with transsexual womanhood, the report glosses *hijras* as the Indian "equivalent of transgender/transsexual (male-to-female) persons," thus not only conflating transgender, transsexual, and *hijra* and eliding gender/sexual diversity among *hijras*, but also, like some Bengali authors, positioning *hijra* as a particular cultural expression of a universal transsexuality (HST 2007: 7).

This tendency is developed further in a 2009 report on transgender communities in eastern India based on a community meeting organized by the NGO SAATHII (Solidarity and Action against the HIV Infection in India) and funded by the United Nations Development Programme (UNDP), which I discuss in more depth in Chapter 6. Partly based on inputs by Kolkata-based trans activists (including Das), this report again defines transgender as a broad umbrella, but—quoting the above definition almost verbatim—says trans persons "usually live . . . in the gender role opposite to the one in which they are born" (SAATHII 2009: 17). The definition describes *kothi* and *dhurani* as "local names" for transgender (ibid.). In effect if not intent, this erases and even reverses the translocal scale and usage of these terms, rescaling and vernacularizing them as local, culturally particular expressions for a universalized transgender category modeled closely on binary transsexuality. This unites hierarchies of scale (local terms vs. trans as implicitly global) and ontology (such categories as particular forms of universal trans ontology). The participation of activists like Das in this vernacularizing process again suggests that this is not subsumption under a Western or Anglophone universal, but rather, under a multicentered transnational transgender discourse buttressed regionally by metropolitan activist articulations of *rupantarkami*/trans identity.

Further, paralleling the positioning of trans as a transnational, universal, and ontologically deeper category than *hijra/kothi*, there happens what may be termed a de-ontologization of the *hijra*—the dismissal of *hijra* as a possible ontological gender/sexual identity.[3] The SAATHII report states: "A few transgender persons also believe in a traditional culture known as *hijra* . . . a historical cult with its own hierarchical social system," both eliding the contemporary dynamicity of *hijra* identities beyond the "traditional" *gharanas* and positioning all *hijras* as basically transgender (SAATHII 2009: 17).[4] Going further, many middle-class trans people reformulate *hijra* as a "profession" of some trans people rather than a gender identity at all, which helps them to protest their social association with the term. In an interview in 2011, a dominant-caste transgender person from Kolkata told me: "Many see my cross-dressed pictures on Facebook and call me *hijra*—I tell them, *hijra* is a specific profession!" Bose, the trans dancer mentioned earlier, says, "Due to . . . the lack of education, people . . . call transgender people as *hijra*. But this '*hijra*' term is not an identity for these people, it is just a profession" ("15 April Ashe" 2018). While, as Reddy (2005) demonstrates, *hijra* identities have multiple dimensions beyond gender, such statements reduce *hijra* identity to only a profession, evacuating gendered difference as a significant constituent. Further, they reinforce a universal-particular hierarchy wherein *hijra* is at best a particular identity of some transgender people, and at worst, not a valid gender identity at all.

Bandyopadhyay herself regards *hijra* as a professional identity adopted by some trans women due to both social discrimination that restricts occupational options and internal *hijra* hierarchies that prevent initiates from leaving. In a public Facebook post celebrating a younger transgender woman who like her successfully became a professor, Bandyopadhyay says such stories show how "trans women are wrongfully forced to remain in a grotesque profession" despite their talents (Bandyopadhyay 2022). In another public post, Bandyopadhyay laments that there are still *hijras* standing like "*bibheeshika*" (horrors) at traffic signals of Kolkata despite increasing options for surgical "body correction," and faults the "professional sexual politics" of *hijra* leaders for preventing *hijras* from accessing gender-affirming treatments so that they are compelled to continue the profession (Bandyopadhyay 2021b). While trans women like herself are associated with anatomical fulfillment and middle-class professional success, *hijra* contrastingly becomes an abject condition to which transgender people are reduced, preventing the realization of their full potential as transgender women both anatomically and professionally. This extends the earlier depiction of *hijras* as unfulfilled transsexuals (Majumdar and Basu 1997: 43).

Rupantarkami *versus* Rupantorito: *Linear Trajectories and Hierarchies*

Beyond reductive interpretations of *hijra* identity, the binary transsexual model may also be used to subordinate or invalidate other narratives of interiority, embodiment, and identification—even elite ones. In a study of middle-class trans women's narratives in Kolkata, Katherine Ewing and Baishakhi Banerjee Taylor note that despite the prominence of the transgender model that assumes a fixed inner self, elite trans women sometimes evoke "Hindu traditions of gender fluidity," such as the aforementioned devotional traditions where devotees assume feminine personas, to articulate shifting or fluid senses of gender that create inconsistencies in their otherwise fixed, binary narratives of identity (Ewing and Taylor 2018: 175–204). Some public figures like the prominent filmmaker Rituparno Ghosh take this tendency beyond occasional departures from stable identities to foreground their gender ambiguity and in-betweenness in films and interviews (Ewing and Taylor 2018: 195–200). Indeed, Ghosh variably positioned themselves as a feminine homosexual male and as a third gender in the media (Dutta 2015).

While such tendencies diversify gender-variant narratives in the Bengali cultural sphere, some trans women try to contain such disruptions and fold such figures back into a binary transitional narrative. After Ghosh's death from cardiac failure in 2013, a fictionalized dialogue between Bandyopadhyay and Ghosh was published in *Abomanob*, a magazine edited by Bandyopadhyay, where Bandyopadhyay states that people like Ghosh who identify as a "third sex" and wish to combine their "*nari mon*" (woman's *mon*) with their "*purush shorir*" (male body) are denying their "*ontorer shotyo*" or inner truth (Chattopadhyay 2014: 18). Bandyopadhyay attributes Ghosh's death to the alleged repression of their true self: "You too would not have died, Ritu, had you become a woman through . . . sex reassignment" (Chattopadhyay 2014: 20).

Others extend the imposition of transsexual ontology to people beyond Ghosh. Bose, the aforementioned dancer, said in her 2018 interview that she planned to "completely transition into a woman," and added: "Some people nurture their *nari shotta* (woman's being) in their *monon* (thinking, subjectivity) . . . while remaining within a male body due to the fear of society . . . others have the courage to change their body" ("15 April Ashe" 2018). Social pressures are thus placed in a dichotomous relation to interiorized femininity in the *monon* (a derivative of *mon*), belying the diverse relations between social influences and interiority or desire explored earlier. Non-transitioning people are cast as repressed, unable to realize their true selves. This narrative thus generalizes a fixed ontology of the *mon* and its relation to embodied transition, which potentially elides the variable understandings of *mon* and interiority in *kothi–hijra* communities—the *mon* may be variably stable or shifting and even a stable internal femininity need not demand linear transition.

Paralleling such elisions of diverse senses of interiority, the discourse of linear male-to-female transition and attaining "complete" womanhood might elide the variable non/linear expressions of femininity within *kothi–hijra* communities. Dipa is a middle-class, Brahmin trans woman who also participates within *kothi* community networks in south Kolkata. As she explained in a conversation in 2014: "Earlier, we knew only *kothi*, our *concept* was that we were all *kothi*; later, we learnt what TG (transgender) is!" Dipa referred to herself as both *kothi* and TG, projecting both terms onto each other—for instance, she once asked me detailed questions about "*kothis* in America," wanting to know how US trans people lived. Paralleling her universalization of the *kothi*, she also saw TG as a term applicable to *kothis* like herself. As she once explained to me, "initially, we thought that *transgender* is simply the English for *hijra*!" She then realized that "we are also TG." She regarded certain elements of transgender narratives as common to all *kothis*—for example, in a 2014 conversation, she asserted that all *kothis*, if given the chance, would want to wear *satra* (female attire), thus generalizing the need for sartorial transition.

While such projections of transgender onto the *kothi* facilitate its adoption within these communities and its expansion beyond metropolitan activist circles, they also potentially accentuate linear understandings of transition over non/linear articulations of *bhel* and *pon*. In 2014, I accompanied Dipa and her friends on a trip to Coochbehar, where Dipa derisively remarked that unlike Kolkata, most *kothis* there "cannot be told apart from *parikhs*." Dipa and her friends asked the activist Sumi why there were so few "*bheli kothis*" in rural Coochbehar and interpreted the lack of feminine-attired *kothis* as an effect of rural conservatism and repression, missing the ways in which the *kodi* (male-attired) *kothis* or *metis* there—such as Suresh and Subesh, the working-class *metis* we met in previous chapters—were already behaviorally *bheli* and publicly feminine. One *kothi/meti*, who desired to wear female attire but faced family opposition, accepted their narrative, telling them during a conversation: "We are the same in the *mon*, but you express yourselves freely by wearing *sarees*, while we are hidden due to the fear of society!" The generalization of *kodi kothis* (the "we") as hidden potentially erases the varied agential negotiations with situational pressures evident among male-attired *kothis*, including *kodi–bheli* alternations or overlaps. The *mon* here becomes the site of an underlying ontological sameness whose expression is charted along a linear teleology of repression to liberation and spatially mapped onto an urban–rural divide—urban trans/*kothi* figures like Dipa become positioned as liberated in contrast to a generalized rural hiddenness.

However, others contested the conflation of *kodi* status and hiddenness. During a subsequent community gathering, Suresh and Subesh compared themselves to the Kolkata-based trans women. Subesh remarked: "(just as) you are doing *bhel* by wearing *sarees*, we are doing *bhel* by putting flowers in our hair!" By combining *kodi* attire with *bheli* adornments (flowers), they claimed *bhel*, flamboyant or overt femininity, as a common property: only the mode of *bhel* varied. Such uses of *bhel* reassert the nonlinearity of *kothi* feminine expression against the generalized imposition of a linear transitional trajectory from *rupantarkami* to *rupantorito* (transformed) or *kodi* to *bheli*—suggesting a nonlinear equality that counters implicit hierarchies between liberated urban and repressed rural subjects.

While delegitimizing *kodi* femininities, transsexual/*rupantarkami* discourse may establish normative linear trajectories of embodied feminization even for people who transition sartorially. Sunita is a young, educated trans woman, estranged from her middle-class family, who entered *kothi* circles at Nadia in the mid-2010s through contacts with *kothis* in her area and later started identifying as transgender and wearing feminine attire. In 2019, she was invited to a Bengali TV show to share her journey as a trans graduate student. However, later, she shared with me that she had a "terrible experience" there: "In the make-up room, someone asked me, are you *rupantarkami* or *rupantorito*? I said *rupantarkami* . . . then I overheard the anchor remarking, she's actually still a boy, not *rupantorito*! . . . they were all concerned whether I still had a penis or vagina!" The distinction between *rupantarkami* (transition-desiring) and *rupantorito* (transformed) thus not only reinforces a linear transitional pathway but also fosters discriminatory and intrusive hierarchies such that one may still be mapped as a "boy" despite sartorial femininity. Sunita thus averred that either everyone should be called *rupantarkami* irrespective of transition, or that an alternative Bengali term should be found that does not connote anatomical status—suggesting contestations of biologically essentialist deployments of transsexual discourse that the next chapter explores further.

Even anatomical transition may be linearly measured as per degree of aesthetic feminization, establishing desirable outcomes according to normative bodily ideals. In a 2012 event organized by a CBO in Kolkata, a trans woman working with an NGO that facilitated access to SRS stated: "Those who want to become complete (*shompurno*), I help them to become complete." In a subsequent workshop, she showed pictures of transitions she deemed successful and those less so: "See, this is an unfortunate case, this patient did only six months of hormone therapy and wanted to have breast implantation done, so we were unable to do anything more." In addition to the conflation of "completeness" with anatomical transition, the marking of bodies through the language of inadequacy or lack reinforces a notion of bodily femininity as a linearly measurable acquisition.

Such hierarchical linearities are variably contested or hegemonically accepted by *kothis*. Ajit, who as mentioned earlier attributed her desire to grow longer hair to *shokh* (fancy) rather than an internal womanhood, was very critical of the narrative of becoming "complete" through SRS. During a discussion at the DIC at Ranaghat in 2012, she protested the imputation that non-transitioned *kothis* were not complete: "What, are we incomplete?" Alluding to her mixed *kodi–bheli* presentation, she added: "To me, this is my completeness (*shompurnota*)!"

Others, however, were more affected by external pressures for transition as transsexual discourse disseminated more widely in community spaces and larger society in the 2010s. I met Roshni, a Dalit *kothi* from a Kolkata slum, in a DIC of the MANAS Bangla network where she worked as low-tier staff in their HIV project while doing sex work on the side. Roshni wore *bheli* dress occasionally, and in 2010, told me that she desired physical transition inconsistently: "this desire works in me 50% of the time." However, she also switched between attires and was sexually versatile or *dupli*, penetrating her male clients if they wanted it. Like her friend Srijan whom we met in the previous chapter, she said her clients could get her in any *pon* (sartorial mode) that they wanted. However, in 2012, she narrated an incident to me when some local men commented on her inconsistent use of padded bras: "Some neighborhood guys made fun of me, saying, one day I have breasts, another day I don't . . . I felt really bad." She was also shamed for her *dupli* sexual behavior by other feminine-attired *kothis* in the DIC. As such experiences accumulated, she seemed to feel more consistent dysphoria, and in 2013, she asked me to help with raising money for her "*sex change operation*," so that she could "fulfill (her) dream of becoming a woman"—something she had never mentioned previously. Here, the articulation of sartorial switching through the *kothi* idiom of *pon* gives way to the desire for a more socially legible womanhood in line with *rupantarkami* discourse.

Predictably, gender intersects with class and caste in structuring these aspirational trajectories. Emergent technologies of "sex reassignment" may be used to assert a sense of superiority to *hijras* who undergo less expensive procedures of *chhibrano* (emasculation). As a middle-class trans and *kothi*-identified person in Kolkata told me in 2014: "I will never do *chhibrano* . . . God! I am saving one *lakh* (hundred thousand) rupees so that I can go to Singapore for SRS. . . . I don't want to be like these *hijras*!"

However, such tendencies do not necessarily translate into a binary divide or hierarchy between trans people and *hijras*, who gradually access emerging technologies and discourses. Sweety, a *kothi* from Kalyani who joined a *hijra* household in the national capital of Delhi in the early 2010s, often boasted to her *kothi* friends during her visits home that *hijras* in Delhi looked like female models, wore branded clothes, and underwent expensive breast augmentation surgeries—although she had initially undergone emasculation through an illicit doctor, her *guru* later helped her get breast implants at a clinic. In comparison to Delhi *hijras*, Sweety derided local small-town *hijras* as "uncultured." Sweety advised her *kothi* friends that they should not join *hijra* lineages unless they were like her elite *gharana*: "If you want to become a *hijra*, become a *hijra* like me! Otherwise, there's no profit (*labh*) in *chhibrano!*" While this extends the transgender–*hijra* divide into an internal hierarchy between *hijras* based on embodiment and class performance, Sweety's pragmatic approach to transition—measuring *chhibrano* in terms of worldly gain, which parallels how some *hijras* cite economic motivations for transition—also marks a shift relative to *rupantarkami* discourse where transition is the realization of a prefixed internal essence.

Conclusion

The aforementioned contestations and shifts suggest that early articulations of transgender and *rupantarkami* identities in Bengali and Indian activist and NGO discourse, closely based on a biomedically informed and binary model of transsexuality, do not acquire absolute dominance or hegemony. Indeed, as the subsequent chapters chart, some key elements of these discourses—such as the emphasis on a linear anatomical transition and distinctions based on degree of transition—are contested not only by marginalized sections of *kothi–hijra* communities but also by middle-class activists and communities during the 2010s. Other features, such as the emphasis on a deeply rooted consistent gendered essence, are not discarded but reconfigured into newer understandings of transgender and genderqueer identity—often emphasizing self-determination over anatomy—that acquire legibility in activist and legal domains, especially after activist challenges to the state's initial attempts at defining and regulating transgender identities.

The hierarchies of ontology and scale related to transgender, however, prove to be durable and the processes of the resignification and rearticulation of transgender by people in *kothi–hijra* communities are repeatedly circumscribed by the continual reestablishment of normative senses of transgender—particularly ones that neatly distinguish it from sexual identities like MSM and gay—that may elide or delegitimize *kothi–hijra* subject positions or practices. The processes of vernacularization studied here are thus subsequently renegotiated on a changing activist and legal terrain.

Chapter 5

REFASHIONING TRANSGENDER

PLURALIZATION AND RE-VERNACULARIZATION

One summer evening in 2010, I had gathered with a group of *kothi* friends in the tiny, rented apartment of Kanchana at Berhampore, Murshidabad. While chatting, Kanchana shared her recent experience of participating in a transgender beauty contest organized by an NGO in a city of North Bengal, where she represented the CBO Sangram—such events, while still new, were becoming increasingly common. Kanchana recalled: "There, they (the organizers) told me what to say. . . . When the judges asked me who I was, I said, I am a woman imprisoned in the cage named a man's body! Everyone clapped so much!" Kanchana demonstrated her delivery of this coached dialogue with a little pirouette and a swish of the arms—gestures more evocative of the consciously performative femininity of *bhel* than the serious pathos of the wrong body narrative. She continued: "Then I said, if a *hijra* could change the story of the Mahabharata, then why don't we have a place of *shomman* (respect) in today's society?" She was referring to Shikhandi, a gender-variant character in the ancient Indian epic Mahabharata who dramatically altered the course of its central war and is sometimes claimed as a precursor to *hijras* (Nagar and DasGupta 2015).

Kanchana's account suggests the multiple frameworks through which "transgender" is mediated and resignified as it increasingly becomes a public identity in the 2010s. While the model of binary womanhood and linear male-to-female transition in *rupantarkami* discourse serves as a standardized narrative that *kothis* are coached to repeat, Kanchana's actual performance of it is more evocative of *kothi* practices like *bhel*. Further, the figure of a separate or third gender, often connected to *hijra* identity and mythic precursors, also serves as a competing template for transgender identity that, as we shall see, increasingly gains prominence alongside and sometimes in tension with the binary transsexual narrative in NGO and state/legal discourse. A woman who later becomes a man, Shikhandi may be regarded as a "half woman" rather than a woman in the wrong body (Nagar and DasGupta 2015: 436). On occasions detailed later, Kanchana variously claimed that she was transgender, *kothi* and/or *hijra*—and not a woman—when asked by peers to transition or behave in normatively womanly ways. While this suggests how transgender may be resignified as a separate gender rather than as a binary gender identity expressed through linear transition, Kanchana was also drawn to the new forms of embodiment exemplified by transgender women. While describing the beauty contest, Kanchana shared how beautiful some trans women activists looked at the event. Already wearing feminine attire consistently, Kanchana later transitioned physically; during this process, she sometimes said she was becoming a woman and at other times continued identifying as a separate gender.

Kanchana's narrative unfolds in the context of the rising prominence of transgender identity and rights within and beyond the NGO and HIV sector. While pioneering activists like Ashok Row Kavi and Shivananda Khan identified as gay and/or MSM, in the late 2000s, transgender activists such as Laxmi Narayan Tripathi formed transgender- and *hijra*-led organizations and began making their voices heard in meetings organized by funders and development agencies such as the UNDP, which assisted the Indian state with implementing its NACP (UNDP 2008).[1] Like other prominent public trans figures within this pioneering generation such as Manobi Bandyopadhyay, Tripathi is also dominant caste—indeed, Brahmin (Tripathi 2015). However, unlike trans women like Bandyopadhyay, Tripathi identifies as *hijra* and as a third or separate gender (TedX 2010).

Alongside increasing trans activism and visibility, the long history of campaigning for governmental recognition by *hijras*, such as a long-standing demand to be not counted as male in government documents and newer demands for welfare provisions, also saw some results (Venkat 2008). In South India, *aravanis*, a group with similar kinship structures and rituals as lineage-based *hijras* who were also mapped as a "vulnerable group" for HIV transmission, used this status to mobilize "to demand their rights" and campaigned both HIV-focused NGOs and the Tamil Nadu state government to address human rights abuses against them, resulting in the government forming an Aravani Welfare Board in 2008 (Venkat 2008). Simultaneously, there was a growing sense among activists and agencies like UNDP that despite the inclusion of transgender within the MSM population in the NACP-III, more specific focus on transgender and *hijra* groups was needed. In 2008, UNDP organized a "national stakeholder consultation" which invited activists from various urban NGOs to assess the "missing pieces" within national HIV policy (UNDP 2008: 4–6). Activists pointed out the lack of specific data regarding the HIV-related risks faced by "TG" (transgender) populations and that HIV interventions, while reaching *kothis*, were reaching a limited number of *hijras* (UNDP 2008: 10–17). However, some participants still considered "TG" as an MSM subgroup. The activist Ashok Row Kavi stated: "Many males, such as eunuchs . . . don't consider themselves men. Advocacy activities . . . should be centered on 'males' who have sex with males rather than 'men.' . . . Transgenders (TG) are a vital part of the picture but NACO has not as yet determined . . . the number of TGs that are most at risk" (UNDP 2008: 10). This sought to reframe MSM more inclusively, locating "TGs" as an understudied group among MSM. This also suggests that an early logic for considering transgender as a distinct subcategory was the drive for gathering more specific and finely graded data on populations at risk for HIV, a tendency predating the focus on transgender (Cohen 2005: 293).

Meanwhile, transgender activists in the consultation urged greater attention to both the "HIV specific needs of TG groups" and to issues beyond HIV such as stigma, discrimination, welfare, and rights (UNDP 2008: 21). Some were dissatisfied with the biologically essentialist subsumption of transgender as a "male" group under MSM. Sharmila, a dominant-caste, middle-class transgender activist and founder of a Kolkata-based CBO who attended the consultation, told me in an interview later in 2010: "I would never call myself male or wish to come under MSM!" In that regard, Tamil Nadu offered a promising example of recognition. Agniva Lahiri, a senior trans-identified activist from MANAS Bangla, lauded the "initiatives undertaken by the Tamil Nadu State government for *hijras* (known as *aravanis* there)" including their recognition of "TGs as a separate gender, at least when seeking government assistance" and efforts to increase their "employment opportunities" (UNDP 2008: 19). Subsequently, development agencies and the Indian state's HIV-control bodies began providing funding for transgender community meetings to map their needs and related events like beauty contests, which presaged the establishment of transgender-focused targeted interventions for HIV prevention in the 2010s.

In that context, this chapter examines contestations and resignifications of the transgender category as it becomes a locus of activist efforts for rights and recognition and gains increased attention from NGOs, funders, and the state, moving beyond—but never entirely superseding—its initial association with biomedical understandings of transsexuality. As transgender disseminates through NGOs and the media, it increasingly intersects with *kothi–hijra* discourses and lifeworlds and is variously claimed and rearticulated by people from these communities, similar to how the term may be used elsewhere in India and the world in ways that exceed its dominant Western senses (Hegarty 2022: 5; Mohan 2013: 30). Indeed, *kothi–hijra* rearticulations may even contest elite Indian significations of transgender identity. Building on fractures and multiplicities within elite transgender discourse, such diverse articulations of transgender mark a freer exchange between various layers of discourse that potentially destabilizes divisions between local, regional, and transnational levels of scale. Simultaneously, contestations emerge around models of rights, with some elite activists evoking binary, respectable transgender womanhood to discipline *kothi–hijra* forms of expression into legitimized models of formal equality, civility, and citizenship, while people from these communities claim transgender identity in ways that contest such disciplining and demand substantive forms of equality—a demand bolstered by the rise of Dalit transgender activism in the 2010s (Banu 2018; Vidya 2013).

However, other tendencies reestablish patterns of vernacularization and delimit institutionally recognized forms of transgender—including an ascendant discourse of third gender identity anchored in a selective understanding of *hijra* subjectivity and authenticity, which potentially overrides *kothi* and non-*gharana hijra* articulations of transgender that differ from this model. Further, as the next chapter shows, the important activist critique of the subsumption of all trans feminine people under MSM gradually prompts an equally reductive separation between MSM and TG categories in NGO and state discourses without concession for potential overlaps, which may elide *kothi/hijra* articulations of transgender that traverse such categorical divides.

Refashioning Transgender

Sumit is a dance teacher from a lower middle-class family in Ranaghat. Bullied for her femininity in high school, Sumit found a classmate like her who knew the *dhurani/kothi* mother figure Bikash, and introduced Sumit to what she described as the *"dhurani* club" that gathered at Bikash's house. Becoming Bikash's daughter around 2009, she subsequently started visiting the DIC at Ranaghat, where she met Kash, a dancer who (unlike Sumit) wore feminine attire and frequented Manas Bangla's DICs in Kolkata where she met transgender activists. Exposed to trans discourse through such friends, Sumit described herself using the common *rupantarkami* trope of an interiorized woman's *shotta* (being) inside a man's *shorir* (body), but with significant twists. In an interview in 2014, she told me:

> We have a separate kind of being (*alada shotta*). I carry a man's body (*purusher deho*) which has a woman's being (*nari shotta*); all my feelings, desires, love, are like women (*meyeder moton*). . . . Our inside (*bhetor*) is like women, but the outside is a male body . . . (but) I don't like dressing up in female attire; I don't have that *nesha* (intoxication) anymore! Sometimes I dress up a little, that's enough for me!

For Sumit, the body-interiority duality did not imply a contradiction demanding resolution through transition. Rather, the "man's body" and "woman's being" become coexisting components of a subject position distinct (*alada*) from men and women, which defies Manobi Bandyopadhyay's insistence that the woman's *mon* and male body cannot be reconciled (Chattopadhyay 2014: 18). But Sumit also articulates the interior (*bhetor*) as "like women" rather than a woman's self per se—a common expression in *kothi–hijra* narratives, as we have seen. Sumit combines this phrasing with the formal, Sanskritic Bengali term *nari shotta* used in *rupantarkami* narratives, where it often describes a total interiorized identification with womanhood ("15 April Ashe" 2018). As Katyal shows regarding sexual desire, apparently contrasting understandings of selfhood may coexist in the same narrative, rather than identitarian frameworks superseding other discourses (2010: 28). Whether her interior is "like women" or harbors the *nari shotta*, it does not imply an identity as a woman or the disavowal of bodily maleness. Further, Sumit's interiorized femininity contrasts with her shifting desire for female attire—expressed as a fluctuating *nesha* (intoxication, addiction). Interiority, while evoked, is not the essential truth or primary determinant of identity—her overall selfhood is composite, encompassing male embodiment, feminine interiority, and changeable desires.

Thus, as transgender and *rupantarkami* tropes enter *kothi-hijra* narratives, they may be transformed through intersections and translations with other ways of articulating interiority and embodiment prevalent in such communities—including idioms like *bhel* and *pon*. Borsha, a middle-class college student who usually wore male attire, temporarily worked as a volunteer at a Manas Bangla DIC in Kolkata. When I first met them at the DIC in 2011, they narrated that they were part of a "*kothimahal*" or *kothi* circle in north Kolkata. Later, in a 2012 interview, they told me: "I have understood the *transgender concept* from the trainer here; though I am a *chhele* (male) in body, in my *mon*, I feel myself as a woman." Borsha referred to trainings of juniors conducted by senior staff—by 2011, "transgender" had entered the terminology taught at such trainings. While evoking NGO language, they then used the language of likeness to elaborate further: "I am male in body, but like behaving like *hijras* for my pleasure." They further said that they liked doing *kolla*—flamboyant, hyperfeminine behavior akin to *bhel*—when with other *kothis*. The received "transgender concept" is thus transformed through the common idiom of likeness (behaving like *hijras*) and distanced from the referent of womanhood. Further, behavioral pleasure in a situational context—doing *kolla* in *kothi/hijra* company—is emphasized over the realization of an identitarian essence through transition. As they said: "What I have outside isn't the issue; I am *transgender*. If someone changes something outside, like making breasts, that is *transsexual*." Borsha thus resists the conflation of transgender and transsexual in some Bengali and Anglophone trans discourse—the importance of external transition to identity is downplayed relative to feelings and being transgender is refashioned as a composite of the feminized *mon* and the male body. Borsha both resignifies transgender using *kothi-hijra* expressions and draws on multiplicity *within* Anglophone discourse (the transgender–transsexual distinction) to articulate a selfhood distinct from dominant versions of transgender or *rupantarkami* identity. Both Borsha's and Sumit's narratives demonstrate a freer negotiation between different discourses relative to the scalar hierarchies of vernacularization that cast *kothi/hijra* as local/particular iterations of the global transgender, suggesting what Mary Pat Brady terms a "queer horizontality" that enables richer connections across locations, rather than a "verticality" that prioritizes discourses positioned at higher global/cosmopolitan scales (2022: 152).

Significantly, Borsha also sometimes designated themselves as gay. One afternoon at the DIC in 2011, they narrated to all of us present how they recently came out in their college, prompted by speculation regarding their non-masculine attire: "I wear narrow jeans to college, so they talk about me behind my back; so, I told them I am *gay*, that is my *orientation*." Later, in the 2012 interview, they told me: "You may say I am *gay*, but *gay* men who take dominant roles in sex, they call me derogatory names for *transgender* people." This marked an awareness of their difference from normatively masculine gay men, but Borsha did not totally separate themselves from gay identity. During a subsequent group discussion at the DIC, Borsha mentioned that their "sexual identity" was gay, while the trainer moderating the discussion described transgender as an "umbrella term" that could include some gay males and *meyeli chhele* (feminine males). Such overlap between the transgender umbrella and some gay males would increasingly be erased in NGO and state discourse, as discussed in the next chapter.

For *kothis* who do identify with a transitional model of transgender, unstable understandings of interiority and desire may mix with characteristic tropes of trans discourse. Sonia, the Kolkata-based activist whom we briefly met in Chapter 3, started to identify as transgender from around 2009 onward, sartorially transitioned from *kodi* to *bheli*, and eventually decided upon gender-affirmative surgery. In 2014, I spent a summer afternoon with her and *kothi* staff members at her CBO office, and the conversation came around to her transition. Interestingly, she explained her desire for genital surgery as per a changeable model of selfhood: "Now what has happened, by repeatedly thinking of myself as a woman (*nijeke meye mone kore kore*), it's like I have lost use of the penis. Now, I don't even ejaculate once in ten days, if I do I feel weak, I don't really want to masturbate . . . so keeping the penis is no longer of any use to me!" Here, similar to some *kothi* narratives, practice rather than a prefixed essence induces a change in her relation to her body, informing her decision to discard an organ that *no longer* has any use rather than having been always inherently irreconcilable.

Such articulations also draw from her understanding of *kodi–bheli* transition. As mentioned in the third chapter, she had once averred that *kothis* who became sartorially *bheli* could never go back to being *kodi*. However, in another conversation in 2013, she observed that she had seen some *kothis* going back from *bheli* to *kodi* embodiment, thus conceding the possibility of "multidirectional movement" within transness (Chen and Cárdenas 2019: 473). During the aforementioned discussion in 2014, she said: "*Kothis* who will come into *ekdom* TG-*pon* (total TG-mode), wear *satra* (female attire) and all, they will do *chhibrano* (emasculation) for sure!" To illustrate, she specifically mentioned one of her *kothi* staff who consistently wore *satra* as someone who would inevitably choose genital surgery, while she was not sure about the other *kothis*. Her phrase "total TG-*pon*," and her distinction between different *kothi* staff, suggests the possibility of different levels of initiation into being TG. While some *kothis* might change back to *kodi*, the *kothi* who comes into "*ekdom* TG-*pon*" would not be able to resist anatomical change—adopting *satra* consistently seemingly induces an inescapable desire for transition.

Sonia thus rearticulated TG as a *pon*—a mode or manner of being—that, like *kodipon* or *bhelipon*, may be adopted to varying degrees, rather than a prefixed identity. While there seemed to be a threshold of no return, her articulation left open the possibility of partial overlap with TG-ness rather than an inherently fixed transgender selfhood.

Transgender, Not Woman: Different Conceptualizations of a Separate Gender

Sumit and Borsha's rearticulations of *rupantarkami* or transgender happen in the context of the rising public visibility of *hijra* activists who also claim a transgender identity. While, as noted earlier, some *hijra* activists like Famila espoused trans-*hijra* solidarity in the early 2000s, up to the late 2000s, many *hijras* not only saw it as an external term but sometimes even expressed suspicion or hostility toward trans activists (especially Anglophone NGO functionaries) who were seen as more class privileged. This was evident in several NGO-organized consultations or meetings with trans and *hijra* communities. Mondira, a Kolkata-based trans/*kothi* activist who attended a consultation in Bangalore (South India) in 2009, recounted acrimonious exchanges between *hijra* and "TG" (transgender) activists in an interview later that year: "It was a *mar-mar kat-kat* (war-like) situation! *Hijras* were attacking TGs, saying you people are privileged, you take money in our name, and so on!" The accusation of NGO leaders misappropriating funds in the name of vulnerable communities would return many times over the years and signals growing discontent with the hierarchical and often untransparent processes of the NGO sector (Shankar 2017).

However, by the early 2010s, some people were also claiming both trans and *hijra* identity, both due to a subsection of transgender activists who started their work in NGOs and later joined *hijra gharanas* and the efforts of non-*hijra* trans activists to build coalitions with *hijras*. For example, in 2009, Sonia's CBO quit the MANAS Bangla network as they felt they were being kept out of an inner group of organizations within that network and worked to build alliances with some *hijra gurus* in Kolkata to increase the membership of an emergent TG network. Later, in 2010, Sonia triumphantly announced to me: "We spoke to several *hijra* leaders, and they said they have no objection to be grouped as TG with us." In Mumbai, Laxmi Narayan Tripathi, who found community with a group of gay men including the activist Ashok Row Kavi during her youth, gradually realized her difference from these people who despite their effeminacy ultimately regarded themselves as men, joined a *hijra gharana*, and founded the CBO Astitva that started working on *hijra* rights in 2006 (Tripathi 2015). While Sonia continued to identify as transgender and not *hijra*, others like Tripathi claimed both identities.

Such activists may resignify transgender as a separate gender rather than in terms of a binary womanhood or male-to-female transition, as evident in a couple of TedX talks by Tripathi in English. In a 2010 talk, she thanked the Indian state's Election Commission for their recent inclusion of the "other" option, which she saw as a recognition of *hijra* citizenship: "I am now a citizen of this country, because now the Election Commission has given me the right of voting out of the boxes of male and female, putting the box of others" (TedX 2010). In a 2011 talk, she identified *hijras* as a "third sex" and said:

> Eunuch is a horrible word, you know . . . it means a castrated man. . . . I deny my gender to be called as man . . . it's what I want you to call! I do not want to even be a woman . . . See the pathetic condition, what happens to the girl child. . . . Better to be a transgender woman or a *hijra* . . . and . . . enjoy both the sides. (Laxmi 2011)

She later explained "both sides" as the ability to understand both men and women's minds (Laxmi 2011). Tripathi thus expresses a politics of gender self-determination in rejecting "eunuch" for its pejorative connotation of a reduced form of manhood, choosing *hijra* and transgender instead. Simultaneously, "transgender" and even the more specific term "transgender woman" are equated with *hijra* and recast as a separate gender that—while encompassing the knowledge of "both sides"—is categorically neither man nor woman, an "other." Such articulations thus model transgender on a particular logic of *hijra* identification as a third sex/gender, which only partially represents the multifarious *hijra* identities we have encountered earlier.

This move potentially reverses the scalar hierarchies between transgender and *hijra* noted in Chapter 4. Rather than the *hijra* being vernacularized in the sense of being positioned as a local and vernacular variation of the global transgender category, *transgender* is redefined as a third/other gender following a certain understanding of *hijra* identity. This process becomes clearer in Tripathi's autobiography, *Me Hijra, Me Laxmi*, where she describes her advocacy for transgender welfare in meetings with the state government of Maharashtra, in which both Tripathi and state officials understand "transgender" as referring to a "third gender," which, in turn, is equated with the *hijra* (2015: 161–2). Such categorical conflations might be understood as the scalar supersession of the "national" over the "transnational," given that *hijra* is commonly mapped as the quintessential example of Indian "third gender" identity (Cohen 1995: 276). Tripathi temporally projects the *hijra* as part of ancient Indian (particularly Hindu) history by equating Sanskrit categories for gender nonconforming people with the *hijra* (2015: 177). This falls within her larger support for Hindu nationalism (Upadhyay 2020); she emphasizes the relation between Hindu traditions and *hijra* cultures and downplays Islamic influences (Tripathi 2015: 178). Spatially, the *hijra* is mapped as nationally prevalent across India with regional variations: "In Urdu, the hijras are also called *khwaja sara* . . . in Telugu we're called *napunsakudu*, and in Tamil, *aravani* . . . Though the nomenclature differs, the concept is the same everywhere" (2015: 171–2). Such subsumption of varied communities under *hijra* has been critiqued for eliding how South Indian trans communities differ from the North Indian *hijra* figure (Tom and Menon 2021: 41). Thus, even as the transnational transgender is rearticulated in terms of the national *hijra*, this move potentially establishes its own forms of vernacularization by positioning other categories as local/regional variants of the national *hijra* or "third gender"— which, as Chapter 6 shows, is reinforced in some legal discourse that constructs transgender as a "third gender."

Insofar as they gain official sanction, such framings of transgender risk eliding other ways of rearticulating trans as a separate gender. Sumit's *alada shotta*— "separate being"—may seem to be an implicit echo of Tripathi's articulation of transgender as third/other. However, as Cohen notes, "all thirdness is not alike" (1995: 277). Unlike Sumit's everyday presentation in conventionally male attire— dressing up only "a little" sometimes—Tripathi equates the "third gender" position with sartorially feminine hijras who are clearly distinct from feminine men. In her autobiography, she ambiguously vacillates between and sometimes combines the narrative of being trapped in a wrong body and that of being a separate gender: "A hijra is neither a man nor a woman. She is feminine, but not a woman. He is masculine, a male by birth, but not a man either. A hijra's male body is a trap—not just to the hijra . . . who suffocates within it, but to the world in general that wrongly assumes a hijra to be a man" (2015: 40). Later, she says: "Hijras . . . feel they are female. . . . Their social behaviour, which includes dress, hairstyle, make-up, jewellery, etc., is also that of women" (2015: 172). It seems the claim to a categorical gendered separateness is rooted in a combination of natal maleness and a psychological and embodied womanhood, without any overlap with male presentation. While in her youth Tripathi switches between male and female attire and mingles with feminine gay men, the adoption of *hijra* identity requires both ritualized initiation under a *gharana*-based *guru* and gradual transition to consistent sartorial femininity (2015: 46–74). While she emphasizes that *hijras* need not be castrated, she distinguishes "real" *hijras* from "men (who) don saris and pretend to be *hijras*" for income—thus displacing authenticity from anatomy to psychological identity without dismantling fake–real divides (2015: 179).

Her aforementioned espousal of gender self-determination is thus implicitly limited by certain expectations around *hijra* identity, which constrain her framing of transgender as a third gender (Tripathi 2015: 161–2). In an afterword, Tripathi's translator R. Raj Rao additionally reinforces a strong, linear *hijra–kothi* distinction where *kothis* are seen as less overtly feminine, heterosexually married men with secretive double lives while *hijras* are entirely marginalized (2015: 199–200). Overall, this model of a third gender is hinged on both psychological and embodied womanhood, clearly distinct from feminine gay men, and exclusive of male-attired or sartorially switching *kothis*.

An increasing number of *kothis* and *akua* (non-emasculated) or non-*gharana* *hijras* also explicitly articulate transgender as a separate gender, but may express composite subject positions that publicly overlap with embodied maleness, thus contravening both normative models of womanhood and the aforementioned versions of third gender identity that gain legibility in state or NGO discourse.

Consider Rima, the *kothi* from a Dalit family in Kolkata whom we met during our discussion of shifting understandings of *kothi* interiority in Chapter 4. One evening in 2013, I was going home with her and another *kothi* friend after attending a meeting preceding that year's pride walk. Rima had begun identifying as transgender in the early 2010s while still referring to herself as *kothi*, and had recently grown out her hair. Earlier that day, she told me: "I will never go back to being *kodi* (male-attired) again!" That evening, she was wearing women's jeans and a T-shirt she described as "unisex," without the stuffed or padded bras that many *hijras* and *bheli kothis* wear. The other *kothi* good-humoredly teased Rima, who naturally lacked facial hair, remarking: "See, she's beardless, *laharanpon* (woman-like), but *nimai!*" *Mai* is a contemporary Bengali colloquialism or slang for the breast: thus, *ni-mai* means no-breast. To her friend's lighthearted aspersion, Rima replied, smiling: "I'll stay *nimai* only. . . . I'm not a woman, I'm *trans!*" Significantly, *nimai* also has an older, unrelated meaning as a well-known nickname of Chaitanya, the spiritual leader of medieval Bengali Vaishnavism— the branch of *bhakti* (devotional) Hinduism in which, as mentioned earlier, men, even heterosexually married ones, may adopt the role of a female devotee while worshipping the male god Krishna, as Chaitanya himself did (Ewing and Taylor 2018: 189). Rima thus indirectly evoked a form of male feminine expression that has some socioreligious sanction in Bengal. Simultaneously, she used *trans* to mark a subject position that—much like the Ulti expression *laharanpon*—marks a simultaneous likeness to and distinction from womanhood, but is also not the sequestered *hijra* identity of Tripathi's narrative. Rima did not identify as *hijra* and her *nimai* presentation set her visibly apart from *hijras*. As the Kolkata-based activist Raina told me on another occasion, not wearing *dharki* (padded bras) was a telltale way in which people could tell *kothis* apart from *hijras*. This, therefore, was a non-*hijra* casting of transgender as a separate gender.

Others like Kanchana at Berhampore combined *kothi*, *hijra*, and trans identification, seeing all of them as standing for a separate gendered position distinct from womanhood. Although she eventually decided to transition surgically in the mid-2010s, for several years prior, Kanchana seemed content to wear *laharanpon* dress without transitioning. In 2007, I witnessed a conversation between her and a *kothi* friend visiting from Kolkata. The friend was transitioning and suggested that Kanchana, too, should do a "sex change" rather than "going about doing *bhel*," since she would look good as a woman. Sensing her friend's implied derision of her current embodiment and lifestyle relative to womanhood, Kanchana defiantly replied, "No, I'm fine just as I am!" In later years, she expressed this subject position in more clearly identitarian terms. One morning in 2011, I accompanied Anik and Kanchana to a district administration office at Berhampore for some bureaucratic paperwork related to the CBO Sangram. Afterward, we were chatting in the waiting area when Anik casually referred to Kanchana as *meye* (girl/ woman): "*Ai meye* (hey girl), where did you get this dress?" Although Kanchana had performed the dialogue of being a woman in a man's body at the trans beauty contest a few months earlier, in this instance, she immediately retorted: "I am not *meye*—I'm *kothi*, I'm *chhibri*, TG!" Anik smiled and went silent.

Kanchana's retort placed TG as contiguous with both *kothi* and *chhibri* (*hijra*) but distinct from woman; TG thus became another name for the overlapping space between *kothi* and *hijra* identities that many sartorially feminine people like her already inhabited, as seen in previous chapters. Kanchana described her attire and presentation sometimes as *laharanpon* (woman-mode) and sometimes as *chhibripon* (*hijra*-mode), and in 2013, a *kothi* visiting Berhampore from Kolkata remarked to me that although Kanchana was the most *lahari* (womanlike) of all *kothis* in Berhampore, she did not wish to present herself as a woman—rather, "she wants to be seen as a *hijra*." This was in reference to her use of *hijra*-like behavior such as performing *thikri* (the clap) and doing *bila*, aggressive behavior, especially with men who harassed her. In 2012, Kanchana even became the disciple of a *hijra* from a different town, although she lived separately, and their connection tapered off after a while. But she also disrupted the typical *hijra* figure. One evening in 2012, I met up with Kanchana and we walked around her neighborhood as she freely flirted with men on the roadside. She wore women's jeans with a "unisex" T-shirt, and at one point, remarked to me: "Tomorrow, I'll have fun, I'll go out wearing breasts (i.e., padded bras)! People in the neighborhood remark how I have breasts one day and another day I don't; I say—that is *pakkipon!*" *Pakkipon* in Ulti denotes a way of being *pakki* (ripe, mature)—able to navigate the world cleverly and strategically. However, as seen in Chapter 1, local *hijra gurus* vehemently derided such inconsistent presentation as *kachchi-pakki*—something that was making *kachchi* (making unripe, spoiling) the social image they had ripened or cultivated. In claiming her inconsistent use of "breasts" as *pakkipon*, Kanchana contradicted *hijra* conceptions of how to be *pakki* in the world.

That year, she also started traveling to Kolkata regularly to avail laser treatment for facial hair reduction, following the example of several transgender women she had met in NGO events, and sometimes said that she would "become a woman" in a few years. Yet, after a session to which I accompanied her, we were traveling back on public transport when she remarked that taking laser treatments meant that she had to shave rather than pluck out remaining facial hair, which caused a residual "greenness" or beard shadow for some days. She then shrugged it off: "It doesn't matter if *hijras* have a little greenness!" Even as womanhood gradually seemed desirable, she thus continued to claim a separate gendered position to justify her embodied difference as needed, oscillating between the model of linear transition (becoming woman) and a separate gendered position.

Sometimes, she even claimed *samakami* identity. In 2014, there was a minor kerfuffle during a gathering at the square field in Berhampore, when some *kodi kothis* like Kajol accused Kanchana of publicly outing hidden *kothis* and pressurizing them to present in feminine attire. Kajol complained: "When I walk down the street, Kanchana will sometimes cry out from afar—hey, you *kothi!*" A trans activist from Kolkata, who was visiting Berhampore, promptly interpreted this as a rift between MSM and TG communities—groups that were being increasingly conceptualized as separate identities, as the next chapter elaborates. However, Kanchana attempted to resolve the conflict, saying: "Some *kothis* say they are being pressured to wear *sarees* . . . this is not true! We are all *samakami*, we all do *same-sex love*; among us, some like me love to wear *sarees*, but that doesn't mean everyone has to do it!" This suggested that she did not always completely dissociate from bodily maleness and same-sex desire and claimed these as common properties she shared with *kodi kothis*—even as, around the same time, she sometimes said she was "becoming a woman" or identified as a separate gender.

Others, however, articulated transgender as a separate gender that was both distinct from *hijras* and exclusive of feminine and gay males. Sharmila, the aforementioned Kolkata-based trans activist, distinguished herself from trans women like Manobi Bandyopadhyay. In her interview in 2010, Sharmila told me: "TG is male body with female soul . . . I would never say I am a woman, though I am like women—I am proud to be TG (transgender). I would respectfully disagree with Manobi—one may wish to keep one's body. To me, the body is like a temple. Besides, how many can afford SRS (sex reassignment surgery)?" Sharmila's phrase "male body with female soul," suggesting coexistence rather than contradiction, parallels Sumit's aforementioned combination of a womanlike interiority and male body. However, Sharmila also emphasized that she was "not a feminine man" and did not want to be grouped with MSM. Further, while de-emphasizing SRS, she associated sartorial transition with the full assumption of TG identity. As I began wearing more conventionally feminine attire from around 2011, she once commented appreciatively: "Nice—you are becoming *bheli*, you're becoming TG!" On other occasions, she derisively referred to *kothis* who inconsistently wore female attire as "part-time TGs." As discussed in the next chapter, she was a strong proponent of a clear separation between MSM and TG communities.

Organizational Evocations of Trans Womanhood

These resignifications of transgender entered into complex negotiations with activist attempts to evoke essentialized ontologies of trans identity to discipline *kothi–dhurani* behaviors such as *bhel* and *bila* and to channel *kothi* femininity toward socially legible forms of embodied womanhood as well as gendered behavior that was deemed to be more respectable or dignified and yet also assertive in correct or proper ways.[2] With the recognition of transgender people as a vulnerable group by the state and funders (whether under MSM or separately), the modes of disciplining discussed in Chapter 3, which try to contain *kothi* femininity within the sanctioned limits of feminine maleness, are increasingly juxtaposed with or superseded by attempts to cast *kothi–dhurani–hijra* femininities within more binarized forms of trans womanhood. As we saw earlier, sartorially and/or behaviorally *bheli kothis* were disciplined within and sometimes even banished from HIV projects, although the pressure of meeting numerical targets counterbalanced such attempts. In the late 2000s, *bheli kothis* became valuable for CBOs in newer ways as organizational representatives in trans-focused consultations, meetings, and events. For instance, while the middle-class activists of Sangram often complained about Kanchana's public behavior, they also gradually became appreciative of her value as a transgender representative. In 2012, I witnessed a conversation where Anik, as a board member of Sangram, informed other *kothis* that she had decided to send Kanchana to a training for emerging "TG-*Hijra*" activists organized by a metropolitan NGO. She explained: "As it's a TG-*hijra* meeting, it would be more suitable for *kothis* like Kanchana who are *arial* (extreme, total) TGs!" Kanchana's status as an *arial kothi*, as per the linear gradation of *kothi* femininity discussed in Chapter 3, translated to her being cast as more totally or extremely TG than other *kothis* and better suited for a TG-*hijra* meeting.

While this apparently greater femininity positioned such *kothis* as good TG representatives, they were also sought to be led away from supposedly exaggerated forms of feminine expression to an ostensibly more natural, ontologically rooted form of womanhood. This was apparent in a transgender beauty contest that Sangram organized in November 2010, following similar events in larger cities. Introducing the contest, the senior activist Arnab gave a speech to an audience of invited dignitaries and journalists:

The aim of this beauty contest is to increase their self-esteem, so that if they dress up, they don't only hear people say, see, a boy has dressed up as a girl, what a shame! But rather, they think that they, too, can win prizes and be appreciated, their life too has value!

Arnab thus suggested that the beauty contest sought to transform derided forms of male effeminacy into socially valued femininity. This involved not simply changing social attitudes but also grooming *kothis* to cut down their "exaggerated" performative femininity and bring out a more subdued yet confident womanhood that was supposedly rooted in their inner truth or gendered essence. A few days before the contest, Ahmed, the activist we met in Chapter 3, supervised the rehearsal for the ramp walk along with Seema, a middle-aged woman who was a local radio artist and an ally to the CBO. The following exchange ensued:

> Ahmed: Do not exaggerate . . . your gait already has a *komoniyota* (gracefulness, elegance) to it, all *kothis* have it . . . no need for such excessive gestures! Since you've become women, you must do it properly . . . Do women do such excessive gestures?
> Kanchana   (smirks): Not women, *hijras*!
> Seema   (ignoring Kanchana): None of you know how to do makeup properly . . . yesterday, you all looked very *utkot* (garish, lurid) . . . we need a beautician!

Ahmed thus sought to guide the *kothis* to express feminine attributes like *komoniyota* that were, apparently, naturally inherent in them—something "all *kothis* have"—rather than an "exaggerated" or "garish" femininity. Reflecting the ontological assumptions of transsexual and *rupantarkami* discourse, womanhood is posited as both an inherent quality and a matter of *becoming*, something one must externally realize in ways that are "properly" rooted in a preexisting essence rather than exaggeratedly performed. Their expectations regarding womanhood naturalized middle-class, dominant-caste ideals of womanhood—gracefulness, elegance—as essential, pre-cultural attributes inherent in all *kothis* which they needed to realize properly. Kanchana's interjection suggested a sarcastic rejection of such an essentialized womanhood, but given the presence of seniors like Seema, other *kothis* were deferentially silent. Later, during the event, Seema introduced the contestants thus:

> These are not your well-groomed models on Fashion TV, some are wearing borrowed clothes, but that's not the main thing . . . they are getting accepted here in their own *roop* (form) which society is not accepting. We are recognizing them in their *ashol* (authentic) *roop*.

What this "authentic *roop*" meant became clearer later when the judges, including local administrators and a Kolkata-based trans activist, asked Guddu, the *kothi* who was eventually crowned the winner, if she could go out publicly in her long flowing dress. She replied: "Why not? Whatever I am outside, inside I am a *meye* (woman/girl)!" Her confident delivery of this assertion met with applause. This episode suggests a significant shift from the previous tendency of mapping *kothis* as essentially male, if feminine—here, there is a recognition of this interiorized womanhood as their true (*ashol*) form and a celebration of their outward realization of this essence.

However, this was not the only tendency at the contest. At one point in Arnab's aforementioned speech, he said: "Today's event is about those who are neither men nor women but in-between, the *kinnars*—it's a *kinnar* beauty contest!" *Kinnar* is a Sanskrit term retrieved from Hindu mythology that some *hijra* activists like Tripathi use as another name for *hijras* to claim traditional sanction for themselves by alluding to their supposed ancient precursors (Tripathi 2015: 150). Given the disparaging connotations of *hijra* in popular usage, some *hijras* may prefer *kinnar* as a better, more respectful term, and it may mark an attempted assimilation within Hindu nationalism (Saria 2021: 4). Arnab's use of *kinnar* was congruent with his citation of Hindu mythological figures such as the *Ardhanariswar* (a half-male, half-female deity) in Sangram's pamphlet, as discussed in Chapter 3. Despite Arnab's allusion to nonbinary subjectivities ("in-between"), later that day, I heard Arnab and other Sangram board members remarking approvingly among themselves that Annapurna, the *hijra guru* who attended as a guest, looked exactly like a well-dressed woman. Thus, the figure of the *kinnar* they were willing to accept was associated with a socially legible femininity rather than nonbinary gender expression.

The winner Guddu's self-expression outside the contest contrasted with both binary trans womanhood and the *kinnar*. Earlier that same day, Guddu, dressed in male attire, participated in a walk to commemorate World AIDS Day organized by various NGOs alongside Sangram. At the streetside gathering preceding the walk, *kothis* indulged in much laughter, *bhel* and *bila* among themselves, teasing each other, cracking jokes with sexual innuendos, and punctuating their sentences with *thikri* (claps). The following exchange ensued between Guddu and a *kodi kothi* who was uncomfortable with such behavior:

The *kothi*:   Hey, why are you giving *thikri*?
Guddu: Why, am I not a *chhibri* (hijra)?
The *kothi* (scoffs):   A *chhibri* in *pant-shirt*!
Guddu (laughs):   Why not? This is *biltaliya*!

Biltaliya, a variant of the word *bila*, here connoted the way she was having fun through unruly behavior. In affirmatively claiming such practices, Guddu's way of being a *chhibri* differs from both the interiorized womanhood that she avowed formally and the Sanskritic high culture version of a separate gender. Yet, Guddu's narrative during the contest also suggests that *kothis* were learning to contextually navigate between different forms of self-expression—a tendency also observed by Vijayakumar among trans persons in Bangalore (2021: 101). This potentially reinforces a form of vernacularization. *Kothis* may perform respectable forms of trans womanhood that have legibility and value in middle-class, formal, or institutional settings, sometimes deploying *rupantarkami* tropes in standard Bengali to do so—suggesting that trans identification may mark an aspirational claim to class mobility and cultural capital (Chatterjee 2018: 314). As the beauty contest suggests, not everyone succeeds equally at this. Meanwhile, *kothi–hijra* discourses and practices like *bila* are reserved for informal, intra-community contexts, although such practices may spill over into public spaces and disrupt the separation.

Respectability, Formal Equality, and Substantive Equality

As trans visibility increased in the late 2000s, the injunction to achieve an ostensibly natural femininity or ontologically rooted womanhood often dovetailed with understandings of rights and citizenship based on notions of formal equality and personal space or privacy. In Chapter 3, we saw how behaviors like *bhel* and *bila* were sought to be restrained in spaces like pride walks on account of further harming the social image or status of the community. A related pattern was an attempt to establish an equation between behaving with responsibility, decency, or dignity and gaining equal rights and/or social respect. For instance, in a post-pride meeting I attended in 2007, an activist from a Kolkata suburb asserted that attendees "shouldn't behave like jokers, (they) should behave responsibly to establish our rights and live with dignity." Another Kolkata-based activist claimed that "indecent" actions by some participants, such as changing clothes publicly during the walk, both "lowered the dignity of the walk" and were "detrimental to the objective of . . . establish(ing) the rights of community people." Such statements were echoed by Anik in Berhampore, who told me in several conversations between 2007 and 2011 that in order to gain *shomman* (respect) in society, one should also behave in ways worthy of *shomman*. In 2011, she specifically criticized the ways in which *kothis* did *bhel*: "The way *kothis* flirt, wink at men in public—people say, why are they forsaking their own *shomman* in this way?" In another conversation in 2010, she derided how *kothis* did *bila*, clapping and abusing people at any provocation: "*Kothis* are losing their own *adhikar* (rights) through their rudeness; they verbally attack people so much, sometimes I wonder, for whose rights are we fighting?" Such tendencies were also evident beyond West Bengal—for example, in a 2010 media article on an activist gathering at Delhi, the gay activist Ashok Row Kavi stated that the way some transgender people behaved during the event, such as lifting up their skirts while dancing and using swear words, hampered the effort to "convince . . . society that we are equal citizens with equal rights" (Afaque 2010).[3]

Despite variations in the specific behaviors targeted, this tendency on the whole assumes a formal equality between citizens who are supposed to interact with each other via seemingly neutral standards of decent, civil, or respectable conduct—if one party breaches this ostensibly neutral civic contract by behaving in ways not regarded as decent, dignified, or respectable, they may lose both social respect and their claim to equal rights. Bridging Western critical social contract theory and critiques of Indian democracy, Christine Keating has argued that the "agreement among equals" that is supposed to underpin liberal democracy is, in fact, profoundly unequal in terms of gender, race, and caste (2011: 4). The attempt to gain equal rights by adhering to seemingly agreed-upon, common standards of conduct—an apparent agreement between equals—marks a claim to formal equality, where marginalized groups such as transgender persons demand to be treated "the same as non-trans people despite gender non-conformity" (Gilden 2008: 85). While implicit in the aforementioned assumptions of common behavioral standards, such a framework of equality was sometimes articulated more explicitly. The pamphlet for the 2011 KRPW stated: "We are humans like you. We are citizens of India. We do not want special favours. We just want the same rights as you" (KRPW 2011). As feminist, queer, Dalit, and critical race theorists have argued, formal equality tends to discount the socioeconomic disadvantages of marginalized groups and reinforce existing inequalities (Daum and Ishiwata 2010; Jain and Kartik 2020). In our context, norms of social respectability or decency based on dominant-caste culture, which typically impose greater restrictions on women's sexual expression than men's, are positioned as part of a seemingly equal exchange, suggesting how dominant-caste morality becomes neutralized as the basis of a formally equal contract between citizens, which, in effect, conceals the unequally gendered nature of such norms. Feminist scholars studying cisgender women's position within Indian democracy and nationhood have demonstrated the profoundly gendered conditions that delimit their citizenship and public participation, albeit in ways differentiated by class and caste (Lukose 2009; Gilbertson 2014). The postcolonial role of women as upholders of a reified notion of national culture and tradition, especially through their nurturing role in the private sphere, often structures their access to the public sphere—respectable women are expected to balance public and private roles and maintain a sense of demureness, sexual modesty, and interiority through their clothing and demeanor in public spaces, although acceptable modes of feminine dress and behavior are changeable (Gilbertson 2014: 122; Lukose 2009: 80).

In that context, the aforementioned equation between achieving rights and maintaining decency or respectability may be seen as an extension of the gendered conditionalities of women's citizenship to trans and *kothi–hijra* people—to become equal rights-bearing citizens, *kothis/hijras* are led away from public behaviors that subvert feminine demureness and modesty. As Andrew Gilden argues in the US context, transgender claims to formal equality might seek to emphasize "the compatibility of trans people with normative social values" and downplay challenges to extant norms (2008: 85).

However, this tendency was complicated by competing understandings of rights and citizenship and changing notions of social propriety and status. As mentioned in Chapter 3, Indian LGBT rights discourse has commonly evoked the liberal ideals enshrined in the Indian constitution to contest social moralities. For instance, the pamphlet of the 2007 KRPW advocated the constitutional right to "freedom of expression" while the 2008 pamphlet evoked the "right to life and personal liberty" to protest against "so-called Indian social values" that proscribe the expression of gender/sexual identity (KRPW 2007, 2008). Both the 2008 and 2009 pamphlets also evoked such rights to contest the state's regulation of sexuality, arguing (in identical language) that Section 377 of the Indian Penal Code, which "criminalizes oral and anal sex even among consenting adults," encroaches upon "a person's democratic rights" and "clearly violates" the constitutional "right to life and personal liberty" (KRPW 2008, 2009). This marks an attempt to safeguard a domain of personal freedom and self-expression from social and state regulation. In the concurrent legal campaign against Section 377 led by large NGOs like the Naz Foundation and their allies, this personal domain was initially associated more with zonal or spatial privacy—private spaces where one should be free to have intimate relations without state encroachment (Dutta 2012b: 130). This approach came under sustained critique from some academics and activists given the unequal access of LGBTQ people to private spaces, and since spatial privacy implicitly allowed the heteronormative ordering of the public sphere to continue unchallenged (Al Baset 2012). Increasingly, however, the understanding of privacy was broadened to decisional privacy, the right to express one's personality and make choices or decisions about one's personal life both privately and in public, as evident in some sections of the Delhi High Court verdict in 2009 that read down Section 377 to exclude consensual non-penile-vaginal sex from its purview, as well as in the 2018 Supreme Court verdict that upheld this position after legal challenges and reversals in the interim (Dutta 2020: 423–29).

Thus, the campaign for such rights posed a potential contradiction to efforts to directly discipline dress or conduct as per ideals of decency or dignity. An attempted reconciliation between norms of respectability and ideals of personal liberty was evident in efforts to distinguish between legitimate forms of self-expression and behaviors not regarded as such. For instance, in a planning meeting preceding the 2009 Kolkata pride walk, one *kothi* activist expressed concerns about the behavior of some *kothis* at pride, saying: "Every year, there is *bila*. We need rules, and I don't mean rules against dressing up!" She thus hinted that the rules should not delimit legitimate self-expression—only behaviors like *bila*.

At their core, such attempts to demarcate legitimate versus non-legitimate behaviors were about distinguishing what legitimately pertained to the sphere of personal liberty and individual autonomy and what did not. The rights to personal liberty and zonal or decisional privacy all pertain to acts or expressions that are seen as belonging to the individual's private and/or personal domain—even if such rights are understood as extending to personal expressions in public. In practice, this meant that acts seen as clearly staying within the personal sphere, and especially expressions seen as stemming from an essential or deeply interiorized personal identity, were more likely to be condoned, while behaviors disrupting normative modes of social interaction that could not be readily attributed to any essential identity remained suspect. In a pre-pride meeting in May 2008, after much discussion on dress codes, the eventual decision was recorded in the minutes thus: "No decision on dress code was taken. Rather, a decision to provide a safe space for dressing and changing was taken." This was in light of some attendees having publicly changed into their dresses in the previous year's walk—this measure was thus meant to facilitate gender nonconforming expression in public, while maintaining a proper public–private divide and containing bodily exposure to private spaces. At a later meeting in June 2009, one attendee opined: "Self-expression is great, but if someone says, my *saree* slipping off my shoulders is about expressing myself—that's a different matter!" Others laughed and agreed—including a gay activist who, in the public gathering following the previous year's pride walk, had made an emotional speech exhorting people to empathize with the "inner pain" of *kothis* who could not accept their bodies and socially assigned identities.

While interiorized gender dysphoria was thus validated, flirtatious or licentious behavior was not seen as legitimately belonging to the domain of personal expression. Proper forms of personal liberty and self-expression were thus defined as per what was seen as proper or fundamental to the gendered self, understood as per ascendant models of trans ontology in Bengali activist discourse that, as seen previously, result in the vernacularization of *kothi–hijra* languages and understandings of selfhood. Indeed, the aforementioned gay activist was associated with *Swikriti Patrika*, the community magazine where Tista Das published her account of transsexual or *lingantarkami* selfhood (Das 2009). Years later, sections of the 2018 Supreme Court judgment that read down Section 377 justified "freedom of expression" based on the supposed naturalness, innateness, and immutability of sexual orientation (Dutta 2020: 430). As legal scholar Saptarshi Mandal notes in his critique of the judgment: "arguments based on immutability provide weak foundations and limited scope to recognition of the rights of those marginalised on account of their sexual orientation or gender identity. . . . It will be instructive to see what traits are deemed intrinsic . . . (or) not, in future cases" (Mandal 2018). Other sections of the judgment condone public gender and sexual expression as long as they do not amount to "indecency" or disturb "public order" (Dutta 2020: 429). Across these instances, essentialized models of gender or sexual ontology that gain validation in formal registers of English and Bengali, over the variable ontologies evident in vernacularized *kothi–hijra* narratives, serve to demarcate legitimate forms of private or personal expression from less legitimate ones, while the gendered norms that structure notions of decency, public order, or formal equality are concealed or neutralized.

An allied tendency was to not externally discipline people through rules on dress or conduct, but rather urge *kothis* to act sensibly or responsibly and refrain from non-legitimate forms of expression. In the aforementioned pre-pride meeting in 2009, one attendee opined: "Why do we need rules—are we children, don't we have any *sense* of our own?" This "sense" could be conflated with an essentialized understanding of selfhood based on naturalized gender norms. In a meeting at Berhampore in 2007, the activist Arnab exhorted *kothis* such as Kanchana to behave responsibly in upcoming pride walks, and added: "Kanchana is quite grown-up, no one should have to take responsibility for her!" Sriroop, a middle-class *kothi*, disagreed: "You are calling Kanchana grown-up? Don't you remember, she once did a pole-dance in a bus?" In an earlier meeting, Sriroop had said that no one had any problem if *kothis* "did full *niharinipona*" (full woman-mode), but behaviors like *bhel* naturally attracted negative attention. She ventured that it was because *kothis* were not able to truly realize who they were that they wore garish makeup "like clowns" and ran after men—self-realization implied embodying a fuller womanhood. Social norms of feminine respectability could be naturalized as aspects of a sensible, responsible selfhood, while defying such norms marked a seeming lack of sense, responsibility, or self-realization.

As per a Foucauldian analytics of power, this may be interpreted as a shift from disciplinary power, which seeks to produce docile bodies through surveillance and control, to a governmental form of power that works by producing apparently free, sovereign, and agential individuals endowed with reason and autonomy, and regulates conduct through guiding the agency of the subject rather than repression (Foucault 2007; Roy 2017). However, as Srila Roy notes, people like poor Global South women may be perceived as "unable to fully exercise such autonomy" and seen as legitimate targets of coercion (2017: 3–4). While *kothis* were exhorted to exercise sense and responsibility, Kanchana was cast as minor (not "grown-up") and hence incapable of doing so, potentially justifying discipline. Overall, access to rights-bearing citizenship becomes conditional—a hallmark of liberal ideologies where equal citizenship is withheld from colonized and subaltern groups through hierarchical conditionalities that mandate them to first become capable sovereign subjects (Skaria 2016: 6). Here, middle-class, dominant-caste groups and norms, rather than colonial authorities or discourses, become the arbiters of such capability.

Of course, such tendencies were hardly uncontested. For instance, Munia was a *kothi* in her twenties from a working-class Dalit family in Kalyani, Nadia, who visited the DIC at Ranaghat frequently. One summer day in 2012, I was returning to Kalyani from Ranaghat with Munia and her friends, and at the railway station, the conversation turned to the Kolkata pride walks. Munia confessed, "I feel embarrassed to go to pride, all the *chishya* (beautiful, good) *kothis* go there. We are nothing to them, so I don't like going!" Her phrase "*chishya kothi*" referenced well-dressed metropolitan queer and trans people from elite class/caste backgrounds who tended to lead pride organizing. Her feelings of inferiority thus suggested the exclusive effects of such dominance at pride walks, which ironically might turn into a shaming experience for *kothis* like her. But then, she added more defiantly: "And what will happen if we go to pride walks? Will we get all our *adhikar* (rights)? They'll give nothing!" Later, in the train, she demonstrated a rather different way of claiming *adhikar* relative to the aforementioned discourses of civility, citizenship, and equality with their hidden conditionalities. We noticed that a middle-aged couple was observing our group—all short-haired and in male attire but wearing makeup and nail polish—and commenting derisively to surrounding people that we were "*meyeli*" (effeminate) boys who wore makeup. Munia said quietly to us, "Wait, let me do *bila* in *chhibripon* (*hijra*-mode)—this is how we will take our *adhikar*!" A little later, when we heard them laugh audibly at us, Munia remarked sharply: "Why won't they laugh? This is laughable indeed!

People behaving like *ladies* despite being boys—totally laughable!" The couple fell into an embarrassed silence. Munia then kept saying that people would naturally laugh at boys who were "half-ladies" and "*chhakka-mowga*" (roughly, faggot/sissy). From time to time, she called out to her friends—"hey, you *ladies!*"—at which they laughed, creating quite a commotion while surrounding people fell uncomfortably silent.

Rather than attempting "full *niharinipona*," Munia and her friends thus emphasized and reclaimed the supposed discordance between "boy" and "*ladies*." Her way of doing *bila* entailed owning the stigma of deviance—taking pejorative words like half-ladies and *chhakka* upon oneself and simultaneously showing that one is not affected by them. Munia repeated and parodied the stigmatizing actions of harassers in a way that effectively rejected their shaming and instead flaunted her group's deviance from norms, using the discomfort occasioned by such gendered difference as a tool to silence abusers and turning their phobic reactions against themselves. This parallels the way *hijras* use their abject status to shame or embarrass people, as noted in earlier chapters and previous ethnographies (Reddy 2005: 136). However, Munia's *chhibripon* unmoored such behavior from the *hijra* body in its socially recognized form and simultaneously linked the performance of *chhibripon* to gaining *adhikar* (rights). While the aforementioned discourses of equality and citizenship premised equal rights on assimilation into an essentialized normative idea of respectable womanhood and/or the unfairly gendered terms of a putatively equal civic contract, this incident suggested a way of claiming rights while reclaiming subject positions and behaviors excluded or abjected by social norms. Munia's *bila* signaled unruly modes of public assertion that sought to "take our rights" while disrupting rather than assimilating into extant norms of civic relationality.

Such tactics found defenders among *kothis* like Kanchana. During a conversation we had in 2010, Kanchana observed that behaving nicely did not always ensure better treatment from people. As she said: "It is because *kothis* are rude that we are able to survive!" She added that being *bhadra* (decent/civil) worked only for "*shamorthowali kothis*"—*kothis* with means—and not for "*khajrawali* (sex worker) *kothis*" like her. While not articulated theoretically, this marked an incipient critique of the aforementioned idea of an abstract formal equality between citizens who supposedly inhabit a "level playing field" (Daum and Ishiwata 2010: 844). Kanchana interrogated the assumption that unprivileged *kothis* share similar conditions with other citizens and may be adjudged as per common standards. If—as noted earlier—she rearticulated transgender identity in ways that contested vernacularizing discourses of transgender or *rupantarkami* womanhood, in these moments, she also interrogated the framework of formal equality buttressed by normative models of transgender.

Changing Activist Tendencies and Self-determination

As the 2010s wore on, such contestations within *kothi–hijra* communities were paralleled by a changing activist terrain that sometimes provided greater openings for *kothi* visibility while also reconfiguring hierarchies and forms of vernacularization. First, some *hijra* activists from relatively elite locations articulated similar critiques of formal equality. Aparna Banerjee, a dominant-caste trans activist based near Kolkata who also belonged to a *hijra gharana*, was asked about the ostensible *ashobhyota* (uncivilized behavior) of *hijras* in a Bengali media interview in 2013; she replied that their *ashobhyota* was much less than that of men who sexually molest others with impunity (Banerjee 2013). She added: "The money we take, that money you didn't allow us to earn. We are not given jobs . . . despite being educated" (Banerjee 2013). Tripathi similarly asserts that the way *hijras* "harass in order to extract money . . . is the *hijra*'s revenge on society for ostracizing her" (Tripathi 2015: 175). Such arguments suggest that *hijras* are not placed in an equal social position and cannot be expected to follow an ostensibly equal contract where all parties behave as per common norms of "civilized" behavior. They defend *hijra* tactics by highlighting the oppression faced by them, and implicitly move from conceptions of the transgender subject based on normative middle-class womanhood (as in dominant-caste *rupantarkami* narratives) to one based on *hijra/kothi* experiences. Concurrently, as traced in the next chapter, transgender activists in the 2010s, particularly Dalit trans activists, went on to demand specific provisions for transgender people to undo oppressive conditions, particularly reservations in jobs and education, going beyond the aforementioned demands for identical treatment as other citizens (Banu 2018; Kumar 2020: 170). Such demands build on provisions for substantive equality in the Indian constitution, which, framed under the leadership of the Dalit visionary B. R. Ambedkar, goes beyond formal equality and promises reservations for oppressed-caste groups (Jain and Kartik 2020: 22). Such tendencies facilitate the reconceptualization of "transgender" from an assimilative framework based on formal equality and normative ontologies of womanhood to a subject of substantive equality in legal and activist discourse.

Second, activist tendencies of behavioral or sartorial policing were further complicated in the 2010s by newer standards of feminine dressing and changing senses of what might properly pertain to the domain of personal liberty. As Amanda Gilbertson demonstrates for middle-class women in Hyderabad, norms of respectability are complicated by newer markers of class status in post-liberalization India, when publicly wearing fashionable clothing and taking part in commodified forms of youth culture and romance become associated with elite practices of consumerism and leisure and mark a cosmopolitan participation in transnational capitalism, as distinct from the supposed provincialism and traditionalism of rural or working-class people—such that middle-class women must balance demands of respectability with the aspirational pursuit of newer forms of status and class distinction (Gilbertson 2014: 124). Further, ideas such as the right to consumption and the freedom of choice of citizen-consumers increasingly inform notions of citizenship in liberalizing India (Lukose 2009: 8).

In the context of Kolkata, a greater emphasis on sartorial choice became apparent when younger generations of activists, many of them gay-identified men, began entering the pride organizing process after a conflict between the

MANAS Bangla network and emergent transgender groups in 2010, detailed in the next chapter, created a vacuum in pride leadership. While still mostly dominant caste and middle class, this group diversified the profile of Kolkata activism as many were employees of multinational corporations rather than HIV or NGO activists and entered LGBTQ communities through emerging social media spaces like LGBTQ Facebook groups rather than CBOs. Several frequented emerging spaces of leisure and consumption such as gay parties in hotels and nightclubs, and some helped organize fund-raising parties where entry fees were used to raise funds for pride.[4] This group was not a consolidated institutional entity like NGOs, but a rather loose network of individuals and informal collectives who floated in and out of pride organizing over the years since 2011 and expressed diverse political outlooks, differing on questions like whether corporate sponsorship should be allowed in pride. Hence, I do not undertake an exhaustive discussion of this complex group here but signal some salient tendencies that intersected with the *kothi–hijra* spectrum. For instance, in general, most among this generation evidenced relatively permissive attitudes regarding dress.

For example, during a pre-pride planning meeting in 2012, two middle-class trans women activists expressed fears that given prevailing fashion trends, people might show up in bikinis, and recommended a dress code. A younger gay activist countered: "If someone has the *shahosh* (courage, boldness) to wear a bikini, they should be able to do so!" Others agreed and no dress code was adopted.[5] This marks the incipient acceptance of a freedom to choose dress that need not be justified via a deep ontological essence—a bold choice is worthy of support in itself. However, concerns about *kothi* behavior remained. During the ensuing discussion, a senior gay activist said: "It is impossible to control dress, but what can be controlled is how people behave with the public—so lots of volunteers are needed!" The younger gay activists concurred, and one of them shared that he had seen a participant of the 2011 pride walk flirting with and groping a minor boy by the roadside. While he did not mention the alleged perpetrator's identity, this specific incident was soon generalized to *kothi/dhurani* behavior. One of the aforementioned trans activists said: "TGs create such problems, especially the ones who cross-dress!" She later referred to such troublemakers as *dhuranis*, suggesting that here "TG" specifically meant the *dhurani–kothi* spectrum. The attempt to control *kothi* behavior through volunteers echoed efforts to prevent practices like *bhel* in previous walks, marking how anxieties around *kothi–dhurani* sexual expression continued despite broadening ideas of sartorial freedom.

Moreover, the acceptance of bold dress did not always extend to *kothi–hijra* sartorial presentation. After the 2011 Kolkata pride walk, some *kothis* from Murshidabad went to visit a cruising area and were harassed by some policemen who suspected them of doing sex work. Several pride organizers conscientiously intervened to extricate them from the situation, but privately, some expressed more ambiguous stances. In a later conversation, one organizer told me that he condemned police harassment, but added: "But, tell me, don't you think that their dress and manner was too *ugra* (strong/garish)?" Such incidents mark a broader

Figure 5.1 Heena posing at the 2015 Kolkata pride walk with a poster stating, "If we are *kothi*, how does that harm you?" Courtesy author.

trend where middle-class expressions of sexuality may be marked as bold or progressive while *kothi–hijra* sartorial or verbal expressions are derided as vulgarly excessive. In the aforementioned media article on an activist gathering at Delhi in 2010, the reporter approvingly mentioned gay and lesbian activists kissing publicly and displaying English slogans such as "un-fuck the world," but "transgenders" who were apparently "lifting their skirts" and "shouting swear words" while dancing to Hindi songs were condemned for such "embarrass(ing)" behavior (Afaque 2010). Later, after the 2013 Kolkata pride walk, I had a conversation with Anurag Maitrayee, a transgender civil rights activist, who pointed out the double standards of elite activists—trans/*kothi* sex workers who had worn low-cut dresses to the walk were criticized by a gay activist for the "inappropriate display of assets," but shirtless middle-class gay men or queer women in fashionably revealing clothing did not elicit such comments. This suggests that the interrogation of gender/sexual norms in middle-class activist circles may not entirely dismantle the gender, caste, and linguistic hierarchies that, as noted in the third chapter, result in the derision of *kothi* sartorial or behavioral expression as vulgar or excessive.

Over the subsequent years, *kothis* and *hijras* faced continuing infrastructural barriers to pride participation and attempted techniques of control involving linguistic hierarchies, even as pride organizers accommodated some ruptures to the status quo, particularly emergent forms of Dalit queer activism. In 2015, beginning from pride walks in South India, Indian pride walks saw a significant upsurge of Dalit queer visibility—urban Dalit queer activists powerfully asserted their presence in both the Delhi and Kolkata walks, reading out a Dalit queer manifesto, walking with "Queer, Dalit and Proud" posters, and declaring that "any LGBTQIA+ fight must include caste" (Jyoti 2017). Pride organizers at Kolkata were seemingly accommodating, and pride pamphlets increasingly mentioned intersectionality and anti-caste struggle "as part of the queer movement's agenda" (Jyoti 2017). However, as Akhil Kang suggests, often, dominant-caste queer allies to these mobilizations meant to exonerate themselves from complicity in caste hierarchies and not critically examine their casteism (2016). Further, Dhrubo Jyoti—who read the Dalit queer manifesto at the 2015 Kolkata walk—suggests that Anglophone, urban Dalit voices might be accommodated more easily than nonmetropolitan, non-Anglophone Dalit people (Jyoti 2017). Despite the seeming inclusion of Dalit critique, in later pride walks, several *kothis* complained to me about the "*tyashpona*" or pretentiously elite, high-handed behavior of volunteers who shouted instructions at them in English, such as injunctions to stay in line and not stray toward the sidewalks. Dalit *kothi*/trans CBO members shared in private conversations that they did not feel comfortable in participating in pride planning meetings since—despite the efforts of some organizers to use Bengali—so much of the discussion defaulted to English that they had difficulty keeping up, which preserved the dominance of middle-class Anglophone people in pride-related spaces. I also observed that while organizers did make meeting minutes available in both languages, in several pride walks between 2018 and 2023, some materials such as online application forms to stage performances during the walk were available only in English, thus reinforcing the relatively vernacularized position of Bengali as a less institutionally recognized language. During the 2019 pride walk, the activist Maitrayee told me: "Initially, they were shouting instructions from the podium and reading the leaflet mostly in English, they'd say something seven times in English and once in Bengali; we went and intervened, only then they started using Bengali!" These tendencies parallel other forms of casteist exclusion through linguistic hierarchies in elite queer social media groups, as noted by Dalit trans persons (Thakur and Zaffar 2023).

However, more promisingly, intersections between LGBTQ, feminist, and Dalit activism in the 2010s also countered moral policing and spurred demands for bodily and gender self-determination. In Kolkata, this became particularly apparent after the gangrape of a young woman in 2012 in Delhi galvanized protests across Indian cities (Dutta 2019). As I have examined elsewhere, protests in Kolkata, often led by university students, featured a spectrum of liberal, radical, and leftist feminists who evidenced divergent political stances on issues like sex work but rallied around slogans against patriarchy, rape culture, and victim blaming, such as "fix your mentality before you ask me to fix my clothes" (Dutta 2019: 14). Some queer, trans, and *kothi* activists joined these protests, and similar slogans turned up in subsequent pride walks. In the 2013 walk, a trans- and *kothi*-led CBO brought an English poster proclaiming, "my body, my right," while a lesbian feminist activist carried a Bengali poster that stated, "my body, my sexuality: my word is the last word." Such slogans, which are broadly interpretable in terms of sartorial and sexual choice as well as gender self-determination, also turned up later in protests against the Indian parliament's transgender bills that tried to restrict the self-identification of gender, addressed in the next chapter. Here, it is relevant that such feminist discourse was gradually mobilized against respectability politics. A case with national repercussions involved the 2017 pride walk in Pune, western India. The organizing CBO Samapathik Trust, which explicitly marked itself as conservative, asked attendees to wear only "decent clothing" and banned "flamboyance," citing previous incidents of sexualized behavior at or near the walk (Horton 2020: 294). In an English media report, Harish Iyer, a Brahmin gay activist, supported the organizers thus: "These rules aren't just for the queer community . . . If it's about dressing as a way of expressing one's sexuality, it does not mean that one comes to Pride in just a bra and panty; this isn't permissible in public even for the heterosexual mainstream" (Lobo 2017).

This statement harkens back to the justification of gendered ideals of decency via the model of formal equality and an ostensibly equal civic contract, as well as the acceptance of sartorial freedom only as long as it legitimately expresses "one's sexuality"—showing the lack of any linear temporal progress. However, such stances were contested. Shyam Konnur, a gay activist, said in the aforementioned report: "Asking the community to dress a certain way is similar to telling a woman how she must dress" (Lobo 2017). Another activist, Rucha Satoor, decried "regressive ideas of 'decency' and 'indecency'" and cautioned that such "moral policing" discouraged the participation of queer and trans women, thus implicitly refuting the supposedly neutral applicability of decency (ibid.). Following such protests, I witnessed a clear consensus in the Kolkata pride meetings that year against moralizing diktats or dress codes, although subtler forms of exclusion like the dominance of Anglophone participants remained. The rising visibility of Dalit trans activists also challenged the policing of self-expression. For instance, Grace Banu, a South Indian Dalit trans activist, has publicly protested against the imposition of dominant-caste standards of dress and conduct. In one media article, Banu spoke out against the "transphobia and casteism" that she and her friends faced when they put up a stall featuring queer/trans literature at the 2023 Chennai Book Fair: "We were told by one of the organisers to dress appropriately and not hug our friends. Who are they to decide what we should wear?" (Koushik 2023).

Figure 5.2 Poster at a protest by the CBO Kolkata Rista in Kolkata, 2013. Courtesy author.

This evolving activist terrain also marks an increasing acceptance of gender self-determination, which has facilitated the ability of *kothis* and *hijras* to identify not only as a distinct gender but also as women without physically transitioning or conforming to norms of womanhood. Over the 2010s, Anglo-American trans discourse has increasingly posited that gender self-identification should not be restricted by anatomical status or sartorial presentation (Asher 2010; Spade 2011). Indian precedents include the 2003 PUCL-K report that demanded gender self-determination. In the 2010s, I observed the increasing expression of such stances in Indian online trans spaces. In this changing context, Aparna Banerjee, the aforementioned trans activist, wrote a Bengali op-ed piece in 2018 where she opined that *rupantar* (change of *roop* or form) was not necessarily "a journey from one body to another" but rather from "one identity to another," and *rupantarkami* people's self-identities are "not defined by genitals" (Banerjee 2018). She thus resignified *rupantar* as the process of claiming an identity different from one's socially assigned gender, independent of physical transition.

Some small-town activists who had some exposure to online and metropolitan activism also started identifying as women irrespective of transition around this period, such as Sumi from Coochbehar. In several conversations we had at her home between 2014 and 2019, Sumi described herself as a *"likam niyei nari"* (woman with a penis). Once, she specified, "I am a woman, but not the kind of woman they are," referring to postoperative trans women. Thus, rather than countering hegemonic womanhood by claiming a distinct gender identity, she claimed a nonnormative form of womanhood. However, while Banerjee sees *rupantar* as an unambiguous shift from "one identity to another" (even if non-anatomical), Sumi sometimes described herself as *byatachhele* (male/man)—especially, but not only, in jocular ways. When we would return home after long days on the field, she would often change out of her *saree*, laugh, and say, "It's so comfortable to become a *byatachhele* again!" Once, for a few months, she shaved off her hair and donned male attire, explaining that she wanted to see what it was like living as a man, and during this period, described herself as "gay" to potential partners. Her trans womanhood was thus not mutually exclusive from maleness. As mentioned earlier, she was quite accepting of the non/linear combination of *kodi* and *bheli* presentations among *kothis* in Coochbehar, and this likely informed her nonbinary womanhood alongside emergent metropolitan discourses of self-determination.

However, while non-transitional claims to trans womanhood become more acceptable, the next chapter shows how gender self-determination may become circumscribed across both activist and legal discourses through the model of a consistent, deep transgender selfhood, clearly distinct from maleness and sexual categories like MSM or gay. Despite the promises of trans politics, such discourses may result in the continuing vernacularization and/or erasure of *kothi–hijra* discourses of selfhood and community that breach the cisgender–transgender boundary.

Conclusion

This chapter has traced the complex interplay between vernacularizing discourses of trans identity, resignifications of transgender within *kothi–hijra* communities, and changing frameworks of equality and rights. We have seen that *kothis* may perform binary discourses of trans identity while also subverting them privately or publicly, and simultaneously, also claim and articulate transgender identity in ways that defy understandings of transgender among both middle-class trans women and relatively elite *hijra* activists. These rearticulations correspond to increasing interrogations of formal equality and emerging demands for substantive equality.

As we shall see, these negotiations become especially fraught as not just binary versions of transgender identity but also some versions of the "third gender" model gain legal and media recognition over the 2010s, even as trans womanhood might be rearticulated in ways departing from the binary and linear transitional model. In this increasingly diverse terrain of trans discourse, attempts to standardize boundaries between trans femininity and cisgender (especially gay or MSM) identities might serve as a stabilizing force, restricting the transgender subject of substantive equality even as transgender becomes reconceptualized from various locations.

Chapter 6

CIS/TRANS DIVIDES AND THE PARTIAL
ERASURE OF THE *KOTHI*

One day in 2016, a member of the West Bengal Transgender Development Board dropped into the office of a CBO in Coochbehar, northern West Bengal. This board had been constituted in 2015 by the West Bengal state government following a landmark judgment by the Indian Supreme Court in 2014 which granted transgender people the right to the self-determination of gender identity as male, female, or transgender and directed central and state governments to protect their constitutional rights and ensure their welfare ("India Court" 2014). Based on exclusive consultations with invited organizations, the state government nominated mostly metropolitan, dominant-caste, and middle-class activists to the board, prompting protests by nonmetropolitan activists (Bhattacharya 2015). The aforementioned board member, a dominant-caste trans woman from Kolkata employed in Coochbehar, announced that she was helping the district administration with issuing voter identity cards to trans people and that the board was aiding the state government with recruiting trans people as lower-level administrative personnel to increase their employment options. Sumi, the secretary of the local CBO Moitrisanjog, recommended some *kothis* who were Dalit and did precarious informal work like making bamboo mats. However, the member doubted their suitability: "The *kothis* here are not exactly *trans* like you or me," she said, adding that they were "double-decker" (sexually versatile), and, in some cases, heterosexually married. She felt that these people were really MSM and did not qualify for welfare as trans, despite their impoverished and marginalized status relative to her.

This incident suggests that while transgender people become gradually conceptualized as subjects of both formal equality (constitutional rights) and substantive equality (welfare measures), the purview of the category and its accessibility to nonmetropolitan *kothi–dhurani–hijra* communities might be limited by the separation of transgender and MSM as mutually exclusive categories without potential for overlap. The construction of a binary divide between MSM and transgender categories in activist and legal discourse was fueled by both the demands of emerging transgender activism and the evolving policies of national and international funders of HIV projects. In the late 2000s, an increasing number of transgender activists were expressing their dissatisfaction with being clubbed under the MSM category in HIV policy and/or a discontent with the perceived dominance of elite MSM and gay leaders in the NGO sector. In parallel, HIV-related policies and the target groups for HIV prevention were being rethought through a series of consultations preceding the fourth phase of the NACP (NACP-IV), which succeeded NACP-III. These consultations often favored established urban, middle-class activists. For instance, all four attendees from West Bengal invited to UNDP's previously mentioned consultation in 2008 were dominant-caste, Kolkata-based activists (UNDP 2008: 3).

As I trace below, developments in such exclusive spaces resulted in the generalization of rubrics of identity formulated largely by relatively elite trans and non-trans activists but also fostered multiple, inconsistent logics of identity separation.[1] While such processes initially influenced HIV-related policies, they later fed into the conceptualization of legal categories. The Indian state's recognition of transgender people has been extensively critiqued for tokenizing trans rights and welfare, policing trans identities, reinforcing discrimination, and even criminalizing some trans people (Semmalar 2014; Banu 2018; Jain and Kartik 2020). However, the relation between the MSM/transgender divide as constructed in NGO and HIV-related activism and the subsequent construction of cisgender/transgender and *kothi/hijra* binaries in legal discourse demands further elaboration. This chapter studies the construction of MSM/trans and cis/trans divides as resulting from multiple and contingently intersecting logics of power, resistance, and distinction. While the initial distinction between MSM and TG categories was influenced by the biopolitics of HIV intervention that demarcated at-risk groups as per their degree of vulnerability to HIV, increasing demands for legal recognition and substantive equality brought transgender identities within the ambit of the governmental classification and enumeration of communities by the modern Indian state, which has, building on colonial practices, tended to categorize the complex religious, ethnic, and caste affiliations of people into mutually exclusive identity groups (Chatterjee 2004; Rao 2009). While HIV-related biopolitics influenced governmental classifications, these logics of power also intersected with transgender contestations of entrenched hierarchies and even *hijra* discourses of authenticity. Paralleling these tendencies, urban gay communities also tended to undergird distinctions between transgender and cisgender gay—even queer—identities. While the precise dynamics of identitarian divides are variable, inconsistent, and contested, overall, the construction of binary divides between transgender and cisgender gay/MSM identities evinces an unstable but powerful layering of multiple dominant discourses of identity and the convergence of various patterns of vernacularization.

Varying Logics of Distinction

In an interview in 2011 in Delhi, a senior employee of an international funding agency told me that the separation of MSM and transgender categories for the purposes of HIV prevention had been undertaken in consultation with communities across the country—a claim also recorded in other HIV-related literature (Lakkimsetti 2020: 113). However, several *kothis* perceived such divisions to be imposed from above. Bijoya, a *kothi* and trans-identified activist from North Bengal, told me in a conversation in 2013: "We are small fry—we don't make these *bhag* (divisions), people above us make them, and then we learn them!"

Indeed, even consultations that included nonmetropolitan or nonelite participants were not really nonhierarchical. The UNDP-funded "Regional Transgender/Hijra Consultation in Eastern India" organized by the NGO SAATHII in 2009, mentioned earlier in Chapter 4, included representatives of several CBOs from nonmetropolitan West Bengal and other states (SAATHII 2009: 3–4). However, partly due to the higher concentration of organizations in Kolkata, half of the forty-two attendees were from Kolkata (ibid.). Dominant-caste activists from Kolkata led the process as members of the "convening committee"—explaining the rationale of the consultation, setting the agendas, and explaining the objectives of group discussions, one of which was to collectively generate a definition of "transgender" (SAATHII 2009: 4–9).

Yet, preceding the discussions, several Kolkata activists already assumed a clear separation between MSM and transgender as communities and identities. Soon after the introductions, Smarajit Jana, a prominent HIV-prevention and sex workers' rights activist associated with NACO, stated in his speech that since NACO was concerned with high-risk sexual behaviors, it had earlier "put MSM, TG and other similar identities into a single high-risk category" based on their "similar sexual practices," but NACO now acknowledged that these groups had "unique identities" and "social position(s)" and thus was "keen to see how social inequities made each of these groups 'differently vulnerable' to HIV" (SAATHII 2009: 5). This extended the biopolitical project of demarcating and enumerating at-risk population groups and calibrating their relative vulnerability to HIV beyond the earlier classification of MSM subgroups.[2]

The earlier UNDP consultation in 2008 had evidenced mixed approaches to such classification—some activists advocated separating MSM and TG populations, some continued subsuming TG under MSM, and some mentioned other differences like those between rural and urban MSM (UNDP 2008: 10–17). But here, the differentiation became simplified to an overarching MSM–TG distinction—Jana stated that NACO expected "TG and *hijra* communities" to "clarify their concerns as different from those of MSM" (SAATHII 2009: 5). Subsequently, Agniva Lahiri, a transgender activist associated with MANAS Bangla, suggested the need for "exclusive TG/Hijra targeted intervention" projects separate from MSM (ibid.). Later, after group discussion sessions, "Lahiri informed all the participants that based on the inputs . . . a common definition would be created" (SAATHII 2009: 15). As discussed in Chapter 4, this "common" definition followed a 2007 HST report in positioning identification with the "opposite" gender as the "usual" identity of transgender people and established scalar hierarchies between the global/universal category of transgender and "local" identities like *kothi* (SAATHII 2009: 17). As relevant here, it also assumed a clear separation between "gender identity" and "sexual preferences," although this point is absent from the discussions summarized earlier in the report:

> Transgender is a gender identity. Transgender persons usually live or prefer to live in the gender role opposite to the one in which they are born. . . . This has got no relation with anyone's sexual preferences. It is an umbrella term which includes transsexuals, cross dressers, intersexed persons, gender variant persons and many more. In eastern India there are various local names and identities, such as Kothi, Dhurani, Boudi . . . Among these, the most common identity is Kothi. (SAATHII 2009: 17)

The list of "local names" left out several terms suggested by participants. One subgroup, comprising participants from districts including my interlocutors Trisha and Kanchana, listed "versatile" as one of the terms corresponding to TG (SAATHII 2009: 15). In 2009, versatile was still a new word in nonmetropolitan communities, but I had observed in several conversations that *kothis* who knew the term typically equated it with *dupli*. The group's inclusion of versatile thus perhaps reflected how *dupli* could be considered a type of *kothi*, as discussed in Chapter 2. However, "versatile" was absent in the final definition. Rather, the sentence "this has got no relation with anyone's sexual preferences," absent in the discussions, was inserted (SAATHII 2009: 16–17). Given the influence of the 2007 HST report, it seems clear that technical expertise and the epistemological assumptions of elite activists were prioritized over actual inputs, even as the "common definition" gained the legitimation of apparent community approval.

For trans activists, the positioning of certain terms (but not others) as transgender was not so much a hierarchizing subsumption as inclusion in an aspirational process of making claims to the state for a broader set of rights beyond sexual health. In the 2008 UNDP consultation, Lahiri had noted how the Tamil Nadu state government's recognition of transgender as a distinct gender facilitated access to welfare and employment opportunities (UNDP 2008: 19). In the 2009 consultation, trans activists noted that the needs of transgender and *hijra* communities "go beyond narrow HIV and sexual health concerns" and the gains made in South India "needed to be replicated" elsewhere (SAATHII 2009: 4). Activists discussed how the link between vulnerability to HIV and social violence could be used to draw the state's attention to violence on trans people; transgender recognition thus potentially made vital concerns of gender-based violence and discrimination visible and legible to the state (SAATHII 2009: 5). The biopolitical construction of transgender as a vulnerable population was thus mobilized for rights-based claims for substantive equality and anti-discrimination measures. As Chaitanya Lakkimsetti argues, the participation of marginalized communities in the state's biopolitical project of HIV control within high-risk groups helped them "demand greater responsibility from the state for their welfare" (2020: 100). Thus, the representation of *kothi–hijra* communities as transgender, and as gender identities, potentially facilitated claims on the state and transnational funders.

In that context, some activists who had earlier identified as *kothi* increasingly emphasized their transgender identity in their activism—such as the Kolkata-based trans activist Sharmila, who was in the convening committee of the 2009 consultation. In her 2010 interview, Sharmila explained: "Internationally, people understand TG, MSM, eunuch—they won't understand *kothi*! Initially, we called ourselves *kothi*, but if we say *kothi* we have to explain a lot, so I've seen that it's more convenient to say TG, because it's globally recognized, and this community needs recognition a lot!" For other activists in the 2009 consultation, transgender also helped consolidate regionally varied communities into a coherent, legible political group: "Sarkar informed that in India different local terms are used as identities among male-to-female TG populations, and there was need for a common term . . . understood by everyone" (SAATHII 2009: 15). Absent from this framing are the forms of transregionalism already evidenced in *kothi–hijra* networks, which become elided relative to the (trans)national scalar reach and legibility of transgender via activist, media, and funding circuits.[3] Simultaneously, transgender holds out the promise of building coalitions "across fine gradations of trans . . . identity" to achieve shared sociopolitical goals (Williams 2014: 234).[4]

However, the 2009 consultation's inclusion of *kothi* as the "most common" trans identity in eastern India proved to be precarious, offering conditional and limited recognition; the diversity of *kothi* identities did not sit well with the equation of transgender with living as the "opposite" gender and the clear distinction from MSM/sexual identities (SAATHII 2009: 17). Its inclusion gradually became contested and even reversed.

Following such consultations, funders and NGOs started assuming that their target communities were readily divisible into MSM and TG (sometimes MSM, TG, and *hijra*) groups, demanding separated data on different populations. In December 2010, SAATHII announced the impending launch of Project Pehchan in eastern India, a project for "Strengthening MSM, Hijra and Transgender Community Systems in India" funded by the Global Fund to Fight AIDS, Tuberculosis and Malaria, an international financing mechanism supported by the UN and various governments, and invited CBOs to a "community consultation" to discuss details.[5] However, belying a truly consultative process, CBOs were asked in advance to send in numbers of "the MSM, transgender and Hijra populations" in their area.[6] This caused confusion within nonmetropolitan CBOs like Sangram in Murshidabad regarding how to divide the *kothi* spectrum in their area into discrete MSM and TG components. During a discussion among CBO members, Srijan, the *kothi* whose alternation between *kodipon* and *bhelipon* was discussed in Chapter 3, commented: "What are they going to call someone like me, who behaves as TG in one place and MSM in another?" No one had a clear answer—common *kothi* practices like switching between *pons* (sartorial/behavioral modes) seemed to confound a neat MSM–TG divide. Eventually, they simply sent numbers of *kothis*, *duplis*, *parikhs*, and *hijras* as per older NACP-III guidelines.

Meanwhile, metropolitan activists evidenced inconsistent approaches to the question of how communities and identities were to be divided as MSM or TG. One simple logic was based on external sartorial presentation, evidenced early on in a residential community convention organized by MANAS Bangla in 2009. Bijoya, the aforementioned trans and *kothi* activist who had worked for MANAS Bangla, recalled in a conversation in 2013: "It all started in that convention, they (senior activists) designated separate accommodations for TG and MSM. It seemed TGs were expected to dress up, grow long hair. That's how we came to know that TG means all this!" Bijoya accordingly mapped the MSM–TG divide onto the distinction between sartorially *bheli kothis* and male-attired or *kodi kothis*: "It is the *bheli kothis* who were being called TG!" Raina, the Kolkata-based trans activist, recalled how the separation failed: "Of course, it didn't work out—at night, everyone stripped down to *genjis* (sleeveless male undershirts)! People changed rooms; everyone visited each other!" The attempted separation between *bheli* and other *kothis* parallels David Valentine's observations of activist attempts to separate gay butch queens and gay fem queens in the NYC ball scene as gay versus transgender (2007). Raina's reminiscence suggests, though, that crossovers between *bheli* and *kodi* subject positions and their shared participation in the same larger community foiled a neat separation.

While the MSM–TG distinction could be translated as a divide among different kinds of *kothis*, some activists positioned *kothis* in general as MSM, as distinct from *hijras* and trans women. The transgender and *hijra*-identified activist Madhuri told me in her 2010 interview: "*Kothis* are MSM, effeminate homosexuals. *Kothis* may sometimes think themselves to be male, sometimes female, but the TG, she will always—while getting up, while sitting down—think of herself as female. Everything about her, even the shoes she chooses to wear, will be feminine. Nowadays everyone calls themselves TG, but they shouldn't!" Madhuri's statement evokes a linear scale of femininity ranging from less consistent to totally consistent femininity ("sometimes" vs. "always" and "everything"), but rather than a continuous linearity, she posits a sharp categorical break between *kothis* (non-TG) and TGs, defining transgender identity as per both a consistent interiorized femaleness and a completely feminine external presentation. The resultant *kothi*–TG divide is reminiscent of the distinction between supposedly inconsistent *kothis* and consistently feminine *hijras* discussed in Chapter 1.

Meanwhile, other emergent understandings of trans identity stressed only interiorized self-identification. As Bijoya told me, she encountered different perspectives among other activists in Kolkata: "During a workshop, a senior activist asked me what transgender is, and I said it's someone who dresses up and all. She said, no, that's not what transgender means! If someone thinks of herself in her *mon* and *pran* (heart/mind and spirit) as a woman, then, even if she has a mustache, she is TG!" I heard the phrases "*mone prane nari*" or "*mone prane* TG" (woman or TG in *mon* and *pran*) in several other conversations as well, used to describe male-attired *kothis* who were perceived as sincerely TG or women. The reference to *mon* in such cases was reminiscent of the stable interiorized essence of transsexual and *rupantarkami* narratives, which, rather than necessitating a linear male-to-female transition, was now posited as sufficient for transgender identification, in keeping with transnational transgender discourse where anatomical status is increasingly de-emphasized relative to self-identification

(Asher 2010). However, the double reference to *mon* and *pran* suggested that for external presentation to be discounted, the interiorized depth and seriousness of self-identification needed to be emphasized all the more, as if compensating for the lack of overt transition—thus, the linear hierarchy of feminine expression was perhaps not totally overcome in such framings.

The linear distinction between fully feminine transgender subjects and less or inconsistently feminine MSM also dovetailed with an understanding of transgender subjects as more vulnerable to HIV and social discrimination. Some activists in the 2008 UNDP consultation had suggested that MSM and TG groups have distinct vulnerabilities (2008: 17). However, some participants in the 2009 consultation suggested transgender people might be *more* vulnerable—one activist noted that two HIV-related studies in 2005 and 2007 had found much higher HIV prevalence rates among *hijras* relative to MSM (SAATHII 2009: 6). As per a NACO document, one of these studies focused on *hijra* sex workers, and studies among other TG populations found variable rates (NACO 2011: 3). Yet, such studies on specific *hijra* groups were cited as data that supported the claim that "TG/hijra populations" in general were "more vulnerable than MSM" to HIV—ignoring other factors like class, caste, or profession (SAATHII 2009: 6). As Khanna notes, the biopolitics of HIV control tends to define identities primarily in terms of their vulnerability, risk, and victimhood (2016: 112). Further, as the second chapter demonstrated, NACP-III guidelines ranked subgroups of MSM as per their lesser or greater risk of HIV infection—a linear gradation that was now remapped onto some versions of the MSM–TG distinction (NACO 2017: 9).

Gradations of vulnerability extended beyond HIV risk. In the 2009 consultation, activists stressed violence as an issue affecting "TG/Hijra people" while not mentioning analogous concerns for MSM, implicitly positioning the latter as less vulnerable (SAATHII 2009: 4–5). In her 2010 interview, Sharmila told me that MSM and gay men "might cross-dress for a night, but then, they go back to their privilege!" She thus understood (un)privilege based on the singular axis of gendered identification and visibility alone, a tendency also apparent in some white trans activism (Lamble 2008: 29). While middle-class and dominant-caste herself, Sharmila did not reflect on how her background privileged her relative to both "TG" and "MSM" people from nonelite locations.

This claim of greater vulnerability was mobilized by emerging transgender activists who felt excluded by hierarchies in the NGO or development sector. Sharmila claimed to me in several conversations that MSM or gay leaders of established NGOs were favored in the disbursal of (trans)national funds or projects, where underpaid trans staff were exploited. Similar concerns about the untransparent and unfair disbursal of HIV projects were raised in national meetings (UNDP 2008: 13). Several trans activists told me in conversations between 2009 and 2014 that during NACP-III (2007–12), CBOs outside MANAS Bangla faced difficulty in procuring funds independently and WBSAPCS allegedly asked them to join the MANAS network if they wanted HIV-prevention projects. However, some activists who joined felt excluded from what they perceived as a preexisting inner circle of CBOs and activists, although MANAS Bangla leaders denied such allegations. Sangeet, a CBO leader in Kolkata, told me: "They never gave equal status to CBOs that joined later; a few people controlled MANAS Bangla." However, this important interrogation of hierarchical NGO structures and the nexus between funders, the state, and elite activists often became generalized into a divide between privileged MSM versus oppressed TG communities, which fueled contests regarding the authenticity of transgender-identified activists and ultimately did not dismantle but merely transformed hierarchical structures.

As the end of NACP-III approached, new funding opportunities provided a window for such CBOs to break entrenched power structures and gain projects independently. Building on the emerging recognition of TG as a vulnerable group, these activists lobbied the state and funders for trans-specific projects. Several Kolkata-based trans activists, including Sharmila and Sonia, joined a new network named Association of Transgender/Hijra in Bengal (ATHB), and Sonia told me how network members approached WBSAPCS several times in 2010 to protest their exclusion from funding and demand TG projects. In May 2010, an ATHB member sent an email to several LGBT mailing lists and funders that alleged that MSM leaders were blocking TG projects to preserve their vested interests: "We all know that TG/Hijra are more vulnerable . . . than MSM. If TG/Hijra will be separated from MSM then these MSM . . . will not be able to digest all the fund that is why they do not want that."[7] While demanding separate projects was a strategy to challenge the dominance of established activists, the claim to greater vulnerability evokes Wendy Brown's argument that minority identities might reinscribe their marginality and become "attached to (their) own exclusion" during the process of political representation (1995: 73–4).

Later in 2010, Sonia and other interlocutors reported that Project Pehchan was announcing new Targeted Intervention projects for MSM, TG, and *hijra* people, while WBSAPCS was launching separate HIV-prevention projects for transgender people. The question of who could claim such funding soon became a contest around transgender authenticity, and several activists were accused of opportunistically switching from MSM to TG to gain projects.

Various external and interiorized logics of MSM–TG division were deployed contingently in these contests. In 2011, Sonia complained to me regarding one MANAS Bangla leader: "He said he's MSM in one place, TG in another: we are waiting to see what he says the third time!" In another conversation, Sharmila alleged: "Sometimes they (rival activists) say they're male, sometimes TG—they identify as whatever is more advantageous to them!" Here, consistency of self-identification was valorized over external presentation or anatomy. Elsewhere, however, it boiled down to sartorial or even anatomical status. The meeting minutes of the consultation preceding the launch of Project Pehchan in eastern India noted: "Questions were raised whether participants . . . were genuine representatives of MSM, TG and Hijra communities specifically . . . some even threatened to remove parts of their clothing."[8] Such conflicts extended transregionally. In 2011, Ajit from Nadia attended a workshop for transgender and *hijra* people organized by a national NGO network as a CBO representative. She told me later: "They (some trans activists) actually pulled off the wig of one participant, saying she was really

MSM, not TG!" In another multiday residential meet outside West Bengal, Anik from Murshidabad went down to dinner in pajamas as was her habit, rather than in overtly feminine garments like the *saree*. "People like you are MSM pretending to be TG," she was told. The aforementioned linear gradation of femininity informs the policing of the MSM–TG divide—people were accused of not really being transgender if deemed not externally feminine enough. Such policing also sometimes reflected the ideals of *hijra* authenticity. As Raina told me: "What they are doing with transgender is just like what happens in *hijra gharanas*—you have to constantly dress in *satra* (women's clothes), ideally, you should get emasculated. . . . Otherwise, they'll say that you are not really transgender!"

The state and funders often responded to such contestations through attempts to reinforce the MSM–TG divide even more clearly through external and/ or interiorized logics of identification, wishing to neatly separate populations, activists, and even entire CBOs as either MSM or TG. Following the arguments in the consultation preceding Project Pehchan, the meeting report stated: "To properly differentiate between MSM, TG and Hijra populations, Project Pehchan would be developing operational guidelines, which would help in . . . population segregation."[9] Meanwhile, in January 2011, I accompanied Srijan and Anik from Murshidabad to Kolkata for a meeting with Majumdar, an officer of WBSAPCS, to advocate for an HIV-prevention project in Murshidabad. Majumdar advised them that upcoming projects were meant for exclusively TG/Hijra organizations since TG activists had complained about anti-trans discrimination in MSM projects. Alluding to the censure of *bheli kothis* in some projects (see Chapter 3), Majumdar said: "I've heard MANAS Bangla had issues; they wouldn't allow anyone to come wearing *sarees-bangles*; thus, there was anger within. Now, there is discussion in the national and international level that for such reasons, transgender projects should be separated." Srijan protested that it was hard to totally separate "TGs" from "MSM" identities, particularly in Murshidabad: "Sexually, TGs are also doing MSM behavior, and feminine males (*meyeli chhele*) may also be TG . . . in Berhampore, many wear shirt-pant but are TG in their *mon* (heart/mind). We don't have such strict divisions in Murshidabad!" Majumdar replied:

> But there is a subtle difference between MSM and TG. MSM means two men having sex, there's no saying that they'd be feminine! Even if one of them takes a female role, he remains a man, what is called homosexuality. . . . To be considered TG, we must gauge how much someone wants to be a woman in their heart/ mind and spirit (*mone prane*), even if physically male.

Here, MSM is collapsed back into homosexuality *pace* its original reference to non-gay-identified males (Boellstorff 2011). Any femininity in homosexual males is seen as less salient than their supposedly more fundamental identification as men, assumed to be mutually exclusive with womanhood. Simultaneously, the interiorized model of womanhood evinced by *rupantarkami* narratives is invoked as a governmental technique for categorizing identities and separating populations—an adjudication of the extent ("how much") of interiorized womanhood and the desire for transition seems necessary for state recognition as TG rather than MSM. Moreover, there is a generalization of specific divides between metropolitan and relatively elite activists or organizations into an overarching classificatory rubric for communities, and a scalar prioritization of discourses that are positioned as (trans)national ("national and international" discussions) over the local (the lack of a clear MSM–TG distinction in Murshidabad).

Kothi *Contestations and Erasure*

To some extent, people like Srijan and Anik contested the imposition of the MSM–TG binary by evoking *kothi* discourses and practices. After the meeting, Srijan defiantly commented: "Let them do whatever division they want here, we'll not let it happen in Murshidabad!" Anik was less optimistic: "Already, this division has started—the *kodi kothis* and *bheli kothis* have become divided in the square field (the main cruising area of Berhampore)." Anik's observation interpreted the *kodi–bheli* divide, usually understood as an intra-*kothi* split, as inaugurating a more definitive separation of MSM and TG identities. Even so, both Srijan and Anik drew on *kothi* practices like alternation between *pons* (behavioral or sartorial modes) to traverse MSM–TG divides. In one conversation in 2011, Srijan boasted of her ability to pass as both MSM and TG: "Sometimes, I do *parikhpon* (*parikh*-mode), but then also do *chhibripon* and *laharanpon* (*hijra*-mode, woman-mode) to get TG projects for Sangram!" Before another meeting with a WBSAPCS officer that year, Anik told me as we waited:

> See, I have brought a wig and a padded bra in my bag; if they say, "this person looks *gay*, this person is MSM, not TG," then I'll take out and put on the wig and bra, and say—look at my *roop* (form)! Look, I was MSM, now I am coming here as TG, next time I'll come as *hijra*!

Here, the trope of switching between *roops*, as mentioned in some *kothi* narratives in Chapter 4, is evoked to jocularly articulate a spontaneous MSM–TG switch rather than the linear male-to-female *rupantar* (transition in *roop*) that officials like Majumdar expect. Such instances corroborate Adnan Hossain's observation that NGO interventions do not simply foster an ossification of identities but also lead to new forms of fluidity as the subjects of such intervention represent themselves contextually based on the identity category for which funding is sought or given (2021: 194). However, there are important limitations to such fluidity, as outlined below.

First, some *kothis* and *hijras* may translate the MSM–TG divide in terms of preexisting tensions and accept its salience. Nandini, for example, is a *hijra gharana* member who temporarily worked in a new trans HIV-prevention project in 2012. During a conversation that year, Nandini reflected back on her youth and said:

My friends and I called ourselves *kothi* . . . We didn't know words like MSM and TG back then. But there were already problems between MSMs and TGs. The *duplis* would harass us, make fun of us; they wouldn't want to be seen with us in public, although behind closed doors, they took it in the ass!

Here, rather than translating the MSM–TG divide into the *bheli–kodi* split, *kothis* are generally understood as TG, while *dupli* are MSM. Nandini reads the MSM–TG split back into the fraught relation between *kothis* and *duplis* of her acquaintance, presuming them as neatly separate identities in a way that potentially elides *kothi–dupli* overlaps in other community circles.

Second, the irreducibility of the *kothi* spectrum to an MSM versus TG split also made the term controversial and contributed to its gradual erasure from activist, state, and legal discourse. As mentioned in Chapter 5, the activist Sharmila understood her trans identity as a separate gender and did not emphasize anatomical transition. Simultaneously, however, she was very suspicious of the flexibility of the *kothi* category. In her 2010 interview, she said:

> I trust and feel comfortable with TGs much more than people who do MSM behavior. The TG always carries her identity with her. . . . The person who does MSM behavior, what's the guarantee that he won't fuck me in the night? Earlier, we called ourselves *kothi*. . . . But there are so many shades among *kothis*. . . . *Kothis* may be *dupli*. . . . I've seen even bisexuals identify themselves as *kothi*. . . . So now, I feel more comfortable saying TG than *kothi*. People who are more feminine, they'll feel more comfortable identifying as TG.

As Sharmila gradually realized the diversity of *kothi* identities and its overlap with MSM, *dupli*, or bisexual people whom she saw as sexually duplicitous and untrustworthy, she publicly adopted transgender instead of *kothi*, which was also prompted by the "globally recognized" nature of transgender, as noted earlier. While I observed that privately she still sometimes referred to herself and her friends as *kothi* and *dhurani*, she expected that "more feminine" *kothis* would naturally adopt transgender as their sole public identity—rather than, for instance, categories like *bhorokti* or *bheli kothi* that demarcate overtly feminine *kothis* while placing them within a larger *kothi* community. Meanwhile, Sonia told me in a conversation in 2011: "*Kothis* may be MSM or TG; each *kothi* should themselves decide whether they are MSM or TG!" Her statement assumes MSM and TG as underlying cross-cultural identities and presumes all *kothis* will neatly fall into one or the other category, presenting this self-designation as an obligatory decision for all *kothis*.

Tensions in metropolitan activist circles came to a head during the consultations preceding the launch of NACP-IV in 2011, which were again somewhat exclusive—Sumi from North Bengal, for example, told me that her CBO was not permitted to attend because older NGOs/CBOs from the region were already coming. Meanwhile, Anik narrated to me how some activists, in collaboration with WBSAPCS officials, insisted that MSM and TG people should sit in separate sections, and *kothis* like herself were compelled to pick a side (she picked TG). When a *kothi* in male attire entered a TG working group discussion and contradicted a trans CBO leader on some issue, they were physically accosted, accused of being an MSM person disrupting TG empowerment, and removed from the group.

Following such contestations, the operational guidelines of NACP-IV placed *kothi* back in the MSM category alongside *panthis* (*parikhs*) and gay men, while mapping *hijras* and trans women as transgender (NACO 2011: 3–8). Concurrently, Project Pehchan's operational guidelines for HIV-prevention projects clearly specified which self-identities corresponded to MSM, TG, and *hijra* categories, stipulating that people identifying as *kothi* would be categorized as MSM, while trans women and *hijras* were classified as TG and *hijra* respectively (Alliance India 2011: 11). These policy developments reversed the earlier inclusion of *kothi* as the most common "local" transgender identity (SAATHII 2009: 17). They also displaced the earlier prominence of *kothi* as a high-risk group. During NACP-IV, NACO (2017: 9) mapped the newly separated category of "H/TG" (*hijra/transgender*) as having higher HIV prevalence than MSM, implicitly indicating its greater vulnerability as per a reconfigured (but still linear) gradation of HIV risk—even though NACO renamed these groups as "key populations" rather than "high-risk groups" following UNAIDS guidelines for less stigmatizing language (Vijayakumar 2021: 195). These policies paralleled the construction of reductive cis/trans binaries and linear gradations of femininity in legal discourse, discussed later, where *kothi* gradually became erased from the transgender category.[10]

However, while the MSM–TG separation became consolidated in policy, breaches of this categorical divide continued below and beyond the level of official representation. In a trans-specific HIV-prevention project administered by Sonia's CBO near Kolkata, I noticed that male-attired *kothis* were counted as transgender to meet the required target number of community members. In a conversation in 2012, Sonia explained: "If TGs were earlier counted within MSM projects, why can't MSM be counted in TG projects? Many *kothis* who are *kodi* here do *bhel* elsewhere." Sonia thus contradicted her aforementioned position that *kothis* must divide themselves as MSM or TG, and conceded both MSM–TG and *kodi–bheli* overlaps. Meanwhile, during a survey on HIV prevalence at a composite intervention for MSM, TG, and *hijra* people funded by Project Pehchan near Kolkata in 2014, I observed that the (mostly *kothi*) staff were categorizing saree-clad *hijras* as MSM on survey forms. One staff person explained to me: "They are not emasculated yet, so we may count them as MSM!" Such practices were possible because usually target group members did not fill up forms directly; rather, as a *kothi* field worker explained, "we talk to them, gauge their feelings, and fill it up later." Another staff member told me privately: "Most of the data in these projects is *khauri* (fake), *parikhs* are counted as *dupli*, *kothis* are counted as *parikhs*!" The pressure of fulfilling numerical targets set for each at-risk category superseded the imperative of neatly separating populations, suggesting that contradictory pressures within the biopolitics of HIV-prevention result in breaches of official cartographies.[11] In our 2012 conversation, Sonia suggested that funders, while demanding population segregation on paper, tacitly tolerated such practices: "WBSAPCS knows very well that these populations are actually overlapping!" But higher levels of representation were a different matter. I noticed that Sharmila was quite tolerant of a *kothi* staff member in her organization who led a parallel life as a heterosexually married man, but publicly attacked a rival trans leader for doing the same. In a conversation in 2013 where I was present, the staff member diffidently asked Sharmila why she tolerated her dual existence. Sharmila replied: "Well, you are not in a leadership position!"

This meant that *kothis* with less involvement in activist politics often continued using terms like transgender and gay nonexclusively—such as Borsha, who, as we saw in Chapter 5, casually combined trans and gay identification while working in an HIV project in this period. Others changed representational strategies contextually, emphasizing an unambiguous trans identity in public or formal representations. Rima, the *kothi* from Kolkata, told me in a conversation in 2016, soon after her sartorial transition, that since funders now understood *kothi* to mean "*meyeli purush*" (feminine men), she felt more comfortable identifying as transgender publicly, although her friend circle continued using *kothi* informally. In a conversation in 2011, Kanchana shared her experience of attending recent trans consultations, and commented: "*Kothi* has become a controversial term, because *kothis* may both fuck and get fucked!" At a pride walk in Kolkata, I observed that she told a reporter: "My only identity is *transgender!*" However, within the community at Berhampore, she continued referring to herself as a *bheli kothi* and, as noted in the last chapter, resisted efforts to divide *kodi* and *bheli kothis* as MSM versus TG—even designating herself as *samakami* in that context. Meanwhile, during a visit to North Bengal in 2013, I met Krishna, a *kothi* who had worked in MANAS Bangla and witnessed attempts at MSM–TG separation. Yet, she interpreted the MSM–TG difference as variations within an overarching *kothi* category. As she said: "There are so many kinds of *kothis*, so many divisions among *kothis*!" Later in the conversation, Sumi, who was also present, reflected on activist efforts to separate MSM and TG: "How much more will they divide *kothis*?" Thus, the use of *kothi* as an overarching umbrella category that could encompass both MSM and trans feminine people also continued.

Rather than either just contextual fluidity or a complete erasure of MSM–TG overlaps, there is thus a process of vernacularization in the sense that certain *kothi* discourses and practices are consigned to private, informal, or unofficial levels, such as quotidian intra-community conversations in Bengali and Ulti, while official or state recognition might be withheld from subject positions that are not seen as conforming to dominant Anglophone categories, such as the aforementioned *kothis* in Coochbehar who were considered ineligible for trans-related benefits.

The politics of MSM–trans separation in HIV projects also elided the class and caste positions of trans leaders. Ironically, despite the aforementioned protests against MSM leaders exploiting trans workers, staff in several new transgender projects told me that the leaders of the associated CBOs, relatively elite trans women, paid them only a part of their official salary, appropriating the rest. Further, while NACP-IV and Project Pehchan salaries were higher than

NACP-III, staff complained that formats and targets had also increased even as there were rampant delays in the disbursement of funds and salaries—up to six months in some WBSAPCS-funded projects during NACP-IV. The separation of MSM and transgender categories thus reinforced a single-axis identity politics that focused on differences of gendered privilege but ignored class and caste differences among newly separated transgender communities and structural exploitation within the HIV industry, which continued in newer forms. Moreover, the HIV industry seemed to be declining as AIDS was internationally perceived as a receding crisis and budgets for HIV projects shrank (Vijayakumar 2021). This compelled CBOs like Sampriti to seek alternative funding (e.g., for human rights work). However, the biopolitics of mapping HIV risk groups had a lasting influence on the legal demarcation of legitimate subjects of substantive equality.

Contrasting Vernacularizations: The Legal Enshrinement of Cis/Trans, Kothi/Hijra Divides

In her book *Legalizing Sex*, Lakkimsetti documents how UNDP, based on inputs from the aforementioned consultations, started advocating for transgender rights with the Indian state and judiciary from 2009 onward (2020: 114). Around 2012, UNDP wrote a letter to NALSA, a state-run agency that provides legal aid to marginalized groups, following which NALSA filed a petition for transgender recognition and rights in the Indian Supreme Court, joined by some trans/*hijra* petitioners such as Tripathi (Lakkimsetti 2020: 115). In 2013, the Indian government's Ministry of Social Justice and Empowerment (MSJE) took cognizance of these developments and organized a meeting to discuss "issues relating to Transgender community such as social stigma, discrimination, lack of education" (MSJE 2014: ii). This meeting included state officials, NGO functionaries, and transgender and *hijra* activists, who recommended the constitution of an expert committee comprising government representatives, academics, and activists to study the problems of transgender communities and suggest remedies (ibid.).

While these developments marked the dawning recognition of transgender people as a vulnerable group beyond HIV, MSJE's meeting and expert committee dispensed with any pretense of democratic process—trans representatives in both cases "were invited" by the ministry (MSJE 2014: ii). No transgender activists from eastern and Northeast India were selected for either. Several Kolkata activists—including some who had participated in the UNDP-funded consultations—told me that they did not know of the NALSA petition or the MSJE committee before they became public. Thus, both the petition and the expert committee report resulted from a consolidation of selective community representation and "expert" knowledges rather than even the token inclusivity of earlier consultations.

The resultant MSJE report draws upon various transnational and domestic sources, including previous UNDP reports, academic studies, and international human rights and LGBTQ rights discourse. Citing the Yogyakarta Principles on rights related to sexual orientation and gender identity authored by international human rights experts in 2006, the report describes gender identity as "a person's internal, deeply felt sense of being either man or woman, or something other or in between" (MSJE 2014: 1). This framing reflects the idea of an "interiorized self with psychic depth" that characterizes modern biomedical discourses of sexuality and gender (Najmabadi 2013: 293). While in *rupantarkami* discourse this deep self is typically associated with cross-gender identification, here, the concept becomes extended to encompass identification as "something other or in between" (MSJE 2014: 1).

However, this significant expansion of (trans)gender identity is limited. First, the report understands any individual's gender as a singular, invariant identity classifiable as one of "the two categories of cisgender and transgender"—either "cis man and cis woman" or "a gender other than the gender assigned" which may be expressed "through several identity terms . . . all of which largely fall under the category of transgender" (MSJE 2014: 7). The binary cis/trans distinction rests on the aforementioned idea of gender as a deeply interiorized identity, either conforming to or clearly distinct from one's socially assigned gender. This elides the possibility of fluctuating relations with one's assigned gender, such as the situational (dis)identifications with maleness and correspondingly diverse ideas of interiority in some *kothi* and *hijra* narratives (see Chapter 4). As A. Finn Enke critiques in the US context, the cis/trans binary might naturalize and ossify gender identities as perpetually stable and elide their contingent production in variable personal and social contexts (2012: 61–73). Although MSJE describes genderqueer persons as those who "may see gender as less rigid," ultimately, they, too, are seen as people who "identify as non cisgender" rather than potentially traversing cis and trans categories (MSJE 2014: 7). Emergent state discourse thus separates "genderqueer" from other, presumably cisgender, queer identities—restricting the potential of "queer" to flexibly encompass varied forms of gender/sexual non-normativity without casting them into rigid identities (Khanna 2016: 30).

Further, while the report recommends the "legal recognition of gender identity of transgender people based on their choice—women, men or a separate gender . . . independent of surgery/hormones," such recognition is made subject to a "psychosocial assessment" by a screening committee including government officials, trans representatives, a psychologist, and a psychiatrist, suggesting that assessing psychic depth is necessary for legally ratifying (trans)gender identity (MSJE 2014: 32–4). The legal requirement of attesting a singular gender identity follows from the postcolonial state's approach to identity classification in general, including religious or ethnic identities—as Partha Chatterjee notes, "one can only be . . . Muslim or not Muslim" to the modern state (2004: 6). However, the report naturalizes this requirement in terms of a universalized psychological understanding of gender as either cis or trans.

Moreover, similar to the tendencies of scalar hierarchization and vernacularization in the SAATHII (2009) report, *kothi* and *hijra* are described as "sociocultural groups of transgender people" and as "local terminologies," which situates them as locally and culturally particular even as transgender is universalized as cross-culturally neutral, subsuming all non-cisgender "identity terms" (MSJE

2014: 2–8). This concretely affects legal recognition since designating oneself through these terms is seen as only signifying affiliation with particular cultural groups: "The criterion/test for qualifying as a transgender person will apply on individual basis and the fact such a person belongs to a known transgender sociocultural group will act as corroborative evidence and not conclusive" (MSJE 2014: 9). Of course, identities like *hijra* have cultural dimensions beyond gender (Reddy 2005)—however, as we have seen, such terms may *also* be used to describe someone's gendered subject position, as when community members distinguish themselves as *hijra/kothi* rather than women or men. Yet, such self-designation is not treated as the "conclusive" declaration of a legally recognizable gender identity in itself, but as "corroborative evidence" of a deeper ontological identity (being transgender or cisgender), thus subordinating *kothi/hijra* understandings of selfhood to the aforementioned psychological model of (trans)gender identity.

Further, a simplistic contrast between *kothis* and *hijras* is established: "*Kothi* persons present themselves as males in most spheres . . . and only reveal their feminine identity in certain social circles, unlike Hijra identified persons who present themselves in their feminine attire all the time" (MSJE 2014: 8). This erases *hijra* overlaps with social maleness, sometimes including heterosexual marriages (Hossain 2021). *Hijra* becomes more closely associated with trans identity than *kothi* based on a linear gradation of feminine presentation—inconsistently versus totally feminine ("all the time")—that parallels similar comparisons between *kothi* and *hijra* femininities in previous HIV-related reports (HST 2007; UNDP 2010). Alongside the *hijra*, South Indian groups like *aravanis* or *jogtas*—often seen as *hijra* equivalents, as Tom and Menon (2021) note—are included in the report's finalized definition of transgender, while *kothi* and related terms that overlap with feminine maleness (like *dhurani* or *zenana*) are relegated to an "etc.":

> Transgender persons: All persons whose own sense of gender does not match with the gender assigned to them at birth. They will include trans-men & trans-women (whether or not they have undergone sex reassignment surgery or hormonal treatment . . . etc.), genderqueers and a number of socio cultural identities, such as kinnars, hijras, aravanis, jogtas, etc. (MSJE 2014: 9)

Meanwhile, another contrasting vernacularizing process also played into legal discourse. As we saw earlier, *hijra* activists like Laxmi Narayan Tripathi recast transgender as a third/separate gender based on a national model of the *hijra*, relative to which other identities are localized. In the 2010s, this redefinition influenced Indian state and media discourse, sometimes superseding other understandings of transgender. This is especially apparent in the text and media reception of the Supreme Court of India's 2014 NALSA judgment on transgender identity and rights, which, apart from the NALSA petition, also drew on a petition by Tripathi (Supreme Court 2014). As demonstrated elsewhere, the judgment text is inconsistent and ambiguous (Semmalar 2014; Dutta 2014). It vacillates between suggesting the psychological testing of gender identity and validating the self-determination of gender (Dutta 2014: 232). Based on an understanding of (trans)gender as an interiorized, innate identity similar to the MSJE report, the final directives grant transgender individuals the right to self-identify as male, female, or a third gender irrespective of transition and disallow any anatomical criteria for legal gender recognition, without explicitly overruling psychological assessment (Dutta 2014: 232; Jain and Kartik 2020: 16). The directives also recognize transgender people as a socially "backward" class eligible for reserved seats in educational institutions and public employment (Supreme Court 2014: 128). However, transgender is treated as a homogenously marginalized category and it is neither specified how oppressed-caste trans people might combine existing caste-based reservations with transgender reservation, nor how trans men or women who desire male/female identification might access trans-specific benefits (Semmalar 2014; Dutta 2014).

Simultaneously, the judgment vacillates between a flexibly broad sense of transgender encompassing even LGB identities and a narrower framing that conflates transgender with *hijra* and third gender identity (Semmalar 2014; Dutta 2014). While it borrows language from previous UNDP (2010) and HST (2007) reports to define transgender as an "umbrella term . . . used to describe a wide range of identities," it also sometimes uses the phrase "*hijras*/transgender persons," loosely conflating these terms (Supreme Court 2014: 8–11). Later, the judgment suggests that gay and lesbian people might be considered within a broad understanding of transgender as "across or beyond gender" but immediately clarifies that it is "not concerned with this aforesaid wider meaning" (Supreme Court 2014: 109). This point was later reinforced by the MSJE, which filed an application to clarify certain points in the judgment, including the distinction between transgender and LGB categories. MSJE's application stated:

> Gay, lesbian, bisexual is based on the "sexual orientation" of the person, while the term "transgender" has to do with the person's own deep sense of gender identity. Worldwide, the term used is LGBT . . . some of the transgender persons may also be gay lesbian or bisexual because of their sexual orientation, but per se, gay, lesbian and bisexual are not transgender persons. ("Gays, Lesbians" 2016)

The Supreme Court responded that this was already clear in the judgment (ibid.). MSJE's reference to LGBT as a "worldwide" term reinforces scalar and conceptual hierarchies between dominant Anglophone concepts that clearly separate gender identity from sexual orientation and other epistemologies that may not understand gender and sexuality as rigidly distinct arenas of experience (Valentine 2007).

Significantly, MSJE concedes that some trans persons may be LGB (e.g., lesbian trans women), but not that some people who are LGB as per their socially assigned gender may *also* be trans. This erases how *kothis* like Borsha, who identify as gay or *samakami* in the sense of feminine males desiring men, might understand such desire as interlinked with their gender variance. As Meredith Talusan (2015) critiques in the US context, dominant understandings of LGB identity tend to erase how some forms of sexual non-normativity might *also* be forms of gender nonconformity. Further, since the MSJE and Supreme Court see trans people as people eligible for measures to ensure substantive equality (like reservations), the LGB–transgender distinction thus constructed also implicitly restricts substantive equality as applicable only to gender variance, disaggregated from sexual nonconformity. Later, non-trans LGB people get constructed as subjects of *formal* equality in the 2018 Supreme Court judgment that decriminalizes nonheterosexual intercourse, declaring that LGBT people have the same constitutional rights as other citizens (Dutta 2020: 427). This tendency is reinforced by elite gay activism that subsequently raises demands for marriage and adoption rights similar to heterosexual citizens, rather than welfare measures (Kumar 2020).

Meanwhile, the NALSA judgment, while discussing gender recognition, prioritizes the recognition of transgender people as a third gender as their "primary" concern while the recognition of trans women or men as female or male is included as an "inter-related" issue that "has also popped up" (Supreme Court 2014: 87). The text then positions *hijra* and related identities as the primary Indian version of transgender: "In this country, TG community comprise of Hijaras, eunuch, Kothis, Aravanis, Jogappas, Shiv-Shakthis, etc. In Indian community transgender are referred as Hizra or the third gendered people [*sic*]" (Supreme Court 2014: 109). As Gee Semmalar (2014) has critiqued, this potentially erases other trans identities and *hijras* who identify as women. At one point, the judgment cites Tripathi's petition to aver that *hijras* are a third gender because they lack "reproduction capacities," harkening back to anatomical ideas of *hijra* authenticity, although the same page contradictorily describes third gender identity as psychological (Supreme Court 2014: 10). Moreover, there is a Hinduization of *hijra* identity as apparently rooted in Hindu mythology, while Islamic influences are downplayed (Semmalar 2014). Thus, the judgment, while granting the right to gender self-determination and prioritizing psychology over anatomy, foregrounds a construction of transgender based on a limited reading of *hijra* identities rather than subsuming the *hijra* as a sociocultural version of the universal transgender as in the MSJE report.

The inclusion of *kothis* is relatively ambiguous. The judgment draws on HIV-focused UNDP and HST reports to locate *kothis* as a "heterogenous group" evincing "varying degrees of femininity" while *hijras*, supposedly, categorically "reject their masculine identity" (Supreme Court 2014: 110; HST 2007: 7; UNDP 2010: 13). Like the MSJE report, the judgment thus reinforces linear gradations between more and less consistently feminine identities based on older HIV-related biopolitics. This tendency, combined with the elision of *kothi* in the MSJE definition of transgender, means that *kothi* and similar identities become implicitly positioned as less ideal subjects of transgender recognition and related measures for substantive equality than the *hijra* and binary trans categories.

Transgender as a "Third Gender"

Following the judgment, media reports claimed that the Supreme Court had recognized "transgender people as third gender" ("India Court" 2014)—eliding the recognition of trans men/women and gender self-determination also offered in parts of the judgment (Nagpaul 2017). During this rearticulation of transgender as a third gender, the old authenticity binaries around real and fake *hijras* were sometimes transposed onto transgender identity. As mentioned in Chapter 1, in 2015, a news portal circulated a viral video of one *hijra* stripping another with the headline "transgender woman beats the heck out of a man posing as one" (Daily Bhaskar 2015). Ideals of *hijra* authenticity may thus translate into biologically essentialist ideas about transgender authenticity.[12]

This tendency sometimes influenced state recognition and welfare. In 2018, the chief minister of West Bengal, Mamata Banerjee, announced that the state wanted to remove *hijras* begging on the streets of Kolkata as they apparently harassed pedestrians and hampered the city's "beautification" ("Morey Morey" 2018). She assured that the state would rehabilitate *hijras* into mainstream professions, but only "*prakrita brihannala*" (real *hijras*) would get opportunities meant for "trans persons" after the police verified whether "they were really third gender" (ibid.). This conflation of transgender, third gender, and the "real" *hijra* instantiated a crude iteration of a broader transnational tendency—the demarcation of deserving trans subjects, worthy of recuperation into society and citizenship, versus others subjected to criminalization, surveillance, and violence (Spade 2015: 18; Pamment 2019: 144–6). The targeting of non-transitioned *hijras* who do *chhalla*, who (as shown earlier) often overlap with *kothi* identity and inhabit the margins of *gharanas*, underlines the precarity of *kothi* inclusion within the transgender category and continues older patterns of the criminalization of "fake" *hijras*. Hierarchies between trans subjects might thus map onto preexisting divides among *hijras*, rather than only schisms between trans women and *hijras* (Mount 2020).

Simultaneously, as they intersect with the transgender category, both the "third gender" and the *hijra* may also be understood in terms of psychological gender identity and/or group affiliation rather than anatomy. Several Kolkata activists condemned the aforementioned attempt to ban *chhalla* and protested the violation of gender self-determination through police verification ("Morey Morey" 2018). Sharmila protested on social media that the "identification of authentic *brihannala* by police" violated the "freedom of self-identification of gender" granted by the NALSA judgment—as mentioned earlier, she emphasized consistent self-identification as TG rather than anatomical transition.[13] The proposed measure was eventually aborted, although administrative attempts to ban *chhalla* and weed out "fake" *hijras* have recurred sporadically ("Nokol Brihannala" 2019).

Meanwhile, some *hijras* cited the NALSA judgment to base legitimate *hijra* status on *gharana* affiliation and profession rather than anatomical authenticity. For instance, Dipika, a *hijra nayak* (senior *guru*) from a district near Kolkata, teamed up with some trans activists who are open about their status as assigned male at birth and established an NGO for *hijra* empowerment and general social welfare around 2014. Later, in 2015, she hosted a public gathering with representatives of several Kolkata-based NGOs at her suburban residence, which I attended. While addressing the guests, she said that "there's no use in hiding anything anymore" and mentioned that her *hijra* household had both emasculated "eunuchs" like herself and non-emasculated "transgender" people. Later, she traced *hijras* back to their supposed ancient precursors in Hindu scriptures, and declared: "The Supreme Court speaks of bringing back this exalted position of *hijras* in ancient scriptures!" She thus underlined the Indian state's judicial support for the place of *hijras* within Hindu religious tradition. However, she associated this venerated status only with *hijras* who performed *badhai* (blessing newborns), the main profession of *hijra gharanas* in Bengal: "Our only income is from *badhai*—the profession of the *buzurg* (venerated elders)! But some people take our *roop* (form/ appearance) and do bad things, like harassing people at traffic signals for money or doing *khajra* (sex work) at night." She thus recast the hierarchy between *gharana*-based *badhaiwali hijras* and other *hijras* not as per biological realness but as per their place within a state-sanctioned religious tradition or lack thereof.

Relative to such varied scripts of *hijra* authenticity, activists like Sharmila instantiate a different interpretation of transgender as a third or separate gender. In her aforementioned protest, Sharmila clarified that she was an ally to *hijras* but wanted to "stick to my identity by not joining Hijra customs." As we have seen, she also distinguished her trans identity from womanhood. Her friend Sonia, meanwhile, did speak of becoming a woman via transition, but felt that trans women should strategically identify as a separate "transgender" category rather than choosing legal female identification. "I know many TGs simply want to be identified as women, but if we all get identity cards as women, we will become *invisible*," she explained to me during a conversation in 2012. This was partly in response to state attempts to count transgender persons through the census (Redding 2021). Both Sonia and Sharmila felt that getting counted as a substantial minority would help in claiming welfare measures.

In that context, some trans activists who identified as a separate gender objected to postoperative trans women claiming the transgender category and potential benefits. In a media report, Ranjita Sinha, a Kolkata-based transgender activist, stated: "If they have converted themselves into women, why should they want the perks . . . reserved for the third gender?" (Dasgupta 2016). Sonia echoed this argument in several conversations. Such stances point to a figure of the "third gender" that is both exclusive of postoperative trans women and distinct from the *hijra*.

Tista Das, meanwhile, strongly critiqued the recognition of transgender people as a "third gender" in a Bengali article: "After much struggle . . . I changed my sex and became a woman. . . . But the state is saying I'm not a woman, I am *tritiyo lingo* (third gender)! . . . In a patriarchal society, men are the first gender. Women are second. And we have become the third" (Das 2014). While she does not mention that some trans people do identify as a separate gender ("third" or not), her critique points to both the denial of self-determination and the hierarchical devaluation latent in the state's segregation of trans people into a "third" category. Manobi Bandyopadhyay, however, sometimes combined her trans womanhood with a claim to the third gender category. In the aforementioned media report, she contested Sinha's argument thus: "When I applied for the post of a principal, it was in the female category . . . Later . . . the rules had been revised with the inclusion of the others category . . . (so) I mentioned myself as the third gender . . . Any transperson who has converted to a woman should get all the facilities that a transgender gets" (Dasgupta 2016). These contestations recall the tensions regarding claims to the transgender category as a subject of substantive equality evinced by earlier demands for MSM–TG separation, with the divide now located between "third gender" and binary trans categories.

The Limits of Self-determination

However, the MSM–TG and cis/trans divides, rather than the various intra-*hijra*, trans-*hijra*, and intra-trans splits, have proved to be more durable in structuring state policy and activist demands. After the NALSA judgment, the MSJE introduced a series of draft bills leading to the Transgender Persons (Protection of Rights) Act of 2019—a process that exacerbated the aforementioned limitations of legal recognition (Banu 2018; Bhattacharya 2019). Given the extensive activist and academic critiques of the bills and act, I will only summarize some key issues relevant here.[14] The MSJE's initial draft bill in 2015 stuck closely to the 2014 committee report, but the 2016 version introduced in the parliament by the minister of social justice and empowerment—the politician in charge of MSJE—disregarded not only several directives of the NALSA judgment but even the MSJE report itself (Jain and Kartik 2020: 18). While the 2015 bill reproduced the MSJE report's definition of transgender and promised trans-specific reservations, the 2016 version excluded reservations and shifted from the report's psychologized understanding of (trans)gender identity to an anatomically inflected definition of transgender persons as "(*A*) neither wholly female nor wholly male; or (*B*) a combination of female or male; or (*C*) neither female nor male" (Jain and Kartik 2020: 35). Simultaneously, the bill subjected legal recognition as transgender to verification through a "screening committee" comprising two government officers, a medical officer, a psychologist, and a trans representative, extending the psychological screening suggested in the MSJE report to potentially include physical screening (Orinam 2016b).[15] Such moves reinforced a medicalized understanding of transgender identity and potentially understood transgender authenticity as per biological framings of *hijra* realness (Bhattacharya 2019: 10). However, the bill also omitted any mention of *hijras* from the definition, recognized only heteronormative families and not *kothi–hijra* kinship structures, and potentially criminalized *hijra* professions (including *badhai*) through provisions against begging (Banu 2018; Orinam 2016b). Thus, contradictorily, there was an abstraction of the "real" *hijra* into the terms of transgender physical difference *and* a disdain for actual *hijra* lives. Other problems included treating sexual violence against trans people less seriously than violence against cis women (Jain and Kartik 2020: 23). Therefore, even trans identities that had hitherto gained some state recognition and legibility, such as trans men/women and the *hijra* or "third" gender, were devalued as citizens.

Thus, the bills garnered intense resistance from trans communities (Bhattacharya 2019). This resistance spurred the formation of coalitions that included both CBO/NGO activists and trans activists critical of the NGO complex, including some oppressed-caste activists and their allies (Shankar 2017). A greater intra-community consensus favoring gender self-determination and opposing the state surveillance of transgender identity emerged in the process. In the years between the NALSA verdict and the 2019 transgender act, activists like Sonia, who were suspicious of MSM people claiming transgender identity for benefits, had terrible experiences with government authorities while trying to get their identity cards changed to the "other" or "transgender" categories that were gradually becoming available. In 2014, Sonia narrated to me her experience of being asked for medical proof of sex change and being laughed at by local administrative officers when her documents were deemed inadequate. Thus, in context of the trans bills, both she and Sharmila came around to the position that the state should accept self-identification for gender change on legal identity documents. In a public meeting on the trans bill in 2016, Sharmila protested against a government lawyer who called a *kodi* (male-attired) *kothi* a "man" and asserted that it was not always possible to adjudge someone's gender externally. Given this emerging consensus against state gatekeeping—even among activists who had earlier policed trans identification themselves—the responses submitted by various trans collectives to the 2015 version of the MSJE's bill all recommended that only self-identification should be required for recognition as male, female, or transgender (as a separate gender) on identity cards, at least when not accompanied by benefits (Orinam 2016a). From 2016 onward, the leaflets of several Kolkata pride walks supported the self-determination of gender and opposed the state's gatekeeping of identification (KRPW 2018). Activists, including some *kothis* and *hijras* connected to CBOs, used the walks to protest against the transgender bills, declaiming Bengali slogans on gender self-determination that evidenced the influence of earlier feminist discourse, such as "*amar shorir, amar mon, dur hato rajshashon*" (my body, my mind/heart: go away state control).

However, activists evinced a more uneven approach to the process of accessing benefits. In their responses to the 2015 bill, several collectives recommended disaggregating the legal identification process from the certification for benefits—recommending self-identification through a notarized legal affidavit as the only requirement for changing gender to male/female or transgender on identity documents, while suggesting that a separate transgender certificate would be required to access benefits like reservations (Orinam 2016a). This potentially resolved the issue of how trans men and women could get male/female identification but also access trans-specific measures, rather than becoming "invisible" within mainstream society as Sonia feared. However, this also allowed for the proposition of a separate screening process for benefits, with contrasting models. The Sampoorna Working Group, a collective of trans and intersex people, proposed certification for benefits based on a "diagnosis" by a licensed mental health professional and not state authorities or intra-community gatekeepers, while the Telangana Hijra Intersex Transgender Samiti (THITS) contrastingly recommended certification by a panel comprising "transgender and intersex people from all the diverse identity backgrounds . . . transwomen, trans men, intersex, hijra, shivashakti, jogappa, mangalmukhi, aravani, jogta, etc. that are locally and culturally relevant" (Orinam 2016a). Rather than the state, authority was sought to be vested on psycho-medical experts or community representatives. While these models became somewhat redundant after the 2016 bill jettisoned reservations and were not included in subsequent activist responses, their proposition suggests that the support for gender self-determination might become qualified when the material stakes of such identification get higher.

Further, the list of identities suggested for the certification panel in the aforementioned THITS response (Orinam 2016a), as well as the definition of transgender in a later consolidated response to the 2016 bill by several collectives (Orinam 2016b), reinforced the previously discussed pattern of vernacularization in the MSJE report by designating non-Anglophone identities as local/cultural and naming only those "cultural" terms—*mangalmukhi, jogappa, jogta, shivashakti, aravani*—that are commonly considered as related to or local variants of the *hijra* (Tom and Menon 2021; Reddy 2005). Meanwhile, *kothi* and related terms like *zenana* were relegated to the "etc." This repeated elision was perhaps related to a relative lack of explicitly *kothi*-identified persons that I observed in the aforementioned collectives, despite their diversity and anti-hierarchical approach. Some *kothi*/trans activists from West Bengal who joined a few anti-bill protests, like Heena and Kanchana, had by then shifted to publicly identifying as transgender and reserved *kothi* as a private intra-community usage, partly due to the aforementioned controversy around *kothi* during the MSM–TG wars and partly due to the greater public legibility and respectability of transgender.[16]

As the government continued to mandate a screening process for identity documents, activist responses voiced stronger demands for gender self-determination while also reinforcing the psychologized model of a consistent, deep-rooted transgender identity without overlap with cisgender or MSM categories. For instance, a press note critiquing the 2018 version of the bill, which eliminated the anatomically inflected definition of transgender but retained the screening committee, stated that "transgender persons have a strong physical and/ or cognitive discomfort" with their assigned genders, while also insisting that trans men and women are men and women "regardless of how they look, or dress" (Bittu et al. 2018: 4). The rejection of any external criteria for assessing transness is accompanied by the assumption of a "strong" dissociation with assigned gender. Further, in 2016, I had online conversations with several metropolitan trans activists involved with anti-bill protests regarding whether the aforementioned MSJE application and the Supreme Court's response ultimately restricted the self-determination of identity by precluding simultaneous gay and trans identification. Most felt that the MSJE was clear that some trans persons could be LGB as per their sexual orientation, and the clarification was fine since it only excluded cisgender LGB people. However, overlap between trans feminine identification and gay or *samakami* identity based on male–male desire, as seen in some *kothi* narratives, is precisely the sort of overlap with "cisgender" LGB identities that the

MSJE clarification disallowed. Some activists sought to preserve a clear gay/trans distinction out of concerns about gay privilege. During an online discussion in 2016, a dominant-caste trans woman expressed the fear that gay activists who led well-funded NGOs might "dress up like us for benefits," depriving trans communities. However, the generalized gay/trans distinction that thus gained hegemonic acceptance potentially elided the overlapping subject positions of people much less privileged than elite gay men.

Eventually, the Transgender Act of 2019 partially responded to activist demands by removing the screening committee and anti-begging provisions and restoring a modified version of the MSJE report's definition:

> "Transgender person" means a person whose gender does not match with the gender assigned to that person at birth and includes trans-man or trans-woman (whether or not such person has undergone Sex Reassignment Surgery . . . or such other therapy), person with intersex variations, genderqueer and person having such socio-cultural identities as *kinner, hijra, aravani* and *jogta.* (Ministry of Law 2019: 2)

Despite the definition not requiring anatomical transition, the act restricted self-determination through a two-tiered system of recognition that allowed certification as transgender based on self-identification through an affidavit submitted to district administration but required proof of medical intervention for identification as male/female (Jain and Kartik 2020: 5). The act thus effectively treated transgender as a separate or third gender identity that could be adopted through a legally binding self-declaration but premised legal recognition as female or male on transition, combining the third gender and binary transitional models into a layered bureaucratic process of recognition. Further, while nonbinary identities are technically included via "genderqueer," the MSJE report from which the definition is adapted understands "genderqueer" as a fixed non-cisgender identity, as discussed earlier. The inclusion of "genderqueer"—an uncommon usage within *kothi–hijra* communities—contrasts with the elimination of the "etc." from the list of "sociocultural" identities. Mapped as the "most common" trans identity in eastern India in the 2009 SAATHII report, *kothi* and related identities become effectively erased from legal discourse by 2019.

This does not necessarily preclude *kothis* from legally identifying as trans—as I observed in Nadia, some *kothis* who usually present in male attire, but are well connected to trans activists, were able to secure transgender certificates from the district administration in 2023 after declaring themselves as transgender in affidavits, although one of them was asked about their clothes and had to argue with government officials that the act did not mandate any sartorial requirements. This signals the success of trans movements in securing at least some degree of self-determination. However, the application process involves submitting online forms and an affidavit in English, such that *kothis* without linguistic privileges must rely on intermediaries like activists and lawyers—in Nadia, lawyers typically demanded Rs. 300 (about $4) per application. Moreover, the act did not stipulate any reservations at the central level, leaving state governments to institute reservations and welfare measures unevenly (Jain and Kartik 2020; Chakrapani 2023).[17] Thus, given the uncertain benefits, many *kothis* of my acquaintance have forgone the process. Even for those willing to navigate the hurdles, legal recognition is premised on an unambiguous public identification as transgender, which perpetuates the containment of terms like *kothi* to the level of intra-community discourse and reinforces the patterns of vernacularization observed through the book.

Gay Vernacularizations

Paralleling the LGB–trans distinctions in legal and activist discourse, less codified processes within urban gay male communities also seek to clearly separate gay from trans identities, but may also subsume *kothi* subject positions and recast them as per middle-class, dominant-caste understandings of gayness, deriding them as incorrect or backward if they contravene such understandings. Several scholars have critiqued gender, class, and caste hierarchies within urban Indian gay and queer communities, both online and offline (Dasgupta 2017; Kang 2016; Khubchandani 2020). For instance, Rohit Dasgupta shows how urban gay men construct their identities in ways aligned with normative masculinity and exclude or otherize effeminate and working-class people in online dating apps and beyond, paralleling transnational tendencies (Dasgupta 2017: 95). Akhil Kang demonstrates how Dalit and Muslim people might be consumed, fetishized, and yet hierarchically subordinated or excluded in dominant-caste gay and queer spaces (2023: 65). Here, I do not offer a detailed analysis of urban gay communities, but rather, highlight some tendencies that reinforce or reconfigure the aforementioned patterns of vernacularization.

As noted in Chapter 2, gay activists in the 2000s lamented that a symmetrically gendered model of gay identity based on supposedly "egalitarian" relationships between two men "does not find a very strong footing in India" relative to ostensibly heteronormative *kothis* who internalize culturally feminine roles and desire mainstream nongay men (Bondyopadhyay and Shah 2007: 36). However, over the ensuing decade, such a model not only became widespread in urban gay spaces, especially with the proliferation of virtual communities from Facebook groups to dating apps, but even in mainstream media and films. In 2020, the Bollywood movie *Shubh Mangal Zyada Saavdhan* became one of the first Indian commercial films to be themed on a gay romance (Roy A. 2020). One reviewer lauded it for breaking "stereotypes about gay men" in earlier Bollywood films that had featured gay males as comic characters who wore "exuberant" clothing and spoke with an "effeminate voice" and "strange hand gestures": in contrast, this film's gay protagonists "both wear normal clothes" (Roy A. 2020). Such valorization of gay men who fit within "normal" social maleness may be seen as symptomatizing the rise of "homonormativity," the politics of assimilation into normative social values and institutions ranging from masculinity to consumerism to marriage (Dasgupta 2017; Rao 2020).

However, various other discourses of gayness also persist—including newer forms of intersection between gay and *kothi* communities that spur anxieties among middle-class gay men seeking social acceptance. In the 2010s, some people within *kothi* communities began using dating apps like Grindr and Blued on smartphones, although I observed that such usage was uneven among working-class *kothis* who could not always afford reliable internet, and older practices of picking up men in streets or parks also continued. Such apps offer users the option to choose a "position" or "role" such as bottom (people who prefer to be penetrated), top (those who prefer to penetrate), versatile (those who prefer both), and side (those into non-penetrative sex). Such English terminology has unevenly entered *kothi* communities, and since the late 2010s, I observed that several younger participants in *kothi* community networks also began referring to themselves as "gay bottom" or less commonly, as "versatile" or "side," while also referring to other *kothis* as sisters and participating in practices like *bhel* (flamboyantly expressed femininity).

For instance, Babai, a young student from a lower-middle-class family in Nadia, was initiated into *kothi* communities through other *kothis* in their neighborhood, but subsequently also interacted with gay communities in Kolkata through dating apps and visits to the city. In an interview in 2015, Babai told me: "We say *kothi* and *parikh*, but my Kolkata friends use *high-class* language like *bottom, top*." Interacting with metropolitan gay men, Babai thus imbibed linguistic and class hierarchies and rendered the *kothi* as a lower-class linguistic equivalent of the gay bottom, reversing the earlier process where the gay category, as a whole, could be seen as an anglicized equivalent of the *kothi* (Gupta 2005). However, Babai also narrated how they sometimes penetrated their partners, thus undoing a rigid notion of the bottom/*kothi* figure as always penetrated. Babai also indulged in *bhel* with their *kothi* sisters, like flirting with men at the local railway station where *kothis* checked out men together. Once, for some months, they grew their hair and wore makeup—although their gay friends encouraged them to revert to a more conventional male presentation. Such gay/*kothi* figures have often attracted disapprobation from middle-class gay men. For instance, in 2020, Suraj Roy, a popular gay social media personality in West Bengal, made a Bengali public post on Facebook that was shared over a hundred times:

> Many of us know the meaning of *same-sex* [sic] but do not follow it. *Samapremi* means a man or woman who is attracted to another man or woman. *Gay* surely does not mean *meye* (girl). . . . I'd still understand if these people were third gender. . . . Why would a guy need to dress as a girl if he likes another guy? Can't a man have relations with another man in a *shadharon* (normal/usual) way? If there's a *nari shotta* (woman's being) in the *mon*, let it stay there; rather than expressing it by clapping and using Ulti language, present yourself in a way that people don't think of you as aliens. (Roy S. 2020)

This post crystallized several tendencies that I had observed in urban gay attitudes to *kothis* in previous years. While overt femininity is acceptable in the "third gender," Roy targets "guys" who wear feminine attire, clap, or use Ulti, suggesting *kothis* who exhibit *hijra*-like behaviors. Such subjectivities and practices are plotted as incorrect as per a definition of gayness or *samaprem* (same-sex love) based on desire between men, where irrespective of role, gay men should behave as "normal" men (significantly, Roy's post was accompanied by a picture of two muscular white men kissing). In a Bengali post in a gay community group on Facebook in 2023, another gay man berated how some "bottoms" call each other "strange nicknames like *kothi*" and "do *meyelipona*" (feminine behavior). He added: "We are *samapremi*, *gay*, men who want other men. Those playing the *bottom role* want men as their partners, your partner also wants a man; if you behave like this, will you get that man?"[18] While devaluing femininity, both posts also prioritize sexual–romantic relations or coupledom between men as the defining element or goal of gay/*samapremi* existence, missing the importance of nonsexual kinship (sisterhood, mother–daughter relations) based on shared femininity among *kothis*.

Further, these posts reference a correct meaning or definition of gay identity in English, relative to which *kothi* linguistic practices like Ulti ("strange nicknames") are derided. Such linguistic hierarchization may be read as an effect of the transnational expansion of a "global gay" identity that has, following Western precedents, emphasized gay masculinity and distinction from trans identities (Altman 2001: 4; Dasgupta 2017: 6). While this process is clearly suggested by Roy's use of an image featuring white gay men, the posts also reference the Sanskritic Bengali term *samapremi*—literally, same-lover—rather than the more common term *samakami* (same-desiring, same-sex-desiring). As I observed in virtual groups, some middle-class gay men see *samakami* as too sexualizing and prefer *samapremi*, while others see such objections as moralistic prudery and continue using *samakami*. In that context, these posts also attempt to establish a preferable Bengali identity category centered on romantic (rather than merely sexual) desire between men. This is thus a multilayered vernacularizing process that seeks to elevate both transnational gay and Bengali *samapremi* discourse above Ulti and "nicknames" like *kothi*, which become positioned as part of a derided, lower-class, and/or conceptually incorrect vernacular.

Even the term "queer," which, as Akshay Khanna (2016: 29) notes, has been used in some metropolitan Indian activism to articulate anti-normative political standpoints and life choices rather than rigid identities, may become resignified as it gains increasing circulation in metropolitan gay spaces in ways that reinforce the cis/trans binary. In posts on virtual community groups between 2018 and 2023, I observed that several Anglophone gay men in Kolkata who identify as queer specify that they are cisgender or cis queer, for example, in expressions like "as a cis queer man, I feel . . . ," thus tending to stabilize the referent of queer as per a clearly demarcated gender identity, despite queer theory's interrogation of sex/gender stability (Enke 2012: 63). As A. Finn Enke reminds us, "meanings do change" when words cross spaces and "queer terminologies" may become simplified or ossified (2012: 60). While for some gay men specifying their cisgender positionality serves to conscientiously index gender privilege, in other cases, "queer" may be recast as per normative gay masculinity. For instance, in one English post in an online gay community group in 2021, a gay man blamed a well-known flamboyantly feminine gay male comedian, who is widely regarded as a *kothi* within community circles (although not self-identified as such), for fueling negative "stereotype(s) associated with being a queer across societies," seeking to dissociate queerness from such effeminacy.[19]

While the *kothi* is fluid in the wrong ways by breaching cis/trans distinctions, more "progressive" urban gay and queer discourse may contrarily see it as too rigid, associated with regressive ideas about feminine and masculine sexual roles, as already evident in the 2000s (Bondyopadhyay and Shah 2007). In 2011, after a pre-pride meeting at Kolkata, I witnessed a conversation between Nakul, a middle-class gay activist involved with pride organizing, and another activist who identified as gay and queer. They critiqued the assumption that feminine males would naturally desire *parikhs* or masculine men. Nakul claimed, "These identities are actually fake, sexuality is much more *fluid!*" He later added, "the *kothi-parikh concept* is gradually becoming obsolete," to which the other activist agreed. While these activists were accepting of gender nonconformity per se, the *kothi* and *parikh* categories were seen as rigidly ossifying gender and sexual binaries. While *kothis* may indeed reproduce gender norms, such stances miss that *kothis* may also switch gender/sexual roles while still distinguishing themselves from mainstream men or *parikhs*, as discussed in Chapter 2. Further, the *kothi* becomes marked as backdated (Reddy 2005: 217); its seeming obsolescence relative to gay and queer identities parallels its increasing erasure within transgender discourse.

Of course, some of these tendencies also prompt contestations. For instance, the aforementioned Facebook posts critiquing *kothi* femininity garnered not only support among gay men but also several dissenting comments—some asserted that some men actually preferred feminine males over masculine men, while others defended attire and behavior as matters of personal choice. Further, as discussed in the ensuing afterword, these tendencies are also countered by an emerging generation of people who combine or switch between *kothi*, gay, and queer identifications, suggesting possibilities beyond vernacularization and erasure.

Conclusion

The processes through which MSM and TG, and later cis LGB and trans categories, become distinguished from each other are multiple and inconsistent, and yet converge around some persistent patterns, like the elision of identities that overlap with feminine maleness. While MSM–TG divides were initially often based on sartorial or even anatomical distinctions, they are increasingly rearticulated as per a logic of consistent psychological identity that delimits gender self-determination. Further, there is no singular, globalized transgender or gay figure that gains ascendance over marginalized communities and discourses. The versions of transgender that gain legitimacy in Indian activist and legal discourse might variably incorporate elements of binary transitional narratives as well as aspects of *hijra* self-representation as a "third" gender, even as thirdness gets reconceptualized in the process.

While the multiple scales of dominant discourses and their varying modes of establishment allow for inconsistencies and contestations, this chapter, and the book overall, has contended that vernacularization—the scalar, conceptual and/ or linguistic subordination of communities, languages, and discourses that do not neatly fit dominant epistemologies of gender/sexuality—has persisted while contextually changing forms. Such processes perpetuate the elision of various *kothi*, *dhurani*, and *hijra* narratives and practices, such as non/linear expressions of femininity that are not neatly categorizable as per linear gradations of femininity and governmental or biopolitical distinctions between different gender/sexual identities. Even as progressive movements push the state toward conceding transgender recognition, LGBTQ rights, and gender self-determination, vernacularizing processes result in selective or constrained forms of legibility, representation, and upward mobility for working-class, oppressed caste, and/or non-Anglophone people. This might seem like a pessimistic conclusion, but an appraisal of such persistent structural processes is necessary if we are to arrive at other possibilities of freer, less hierarchized intersections and translations between diverse languages and concepts of gender/sexual difference. In that regard, the afterword looks to ongoing intersections between *kothi*, gay, trans, and queer discourses that might help disrupt the subordinations and erasures of multiple vernacularizations.

AFTERWORD

AFTERLIVES OF THE VERNACULARIZED

This book studies ongoing processes that do not lend themselves to any definitive closure. While legal or even activist discourse might seem to arrive at a particular consensus around gender/sexual terminologies and definitions, such seeming unity is often internally ruptured and there may be multiple superseding understandings, as in the case of transgender in India. Further, scholars remind us that epistemologies or ways of understanding identity, selfhood, or community that challenge or exceed such models often persist. As Chiang, Henry, and Leung note: "regional histories and practices in most Asian contexts show that gender and sexual identities continue to remain entangled even in the face of the globalizing pressure to become separate" (2018: 308). Indeed, "globalizing" concepts may themselves intersect with seemingly local formations, or with non-Anglocentric transregional discourses, in ways that displace settled meanings and create new possibilities. In that context, this afterword explores some ways in which intersections between "globalizing" terminologies and *kothi–hijra* communities have continued and may both reinforce and suggest ways beyond the erasures of vernacularization, granting a rich afterlife to identities and discourses that become seemingly superseded or erased.

Tara, for instance, is a young person in their twenties who belongs to a Nepali-speaking ethnolinguistic minority in West Bengal. Tara lives in a working-class neighborhood of Kalyani, Nadia, which has an intergenerational community network of *kothis* and *hijras*, but having had some English education, also interacts with middle-class gay communities in Kolkata and uses gay dating apps. Tara often boasts of their ability to do *bhel*: once, while visiting my home at Kalyani, they demonstrated their ability to attract men through seductive gestures (e.g., suggestively passing their hands over their body), and exclaimed at the end of the performance: "I am a *bheli kothi*!" Simultaneously, Tara usually wears conventionally male attire and identifies themselves as a gay bottom on dating apps. In one conversation, Tara shared with me that they sometimes felt uncomfortable referring to themselves as *kothi* in gay circles since some gay men use *kothi* as a slur to mock others: "You know, some people use *kothi* as a *gali* (insult)!" Tara also described how some gay men they dated wanted them to present in more masculine ways: "They say, what's the point of dating a *girlish bottom*, then they might as well date a girl!" This assertion, which I heard from other gay men as well, presumes a binary gay-straight distinction—a man either desires a man or a woman, and *kothi* femininity becomes inherently undesirable as a poor substitute for either. However, Tara has not only found *parikhs* who do like them, but has also continued to use *kothi* to refer to themselves and others in public. For example, at a recent pride walk, they excitedly introduced me to a group of new friends they had made: "Come, meet all these *kothis!*"

Tara has also picked up words like "nonbinary" and "queer" from metropolitan and online spaces and occasionally adopts such terms for themselves. Once, they shared a reel (short video) of a person posing in androgynous attire on Facebook with the English caption: "Hey, are you non-binary? I am!" Another day, they shared a group picture with their *kothi* sisters, captioning it "queer friends." Their eclectic, experimental use of terms suggests potentially freer and more horizontal interchanges between Anglophone queer discourse and *kothi* language, suggesting possibilities of self-construction and expression that exceed or contradict the tiered hierarchies of vernacularization.

However, middle-class metropolitan queer or nonbinary people may not always manifest solidarity with their less elite counterparts. In the Kolkata queer circles, I met a corporate employee in their twenties who had their gender designated as "queer" on their Grindr profile and who wore daring and stylish costumes to pride walks—combining gowns, nail polish, and nose rings with a pronounced beard. However, several *kothis* from Kalyani who were intrigued and wanted to make their acquaintance were disappointed. As one *kothi* told me: "I saw this person at a poster-making workshop for pride, but these *high-profile* people don't really want to talk with us!" Such cases suggest the emergence of elite or "high-profile" forms of queerness associated with upper-class forms of fashion and consumerism (expensive makeup, stylish dress) that remain relatively inaccessible to *kothis* and *hijras* from nonelite, nonmetro locations, as Khubchandani (2020: xxi) also notes in Bangalore.

Such missed intersections between queer and *kothi–hijra* communities are amplified by the tendency to see nonbinary identities as a foreign emergence or as neatly separate from existing trans communities. One Bengali handbook on gender/sexual terminology, for example, says that some people "want to retain some signs of both the genders, and rather than designating themselves as a woman or a man, they . . . identify themselves as *trans*. In our country such people are very few in number, but abroad there are separate communities of such people" (Sappho for Equality 2013: 46). This tendency may be paralleled by emergent forms of nonbinary or genderqueer identity politics in metropolitan cities, whose proponents might neatly distinguish themselves from both *hijras* and trans men/ women. For example, a genderqueer person from a dominant-caste background who spoke at an open mic event during a queer literary festival at Kolkata in 2019 opined that both trans women and "our *hijra* sisters" were wrongly represented in India as a third gender rather than as women, and the "other" gender category should be reserved for nonbinary people like themselves. The speaker described how they had encountered the word "genderqueer" through exposure to communities abroad and lamented that they had no corresponding culture or tradition in India. Such an attempt to neatly sequester nonbinary from binary trans identities potentially elides subjectivities and practices within *kothi–hijra* communities that not only breach the man/woman binary but may also combine or switch between womanhood and a third/separate position.

The recent interventions of some Dalit queer scholars and activists point to more promising horizontal intersections between queer, trans, and *kothi* discourses. Saptarshi Bairagi, for instance, is a queer anthropologist who has publicly claimed both nonbinary trans and *kothi* identities and protested against casteist and transphobic exclusion in queer spaces. A media article on Dalit queer voices states:

> Saptarshi Bairagi, 26, whose pronouns are also they/them . . . belongs to the marginalized Namasudra caste. They identify as Kothi, an Indigenous group wherein a male takes on an effeminate role in same-sex relationships. "People from Indigenous communities like mine aren't able to reclaim their pride even among the queer community. The online spaces aren't any different but rather a reflection of our real world," they said. (Thakur and Zaffar 2023)

In the 2022 Kolkata pride walk, Bairagi raised English, Bengali, and Ulti slogans that foregrounded Dalit and *kothi* self-assertion, such as "Dalit rights, human rights, let us join, let us fight" and "*ami koti ami dhurai, dhuriye dhuriye bhaat khai*" (roughly: I am a *kothi*, I have sex, through my sex work I feed myself). As I observed, several *kothis* and *hijras* from the districts also joined in voicing such slogans as we marched down Kolkata streets together. Given that pride walks have often served as arenas of the policing and disciplining of *kothi–hijra* self-expression, one can only hope that such moments herald a genuine democratization of metropolitan queer spaces.

The emergent forms of intersection between communities and discourses noted here are thus sometimes hierarchizing and sometimes disruptive of class, caste, and linguistic hierarchies, suggesting multiple future trajectories with contrary political possibilities. In that context, I end this book with the hope that this work may, in some small way, open up space for a more encompassing future in which a diverse variety of marginalized and vernacularized communities and discourses may not just continue to exist, but flourish.

NOTES

Introduction

1 In June 1969, LGBT individuals who had gathered at the Stonewall Inn in New York demonstrated against a police raid, an event that has acquired iconic status in transnational queer histories (Carter 2010).

2 I use pseudonyms to designate most people to ensure confidentiality, barring public figures and people who generously allowed me to use their names. I have not distinguished between real names and pseudonyms.

3 On economic liberalization in India since the 1990s and related gender/sexual transformations, see Lukose (2009), Gilbertson (2014), and Roy (2022).

4 On *hijra* communities, see Nanda (1999), Reddy (2005), Saria (2021), and Hossain (2021). While these ethnographies include *kothis*, fewer books focus specifically on *kothi* communities or related identities (Nagar 2019; Nandi 2024). Except these monographs and some preceding articles (Hall 2005; Dutta 2012a), scholarship on the *kothi* category has often focused on its relation to HIV-related activism rather than community dynamics (Cohen 2005; Boyce 2007; Khanna 2016).

5 On such languages, called Farsi elsewhere, see Hall (2005) and Nandi (2024).

6 As Reddy (2005) argues, their nonconformity, variance, or liminality with respect to social gender and sexual norms encompasses only a part of their subject positions. Yet, being labeled as and sometimes adopting terms like MSM and transgender, these groups have been increasingly marked in terms of gender and sexual difference. In that context, I use "gender/sexually variant" as a provisional, inadequate descriptor.

7 The phrase representational politics has varied connotations, ranging from the politics of textual representation (Meeker 2005) to representative participation within political institutions (Rushton 2014). I use it here to signal a variety of processes (including textual representation) through which LGBTQ identities are constituted, spoken for, and made legible in the public sphere.

8 On the complex mediation and translation between various discourses and idioms in Indian LGBTQ activism, see Katyal (2016) and Khanna (2016).

9 Some of these arguments have appeared partially in some of my previously published articles (Dutta 2012a, 2013), and in my portions of a coauthored essay (Dutta and Roy 2014). However, the central argument about vernacularization has not been published before. Arguments from previous publications are revised and updated rather than reproduced verbatim, and accordingly, previous articles are cited in some chapters as research I am building on.

10 The diffusionist model of "global queering" or a homogenizing globalization of Western-origin categories has been extensively critiqued; for instance, Boellstorff shows how "gay" identity in Indonesia is not derivative of the West but represents a form of transformative translation (2005: 6). Rahul Rao argues that even normative capitalist queer discourses are coproduced by domestic elites rather than transplanted from the West (2020: 150).

11 Following Michel Foucault ([1976] 1990), queer scholarship has traced the emergence of "sexuality" as a basis for the formation of interiorized identities and population groups during the expansion of capitalist modernities (Jackson 2009; Khanna 2016). My project traces the imbrications of this process with logics that are irreducible to capitalist modernization, as elaborated later.

12 For a critique of developmentalism, see Chakrabarty (2000); for critiques of queer developmentalism, see Mason (2018).

13 For a critique of rigid metropolitan versus nonmetropolitan binaries, see Blackwood (2010).

14 For a critique of the gender/sexuality distinction in LGBT discourses, see Valentine (2007).

15 See Sadana (2012: 17–18).

16 On the use of queer in Indian activism as both an umbrella term and as a political framework that interrogates the normalization and fixity of social gender/sexual identities, see Khanna (2016).

17 See Vidya (2013).

18 A prominent Marxist-feminist tradition also emphasizes how capitalism depends on other logics like sexism and gendered labor (Oksala 2016).

Chapter 1

1 On potential religious sources of such beliefs, see Nanda (1999).

2 See Nanda (1999: 15).

3 Some sections of this chapter are revised from Dutta (2012a).

4 For narrow and broad definitions, see Daily Bhaskar (2015) and Mok and Linning (2015), respectively.

5 See Hall (1997).

6 Chapter 3 elaborates this.

7 See Reddy (2005: 66) and Hall (2005: 131).

8 Also see Boyce (2007: 179).

9 Also see Reddy (2005) and Nandi (2024).

10 On *badhai*, see Hossain, Pamment, and Roy (2023).

11 On such hierarchies, see Reddy (2005: 6).

12 See Cohen (1995: 276).

13 Also see Vidya (2013: 82).

14 Also see Tom and Menon (2021).

15 However, implementation was uneven (Hinchy 2019).

16 See Reddy (2005: 124).

17 Also see Hossain (2021: 71).

18 On similar exchanges, see Hossain (2021: 72).

19 Also see Hossain (2021: 151).

20 Hossain (2021: 89) similarly notes the secrecy around Ulti and *hijra* sexuality in Bangladesh, but his analysis differs from my framework of vernacularization.

21 Chapter 6 elaborates this.

22 Goel (2016) reports a similar hierarchy in Delhi.

23 Non-emasculated *hijras* within Bangladeshi lineages also do this to prove their authenticity (Hossain 2021: 152).

24 Also see Nandi (2024).

25 Citation withheld to maintain confidentiality.

Chapter 2

1 Althusser describes interpellation as acts of "ideological recognition," manifested in everyday rituals and gestures, through which individuals are constituted as subjects, and sees this process as a function of all ideology, not just dominant ones (1971: 174–6). Accordingly, I interpret acts of recognizing and calling out people as *dhurani* (or similar categories) as forms of interpellation that contradict dominant ideologies of gender/sexuality that interpellate people like Susanta as "men."

2 Relatedly, Cohen shows how the language of shared play and similitude, for example, *aise* (like this/these), was used to identify prospective friends in parks of Varanasi in the 1990s without signaling a consistent subjectivity outside (1995: 280).

3 On this issue, see Dutta (2012a).

4 Some of these arguments appear partially in previous publications (Dutta 2012a, 2013); they are here revised and integrated with the framework of vernacularization.

5 Boyce (2007: 182) notes dissonances between institutional definitions of *kothi* and *kothi* self-perceptions but does not relate them to institutional–subcultural mediations.

6 For more on their journey, see DasGupta (2012).

7 Khanna (2016: 169) notes similar tendencies around *dhurani*.

8 See Butler (1993).

9 For critiques of such linear spectra, see Halberstam (1998) and Castleberry (2019).

10 Chapter 6 elaborates on tensions and overlaps between gay and *kothi* identities.

11 On Hindi sexual slang, see Hall (2005: 141).

12 Also see Saria (2021: 203).

Chapter 3

1 See Reddy (2005: 134).

2 For Bengali literature on *kothi* subtypes, see Majumdar and Basu (1997).

3 Vijayakumar (2021) argues that ideals of respectability are both reinforced and contested in HIV projects in Bangalore, but does not focus on *kothi/hijra* languages and their intersections with activist discourse.

4 On such gestures among *jananas*, see Nagar (2019: 89).

5 I heard *bhorokti, bhelki,* and *lahari* more in Kolkata and Nadia and *bheli* more at Murshidabad. With increasing translocal contact, *bheli* (or *bhelki*) was understood by many community members across my field areas. There are also terms like *satrawali* (female-attired) *kothi* that specifically denote attire without behavioral connotations.

6 The suffix *taal* is also used similarly—*kodi-taal, bhel-taal.*

7 Nagar notes a similar use of "*kade*" in North India (2019: 210).

8 On such tendencies within the anti-377 movement, see Dutta (2020).

9 On developmentalism in transnational LGBT activism, see Mason (2018).

10 Hall notes similar injunctions against "cross-dressing" in HIV projects in Delhi (2005: 134).

11 This tendency evokes rough parallels with the deferral of trans rights in Western activism (Greer 2018).

12 On gay abjections of *hijra*, see Khubchandani (2020: xxi).

13 Cited from minutes circulated by email among attendees, including myself.

14 On the sartorial androgyny of some Bangladeshi *hijras*, see Hossain (2021: 34).

Chapter 4

1 Several NGO activists critiqued these measures as inadequately implemented (Bhattacharya 2005).
2 The idiom of *bhab* expresses an interiorized condition that may be stable or fleeting; it has a rich history in religious traditions (Ewing and Taylor 2018).
3 On this issue, also see Boyce and Khanna (2023: 508).
4 On the reductive representation of *hijra* practices as "traditional," see Hossain, Pamment, and Roy (2023: 15).

Chapter 5

1 Tripathi formed Astitva in 2006 (Tripathi 2015: 90).
2 On attempts to balance respectability and assertion in HIV projects in Bangalore, see Vijayakumar (2021: 89). On making *hijras* into respectable citizens, see Pamment (2019: 144).
3 For more on such tendencies, see Dutta (2012b: 110).
4 On gay/queer metropolitan communities and spaces, see Khubchandani (2020) and Dasgupta (2017).
5 On contestations of feminine sartorial respectability, see Vijayakumar (2021: 95).

Chapter 6

1 Some sections of this chapter are revised from Dutta (2013).
2 On HIV-related biopolitics, also see Lakkimsetti (2020) and Khanna (2016).
3 On the localization of identities relative to transgender, see Mauro Cabral's section in Boellstorff et al. (2014: 436), although Cabral does not mention preexisting forms of transregionalism beyond trans.
4 On transgender solidarity networks in the Global South, see Billard and Nesfield (2020: 81).
5 As per a publicly circulated email sent to many CBOs on December 8, 2010.
6 As per the same email.
7 As per a publicly circulated email sent to several listservs, including lgbt-india@yahoogroups.com.
8 'Minutes of West Bengal Community Consultation for Project Pehchan,' personal email communication (December 2010).
9 Ibid.
10 Also see Boyce and Khanna (2023: 506).
11 On the pressure of targets, see Aneka and KSMF (2011).
12 Also see Bhattacharya (2019).
13 The citation is withheld to maintain Sharmila's confidentiality.
14 See, for example, Banu (2018), Nagpaul (2017), Bhattacharya (2019), and Jain and Kartik (2020).
15 Responses by trans collectives are archived together on webpages maintained by Orinam, a South India-based LGBTQ+ collective, and are hence cited together; this does not imply that Orinam necessarily shares these viewpoints.

16 Also see Boyce and Khanna (2023: 504).
17 In resistance, Dalit trans activists have demanded horizontal reservations that would allow oppressed-caste trans persons to access reserved seats within existing caste-based quotas rather than being lumped with dominant-caste trans people as a single backward class, which nuances the aforementioned assumption of homogenized transgender vulnerability (Chakrapani 2023).
18 The names of the author and group are withheld to maintain confidentiality.
19 Citation withheld to maintain confidentiality.

GLOSSARY

The following list briefly explains some Bengali and Ulti words referenced frequently in the book. For ease of reading, I have not used diacritics but transliterated them following their phonological realization as closely as possible.

Akua —a *hijra* or *kothi* who is not emasculated.
Arial —very, extreme, total.
Badhai —an occupation where *hijras* bless newborn children or newlyweds.
Bila —bad; also connotes disruptive, aggressive, or troublemaking behaviors.
Bhab —feeling, affect, demeanor.
Bhel —a term connoting various gestures or expressions socially regarded as feminine.
Bheli —visibly feminine, flamboyant, wearing socially feminine attire.
Chhalla —asking for money in trains, streets, or shops.
Chhibrano —emasculation (castration and penectomy).
Chhibri —intra-community word for *hijra* (literally, emasculated).
Chhibripon or hijrepon —*hijra*-like behavior, looks, or attire.
Chipti —vagina; sometimes anus.
Chishya —good, beautiful.
Dhurano —to have sex.
Dhurani —an older usage in Bengal corresponding to *kothi*; a sexually promiscuous *kothi*.
Gharana —a *hijra* lineage.
Hijra —roughly, feminine-identified people who may form lineage-based groups with distinct customs.
Kachchi —unripe, immature.
Khajra —sex work.
Khajrawali —sex worker.
Kodi —sober, restrained, socially male-presenting.
Kothi or koti (IPA: koṭi) —roughly, spectrum of feminine males and trans feminine persons.
Lagan —dancing at weddings and festivals in feminine attire.
Likam —penis.
Meyeli —feminine, girlish.
Meti —a word used interchangeably with *kothi* in North Bengal.
Mon or mana —heart, mind, psyche.
Niharini / laharan —woman.
Niharinipon or laharanpon —womanlike behavior or attire.
Nirvan —a *hijra* or *kothi* who has undergone emasculation.
Pakki —ripe, mature.
Roop —form, appearance.
Rupantarkami—transgender, transsexual.
Samakami —homosexual, gay.

Saree —draped garment usually worn by women.
Satra —clothes, usually feminine attire.
Shotta —being, selfhood.
Thikri —a loud clap used by *hijras* and *kothis*.
Tonna —man, young man.
Tonnapon —manlike behavior or attire.

REFERENCES

"15 April Ashe Jay! Guinness-Joyi Surojitra Ekhono 'Hijra,'" (2018), *Prothombarta*, January 28. Available online: https://prothombarta.news/archives/25059 (accessed July 4, 2020).

Abraham, J. (2014), "Contingent Caste Endogamy and Patriarchy: Lessons for Our Understanding of Caste," *Economic and Political Weekly*, 49 (2): 56–65.

Afaque, Z. (2010), "Let's Keep The Pride," *Hindustan Times*, July 4: 5.

Ahmed, S. (1995), "Mograhaater Ajoy Ekhon Shyamoli," *Ajkal*, November 9: 3.

Ahmed, Z. (2009), "Mumbai Gays' Long Fight for Recognition," *BBC*, July 2. Available online: http://news.bbc.co.uk/2/hi/south_asia/8131476.stm (accessed February 2, 2018).

Al Baset, Z. (2012), "Section 377 and the Myth of Heterosexuality," *Jindal Global Law Review*, 4 (1): 89–109.

Alliance India. (2011), *Management Information System (MIS) Toolkit: A Handbook for Pehchan Project Implementing CBOs*, New Delhi: Alliance India.

Alpo Jana Golpogulo: The Lesser Known Stories. (2019), [Film] Dir. Sudarshana Chakraborty, India: Moitrisanjog Society.

Althusser, L. (1971), *Lenin and Philosophy and Other Essays*, trans. B. Brewster, New York: Monthly Review Press.

Altman, D. (2001), "Global Gaze/Global Gays," in J. C. Hawley (ed.), *Postcolonial and Queer Theories: Intersections and Essays*, 1–18, Westport: Greenwood Press.

Anandabazar Desk. (1995), "Prokashye Bikri Hochhe Samakami Patrika," *Anandabazar Patrika*, July 9: 3.

Aneka and Karnataka Sexual Minorities Forum (KSMF). (2011), *Chasing Numbers, Betraying People: Relooking at HIV Related Services in Karnataka.* Bangalore.

Annamalai, E. (2014), "Death by Other Means: Neo-Vernacularization of South Asian Languages," in H. C. Cardoso (ed.), *Language Endangerment and Preservation in South Asia*, 3–18, Honolulu: University of Hawai'i Press.

Arondekar, A. (2023), *Abundance: Sexuality's History*, Durham: Duke University Press.

Arondekar, A. and G. Patel. (2016), "Area Impossible: Notes toward an Introduction," *GLQ: A Journal of Lesbian and Gay Studies*, 22 (2): 151–71.

Asher. (2010), "Not Your Mom's Trans 101," *Tranarchism*, November 26. Available online: https://transreads.org/not-your-moms-trans-101/ (accessed August 2, 2023).

Bandyopadhyay, M. (2018), "Notun Kore Swadhinota'r Swad Pelam Aj: Manobi," *Anandabazar Patrika*, September 6: 3.

Bandyopadhyay, M. (2019), *Rupantarkami noi rupantorito nari* [Facebook], July 17. Available online: https://www.facebook.com/manobi.bandyopadhyay/posts/pfbid0M uoHcdmcAuqiVobGoFtr37CBins7R5g34u9rzwQKBTND7MzE9W8AyWi76BB2eSQxl (accessed July 31, 2023).

Bandyopadhyay, M. (2021a), *Goto shombar shosrumata'r sraddhobarshik* [Facebook], June 5. Available online: https://www.facebook.com/manobi.bandyopadhyay/posts/pfbid02 Psp7nzp9xYtvZJemsQbxDVb57j9aondKWvf78kuvSt1o8yYHhyVWjf7d1Srf7BW6l (accessed July 21, 2023).

Bandyopadhyay, M. (2021b), *Dilli'r ekjon doctor* [Facebook], December 20. Available online: https://www.facebook.com/manobi.bandyopadhyay/posts/pfbid0342jjZf1R WeMyTWwzkChnErMUVAoSmHYvRrmuR8SRnuCKMM7SRcjEZH3XXSxPGEQBl (accessed July 20, 2023).

Bandyopadhyay, M. (2022), *Shuru holo amar poth chola* [Facebook], June 1. Available online: https://www.facebook.com/manobi.bandyopadhyay/posts/pfbid02zigaCEexynZyYSkZ terRqvCRjb5krNf4Cow3jTPa4XuWTjrYLEx9YRQqKRTk5eR6l (accessed July 20, 2023).

Bandyopadhyay, M. and J. M. Pandey. (2017), *A Gift of Goddess Lakshmi*, New Delhi: Penguin.

Bandyopadhyay, S. (2004), *Caste, Culture, and Hegemony: Social Domination in Colonial Bengal*, New Delhi: Sage.

Bandyopadhyay, S. (2019), "Nagarkitan Amar Jibon, Obhinoy Korte Hoyni: Manobi," *Anandabazar Patrika*, February 12: 7.

Banerjee, A. (2013), "Jiboner Prothom Kannata Kintu Amader Manusher Motoi Chhilo, Biraler Moto Na," *Whatzup Kolkata*, October 6. Available online: http:// whatzupkolkata.com/249/?fb_action_ids=246518142163035 (accessed December 23, 2018).

Banerjee, A. (2018), "Jounango Amake Define Kore Na," *Ei Samay*, April 7: 3.

Banerjee, S. (1989), *The Parlour and the Street: Elite and Popular Culture in Nineteenth-Century Calcutta*, Kolkata: Seagull Books.

Banu, G. (2018), "Where are the Archives of our Dalit Trans Foremothers and Forefathers?" *The Print*, April 29. Available online: https://theprint.in/opinion/dalit -history-month/dalit-trans-resilience-is-a-fight-against-caste-and-patriarchy-though -we-are-missing-from-written-archives/53509/ (accessed July 20, 2023).

Besnier, N. (1997), "Sluts and Superwomen: The Politics of Gender Liminality in Urban Tonga," *Ethnos*, 62 (1–2): 5–31.

Bhaduri, N. P. (2014), "Tritiya Prakritir Kotha Amra Bohukal Jani," *Anandabazar Patrika*, April 30: 4.

Bhattacharya, C. (2005), "'Third Sex' in Passports?" *The Telegraph*, March 9: 3.

Bhattacharya, S. (2015), "Board of Mysteries," *Kindle*, July 1. Available online: https:// kindlemag.in/board-mysteries/ (accessed July 27, 2023).

Bhattacharya, S. (2019), "The Transgender Nation and its Margins: The Many Lives of the Law," *South Asia Multidisciplinary Academic Journal*, 20: 1–19.

Billard, T. J. and S. Nesfield. (2020), "(Re)making 'Transgender' Identities in Global Media and Popular Culture," in J. M. Ryan (ed.), *Trans Lives in a Globalizing World: Rights, Identities and Politics*, 66–89, London: Routledge.

Bittu, Jamal, Meera and Anindya. (2018), "Press Note: For Immediate Release," [Mimeograph].

Blackwood, E. (2010), *Falling into the Lesbi World: Desire and Difference in Indonesia*, Honolulu: University of Hawai'i Press.

Boellstorff, T. (2005), *The Gay Archipelago: Sexuality and Nation in Indonesia*, Princeton: Princeton University Press.

Boellstorff, T. (2011), "But Do Not Identify as Gay: A Proleptic Genealogy of the MSM Category," *Cultural Anthropology*, 26 (2): 287–312.

Boellstorff, T., M. Cabral, M. Cárdenas, T. Cotten, E. A. Stanley, K. Young, and A. Z. Aizura. (2014), "Decolonizing Transgender: A Roundtable Discussion," *Transgender Studies Quarterly*, 1 (3): 419–39.

Bondyopadhyay, A. and V. Shah. (2007), *My Body is Not Mine: Stories of Violence and Tales of Hope*, New Delhi: Naz Foundation International.

Boyce, P. (2007), "Conceiving Kothis: Men Who Have Sex with Men in India and the Cultural Subject of HIV Prevention," *Medical Anthropology*, 26 (2): 175–203.

Boyce, P. and A. Khanna. (2011), "Rights and Representations: Querying the Male-to-Male Sexual Subject in India," *Culture, Health & Sexuality*, 13 (1): 89–100.

Boyce, P. and R. K. Dasgupta. (2017), "Utopia or Elsewhere: Queer Modernities in Small Town West Bengal," in T. Kuldova and M. A. Varghese (eds.), *Urban Utopias: Excess and Expulsion in Neoliberal South Asia*, 209–26, London: Palgrave Macmillan.

Boyce, P. and A. Khanna. (2023), "Subjectivities, Knowledge, and Gendered and Sexual Transitions," in C. McCallum, S. Posocco, and M. Fotta (eds.), *The Cambridge Handbook for the Anthropology of Gender and Sexuality*, 491–519, Cambridge: Cambridge University Press.

Brady, M. P. (2022), *Scales of Captivity: Racial Capitalism and the Latinx Child*, Durham: Duke University Press.

Brown, G. (2012), "Homonormativity: A Metropolitan Concept that Denigrates 'Ordinary' Gay Lives," *Journal of Homosexuality*, 59 (7): 1065–72.

Brown, W. (1995), *States of Injury: Power and Freedom in Late Modernity*, Princeton: Princeton University Press.

Butler, J. (1993), *Bodies that Matter: On the Discursive Limits of Sex*, New York: Routledge.

Butler, J. (2004), *Undoing Gender*, New York: Routledge.

Butler, J. (2009), "Performativity, Precarity and Sexual Politics," *AIBR: Revista de Antropología Iberoamericana*, 4 (3): i–xiii.

Canagarajah, S. and P. De Costa. (2016), "Introduction: Scales Analysis, and its Uses and Prospects in Educational Linguistics," *Linguistics and Education*, 34: 1–10.

Carter, D. (2010), *Stonewall: The Riots that Sparked the Gay Revolution*, New York: St. Martin's Griffin.

Castleberry, J. (2019), "Addressing the Gender Continuum: A Concept Analysis," *Journal of Transcultural Nursing*, 30 (4): 403–9.

Chakrabarty, R. (2004), "Itihasher Prekkhapote Shomaj o Prantik Jounota," *Swikriti Patrika*, 2: 25–32.

Chakrabarty, D. (2000), *Provincializing Europe: Postcolonial Thought and Historical Difference*, Princeton: Princeton University Press.

Chakraborty, K. and S. Chakraborty, eds (2023), *The Queer and the Vernacular Languages in India: Studies in Contemporary Texts and Cultures*, New Delhi: Routledge.

Chakrapani, S. (2023), "More Reservation, More Rights, Says TN Trans Community," *Socialstory*, May 17. Available online: https://yourstory.com/socialstory/2023/05/more-reservation-more-rights-say-tn-trans-people. (accessed August 2, 2023).

Chatterjee, P. (1989), "The Nationalist Resolution of the Women's Question," in K. Sangari and S. Vaid (eds.), *Recasting Women: Essays in Colonial History*, 233–53, New Delhi: Kali for Women.

Chatterjee, P. (2004), *The Politics of the Governed: Reflections on Popular Politics in Most of the World*, New York: Columbia University Press.

Chatterjee, P. (2017), "Govt to Provide Transgenders with Medical Assistance," *Millennium Post*, January 9. Available Online: https://www.millenniumpost.in/govt-to-provide-transgenders-with-medical-assistance-178308 (accessed March 24, 2024).

Chatterjee, S. (2018), "Transgender Shifts: Notes on Resignification of Gender and Sexuality in India," *Transgender Studies Quarterly*, 5 (3): 311–20.

Chattopadhyay, M. (2014), "Sotyi Holeo Golpo Bodhoy," *Abomanob*, January: 16–23.

Chaudhuri, S. R. (2006), "We Are Also Women, Say Transsexuals," *DNA*, March 6: 3.

Chen, J. N. and Cárdenas, M. (2019), "Times to come: Materializing Trans Times," *Transgender Studies Quarterly*, 6 (4): 472–80.

Chiang, H. (2021), *Transtopia in the Sinophone Pacific*, New York: Columbia University Press.

Chiang, H. and A. K. Wong. (2016), "Queering the Transnational Turn: Regionalism and Queer Asias," *Gender, Place & Culture*, 23 (11): 1643–56.

Chiang, H., T. A. Henry, and H. H. Leung. (2018), "Trans-in-Asia, Asia-in-Trans: An Introduction," *Transgender Studies Quarterly*, 5 (3): 298–310

Chimhundu, H. (1993), "The Vernacularization of African Languages after Independence," *Diogenes*, 41 (161): 35–42.

Chowdhury, S. (2015), "Ki Kore Manobi Holam," *Anandabazar Patrika*, June 6: 6.

Chu, A. L. and E. H. Drager. (2019), "After Trans Studies," *Transgender Studies Quarterly*, 6 (1): 103–16.

Cohen, L. (1995), "The Pleasures of Castration: The Postoperative Status of Hijras, Jankhas and Academics," in P. R. Abramson and S. D. Pinkerton (eds.), *Sexual Nature/Sexual Culture*, 276–304, Chicago: University of Chicago Press.

Cohen, L. (2005), "The Kothi Wars: AIDS Cosmopolitanism and the Morality of Classification," in V. Adams and S. L. Pigg (eds.), *Sex in Development: Science, Sexuality, and Morality in Global Perspective*, 269–303, Durham: Duke University Press.

Coupland, N. (2009), "The Mediated Performance of Vernaculars," *Journal of English Linguistics*, 37 (3): 284–300.

Daily Bhaskar. (2015), "Transgender Woman Beats the Heck Out of a Man Posing as One," September 24. Available online: https://dbvideos.bhaskar.com/trending/transgender-woman-beats-man-posing-as-one-8916.html (accessed January 28, 2018).

Das, T. (2009), "Bibhatsa Bibar," *Swikriti Patrika*, 7: 9–15.

Das, T. (2013), "Ami Kichhutei Tomar Chhele Hote Chai Na Ma," *News Bangla*, June 21: 5.

Das, T. (2014), "Shomaje Ebar Tritiyo Holam, Kintu Shoman Holam Koi," *Ebela*, April 16: 5.

Dasgupta, P. (2016), "Who is Eligible to be called a Transgender in Kolkata," *Times of India*, July 21: 3.

DasGupta, D. (1996), "STD/HIV Outreach Among Sexual Networks of Men Who Have Sex with Men in Calcutta: The Naz (Calcutta) Project," (Abstract), *NLM Gateway*. Available online: http://gateway.nlm.nih.gov/MeetingAbstracts/ma?f=102220874.html (accessed July 28, 2012).

DasGupta, D. (2012), "Trans/Nationally Femme: Notes on Neoliberal Economic Regimes, Security States, and My Life as a Brown Immigrant Fag," in M. B. Sycamore (ed.), *Why Are Faggots Afraid of Faggots?* 15–23, Oakland: AK Press.

Dasgupta, R. K. (2017), *Digital Queer Cultures in India: Politics, Intimacies and Belonging*, New York: Routledge.

Dasgupta, S. (2009), *The Bengal Renaissance: Identity and Creativity from Rammohun Roy to Rabindranath Tagore*, Ranikhet: Permanent Black.

Dave, N. (2012), *Queer Activism in India: A Story in the Anthropology of Ethics*, Durham: Duke University Press.

Daum, C. W. and E. Ishiwata. (2010), "From the Myth of Formal Equality to the Politics of Social Justice: Race and the Legal Attack on Native Entitlements," *Law & Society Review*, 44 (3–4): 843–76.

Derrida, J. (2004), *Positions*, trans. A. Bass, London: Continuum.

Dhaliwal, G. (n.d.), "A Little Hope… A Little Happiness," [Blog]. Available online: http://gazalhopes.blogspot.com/ (accessed July 21, 2023).

Dhall, P. (2005), "Solitary Cruiser," in A. Narrain and G. Bhan (eds.), *Because I Have a Voice: Queer Politics in India*, 115–22, New Delhi: Yoda Press.

Dum Dum Swikriti Society (DDSS). (2008), "Pamphlet," [Mimeograph].

Dutta, A. (2012a), "An Epistemology of Collusion: Hijras, Kothis and the Historical (Dis) continuity of Gender/Sexual Identities in Eastern India," *Gender & History*, 24 (3): 825–49.

Dutta, A. (2012b), "Claiming Citizenship, Contesting Civility: The Institutional LGBT Movement and the Regulation of Gender/ Sexual Dissidence in West Bengal, India," *Jindal Global Law Review*, 4 (1): 110–41.

Dutta, A. (2013), "Legible Identities and Legitimate Citizens: The Globalization of Transgender and Subjects of HIV-AIDS Prevention in Eastern India," *International Feminist Journal of Politics*, 15 (4): 494–514.

Dutta, A. (2014), "Contradictory Tendencies: The Supreme Court's NALSA Judgment on Transgender Recognition and Rights," *Journal of Indian Law And Society*, 5: 225–36.

Dutta, A. and R. Roy. (2014), "Decolonizing Transgender in India: Some Reflections," *Transgender Studies Quarterly*, 1 (3): 320–37.

Dutta, A. (2015), "Beyond the Binary: (Trans) Gender Narratives and Class Distinction in Rituparno Ghosh's Later Films," *South Asian History and Culture*, 6 (2): 263–76.

Dutta, A. (2019), "Dissenting Differently: Solidarities and Tensions between Student Organizing and Trans-Kothi-Hijra Activism in Eastern India," *South Asia Multidisciplinary Academic Journal*, 20: 1–20.

Dutta, A. (2020), "The End of Criminality? The Synecdochic Symbolism of §377," *NUJS Law Review*, 13 (3): 412–32.

Enke, A. F. (2012), "The Education of Little Cis: Cisgender and the Discipline of Opposing Bodies," in A. Enke (ed.), *Transfeminist Perspectives in and Beyond Transgender and Gender Studies*, 60–77, Philadelphia: Temple University Press.

Ewing, K. P. and B. B. Taylor. (2018), "The Ungendered Self: Sex Reassignment, the Third Gender, and Gender Fluidity in India," in C. Strauss and Jack. R. Friedman (eds.), *Political Sentiments and Social Movements: The Person in Politics and Culture*, 175–204, New York: Palgrave Macmillan.

Farmer, B. (2011), "Loves of Siam: Contemporary Thai Cinema and Vernacular Queerness," in P. Jackson (ed.), *Queer Bangkok: 21st Century Markets, Media, and Rights*, 81–98, Hong Kong: Hong Kong University Press.

Foucault, M. ([1976] 1990), *The History of Sexuality, Volume One: An Introduction*, trans. R. Hurley, New York: Vintage Books.

Foucault, M. (1988), "Technologies of the Self," in L. H. Martin, H. Gutman, and P. H. Hutton (eds.), *Technologies of the Self: A Seminar with Michel Foucault*, 16-49. London: Tavistock.

Foucault, M. (2007), *Security, Territory, Population: Lectures at the College de France, 1977-1978*, trans. G. Burchell, New York: Palgrave Macmillan.

Gannon, S. (2009), "Translating the Hijra: The Symbolic Reconstruction of the British Empire in India," Ph.D. diss., University of Alberta, Edmonton.

"Gays, Lesbians, Bisexuals are not Third Gender: SC," (2016), *The Hindu*, June 30: 4.

Gibson-Graham, J. K. (1996), *The End of Capitalism (As We Knew It): A Feminist Critique of Political Economy*, Oxford: Blackwell.

Gidwani, V. (2008), *Capital, Interrupted: Agrarian Development and the Politics of Work in India*, Minneapolis: University of Minnesota Press.

Gidwani, V. and J. Wainwright. (2014), "On Capital, Not-Capital, and Development: After Kalyan Sanyal," *Economic & Political Weekly*, 49 (34): 40–7.

Gilbertson, A. (2014), "A Fine Balance: Negotiating Fashion and Respectable Femininity in Middle-Class Hyderabad, India," *Modern Asian Studies*, 48 (1): 120–58.

Gilden, A. (2008), "Toward a More Transformative Approach: The Limits of Transgender Formal Equality," *Berkeley Journal of Gender, Law & Justice*, 23 (1): 83–144.

Goel, I. (2016), "Hijra Communities of Delhi," *Sexualities*, 19 (5–6): 535–46.

Gray, S. (2011), "Hillary Clinton: Being Gay is Not a Western Invention, but a Human Reality," *PinkNews*, December 7. Available online: http://www.pinknews.co.uk/2011/12/07/hillary-clinton-being-gay-is-not-a-western-invention-but-a-human-reality/ (accessed January 28, 2018).

Greer, E. (2018), "Powerful Gay Rights Groups Excluded Trans People for Decades – Leaving Them Vulnerable to Trump's Attack," *The Washington Post*, October 29. Available online: https://www.washingtonpost.com/outlook/2018/10/29/trumps-attack-trans-people-should-be-wake-up-call-mainstream-gay-rights-movement/ (accessed April 3, 2022).

Gupta, A. (2005), "Englishpur ki Kothi: Class Dynamics in the Queer Movement in India," in A. Narrain and G. Bhan (eds.), *Because I Have a Voice: Queer Politics in India*, 136–57, New Delhi: Yoda Press.

Gupta, S. (2015), "The History of Hijras: South Asia's Transsexual and Transgender Community," *India.com*, September 16. Available online: http://www.india.com/lifestyle/the-history-of-hijras-south-asias-transsexual-and-transgender-community-540754/ (accessed January 28, 2018).

Halberstam, J. (1998), *Female Masculinity*, Durham: Duke University Press.

Halberstam, J. (2005), *In a Queer Time and Place: Transgender Bodies, Subcultural Lives*, New York: New York University Press.

Hall, K. (1997), "'Go Suck Your Husband's Sugarcane!' Hijras and the Use of Sexual Insult," in A. Livia and K. Hall (eds.), *Queerly Phrased: Language, Gender, and Sexuality*, 430–60, New York: Oxford University Press.

Hall, K. (2005), "Intertextual Sexuality: Parodies of Class, Identity, and Desire in Liminal Delhi," *Journal of Linguistic Anthropology*, 15 (1): 125–44.

Hegarty, B. (2022), *The Made-Up State: Technology, Trans Femininity, and Citizenship in Indonesia*, Ithaca: Cornell University Press.

Hickel, J. (2012), "Neoliberal Plague: The Political Economy of HIV Transmission in Swaziland," *Journal of Southern African Studies*, 38 (3): 513–29.

Hinchy, J. (2013), "Troubling Bodies: 'Eunuchs', Masculinity and Impotence in Colonial North India," *South Asian History and Culture*, 4 (2): 196–212.

Hinchy, J. (2017), "The Eunuch Archive: Colonial Records of Non-Normative Gender and Sexuality in India," *Culture, Theory and Critique*, 58 (2): 1–20.

Hinchy, J. (2019), *Governing Gender and Sexuality in Colonial India: The Hijra, c. 1850-1900*, Cambridge: Cambridge University Press.

Horton, B. A. (2020) "Fashioning Fabulation: Dress, Gesture and the Queer Aesthetics of Mumbai Pride," *South Asia: Journal of South Asian Studies*, 43 (2): 294–307.

Hossain, A. (2017), "The Paradox of Recognition: Hijra, Third Gender and Sexual Rights in Bangladesh," *Culture, Health & Sexuality*, 19 (12): 1418–31.

Hossain, A. (2021), *Beyond Emasculation: Pleasure and Power in the Making of Hijra in Bangladesh*, Cambridge: Cambridge University Press.

Hossain, A., C. Pamment, and J. Roy. (2023), *Badhai: Hijra-Khwaja Sira-Trans Performance Across Borders in South Asia*, London: Methuen Drama.

Humsafar Trust (HST). (2000), "1st Baseline Study," [Mimeograph].

Humsafar Trust (HST). (2004a), *Safarnaama (Travelogue): The Humsafar Journey Document 1994-2004*, Mumbai: HST.

Humsafar Trust (HST). (2004b), "Explanation of MSM Sub-groups," [Mimeograph].

Humsafar Trust (HST). (2007), *Sexual and Social Networks of Men Who Have Sex with Men (MSM) and Hijras in India: A Qualitative Study*, Mumbai: HST.

"India Court Recognises Transgender People as Third Gender," (2014), *BBC*, April 15. Available online: https://www.bbc.com/news/world-asia-india-27031180 (accessed August 3, 2023).

"Indian Eunuchs Given Separate IDs," (2009), *BBC*, November 13. Available online: http://news.bbc.co.uk/2/hi/south_asia/8358327.stm (accessed March 24, 2024).

INFOSEM. (2006), "History of INFOSEM," *Infosem*. Available online: http://www.infosem.org/about.htm (accessed March 3, 2018).

International Development Association (IDA). (2009), "Prevention Measures Stem the Spread of HIV-AIDS," *World Bank*. Available online: http://web.worldbank.org/WBSITE/EXTERNAL/EXTABOUTUS/IDA/0,,contentMDK: 21917859~pagePK:51236175~piPK:437394~theSitePK:73154,00.html (accessed August 15, 2019).

Iyer, N. and B. Zare, eds (2009), *Other Tongues: Rethinking the Language Debates in India*, Amsterdam: Rodopi.

Jackson, P. (2009), "Capitalism and Global Queering: National Markets, Parallels among Sexual Cultures, and Multiple Queer Modernities," *GLQ: A Journal of Lesbian and Gay Studies*, 15 (3): 357–95.

Jain, D. and K. Kartik. (2020), "Unjust Citizenship: The Law That Isn't," *NUJS Law Review*, 13 (2): 1–44.

Jain, D. and K. M. Rhoten. (2020), "Epistemic Injustice and Judicial Discourse on Transgender Rights in India: Uncovering Temporal Pluralism," *Journal of Human Values*, 26 (1): 30–40.

Jarrin, A. (2016), "Untranslatable Subjects: Travesti Access to Public Health Care in Brazil," *Transgender Studies Quarterly*, 3 (3–4): 357–75.

Joseph, S. (2005), *Social Work Practice and Men Who Have Sex With Men*, New Delhi: Sage.

Jyoti, D. (2017), "Being a Queer Dalit and The Assertion of Dalit Identities in Pride Marches," *Feminism in India*, June 22. Available online: https://feminisminindia.com/2017/06/22/queer-dalit-assertion-pride-marches/ (accessed March 24, 2024).

Kang, A. (2016), "Casteless-ness in the Name of Caste," *Round Table India*, March 4. Available online: https://www.roundtableindia.co.in/casteless-ness-in-the-name-of-caste/ (accessed July 28, 2023).

Kang, A. (2023), "Savarna Citations of Desire: Queer Impossibilities of Inter-caste Love," *Feminist Review*, 133: 63–78.

Kapur, R. (1999), "'A Love Song to Our Mongrel Selves': Hybridity, Sexuality and the Law," *Social and Legal Studies*, 8 (3): 353–68.

Katyal, A. (2010), "No 'Sexuality' for All: Some Notes from India," *Polyvocia: The SOAS Journal of Graduate Research*, 2: 21–9.

Katyal, A. (2016), *The Doubleness of Sexuality: Idioms of Same-Sex Desire in Modern India*, New Delhi: New Text.

Kaviraj, S. (2015), *The Invention of Private Life: Literature and Ideas*, New York: Columbia University Press.

Keating, C. (2011), *Decolonizing Democracy: Transforming the Social Contract in India*, University Park: Pennsylvania State University Press.

Khaleeli, H. (2014), "Hijra: India's Third Gender Claims its Place in Law," *The Guardian*, April 16. Available online: https://www.theguardian.com/society/2014/apr/16/india-third-gender-claims-place-in-law (accessed January 28, 2018).

Khan, S. (1997), *Sex, Secrecy and Shamefulness: Developing a Sexual Health Response to the Needs of Males Who Have Sex with Males in Dhaka, Bangladesh*, London: Naz Foundation International.

Khan, S. (2000), [Untitled essay], *Naz ki Pukaar*, October: n. p.

Khan, S. (2004), *MSM and HIV/AIDS in India*, Lucknow: Naz Foundation International.

Khanna, A. (2016), *Sexualness*, New Delhi: New Text.

Khubchandani, K. (2020), *Ishtyle: Accenting Gay Indian Nightlife*, Ann Arbor: University of Michigan Press.

Kolkata Rainbow Pride Walk (KRPW). (2007), "Rainbow Pride Week 2007," [Mimeograph].

Kolkata Rainbow Pride Walk (KRPW). (2008), "Rainbow Pride Week: June 24–29, 2008," [Mimeograph].

Kolkata Rainbow Pride Walk (KRPW). (2009), "Rainbow Pride Week: June 28–July 5, 2009," [Mimeograph].

Kolkata Rainbow Pride Walk (KRPW). (2010), "Rainbow Pride Walk 2010," [Mimeograph].

Kolkata Rainbow Pride Walk (KRPW). (2011), "Kolkata Rainbow Pride Festival 2011," [Mimeograph].

Kolkata Rainbow Pride Walk (KRPW). (2018), "Kolkata Rainbow Pride Walk, 2018," [Mimeograph].

Koushik, J. (2023), "'Dress Appropriately, No Hugs': Transgender Rights Activist Grace Banu Alleges Transphobic Treatment at Chennai Book Fair," *Indian Express (Chennai)*, January 11: 4.

Kullberg, C. and D. Watson, eds (2023), *Vernaculars in an Age of World Literatures*, London: Bloomsbury Academic.

Kumar, P. (2016), "In Nakhadha We Can Outshine Women but Can't Give Birth: Kothis in Provincial Cities of Western India," in T. Mukherjee and N. R. Chatterjee (eds.), *Androgyny and Female Impersonation in India: Nari Bhav*, 191–204, New Delhi: Niyogi Books.

Kumar, P. (2020), "Mapping Queer 'Celebratory Moment' in India: Necropolitics or Substantive Democracy?" *Community Development Journal*, 55 (1): 159–76.

Kunihiro A. (2022), "Against Taxonomy and Subalternity: Reconsidering the Thirdness and Otherness of Hijras of Gujarat," *South Asia Multidisciplinary Academic Journal*, 28: 1–19.

Lakkimsetti, C. (2020), *Legalizing Sex: Sexual Minorities, AIDS, and Citizenship in India*, New York: New York University Press.

Lamble, S. (2008), "Retelling Racialized Violence, Remaking White Innocence: The Politics of Interlocking Oppressions in Transgender Day of Remembrance," *Sexuality Research and Social Policy*, 5 (1): 24–42.

Laxmi Tripathi at TEDx Sabarmati. (2011), [YouTube] TedXSabarmati, June 17. Available online: https://www.youtube.com/watch?v=kxZuLPuiSDM (accessed August 3, 2023).

Leung, H. H. (2016), "Always in Translation: Trans Cinema across Languages," *Transgender Studies Quarterly*, 3 (3-4): 433–47.

LGBT India. (1999), "LGBT India Walks for Rights," [Mimeograph].

Lobo, D. (2017), "Flamboyance or Decency? Queer Community in a Dilemma," *The Times of India*, June 7. Available online: https://timesofindia.indiatimes.com/city/pune/pune-pride-2017-social-media-notice/articleshow/59021349.cms (accessed September 21, 2023).

Lothspeich, P. (2008), *Epic Nation: Reimagining the Mahabharata in the Age of the Empire*, New Delhi: Oxford University Press.

Lukose, R. (2009), *Liberalization's Children: Gender, Youth, and Consumer Citizenship in Globalizing India*, Durham: Duke University Press.

Madhya Banglar Sangram (MBS). (2009), "Pamphlet," [Mimeograph].

Majumdar, A. and N. Basu. (1997), *Bharoter Hijre Shomaj*, Kolkata: Deep Prakashan.

Majumdar, A. and N. Basu. (2005), *Samaprem*, Kolkata: Deep Prakashan.

Mandal, S. (2018), "Section 377: Whose Concerns Does the Judgment Address?" *Economic and Political Weekly (Engage)*, 53 (37): 1–9.

Marston, S. A., J. P. Jones III, and K. Woodward. (2005), "Human Geography without Scale," *Transactions of the Institute of British Geographers*, 30 (4): 416–32.

Martinez, E. J. (2012), *On Making Sense: Queer Race Narratives of Intelligibility*, Stanford: Stanford University Press.

Mason, C. ed. (2018), *Routledge Handbook of Queer Development Studies*, London: Routledge.

Massad, J. (2007), *Desiring Arabs*, Chicago: University of Chicago Press.

Mathew, P. (2015), "Viral Video of a Transgender Person Beating Up a 'Fake' Shows How Little We Know about Them," *The News Minute*, September 23. Available online: https://www.thenewsminute.com/article/viral-video-transgender-person-beating-%E2%80%98fake%E2%80%99-shows-how-little-we-know-about-them-34571 (accessed January 28, 2018).

McDaniel, J. (1995), "Emotion in Bengali Religious Thought: Substance and Metaphor," in J. Marks and R. T. Ames (eds.), *Emotions in Asian Thought: A Dialogue in Comparative Philosophy*, 39–63, Albany: SUNY Press.

Meeker, M. (2005), "A Queer and Contested Medium: The Emergence of Representational Politics in the 'Golden Age' of Lesbian Paperbacks, 1955-1963," *Journal of Women's History*, 17 (1): 165–88.

Merry, S. and P. Levitt. (2017), "The Vernacularization of Women's Human Rights," in S. Hopgood, J. Snyder and L. Vinjamuri (eds.), *Human Rights Futures*, 213–36, Cambridge: Cambridge University Press.

Michelutti, L. (2007), "The Vernacularization of Democracy: Political Participation and Popular Politics in North India," *The Journal of the Royal Anthropological Institute*, 13 (3): 639–56.

Ministry of Law and Justice. (2019), *The Transgender Persons (Protection of Rights) Act, 2019*, New Delhi: Gazette of India.

Ministry of Social Justice and Empowerment (MSJE). (2014), *Report of the Expert Committee on the Issues Relating to Transgender Persons*, New Delhi: MSJE.

Mohan, S. (2013), *Towards Gender Inclusivity: A Study on Contemporary Concerns around Gender*, Bangalore: Alternative Law Forum and LesBiT.

Mok, J. and S. Linning. (2015), "Hidden World of the Hijras: Inside India's 4,000-year-old Transgender Community where Religious Respect Doesn't Protect Them from Modern-Day Discrimination," *Daily Mail*, June 30. Available online: http://www.dailymail.co.uk/news/article-2852834/Hidden-world-hijras-Inside-India-s-4-000-year-old-transgender-community-religious-respect-doesn-t-protect-modern-day-discrimination.html#ixzz55WZQw3oJ (accessed January 28, 2018).

Mokkil, N. (2019), *Unruly Figures: Queerness, Sex Work, and the Politics of Sexuality in Kerala*, Seattle: University of Washington Press.

Morcom, A. (2013), *Illicit Worlds of Indian Dance: Cultures of Exclusion*, New York: Oxford University Press.

"Morey Morey Brihannalader Shorate Chan Mamata," (2018), *Anandabazar Patrika*, November 22: 2.

Mountz, A. and J. Hyndman. (2006), "Feminist Approaches to the Global Intimate," *Women's Studies Quarterly*, 34 (1–2): 446–63.

Mount, L. (2020) "'I am Not a Hijra': Class, Respectability, and the Emergence of the 'New' Transgender Woman in India," *Gender and Society*, 34 (4): 620–47.

Nagar, I. (2019), *Being Janana: Language and Sexuality In Contemporary India*, New York: Routledge.

Nagar, I. and D. DasGupta. (2015), "Public Koti and Private Love: Section 377, Religion, Perversity and Lived Desire," *Contemporary South Asia*, 23 (4): 426–41.

Nagpaul, S. R. (2017), "Promised Empowerment of Trans People and the New Dealers of a False Liberty," *The Indian Express*, August 5: 3.

Najmabadi, A. (2013), *Professing Selves: Transsexuality and Same-Sex Desire in Contemporary Iran*, Durham: Duke University Press.

Nanda, S. (1999), *Neither Man nor Woman: The Hijras of India*, Belmont: Wadsworth Publishing Company.

Nandi, E. (2024), *Embedding Subversion and Gender Identity: 'Ulti', the Secret Language of the Hijra-Koti Community*, Delhi: Tulika Books.

National AIDS Control Organization (NACO). (2007), *Targeted Interventions under NACP III: Core High Risk Groups*, New Delhi: Ministry of Health and Family Welfare, Government of India.

National AIDS Control Organization (NACO). (2011), *Strategic Approach for Targeted Intervention among Transgender and Hijra: Working Draft*, New Delhi: Ministry of Health and Family Welfare, Government of India.

National AIDS Control Organization (NACO). (2017), *National Strategic Plan for HIV/AIDS and STI: 2017-24*, New Delhi: Ministry of Health and Family Welfare, Government of India.

Naved, R. T., S. Chowdhury, S. Arman, and K. Sethuraman. (2007), "Mobility of Unmarried Adolescent Girls in Rural Bangladesh," *Economic and Political Weekly*, 42 (44): 63–70.

Naz Foundational International (NFI). (2011), *Supporting the Scale up of HIV Services for Males who have Sex with Males (MSM) in India*, Lucknow: NFI.

News18 Bangla. (2023), *Je Shomosto Hijrader Dekhchhen, Tara Kara* [Facebook], January 19. Available online: https://www.facebook.com/watch/live/?ref=watch_permalink&v =1100004067337792 (Accessed March 24, 2024).

Newton, E. (1972), *Mother Camp: Female Impersonators in America*, Chicago: University of Chicago Press.

"Nokol Brihannalader Utpater Obhijog," (2019), *Anandabazar Patrika*, September 16: 4.

Okafor, O. and E. Krooneman. (2011), *Vernacularization of Universal Human Rights: A Step towards Realizing Human Rights in the Local Social Setting*, Wageningen: Wageningen University Law and Governance Group.

Oksala, J. (2016), "Affective Labor and Feminist Politics," *Signs: Journal of Women in Culture and Society*, 41 (2): 281–303.

Omni, V. U. and L. A. Harris. (2023), "Who is They? Black Queer/Trans Vernacular Grammars," *Transgender Studies Quarterly*, 10 (3–4): 212–25.

Oostvogels, R. and S. Menon. (1993), *Men Who Have Sex with Men: Assessment of Situation in Madras, Third Draft Prepared for the Government of Tamil Nadu*, [Mimeograph].

Orinam. (2016a), "MSJE Rights of Transgender Persons Bill 2015," *Orinam*, January. Available online: http://orinam.net/resources-for/law-and-enforcement/nalsa-petition -tg-rights-india/msje-rights-of-transgender-persons-bill-2015/ (accessed July 28, 2023).

Orinam. (2016b), "The Transgender Persons (Protection of Rights) Bill 2016," *Orinam*, November. Available online: http://orinam.net/resources-for/law-and-enforcement /nalsa-petition-tg-rights-india/trans-persons-protection-rights-bill-2016/ (accessed July 28, 2023).

Paik, S. (2022), *The Vulgarity of Caste: Dalits, Sexuality, and Humanity in Modern India*, Stanford: Stanford University Press.

Pamment, C. (2019), "The *Hijra* Clap in Neoliberal Hands: Performing Trans Rights in Pakistan," *TDR: The Drama Review*, 63 (1): 141–51.

Patel, R. (2016), "Being LGBT in India: Some Home Truths," *LiveMint*, August 27. Available online: http://www.livemint.com/Sundayapp/sAYrieZdZKEybKzhP8FDbP/ Being-LGBT-in-India-Some-home-truths.html (accessed February 2, 2018).

Pattanaik, D. (2012), *The Man Who Was a Woman and Other Queer Tales from Hindu Lore*, London: Routledge.

People's Union for Civil Liberties, Karnataka (PUCL-K). (2003), *Human Rights Violations Against the Transgender Community: A Study of Kothi and Hijra Sex Workers in Bangalore, India*, Bangalore: PUCL-K.

Pollock, S. (2006), *The Language of the Gods in the World of Men: Sanskrit, Culture, and Power in Premodern India*, Berkeley: University of California Press.

Praajak. (1997), *Needs Assessment of Males Who Have Sex with Males in Calcutta and its Suburbs*, [Mimeograph].

Praajak. (2005), "*Manash*: Blurb," [Mimeograph].

Pramanik, T. (2014), "Bhejal Brihannalar Julume Atishto Shahar," *Ei Samay*, March 3. Available online: https://eisamay.indiatimes.com/city/kolkata/copy-on-brihannalas/ articleshow/31292942.cms (accessed January 28, 2018).

Preston, L. W. (1987), "A Right to Exist: Eunuchs and the State in Nineteenth-Century India," *Modern Asian Studies*, 21 (2): 371–87.

Puri, J. (2016), *Sexual States: Governance and the Struggle over the Antisodomy Law in India*, Durham: Duke University Press.

Ramamurthy, P. (2004), "Why Is Buying a 'Madras' Cotton Shirt a Political Act? A Feminist Commodity Chain Analysis," *Feminist Studies*, 30 (3): 734–69.

Rao, A. (2009), *The Caste Question: Dalits and the Politics of Modern India*, Berkeley: University of California Press.

Rao, R. (2020), *Out of Time: The Queer Politics of Postcoloniality*, New York: Oxford University Press.

Redding, J (2021), "Surveillance, Censure and Support: Gender Counting in South Asia," *South Asia: Journal of South Asian Studies*, 44 (6): 1056–74.

Reddy, G. (2003), "'Men' who Would be Kings: Celibacy, Emasculation, and the Re-production of 'Hijras' in Contemporary Indian Politics," *Social Research*, 70 (1): 163–200.

Reddy, G. (2005), *With Respect to Sex: Negotiating Hijra Identity in South India*, Chicago: University of Chicago Press.

Row Kavi, A. (2008), "Criminalizing High-Risk Groups Such as MSM," *Infochange Agenda*. Available online: http://infochangeindia.org/agenda/hiv/aids-big-questions/ criminalising-high-risk-groups-such-as-msm.html (accessed March 28, 2018).

Revathi, A. (2010), *The Truth About Me: A Hijra Life Story*, trans. V. Geetha, Delhi: Penguin.

Roy, A. (2020), "4 Irritating Myths About Indian Gay Men That The 'Shubh Mangal Zyada Saavdhan' Trailer is Demolishing," *ED Times*, January 21. Available online: https://www

.edtimes.in/4-irritating-myths-about-indian-gay-men-that-the-shubh-mangal-zyada
-saavdhan-trailer-is-demolishing/ (accessed July 29, 2023).

Roy, S. (2017), "Enacting/Disrupting the Will to Empower: Feminist Governance of
'Child Marriage' in Eastern India," *Signs: Journal of Women in Culture and Society*, 42
(4): 1–25.

Roy, S. (2022), *Changing the Subject: Feminist and Queer Politics in Neoliberal India*,
Durham: Duke University Press.

Roy, S. (2020), *Same Sex er Mane* [Facebook], March 6. Available online: https://www
.facebook.com/permalink.php?story_fbid=1331534893701390&id=100005346768711
(accessed July 31, 2023).

Rupantar (2008), [Film] Dir. Amrita Sarkar, India: SAATHII.

Rushton, C. (2014), "Whose Place is it Anyway? Representational Politics in a Place-Based
Health Initiative," *Health & Place*, 26: 100–9.

Sadana, R. (2012), *English Heart, Hindi Heartland: The Political Life of Literature in India*,
Berkeley: University of California Press.

Sangari, K. and S. Vaid, eds (1989), *Recasting Women: Essays in Colonial History*, New
Delhi: Kali for Women.

Sanyal, K. (2013), *Rethinking Capitalist Development: Primitive Accumulation,
Governmentality and Post-colonial Capitalism*, Delhi: Routledge.

Saria, V. (2021), *Hijras, Lovers, Brothers: Surviving Sex and Poverty in Rural India*, New
York: Fordham University Press.

Sartori, A. (2008), *Bengal in Global Concept History: Culturalism in the Age of Capital*,
Chicago: University of Chicago Press.

Sawhney, S. (2008), *The Modernity of Sanskrit*, Minneapolis: University of Minnesota Press.

Saxena, A. (2022), *Vernacular English: Reading the Anglophone in Postcolonial India*,
Princeton: Princeton University Press.

Scott, J. (1999), *Seeing Like a State: How Certain Schemes to Improve the Human Condition
Have Failed*, New Haven: Yale University Press.

Semmalar, G. (2014), "Gender Outlawed: The Supreme Court judgment on third gender
and its Implications," *Round Table India*, April 18. Available online: https://www
.roundtableindia.co.in/because-we-have-a-voice-too-the-supreme-court-judgment-on
-third-gender-and-its-implications/ (accessed July 28, 2023).

Sengupta, V. (2005), "Oh! Calcutta!" *The Telegraph*, August 7.

Shankar, K. (2017), "Hijra has become a political identity," *The Hindu*, July 19. Available
online: https://frontline.thehindu.com/social-issues/hijra-has-become-a-political
-identity/article9776856.ece (accessed January 27, 2019).

Shankar, S. (2012), *Flesh and Fish Blood: Postcolonialism, Translation, and the Vernacular*,
Berkeley: University of California Press.

Singh, S., S. Dasgupta, P. Patankar, and M. Sinha, (2012), *A People Stronger: The
Collectivization of MSM and TG groups in India*, Delhi: Sage.

Sircar, O. (2021), "A Brief Prehistory of Queer Freedom in the New India," in P. Kumar
(ed.), *Sexuality, Abjection and Queer Existence in Contemporary India*, 226–50, Delhi:
Routledge.

Skaria, A. (2016), *Unconditional Equality: Gandhi's Religion of Resistance*, Minneapolis:
University of Minnesota Press.

Solidarity and Action Against the HIV Infection in India (SAATHII). (2009), *Report of the
Regional TG/Hijra Consultation in Eastern India*. Available online: http://www.saathii
.org/orissapages/tg_hijra_issues_consultation%20.html (accessed January 28, 2018).

Spade, D. (2011), "About Purportedly Gendered Body Parts," *Deanspade.net*. Available online: https://www.deanspade.net/wp-content/uploads/2011/02/Purportedly -Gendered-Body-Parts.pdf (accessed August 2, 2023).

Spade, D. (2015), *Normal Life: Administrative Violence, Critical Trans Politics, and the Limits of Law*, Durham: Duke University Press.

Springer, S. (2014), "Human Geography without Hierarchy," *Progress in Human Geography*, 38 (3): 402–19.

Spivak, G. C. (1988), "Can the Subaltern Speak?" in C. Nelson and L. Grossberg (eds.), *Marxism and the Interpretation of Culture*, 271–315, Chicago: University of Illinois Press.

Still, C. (2011), "Spoiled Brides and the Fear of Education: Honour and Social Mobility among Dalits in South India," *Modern Asian Studies*, 45 (5): 1119–46.

Sukthankar, A. (2005), "Complicating Gender: Rights of Transsexuals in India," in A. Narrain and G. Bhan (eds.), *Because I Have a Voice: Queer Politics in India*, 164–73, New Delhi: Yoda Press.

Supreme Court of India. (2014), *National Legal Services Authority versus Union of India and Others*, New Delhi: Supreme Court of India.

Sappho for Equality. (2013), *Proshnottore Jounota: Kotha Tothyo Alochona*, Kolkata: Sappho for Equality.

Stone, S. ([1987] 2014), "The Empire Strikes Back: A Posttranssexual Manifesto," *Sandystone.com*. Available online: https://sandystone.com/empire-strikes-back.pdf (accessed July 21, 2023).

Stryker, S. (2009), "We Who Are Sexy: Christine Jorgensen's Transsexual Whiteness in the Postcolonial Philippines," *Social Semiotics*, 19 (1): 79–91.

Tagore, R. ([1914] 2008), "Keno Tomra Amay Dako," *Geetabitan.com*. Available online: https://www.geetabitan.com/lyrics/K/keno-tomra-aamay-lyric.html (accessed July 21, 2023).

Talusan, M. (2015), "The Mirror Stage," *The New Inquiry*, July 23. Available online: https://thenewinquiry.com/the-mirror-stage/ (accessed August 2, 2023).

Tannehill, B. (2013), "Myths about Gender Confirmation Surgery," *Huffington Post*, December 8. Available online: http://www.huffingtonpost.com/brynn- tannehill/myths-gender-confirmation- surgery_b_4384701.html (assessed July 21, 2023).

TEDxMumbai - Lakshmi Tripathi. (2010), "[YouTube] TedX Talks," April 19. Available online: https://www.youtube.com/watch?v=dhQTBRQlapw (accessed August 3, 2023).

Thakur, J. and H. Zaffar. (2023), "The Need to Make Space for Dalit Queer Voices in India," *New Lines Magazine*, March 16. Available online: https://newlinesmag.com/reportage/the-need-to-make-space-for-dalit-queer-voices-in-india/ (accessed August 2, 2023).

Thomas, H. and T. Boellstorff. (2017), "Beyond the Spectrum: Rethinking Autism," *Disability Studies Quarterly*, 37 (1): n.p.

Tom, L. and S. Menon. (2021), "Living with the Norm: The Nirvanam Ritual in South Indian Transfeminine Narratives of Self and Transition," *GLQ: A Journal of Lesbian and Gay Studies*, 27 (1), 39–59.

Tripathi, L. N. (2015), *Me Hijra, Me Laxmi*, trans. R. R. Rao and P. G. Joshi, Delhi: Oxford University Press.

United Nations Development Programme (UNDP) (2008), *Missing Pieces: HIV Related Needs of Sexual Minorities in India*, New Delhi: UNDP.

United Nations Development Programme (UNDP) (2010), *Hijras/Transgender Women in India: HIV, Human Rights and Social Exclusion*, New Delhi: UNDP.

UNICEF (2002), *The Humsafar Trust: Grounded in its Community*. Kathmandu: UNICEF Regional Office South Asia.

Upadhyay, N. (2020), "Hindu Nation and its Queers: Caste, Islamophobia, and De/coloniality in India," *Interventions*, 22 (4): 464–80.

Valentine, D. (2007), *Imagining Transgender: An Ethnography of a Category*, Durham: Duke University Press.

Valentine, D. (2012), "Sue E. Generous: Toward a Theory of Non-Transexuality," *Feminist Studies*, 38 (1): 185–211.

Vanita, R. and S. Kidwai, eds (2000), *Same-Sex Love in India: Readings from Literature and History*, New York: Palgrave.

Venkat, V. (2008), "From the Shadows," *Frontline*, February 29. Available online: https://frontline.thehindu.com/other/article30194752.ece (accessed August 3, 2023).

Vijayakumar, G. (2018), "Collective Demands and Secret Codes: The Multiple Uses of 'Community' in 'Community Mobilization'," *World Development*, 104: 173–82.

Vijayakumar, G. (2021), *At Risk: Indian Sexual Politics and the Global AIDS Crisis*, Stanford: Stanford University Press.

Vidya, L. S. (2013), *I am Vidya: A Transgender's Journey*, Delhi: Rupa.

"Walk to Remember, A," (2010), *Gaylaxy*. Available online: http://www.gaylaxymag.com/exclusive/a-walk-to-remember/#gs.9v1QhMc (accessed January 28, 2018).

Werbner, P. (2006), "Vernacular Cosmopolitanism," *Theory, Culture and Society*, 23 (2–3): 496–8.

Weston, K. (1995), "Get Thee to a Big City: Sexual Imaginary and the Great Gay Migration," *GLQ: A Journal of Lesbian and Gay Studies*, 2 (3): 253–77.

Williams, C. (2014), "Transgender," *Transgender Studies Quarterly*, 1 (1–2): 232–4.

Zimman, L. and K. Hall. (2010), "Language, Embodiment, and the 'Third Sex'," in C. Llamas and D. Watt (eds.), *Language and Identities*, 166–78, Edinburgh: Edinburgh University Press.

INDEX

Note: *Italicized* and **bold** page numbers refer to figures and tables. Page numbers followed by "n" refer to notes.